THE MASCULINE SELF

CHRISTOPHER T. KILMARTIN
Mary Washington College

Macmillan Publishing Company
New York

Maxwell Macmillan Canada
Toronto

Editor: Christine Cardone
Production Supervisor: WordCrafters Editorial Services, Inc.
Production Manager: Francesca Drago
Cover Designer: Curtis Tow
Cover Photograph: Francesca Drago
Cover Model: Roger Vergnes
Photo Researcher: Diane Kraut
Illustrations: AmeriComp
This book was set in Palatino by AmeriComp
and was printed and bound by Book Press.
The cover was printed by New England Book Components, Inc.

Macmillan Publishing Company
866 Third Avenue, New York, New York 10022

Macmillan Publishing Company is part of
the Maxwell Communication Group of Companies.

Maxwell Macmillan Canada, Inc.
1200 Eglinton Avenue East, Suite 200
Don Mills, Ontario M3C 3N1

Library of Congress Cataloging-in-Publication Data
Kilmartin, Christopher T.
    The masculine self / Christopher T. Kilmartin.
        p.   cm.
    Includes bibliographical references and index.
    ISBN 0-02-363611-4
    1. Masculinity (Psychology)   2. Men—Psychology.   3. Men.
    I. Title.
    BF692.5.K55   1994
    155.3′32—dc20   93-1920
                                                       CIP

Text Credits:
p. 129: "We Real Cool" is copyright by Gwendolyn Brooks, © 1991. Published by Third
World Press, 1991.
p. 167: "Sixteen Tons" (Merle Travis) © 1947 UNICHAPPELL MUSIC INC. and ELVIS
PRESLEY MUSIC. All rights on behalf of ELVIS PRESLEY MUSIC administered by
UNICHAPPELL MUSIC INC. All Rights Reserved. Used By Permission.
p. 277: "A New Kind of Man." Written by Van Morrison. Copyright © 1984 by Essential
Music. Used by permission. All rights reserved.

Printing: 1 2 3 4 5 6 7   Year: 4 5 6 7 8 9 0

To the loving memory of my father:
James Edward Kilmartin (1929–1980)

PREFACE

I have been interested in men's studies for nearly my entire professional career. It has been gratifying to see a burgeoning literature in this area produced in the 1980s and early 1990s. College courses on the subject are no longer a rarity, and serious scholarship is well under way.

I had three broad goals for the content of this text, and these goals are reflected in the three parts of the book. First, I wanted to introduce the reader to contemporary concepts of gender and masculinity. Only recently have men begun to understand the difference between being male and being a "generic human being." As you shall see, the distinction is an important one.

Second, I wanted to bring male gender-role theory into the mainstream of psychology. I undertook this task in Chapters three through six by applying concepts of masculinity to the four major theoretical schools of personality. These four chapters contribute perspectives on masculine development against the backgrounds provided by great thinkers such as Freud, Jung, Bem, Maccoby, and Rogers. You may disagree with some of their positions, but you will find the application of their theories to masculinity stimulating and enlightening. Bruce Rybarczyk's description of the diversity among men provides a focus on the effects of age, race, and ethnicity. Only recently has social science begun to seriously consider these factors.

Third, I wanted to organize and summarize the available research on men and masculinity. I did so by identifying themes or issues common to many men, and then reviewing the available scholarship in each area —a body of literature that is constantly changing and growing. This book is a snapshot in time—a map of a territory that continues to evolve.

As I wrote, I tried to keep in mind that my primary aim is to teach. This book is intended to introduce the college student to the theoretical and scientific study of men without losing sight of the fact that we are talking about real human beings. I use examples, whenever possible, to move a concept from the abstract into the real world. I especially enjoyed writing the many "boxes" that are contained throughout the text. My goal in including these features was to give the book a "face" and provide illustrations of various concepts in some depth. You may find that these boxes can serve as "appetizers" to introduce you to a topic, or as "desserts"—enjoyable finishing touches. In many cases, I also included some questions for critical thinking in these features. You may find them useful for starting discussions, either in the classroom or in less formal settings.

I am grateful to a number of people who have contributed to this work directly and indirectly. The following reviewers contributed their time and gave valuable suggestions for revising earlier versions of the manuscript: Karen W. Bauer, University of Delaware; Carol S. Wharton, University of Richmond; Clyde W. Franklin, II, The Ohio State University; Nyla Branscombe, University of Kansas; Michael A. Messner, University of Southern California; and Lee D. Millar Bidwell, Longwood College. Mary Washington College has supported this project through a grant, as well as through the provision of a campus atmosphere conducive to scholarship. The Michigan State University Library's "Changing Men" special collection was a unique set of resources. Library personnel working in this area were helpful and supportive on my visit there. My good friends Drew Gallagher and Tim Goecke helped to secure photographs, illustrations, and permissions for copyrighted material. Christine Cardone, Executive Editor at Macmillan, has been encouraging and supportive throughout the process. Macmillan's Bill Beville was instrumental in originating the project. Cynthia Kilmartin provided the title for the book. Finally, many people provided support through their interest and encouragement.

C.T.K.

CONTENTS

The Price of Experience

What is the price of Experience? Do men buy it
    for a song?
Or Wisdom for a dance in the street? No, it is
    bought with the price
Of all that a man hath, his house, his wife, his
    children.
Wisdom is sold in the desolate market
    where none can come to buy
And in the wither'd field where the farmer
    plows for bread in vain.

                    —*William Blake*

PART ONE

Frameworks for Understanding Men

Dan Bosler/Tony Stone Worldwide

CHAPTER ONE

Introduction

The biological categorization of sex is the most basic division of human beings. Probably the first characteristic we notice about someone is whether that person is male or female. There is evidence to suggest that children as young as a year old are able to make this distinction (Maccoby, 1987), and a profound distinction it is. Every culture in the world prescribes norms for behavior that are assigned on the basis of sex. Obviously, reproductive roles (impregnation, childbirth, and lactation) are biologically assigned, but the division of behavior based on sex goes far beyond these roles into areas of work, child care, and society. Even personality characteristics such as aggressiveness or nurturance are often ascribed disproportionately to one sex or the other.

Psychological literature abounds with studies of differences in the socialization of males and females as well as speculations about the effects of these differences on the personalities of adult men and women (Lytton & Romney, 1991). Biological psychologists search for differences in brain structure and hormone levels and attempt to describe the influences of these differences on behavior. And, of course, other social scientists, including sociologists, anthropologists, economists, and philosophers, have long been interested in the study of male and female.

Beginning around the 1960s, modern feminist writers began to make strong critiques of mainstream psychological theory and research methods. New ideas about female development and functioning gave rise to a new field, the psychology of women. Theorists and researchers in this area urged the rest of psychology to take seriously the notion that a person's gender has important effects on his or her behavior. If we want to understand human behavior in all of its complexity, we would do well to take these effects into consideration when we construct our theories and research designs. Thus, the psychology of women created a stronger awareness of people as *gendered beings.*

In the early 1970s, this awareness was expanded into a new area, the psychology of men. Scholars in this field began to ask the question, "If the experience of being female has a profound effect on a woman's behavior and on others' reactions to her, does the experience of being male also have powerful implications for a man?" The answer would seem to be an emphatic yes.

The idea that men need their own psychology was (and still is) greeted with skepticism. It has been argued that *all* psychology is the psychology of men because mainstream psychological theory was constructed largely by males. In fact, many research studies were undertaken using only male subjects, as if male behaviors generalized to the whole human race. It was said that "even the rat was male." Thus, the argument against the existence of such a field is that, since men have been studied as the *normative referent* for psychology, we do not need to identify a new area of psychology to investigate male behavior and experience.

Joseph Pleck (1988) makes a compelling counterargument in favor of distinguishing the study of men as a normative referent from the study of men from a *gender-aware perspective.* The literature is replete with models of men as "generic human beings," but (prior to the emergence of the psychology of men) it was difficult to find reference to men as *gendered beings.* Men are powerfully affected by the experiences of growing up male, having people respond to them as male, expecting and having others expect certain behaviors based on "male gender roles," and having feelings about their masculinity.

Brod (1987b) points out that traditional scholarship is "about men only by virtue of not being about women" (p. 264). Men's studies move masculinity from the periphery of inquiry into the center. The subject of study is not, as in most traditional scholarship, men as historical, political, and cultural actors, but rather men *as men.*

There is a good deal of confusion about the psychology of men. When I tell people that I am a psychologist specializing in the study of men or "men's issues," the typical reactions are:

1. "Why do we need to look at men's issues? Men have all the power and get to do whatever they want."
2. "Men are becoming a bunch of complainers who can't deal with women being strong."
3. "It's surprising that a psychologist would be 'antiwoman' or antifeminist."
4. "What are 'men's issues'? I didn't know men had any issues."

These reactions come from both men and women, and they reveal misunderstandings about, and biases against, the study of men from a gender-aware perspective. I would respond to these reactions with the following:

1. While it is true that many men have a good deal of power and often get to do what they want, there are also many men who feel quite powerless and have been damaged by harsh masculine socialization (see number 4 below). By virtue of their greater social power, men are also in a unique position to help shift this power into better balance. An understanding of the effects of masculine privilege is needed in order to do so.

2. Many men do have a lot of trouble dealing with strong women. Men are raised to believe that they should be strong and dominant. Therefore, they may feel that strong women are a threat to their masculinity. This is an issue for men that must be addressed, because women *are* powerful, and men must learn to accept and deal with them in appropriate ways.

3. Although there are some men's studies scholars and "men's movement" leaders who might be considered antiwomen or antifeminist, there are others who can be characterized as just the opposite. The purpose of studying men from a gender-aware perspective is not to further oppress women, but to address quality-of-life issues for men and women. Men's issues are often very compatible with women's issues. For instance, if we can understand the nature of the threat that many men feel when confronted with the power of women, we can perhaps take steps to decrease or prevent that threat. As a result, men would become both more comfortable with themselves *and* respectful of women.

4. What are "men's issues"? Consider the following:

- Men spend most of their childhood years with women (mainly mothers and female teachers). This may have important effects on their development.
- Males are encouraged from an early age to deny the experience of most of their emotions. This may lead to a variety of psychological, physical, and social problems.
- Many men have been raised in a way that creates problems with intimacy, which is regarded by many as a basic human need.
- Following the breakup of a marriage or other primary relationship, men are more likely than women to suffer psychological problems or be admitted to mental hospitals. It is doubtful that men are as emotionally independent as the social image of masculinity would have us believe.
- Most acts of violence are committed by men.
- The vast majority of incarcerated and homeless people are men.

- A man's average life span is 6 to 8 years shorter than a woman's average life span.
- Many men have strong feelings of being disappointed with their fathers.
- The general quality of men's relationships with others is often impoverished.
- Definitions of masculinity are changing.

This is a partial list. As you read this book, you will come across many more men's issues. It should be clear from this list that all is not well with men. While there are many positive facets to traditional masculinity, there are also many destructive ones, both for individual men and for others around them.

Describing Masculinities

"Snips and snails and puppy dog tails" is the first description of maleness I remember hearing as a child, the answer to the question, "What are little boys made of?" What are little girls made of? "Sugar and spice and everything nice." These sayings are supposed to describe personality differences between the sexes. It is not too difficult to interpret the statement about girls. Sugar and spice are pleasant and palatable. A "sweet" person is someone who can evoke positive responses from others, someone who cares about people. The statement about boys is more cryptic, but it seems to create images of being dirty, scattered, and hyperactive (puppy dog tails don't remain still for very long).

From the earliest days of childhood, males are bombarded with messages about what it means to be masculine. These messages serve to communicate expectations for their behavior. Some messages, like the one just described, are verbal. Others are more subtle, such as a parent's communication of silent approval for behaviors like refusing to cry when one is sad or hurt. Because a good deal of behavior is learned through imitation, many of these messages are received through merely observing the behaviors of men in the family, the neighborhood, the media, and the culture.

These messages have powerful impacts on boys. They learn to act in a "masculine" way and avoid behaviors that are considered "unmasculine." The social settings in which adult men find themselves tend to reinforce these standards. For example, a man who displays aggression at a business meeting might gain the approval of his colleagues, whereas a woman might get disapproval for exactly the same behavior.

What is masculinity? How do we define it? We see romanticized views of masculinity in Boxes 1.1 and 1.2. The stereotypical "real man" in the United States can be described as having certain personality traits:

strong
independent
achieving
hard working
dominant
heterosexual
tough
aggressive
unemotional
physical
competitive
forceful

We could also describe him in terms of activities or behaviors, that is, what a man *does*:

earns money
initiates sex
solves problems
gets the job done
takes control
takes action
enjoys "masculine" activities (e.g., hunting, sports, drinking)
takes physical risks
supports his family financially

We can describe him in terms of prohibited activities, that is, what a man *does not do* (see Box 1.1):

cry
express feelings other than anger
perform "women's work" (e.g., wash dishes, change diapers)
back down from a confrontation
get emotionally close to other men

We can describe him in terms of *roles*:

athlete
professional

Box 1.1
A Negative Description of Masculinity

Following is a definition of *gentleman* from the handbook of the Virginia Military Institute:

> Without a strict observance of the fundamental code of honor, no man, no matter how "polished" can be considered a gentleman. The honor of a gentleman demands the inviolability of his word and the incorruptibility of his principles. He is the descendant of the knight, the crusader, he is the defender of the defenseless and the champion of justice—or he is not a gentleman.
>
> A gentleman *does not* discuss his family affairs in public or with acquaintances.
>
> *Does not* speak more than casually about his wife or girlfriend.
>
> *Does not* go to a lady's house if he is affected by alcohol. He is temperate in the use of alcohol.
>
> *Does not* lose his temper nor exhibit anger, fear, hate, embarrassment, ardor, or hilarity in public.
>
> *Does not* hail a lady from a club window.
>
> *Never* discusses the merits or demerits of a lady.
>
> *Does not* borrow money from a friend, except in dire need. Money borrowed is a debt of honor and must be repaid as promptly as possible. Debts incurred by a deceased parent, brother, sister, or grown child are assumed by honorable men as a debt of honor.
>
> *Does not* display his wealth, money, or possessions.
>
> *Does not* put his manners on and off, whether in the club or in a ballroom. He treats people with courtesy, no matter what their social positions may be.
>
> *Does not* slap strangers on the back nor so much as lay a finger on a lady.
>
> *Does not* "lick the boots of those above him" nor "kick the face of those below him on the social ladder."
>
> *Does not* take advantage of another's helplessness or ignorance and assumes that no gentleman will take advantage of him.
>
> A gentleman respects the reserves of others but demands that others respect those which are his.
>
> A gentleman *can* become what he wills to be. . . .

Notice that the positive parts of the description (what gentlemen *are* and what they *do*) are rather vague: defender of the defenseless, champion of justice, and so on. These are high ideals that do not necessarily transfer easily into a prescription for any specific behavior. When the description turns to negative guidelines (what gentlemen *do not do*), however, very specific behaviors are stated. You might notice the prohibitions against acknowledging a connection to another person ("never speaks more than casually about his wife or girlfriend"), expressing emotion ("does not exhibit fear, hate, ardor . . ."), and being vulnerable or in need of help ("does not borrow money from a friend . . ."). The last line reflects the masculine value on self-determination.

worker
father
husband
buddy
playboy
leader

What do these varying definitions have in common? Robert Brannon's classic (1976) essay describes four major themes of traditional U.S. masculinity:

1. *Antifeminity.* Males are encouraged from an early age to avoid behaviors, interests, and personality traits that are considered "feminine." Among these are expression of feeling, emotional vulnerability, sexual feelings for men, and feminine professions (e.g., elementary school teacher, nurse, secretary). Brannon labels this masculine norm *"No Sissy Stuff."*
2. *Status and achievement.* Men gain status by being successful in all they do, especially sports and work. Powerful men earn the respect and admiration of others. Brannon calls this dimension *"The Big Wheel."*
3. *Inexpressiveness and independence.* Men are expected to maintain emotional composure and self-control even in the most difficult of situations, solve problems without help, keep their feelings to themselves, and disdain any display of weakness. This dimension is *"The Sturdy Oak"* or *"The Male Machine."*
4. *Adventurousness and aggressiveness.* Masculinity is characterized by a willingness to take physical risks and become violent if necessary. Brannon calls this masculine norm *"Give 'Em Hell."*

Box 1.2
Thinking about Masculinity

Following is Rudyard Kipling's classic poem "If-," which reflects a romanticized view of masculinity. As you read the poem, try to answer the following questions:

1. What kinds of masculine traits is Kipling describing?
2. Which of these traits are positive, negative, or neutral? Why?
3. Are there differences in what is judged to be positive or negative for the *individual* compared with *society*?
4. In what ways is modern masculinity different or similar to Kipling's description?

If-

If you can keep your head when all about you
   Are losing theirs and blaming it on you,
If you can trust yourself when all men doubt you,
   But make allowance for their doubting too;
If you can wait and not be tired by waiting,
   Or being lied about, don't deal in lies,
Or being hated, don't give way to hating,
   And yet don't look too good, nor talk too wise.
If you can dream—and not make dreams your master;
   If you can think—and not make thoughts your aim;
If you can meet with Triumph and Disaster
   And treat those two imposters just the same;
If you can bear to hear the truth you've spoken
   Twisted by knaves to make a trap for fools,
Or watch the things you gave your life to, broken,
   And stoop and build 'em up with worn-out tools;

If you can make one heap of all your winnings
   And risk it on one turn of pitch-and-toss,
And lose, and start again at your beginnings
   And never breathe a word about your loss;
If you can force your heart and nerve and sinew
   To serve your turn long after they are gone,
And so hold on when there is nothing in you
   Except the Will which says to them: "Hold on!"

If you can talk with crowds and keep your virtue,
   Or walk with Kings—nor lose the common touch,

> If neither foes nor loving friends can hurt you,
>   If all men count with you, but none too much;
> If you can fill the unforgiving minute
>   With sixty seconds' worth of distance run,
> Yours is the Earth and everything that's in it,
>   And—which is more—you'll be a Man, my son!
>
> Note: From *Rudyard Kipling's Verse: Definitive Edition*, 1940, Garden City, NY: Doubleday.

There are variations in cultural definitions and stereotypes of masculinity (and femininity). For example, African-American men are considered more emotionally expressive than white American men (Basow, 1992). Jewish men are encouraged to incorporate a love of knowledge into their concept of masculinity, in contrast with some other groups of men (Brod, 1987a). At the same time, there is a good deal of cross-cultural similarity in gender roles. Williams and Best (1990) found that men were described as forceful, active, and strong across a variety of cultures.

Most men are raised to be unemotional, task and achievement oriented, aggressive, fearless, and status seeking. Male gender roles are powerful influences on behavior partly because men who are seen as "masculine" receive many social rewards. For instance, financially successful men gain the admiration of others and are seen as more sexually desirable than other men. Actress Zsa Zsa Gabor (quoted in James, 1984) said, "No rich man is ugly." Competitive and inexpressive men are seen as good candidates for promotion in many work environments. The man who shows a willingness to be "one of the boys" may enjoy the approval of others and have a large circle of friends.

On the other hand, men who are seen as "unmasculine" may receive social punishment. Gay men are subject to abusive comments, stigmatization, and even unprovoked violence. Men who are willing to talk about personal problems or admit weakness are judged to be unhealthy (Lewis & McCarthy, 1988; Derlega & Chaikin, 1976). Male politicians who display out-role behaviors may damage their chances for election (Tobin, 1991).

In general, men who fail to live up to accepted standards of masculinity risk losing their self-esteem, health, connectedness with others, or lives. Men commit suicide at least three times more often than women (Robins, 1985). There are over 15 times more men in prison than women, and males comprise close to 80% of the U.S. homeless population (Christenson, 1989).

Consequences of Male Gender Roles

Cultural norms of masculinity are enforced and maintained through expectations, rewards, and social sanctions. Adhering to traditional male gender roles has both positive and negative effects on individual men and on society.

Benefits

The man who is able to live up to male gender-role demands has the opportunity to reap many rewards. Chief among these are money, status, and privilege. Men who are "winners" are often able to live in the lap of luxury, enjoy the admiration of others, and do basically what they want to do. The traditional man bases his self-esteem in work, wealth, and achievement. Men who acquire large amounts of these things may feel quite good about themselves, and they are often viewed as desirable lovers, friends, and associates. As Farrell (1991) put it, financially successful men are comparable to beautiful women; they have "centerfold" status.

Work, wealth, and achievement are often very quantifiable. It is much easier for a man to evaluate success by how much money he has made rather than by how good a parent he has been. The latter (which has been traditionally defined as "women's work") is a more difficult judgment because it is qualitative. Thus, a traditional man can operate in somewhat of a "closed system," with his worth measured by a convenient and relatively unambiguous "yardstick." Such a man can be singular in his purpose; he rarely has to deal with mixed feelings.

The traditional man is a "breadwinner" who supports his family financially by working hard. Whether or not he is a "big wheel," a man can take a great deal of pride in fulfilling this role. Working hard every day so that you and your family can have food and shelter is a very loving thing to do. The contribution of the provider role to family is one of the most positive aspects of traditional masculinity. Men have also usually participated in other aspects of family life such as physical work in and around the house, money management, and everyday problem solving. Certain aspects of male gender roles are well suited to these important activities.

The masculine achievement and problem-solving orientation has resulted in a great number of positive contributions to society and the world. Men's achievements in engineering, literature, and the sciences, for example, should not be overlooked, nor should the contributions of working men who produce goods, build houses, and otherwise labor for the greater good. This is not to deny that women have made significant contributions (a fact that has historically been downplayed), but only to note that the traditional masculine ethic of "getting the job done" has had enormous positive implications for the quality of life. This is one aspect of male gender roles that deserves to be celebrated.

Costs

It is clear that being a "real man'" has many tangible rewards. However, there has also been a price to pay for some aspects of traditional masculinity, both for society and for individual men. Living up to male gender demands is largely an impossible task that exacts a heavy toll.

The expectations that men compete, achieve, are "on top," and always look for more have left many men feeling driven, empty, disillusioned, and angry. No matter how talented and hard working a man is, winning every time is an impossibility. There is always another man who has more money, higher status, a more attractive partner, or a bigger house. The traditional man can never get enough, and thus he can never really enjoy what he has. He must constantly work harder and faster. Such a life style often results in stress-related physical and psychological symptoms.

To strip a man of his emotional life is to take away one of the most basic aspects of human existence. The experience of positive emotion is profoundly important. When a man is made into a machine, he loses his humanity. He is rendered less capable of having empathic, caring, intimate relationships with other people. Emotional intimacy requires people to share power, be vulnerable, and disclose themselves. Traditional masculine socialization is antithetical to these behaviors (Jourard, 1971). The damage that male gender roles do to the quality of connectedness to other people and to feelings about the self can hardly be overestimated. Many men feel alienated from their partners, children, and other men, and these feelings are often mutual.

The most serious result of unconnectedness to others is its influence on men's willingness to do physical and psychological harm to others. It is easier to hurt people when you cannot identify or empathize with them. Violence is first and foremost a failure of empathy (Jolkovski, 1989). Men are socialized away from empathy and this enables them to be cruel toward anyone who gets in their way. The disproportionate participation of men in war, violence, damage to the planet, the oppression of marginalized social groups, and psychological cruelty must (at least partly) be laid at the doorstep of traditional masculinity.

The Organization of This Book

The Masculine Self is oriented toward understanding masculinity in the contexts of personality theory and cultural forces. This first chapter describes male gender roles. Chapter 2 provides the necessary background for conceptualizing gender from historical and research perspectives.

Part Two (Chapters Three through Seven) provides some theoretical viewpoints of men and masculinity as seen by scholars in five major schools of psychological thought (biological, psychoanalytic, social learning, phenomenological, and cross-cultural). My good friend and colleague, Dr. Bruce Rybarczyk, contributed his expertise on ethnic men by writing Chapter Seven.

Part Three (Chapters Eight through Fifteen) examines research findings and other scholarship related to various themes that have been identified as "men's issues." The final chapter describes various social movements that are concerned with the state of masculinity in U.S. culture.

Summary

1. The distinction between the sexes is learned very early in life, and roles are culturally assigned based on this distinction. Only recently have researchers and theorists begun a serious investigation of the effect of gender roles on men. This study has met with a good deal of resistance due to misunderstanding and mistrust. Nevertheless, a growing body of literature suggests that masculinity is an important psychological construct highly worthy of investigation.

2. From very early in life, males are given messages about what it means to be a man. These messages are communicated through interpersonal relationships and the culture, and they are later reinforced in adult social settings. There is considerable similarity in gender-role definitions across cultures.

3. Traditional gender roles provide expectations that men be unemotional, independent, aggressive, competitive, achieving, and unfeminine. Living in these roles can have positive results, such as financial rewards, social status, contribution to family, and contribution to society. However, there can also be negative effects, including overattention to work, an impoverished emotional life, poor relationships, and violence.

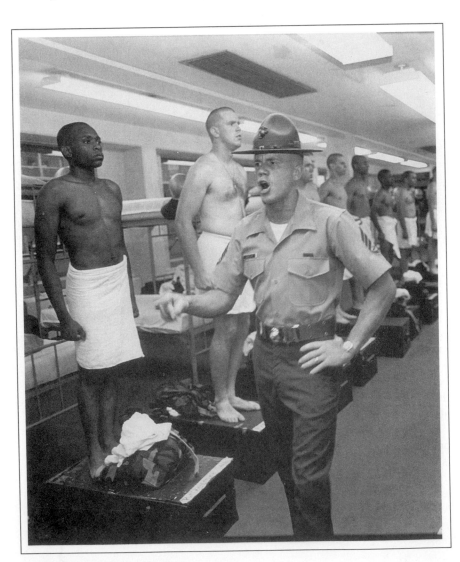

David Wells/The Image Works

CHAPTER TWO

Models for
Understanding Masculinity

Masculinity can be understood as a set of role behaviors that men often perform. In this chapter, we examine the nature of roles, the historical development of models for understanding gender roles, and various attempts to measure gender-role characteristics.

Roles and Gender Roles

A **role** is a collection of behaviors of a person in a given situation. The most familiar use of this term is as a description of a person's behavior in a movie, play, or other acting situation. **Social roles** define a set of expected behaviors for a person in any given social position. For example, the social role of *student* includes the expectations that the person will attend classes, take tests, and complete assignments.

A **gender role** is a kind of generalized social role. Gender role can be defined as a set of expectations for behaving, thinking, and feeling that is based on a person's biological sex. The term **sex role** is also used throughout psychological literature as an equivalent term. This is problematic because this term uncritically combines a biological category (sex) with a set of social behaviors (role) (Sherif, 1982). This may result in the impression that "sex-role behaviors" are determined by biological processes. For example, a writer who describes aggressiveness as a characteristic of the "male sex role" might lead a reader to assume that men are more aggressive than women because they have "aggressive genes" or "aggressive hormones."

The extent of biological bases for sex-typed behavior is open to question (and discussed in Chapter Three). When one is speaking about such behaviors *without* implicating biology, the term *gender role* is more accurate than the term *sex role*. Nevertheless, the two terms continue to be used interchangeably. Do not be misled when you see the term *sex role*.

Components of Gender Roles

Gender roles are usually described as sets of behaviors that are assumed to characterize men or women. There are several components to gender roles. They include **stereotypes**, which are culturally based overgeneralizations about the characteristics of people who belong to the biological category of male or female. These beliefs are a part of the social fabric (Basow, 1992). Stereotypes take the form of unquestioned, socially shared beliefs and images of how men and women *are* (Pleck, 1981a). For instance, in mainstream U.S. culture, it is widely believed that men are competitive and that women are not.

Many stereotypical masculine and feminine traits are widely believed to be opposites from one another (Tavris, 1992; Deaux & Lewis, 1984). For example, women are believed to be very neat, and men are believed to be very sloppy (Broverman, Vogel, Broverman, Clarkson, & Rosenkrantz, 1972). The use of the term *opposite sex* rather than *other sex* reflects the tendency to think in this way. Although a good deal of research refutes this bias, people tend to characterize masculinity and femininity as anitithetical to one another (Marsh, Antill, & Cunningham, 1989).

Gender roles also include **norms,** which are *prescriptive* and *proscriptive* beliefs. That is, they are beliefs about how males and females *should be* (prescriptive) and *should not be* (proscriptive). A norm in a social role is analogous to a script in an acting role. For example, one might believe that, although faithfulness is uncharacteristic of men (a stereotype), men *should be* faithful (a norm).

It is quite possible for a gender-role stereotype to conflict with a gender-role norm. For instance, one might have a conception that "real men" are confident (a prescriptive norm), but that "most men" are unconfident (a gender stereotype). The term *real man* appears to have become shorthand for the description of male gender-role norms, for example, "real men" make a lot of money, don't cry, and (as in the popular book title) don't eat quiche (Feirstein, 1982).

Discrepancies between gender-role stereotypes and norms are rather commonplace. In one research study, college students reported beliefs that males and females differed on over 50 characteristics (gender-role stereotyping), but that they *should* differ only on 12 characteristics (gender-role norms) (Ruble, 1983).

Gender-role norms and stereotypes are also applied to the self. A man may have a conception of "how men are" (stereotype) that is in conflict with "how I am" (**self-concept**). It would not be unusual for a man to view men in general as aggressive and at the same time view himself as unaggressive, even though he is a man.

Norm-based beliefs also apply to the individual. I have beliefs about "how I should be" (**ideal self-concept**) and these may conflict with the other components already mentioned. Thus, I may believe that men are dominant (stereotype), men should not be dominant (norm), I am not dominant (self-concept), and I should be more dominant (ideal self-concept). Martin (1987) found that a sample of college students reported the belief that males and females differ in 32 characteristics. When asked to rate themselves with regard to these characteristics, however, males and females differed significantly on only five of them. Bem's (1981a) summary of several studies revealed that less than half of college students' self-descriptions fit traditional gender stereotypes. Discrepancies between self-concept and stereotype, then, are more the rule than the exception.

I have described these components of gender roles as "beliefs," but they are really more complex than mere beliefs. Gender roles also include *cognitive, affective,* and *behavioral* aspects, and these can also be discrepant from one another (Deaux & Kite, 1987). So far, I have only discussed the cognitive aspect, that is, what a person thinks about men in general or about the self as a man. However, a person also has feelings (affective aspect) and acts in a certain way (behavioral aspect). For example, a person might believe that men are aggressive (cognitive), feel uncomfortable about it (affective), and avoid men (behavioral).

In the preceding example, the three aspects go together logically and consistently, but it does not always work this way. For instance, I might think that men should be emotionally expressive (cognitive), but I feel anxiety in the presence of an emotionally expressive man (affective), and I cut conversations short with such men (behavioral). These different components of gender roles are summarized in Box 2.1.

To make matters more complicated, there are probably *conscious* and *unconscious* aspects to each component as well. An individual can have a definite sense of what men should be. He or she may feel and behave in consistent and distinctive ways toward men, and at the same time be unaware of these behaviors and attitudes. Most parents *state* that they treat their sons and daughters similarly (Antill, 1987). Nevertheless, there is research evidence that most parents discourage their children (especially their sons) from engaging in behaviors associated with the other sex (Lytton & Romney, 1991).

Box 2.1
Components of Gender Roles

Self

Descriptive: **Self-Concept**—"How I am as a man"

- "I am independent" (cognitive)
- Feeling anxious when dependent feelings emerge (affective)
- Avoiding situations that highlight dependence (behavioral)

Prescriptive: **Ideal Self-Concept**—"How I should be as a man"

- "I wish I were a good leader" (cognitive)
- Feeling ashamed that I am not a good leader (affective)
- Using drugs to soothe discomfort (behavioral)

Proscriptive: **Ideal Self-Concept**—"How I should not be as a man"

- "I should not be weak" (cognitive)
- Depressed feelings (affective)
- Bragging to cover up feelings (behavioral)

Others

Descriptive: **Stereotypes**—"How men are"

- "Men are distant" (cognitive)
- Feeling frustrated in the company of distant men (affective)
- Demanding that the man come closer emotionally (behavioral)

Prescriptive: **Norms**—"How men should be"

- "Men should be caring" (cognitive)
- Feeling affectionate toward caring men (affective)
- Keeping company with men perceived as caring (behavioral)

Proscriptive: **Norms**—"How men should not be"

- "Men should not be cowards" (cognitive)
- Feeling disgusted with men who won't fight to protect someone (affective)
- Ridiculing the man (behavioral)

The Power of Roles

If you were to obtain a part in a stage play, you would have a script that told you what to say and how to behave while acting. On occasion, actors will say or do things that are not in the script (improvising). If you decided to improvise, the director of the play might or might not tolerate it, depending on his or her rigidity and on whether or not your improvising was consistent with the role. However, if you were to improvise too extensively or in a way that was inconsistent with the role, the director would probably discipline you or throw you out of the play.

Actors and actresses know that they have to stick to their roles in order to keep their jobs. Social roles are a little less well defined than stage roles; nobody gives a boy an explicit script telling him how to act as a man. But social roles and gender roles are every bit as powerful. A person may incur severe punishment for stepping outside of his or her prescribed role. In the gender-role arena, for instance, a boy who cries or plays with girls may be ostracized by his male peers. The power of gender roles is most evident when the prescriptions of the role are violated. If you want to experience the power of male gender-role demands first hand (and you are a man), try some of the behaviors that are described in Box 2.2. If you are a woman, try to think of equivalent behaviors that would violate feminine gender-role demands.

Who are the "directors" of the "plays" when it comes to gender-roles? They are everyone who can reward the individual for staying

---

Box 2.2
Male Gender-Role Violation Exercises

Chose a behavior from the following list. Evaluate your thoughts and feelings as well as the reactions of those around you as you perform the behavior.

1. Wear nail polish to class or some other public place.
2. If you are in a satisfying relationship with a woman, talk at length with some male friends about how much you love your girlfriend and how good she makes you feel.
3. Tell a male friend how much you value his friendship.
4. Spend a half-hour in a conversation with a group of people without interrupting or telling a story.
5. Walk to class carrying your books at your chest.
6. Sit with your legs crossed at the knee in some public place.
7. Make a comment about the physical attractiveness of some man.

How did it feel for you to perform these behaviors? How did others react to you? Was there a difference in the reactions of men and women? Of older and younger adults? Of people who know you well and people who do not? What does your experience of gender-role violation tell you about masculinity, yourself, and the culture?

within gender-role boundaries and everyone who can punish the person for stepping outside of those boundaries. Families, friends, employers, romantic partners, and others all have the power to enforce gender-role norms. Sometimes their sanctions are subtle; sometimes they are clearly visible.

Because men (and women) are socialized in a sex-typed society, they internalize gender roles and become their own "directors" to some extent. A great many men incorporate masculine stereotypes and norms into their ideal self-concepts and attempt to live up to those standards. If a man accepts such standards uncritically, then the content of male gender-role norms becomes the yardstick by which the man judges his worth. Pleck (1981b) described such men as "prisoners of manliness" who compulsively conform their behavior to masculine role norms and lose sight of their individuality in the process.

Functions of Gender Roles

From the foregoing discussion, you might ask "Why do gender roles exist?" Answers to this question might involve explanations about reproductive roles (see Chapter Three), the history of work (see Chapter Ten), or social conditions such as the struggle for power and the competition for scarce resources. However, gender roles also seem to be at least partly the result of the human tendency to simplify our complex perceptual worlds by putting things into categories.

By the time we become adults, we have experienced a countless number of objects and events. In order to function effectively, we must learn to separate the important from the unimportant. Part of this process involves thinking about events (objects, perceptions, thoughts, people) in terms of categories. This allows us to reduce data and thereby process a great deal of information. For instance, a child learns that shoes, shirts, and underwear all belong to the general category of "clothing." This allows the child to understand and respond to a new shirt without having to learn about its significance all over again. Being able to think in generalities helps us to predict the value of a new object in a category that we have encountered before, and thus respond to the world more efficiently.

In the same way, we have a propensity for categorizing people. Since biological sex is one of the most basic, visible, and obvious divisions among human beings, it is easy to think about people in these dualistic terms. This categorizing may guide what we notice and remember about a person, how we interpret his or her behavior, and what information we seek from this person (Hamilton, 1979). If you meet a man for the first time, you might notice the size of his biceps but not his hips, remember how loud he laughed rather than how interested he seemed to be in you, and ask about his job rather than about his children.

We also tend to pay attention to and remember information that fits our stereotypes and ignore or discard information that does not (Boden-hausen, 1988; Bem, 1981b). A man who seeks sex indiscriminately may confirm a stereotype. On the other hand, little or no attention might be paid to a man who is monogamous and loving, or else he is seen as an exception. Thus, stereotypes have a self-perpetuating nature (Lips, 1988).

Negative stereotypes about a group are tempered when we have frequent and meaningful contact with group members who do not con-firm our expectations. The more information we have about an individ-ual, the more likely we are to respond to the person and not the stereotype (Swim, Borgida, Maruyama, & Myers, 1989).

Because we tend to be sensitive to other people's expectations, there is a tendency to behave as we think the other person wants us to behave, and this is especially true when we want a person to like us or approve of us (Lips, 1988). Consider the following scenario: Two men are becom-ing friends on the basis of a shared interest in a sport. After a while, each man may have the desire (which is perhaps not even conscious) to ex-pand and deepen the friendship. To do so would involve communicating information that is more personal. Of course, neither one knows that the other has this desire, and both may believe that "real men" don't talk about their families, feelings, or fears. Therefore, each man continues to play a stereotypical male role by talking about sports and maintaining emotional distance whenever he sees the other man. A rigid behavioral pattern is established, and the view that men are only interested in sports becomes a self-fulfilling reality for these men and for people who observe them. Each man has behaved in a way that confirms the other's expec-tations.

We tend to create cognitive structures that represent the essences of masculinity and femininity in order to predict events. However, in our effort to simplify, we tend to oversimplify by exaggerating the similarities of things within a group and by exaggerating differences between these things and those from other groups (Taylor, 1981). The result is an over-estimation of the similarities within each sex and an underestimation of the similarities *between* men and women. Together with the bias toward thinking of the sexes as opposite, this over- and undergeneralization is at the root of gender-role stereotyping.

One way to observe your tendency to categorize and stereotype is to use imagery. Picture in your mind the following people: a basketball player, a housekeeper, a corporation executive, and a nurse. Any of these people could be male or female, but you probably pictured the basketball player and executive as males and the housekeeper and the nurse as females. If you continue to think about these people, some other charac-teristics will emerge. You may find yourself thinking of the basketball player as tall, the nurse as kind, and so on.

It is important to notice that these categorizations may be somewhat useful, as there are fewer male than female nurses, more tall than short basketball players, and so forth. However, problems arise when we over-attend to a category and underattend to an individual (or to the self). Within the realm of gender, people who do not fit stereotypes often have to battle against others' tendencies to attribute gender characteristics to them and respond to them on the basis of these attributions.

There are differences among people in the degree to which they rely on the concepts of masculinity and femininity in processing information. People who are highly attuned to these concepts in their everyday think-ing are called **gender schematic.** Not only do they tend to see the world in these terms, they are more motivated than others to comply with gender stereotypes (Fiske & Taylor, 1991).

Although we may sometimes need to categorize people in order to make sense of the world, there are a variety of schemata other than sex that we can use. Because so many people do not fit gender stereotypes, the use of alternative and multiple schemata helps to avoid the unfortu-nate tendency to deny a person's individuality.

Sexism

Sexism is differential treatment of people based on their biological status as male or female. For example, you might comfort a female friend when she exhibits vulnerability, but avoid a male friend who exhibits the same behavior. Or a man's assertive behavior might be described as "forceful" while the identical behavior, performed by a woman, might be labeled "bitchy." Because gender roles are sometimes subtle, because of our nat-ural propensity toward categorizing and stereotyping, because there are affective and unconscious aspects to gender roles, and because we have all been socialized in a sexist society, we are all sexist in some measure.

While it may be difficult to change sexist *behaviors,* it is often even more difficult to change sexist *reactions* that may be emotional and un-conscious. If you are committed to reducing your own sexism, realistic goals include expending efforts to understand your own socialization and gender-role attitudes, to recognize when you are engaging in stereotyp-ical thinking, and to resist urges to behave in sexist ways. Because sexism involves the disrespect of individuals, these are laudable goals. It is prob-ably not very realistic to believe that anyone can ever become *completely* nonsexist.

Since we live in a patriarchal society in which males wield the vast majority of institutional power, most sexism involves the disrespect of women. A woman who makes less money than a man in the same job is a victim of **institutional sexism.** An adult woman who is called a "girl" or addressed as "honey" when these labels are offensive to her is a victim of **interpersonal sexism.** And a woman who limits her own potential because she has received repeated messages that she is incompetent (and she believes these messages) is a victim of **internalized sexism.** Although these forms of sexism are presented here as distinct categories, they are interrelated. The sexist culture perpetuates all forms of sexism.

It is only recently that people have begun to recognize sexism toward men. Here are some examples of antimale sexism in each of the broad categories just described:

- **Institutional**
    1. Drafting only men for military duty and combat assignments.
    2. In divorce proceedings, awarding custody to a woman when a male is equally or better suited as a parent.
    3. "Bachelor Auctions" (see Box 2.4).
    4. Higher car insurance rates for men.

Box 2.3
Male Bashing

The following are examples of the disrespect of men. Try to imagine the cultural reaction of equivalent messages directed against women or ethnic minorities.

1. *Sign in an office*: "Of course God created man before woman. You always do a rough draft before the final masterpiece."
2. *Lapel button*: "Men are living proof that women can take a joke."
3. *Television commercial*: "When you're looking for a car, and the dealer doesn't have it in stock, that's a slap in the face." (male actor gets slapped)
4. *Radio commercial*: A man is talking to his girlfriend and you hear her punch him in the stomach. Man: "What did you do that for?" Woman: "Because you look so cute when you're doubled over!"
5. Best-selling book: *Men: An Owner's Manual. A Comprehensive Guide to Having a Man Underfoot.* (Brush, 1984)
6. *Greeting card*: Front: "Men are scum." Inside: "Excuse me. For a second there, I was feeling generous."

Many other examples can be found in Farrell (1986). Why has "male bashing" become socially acceptable, and even fashionable, in some segments of society?

Box 2.4
The Bachelor Auction

Bachelor auctions are events in which men offer an expensive date to the highest bidder, with the proceeds going to charity. The bachelor auction represents sexism in addition to many of the destructive aspects of the male gender role:

1. The man is for sale. If women were in a similar situation, many would be rightfully outraged.
2. The "most eligible" bachelors are those who make the most money and have the most prestigious jobs. Not only are they "good catches" as defined socially, but they are able to offer the most expensive dates to auction. This reinforces the social norm that a man's worth as a person is determined by his income and occupational status.
3. Some women who bid on dates with these men expect the bachelor to have sex with them. This reinforces the stereotype that men are always willing to engage in sexual behavior with any willing female.
4. Men are not allowed to bid on the bachelors. Thus, the event is heterosexist.

When asked to justify such events, two rationales are usually given: (1) it's for a good cause and (2) the bachelors do not mind; in fact, they enjoy it. Are these rationales good enough justification?

- **Interpersonal**
  1. Display of negative stereotypes of men in the media.
  2. "Man Bashing" (see Box 2.3).
- **Internalized**
  1. Feelings of incompetence in social relationships.
  2. Guilt around emotional vulnerability.
  3. Refusal to give in to a desire to do "feminine" activities.

Sex Comparison

A commonly held social belief is that men and women are very different in many ways. The areas of difference most often cited include aggressiveness, nurturance, mathematical ability, verbal ability, achievement motivation, competitiveness, dominance, moral development, conformity, and communication styles. Many television shows and popular books have capitalized on people's tendency to think in gender dualisms by displaying "experts" who make sweeping generalizations about sex differences.

Are males and females really different? More accurately, we might ask, *How* different are males and females? or *How* similar are the sexes? These questions are empirical. We cannot know the answers without careful scientific investigations.

Researchers have made comparisons between males and females on a variety of dimensions. Historically, this area of research has been referred to as the study of *sex differences* rather than *sex similarities* or *sex comparisons.* The use of this term indicates that many researchers believed that important sex differences do exist (Deaux, 1985) and that the scientific task is to find these differences and describe them.

The Measurement of Characteristics

If we measure enough people in a population on any dimension and then graph the results, the picture that emerges almost always approximates a normal curve (Figure 2.1). This means that most people's scores cluster around the middle (average) of the distribution, and relatively few people's scores are found at the extremes. For example, if we were to give an intelligence test to 10,000 people, most would score around the average, a few people (the intellectually gifted) would have very high scores, and a few people (the mentally impaired) would have very low scores. The majority of people would score somewhere between these two extremes.

Sex-difference research tends to treat males and females as two different populations. Comparisons are made between the population of

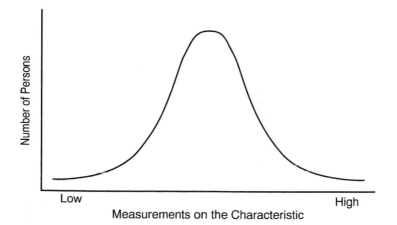

FIGURE 2.1   The Normal Curve

males and that of females with reference to the characteristic of interest. Within each group, the distribution of scores would again approximate the normal curve. The sex-comparison question is, To what extent do the curves overlap? A large sex difference would look like Figure 2.2. A small difference would look like Figure 2.3.

Differences (or similarities) are almost always a matter of *degree* because there are so few behaviors that are seen exclusively in one sex. Men may be more aggressive, but obviously women also display aggressive behaviors. Women may be nurturant more often, but men can also be nurturant. In fact, the only behaviors seen exclusively in one sex or the other are associated with reproductive roles: women can menstruate, give birth, and lactate; men can impregnate (Money, 1987a).

Research in Sex Comparison

An in-depth review of the voluminous sex-comparison literature is far beyond the scope of this book. What follows is the barest summary of some studies that have organized large amounts of research.

In 1974, Eleanor Maccoby and Carol Jacklin published an extensive review of child sex-difference literature. They concluded that, despite the efforts of researchers to find sex differences in a wide variety of areas, very few true differences were convincingly demonstrated. Differences were found in four areas: girls had greater verbal ability and boys had greater mathematical and visual-spatial ability and were more aggressive. While these differences were statistically significant, in every case the amount of difference *between* sexes was vastly smaller than the variability *within* the population of males or the population of females. Graphic displays of differences resembled Figure 2.3, not Figure 2.2. This

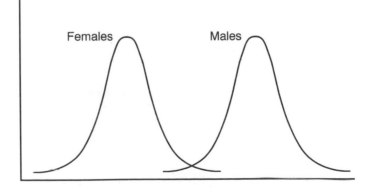

FIGURE 2.2   A Large Sex Difference

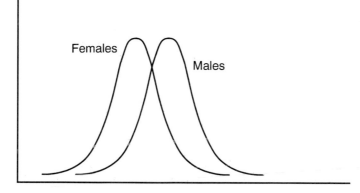

FIGURE 2.3   A Small Sex Difference

means that, for instance, while boys as a group outperformed girls as a group in mathematics, girls who did very well still outperformed the vast majority of boys; boys who did very poorly were still outperformed by the vast majority of girls.

Other researchers using meta-analysis (statistical techniques that combine data from many different studies) have reported similar results (Hyde, 1981; Sherman, 1978; Cohn, 1991; Roberts, 1991; and many others). Deaux (1985) noted that reported sex differences, if found at all, accounted for very small amounts of total variance, usually less than 5%, at the time her research was published.

What is the meaning of these differences? On the one hand, it is clear that predicting an individual's behavior based on his or her biological sex is not a very fruitful enterprise and that generalizing about men and women ought to be done with extreme caution. On the other hand, as Deaux (1985) pointed out, a small difference at the midpoint of a distribution is accompanied by a relatively large difference at the extremes of the distribution. For example, although there is a very small difference between *normal* men and women on aggression, there are many more highly aggressive men than there are highly aggressive women. In fact, men commit nearly eight times more violent crimes than women (FBI, 1992). Thus, small sex differences have important implications when behavioral extremes have major consequences (as is the case with violent behaviors). Clearly, however, saying that "all men" are aggressive, uncaring, disrespectful, and so on is a gross inaccuracy.

When differences exist, even when they are small, they give us clues as to where the strengths, weaknesses, and struggles of men and women lie, and these clues contribute to the awareness of the psychological importance of gender.

Models of Masculinity and Femininity

As knowledge about gender roles has increased and as sex-comparison research has proceeded, frameworks for understanding the psychological implications of gender-roles have been created and revised.

The Gender-Identity Model

The earliest models of gender roles assumed it was important that a person display appropriately "masculine" (for males) or "feminine" (for females) behaviors. From this perspective, sex differences are understood to be based in biology and/or some sort of "natural order." The position here is that men are (and should be) different from women because of differences between the sexes in natural social roles. These differences were thought to be so profound that they pervaded virtually every sphere of human experience. The belief advanced in this system is that the most healthy and productive men are those who are the most masculine, and masculinity is roughly defined as the masculine stereotype (aggressive, unemotional, task oriented, etc.). These traits were thought to be *opposite* from "feminine" traits (nurturant, loyal, dependent, etc.).

The gender-identity model makes a variety of assumptions about the importance of masculinity to the healthy development and general functioning of the man. First and foremost is the assumption that a fundamental developmental task for every boy is to establish an appropriate "gender-role identity," or a solid and appropriate sense of himself as masculine. Ideally, this gender-role identity is built through the boy's relationship with his father or some other appropriate male role model (Pleck, 1981a). The most positive personality development is seen as one in which a boy spends a good deal of time with his father or "father figure," who shows the boy how to "be a man."

The gender-identity model also assumes that "being like a woman" (because it is defined as being unlike a man) is a negative outcome in personality development. This was thought to occur if the boy's father is absent, distant, or passive. A domineering or overpowering mother was also thought to thwart masculine identity, as was the "feminizing" influence of the early school years, when most teachers are women. These kinds of mother-blaming explanations were quite popular with many psychoanalytic theorists. In the last few decades, gender roles have become somewhat blurred, and those who subscribe to the gender-identity model would propose that this has led to a "masculine insecurity" in young men (Lederer & Botwin, 1982).

In fact, any feminine activities can be seen as a threat to masculine identification. There are many parents (especially fathers) who feel that it is extremely unhealthy for their boys to play with dolls, express emotions, do domestic chores such as washing dishes, or spend a lot of time with female playmates or adult women. Likewise, the failure to engage in activities defined as appropriately masculine is also seen as unhealthy. Parents and other adults may worry about a boy who shows little interest in sports or mechanical things (Antill, 1987).

What are the outcomes if appropriate male gender-identity development is not achieved? Freud ([1910] 1989) believed that homosexuality was one possible result, and it would not be difficult to find people that agree. The logic may proceed like this: If a boy does too many feminine things, he might end up identifying with women. He would then end up being like a woman in every way, including having a sexuality that is oriented toward men. However, Kurdek (1987) reported that gay men and lesbians are more likely to exhibit a mixture of masculine and feminine characteristics as opposed to a set of characteristics usually seen in the other sex. In other words, they tend to be broader in their gender expression than heterosexuals, not "inverted," as Freud thought. It should also be noted that there is a great deal of variation in gender-role behavior in the populations of gays and lesbians, just as there is in the population of heterosexuals.

Historically, some theorists (Toby, 1966; Adorno, Frenkel-Brunswik, Levinson & Sanford, 1950) have proposed that an insecure male gender identity leads men into exaggerated masculine behaviors that are attempts to prove their masculinity to others as well as to themselves. These behaviors have been labeled *hypermasculine* and include violence, physical risk taking, and hostility directed toward women and gays. The picture that emerges is of a man who is not really masculine, but is more of a *caricature* of masculinity—the man who puffs out his chest, spits on the ground, beats up gays, and hates women. These activities are ways of covering up the part of the man that is a frightened, insecure little boy, because he has never come to a sense of secure masculinity. This man is like a schoolyard bully who attacks other children because of his own poor self-esteem.

The Androgyny Model

In the 1970s, gender-role theorists and researchers began to question the assumptions of a gender-identity model that viewed masculinity and femininity as opposites. Figure 2.4 depicts the traditional view of gender roles as a single, bipolar dimension. From this (gender identity) perspective, becoming more feminine would mean that a person was less masculine, and vice versa.

As we have seen, however, the sexes are not really opposite. Sandra Bem (1974) and many of her contemporaries believed that it was possible (and desirable) for people to have *both* masculine and feminine traits.

Masculinity   Femininity

FIGURE 2.4   A Bipolar View of Gender-Role Identity

Thus, a person could be strong *and* gentle, task oriented *and* emotionally expressive, and connected *and* independent.

The person with these qualities is defined as **androgynous.** The concept of androgyny is derived from a view of masculinity and femininity as independent dimensions (Figure 2.5). A person can be high in masculinity and low in femininity. This person is traditionally masculine. The gender-identity model would define this as the ideal for a male. The person who is high in femininity and low in masculinity is described as traditionally feminine (the gender-identity ideal for a female).

The person who possesses high levels of both sets of attributes is androgynous (the ideal from the perspective of this model). It is also possible for a person to have low levels of both masculinity and femininity. Such a person is labeled **undifferentiated.** All of these categorizations are independent of the person's biological sex. Although most traditionally masculine people are men, some women also fit this description.

Traditional femininity and masculinity are thought to be strategies for adaptation. Sometimes it is adaptive to express one's feelings (feminine); sometimes it is adaptive to shut down one's emotions and get the job done (masculine). In stereotypical personality development, each sex learns about half of the attitudes, skills, and behaviors necessary for

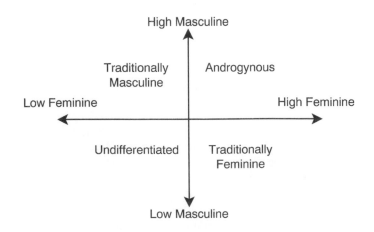

FIGURE 2.5   Masculinity and Femininity as Independent Dimensions

coping in the world. Theoretically, the person who can incorporate both the masculine and feminine into the personality will have a wide repertoire of coping strategies at his or her disposal, and this renders the person more adaptive than a sex-typed person. Thus, for some theorists, androgyny is seen as a mental health ideal.

Whether or not androgyny is associated with better mental health is an empirical question, and there has been an explosion of research on this question in the last two decades (Cook, 1985). This research is summarized in Chapter Fourteen.

Pleck (1981a) described the importance of the shift from gender-identity models to androgyny models. In the former, traditional gender roles were seen as ideal, while in the latter, they were viewed as limiting and constricting a person's functioning. The demand to be masculine or feminine limits behavioral flexibility and shuts the person off from half of the potentially fulfilling experiences of the human race. The gender-identity model views gender roles as emerging from within the individual; whereas the androgyny model sees gender-role prescriptions as imposed through socialization.

This shift in thinking can have important effects on parenting practices. The gender-identity model regards the parents' role as allowing the natural process of sex typing to occur by exposing the child to the same-sex parent, rewarding sex-typed behaviors, and punishing out-role behaviors. The androgyny model regards the parents' role as socializing the child to both masculine and feminine behaviors. Whereas the gender-identity model sees it to be dangerous to let a boy play with dolls, the androgyny model views this activity as important for the boy in developing nurturing (feminine) characteristics.

If we look closely at this model, is it possible to take the position that androgyny is no less of a demand on the individual than masculinity or femininity? Is it possible that there is more to personality than socialization? Joseph Pleck (1981a), in his landmark book *The Myth of Masculinity*, addressed these questions in light of the available androgyny research and proposed a new model.

The Gender Role Strain Model

While the androgyny model emphasizes the limited adaptive quality of sex-typed behavior, the gender role strain model emphasizes that some sex-typed behavior is downright *maladaptive*. In addition, some theorists (O'Neil, 1982; Pleck, 1981a, 1981b) argue that trying to become androgynous means living up to a set of rather stringent demands, and that perhaps these are even greater than the demands to live up to traditional gender roles. For men, traditional gender roles demand competitiveness, aggression, and task orientation. Androgyny demands emotional expression, relationship orientation, and gentleness *in addition to* the demands of traditional masculinity.

Gender role strain is a psychological situation in which gender-role demands have negative consequences for the individual or others (O'Neil, 1981a). The negative consequences of male gender role strain can be described in terms of stress, conflict, health, and mental health problems for the individual. Violence and poor relationships are potential negative consequences for others who come into contact with the individual.

Gender role strain is experienced when gender-role demands conflict with the person's *naturally occurring tendencies.* For example, males in most Western cultures are socialized to be unemotional. For a naturally emotional man, the demand created by this socialization may cause him to feel a good deal of pressure to conform his behavior to the cultural norm. As a result, he may experience negative consequences, such as depression or high blood pressure. The net effect of gender role strain is the restriction of the person's ability to reach his or her full human potential (O'Neil, 1981a). In this example, the man's depression or high blood pressure may restrict his potential by lowering his functioning in his work, affecting his relationship with his partner, or even shortening his life.

O'Neil's (1981a) conceptualization of gender-role strain is illustrated in Figure 2.6. (The theoretical basis for the gender-role strain model is examined in Chapter Six.)

Pleck (1981a) outlined a set of 10 propositions defining the gender role strain model. (Pleck used the term *sex role strain paradigm.*) Words in italics are Pleck's propositions, directly quoted:

1. *Sex roles are operationally defined by sex-role stereotypes.* As discussed earlier in this chapter and in Chapter One, people tend to hold beliefs about how men and women are and how they should be.

2. *Sex roles are contradictory and inconsistent.* It is impossible for anyone to fulfill all of the demands of the masculine or feminine gender role. For instance, men are socialized to avoid everything feminine, but are expected to marry and be intimate with women (Jourard, 1971).

3. *The proportion of individuals who violate sex roles is high.* For men, this is because masculine gender-role demands are contradictory, but also because some demands border on the impossible and because the inner psychological needs of the person can outweigh the social (gender-role) demands.

To illustrate, one gender-role demand is for men to make a great deal of money. Socioeconomic conditions make it impossible for many men to do so. Another demand is for men to be strong and athletic, but the native endowment (natural physique, cardiovascular capacity, eye-hand coordination, etc.) of some men renders this virtually impossible.

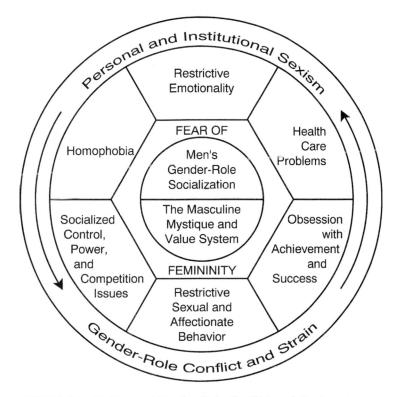

FIGURE 2.6   Patterns of Gender-Role Conflict and Strain
Emanating from Men's Gender—Role Socialization, the Masculine
Mystique, and the Fear of Femininity,   (From "Patterns of Gender
Role Conflict and Strain: Sexism and Fear of Femininity in Men's Lives"
by J. M. O'Neil, 1981, *Personnel and Guidance Journal*, pp. 203–210. © 1981
American Counseling Association. Reprinted with permission. No further
reproduction authorized without written permission of American
Counseling Association.)

Men are sometimes expected to take physical risks to defend their
"honor" (or someone else's). However, safety is a basic (inner) human
need, and it may often win out over the gender-role (social) demand.
Pleck proposes that even the most traditionally masculine, successful,
physical men may feel that they fail to live up to masculine gender-role
norms.

4. *Violating sex roles leads to social condemnation.* Men who exhibit out-
role behavior may be socially ostracized or experience other punishment.

5. *Violating sex roles leads to negative psychological consequences.* A
man who accepts male gender-role norms and fails to fulfill them (which,
as noted, is virtually inevitable) will experience negative emotional consequences such as anxiety or depression. Such men are victims of internalized sexism.

6. *Actual or imagined violation of sex roles leads individuals to overcon-form to them.* Male gender-role strain theorists offer this as a hypothesis for hypermasculinity. Pleck's proposition is that failure in gender role leads the man to compensate for negative emotions by exaggerating the male role behaviors that are the most obvious. He might do so by being aggressive, making negative statements about women and gays, and/or exaggerating his independence. For example, sexual feelings toward other men are clearly not tolerated by the masculine gender role. Men who experience homosexual feelings may compensate for the anxiety that accompanies these feelings by attacking gay men verbally or even physically.

It is important to draw a distinction between this theory of hypermasculinity and the theory proposed by the gender-identity model. In the latter, hypermasculine behavior is thought to be the result of blocking natural (masculine) personality development. In contrast, the gender role strain model views hypermasculinity as a result of the conflict between individual tendencies and social expectations. In the last example, the gender role strain theorist proposes that, if society were to define homosexual feelings as acceptable, the man would feel less anxious about his sexuality and thus have less of a need to compensate for these feelings. If it were culturally acceptable for men to act in stereotypically unmasculine ways, there would be no need to exaggerate one's masculinity.

7. *Violating sex roles has more severe consequences for males than females.* Pleck cites a number of studies that demonstrate greater negative social sanction for male out-role behavior. It should be noted, however, that males can conform to gender-role demands and maintain a good deal of social power, whereas females who conform to their gender-role demands suffer from having much less social and economic power.

8. *Certain characteristics prescribed by sex roles are psychologically dysfunctional.* For instance, aggressive behavior may lead to relationship and/or legal problems.

9. *Each sex experiences sex-role strain in its work and family roles.* The pressures to be a good provider, a good husband, and a good father sometimes conflict with each other. There is always the demand to work harder, make more money, spend more time with one's children, and relate to one's partner better. It is quite difficult to continually do all of these things at the same time.

10. *Historical change causes sex-role strain.* For example, the traditional gender-role demand that men dominate women has become more stressful as women increasingly claim more of their fair share of institutional and economic power. Although changing traditional masculinity is important, it does create anxiety for many men, who feel that they are losing the basic emotional anchor of manliness.

A Comparison and Contrast

The gender role strain model has features in common with both the gender-identity and androgyny models. Both the gender-identity and gender role strain models stress the importance of *naturally occurring tendencies* within the individual. Gender-identity theorists consider these to be sex typed, whereas gender role strain theorists consider them to be more specific to the individual. By contrast, the androgyny model de-emphasizes the importance of the naturally occurring parts of personality. Instead, the emphasis is on the *learned* aspects of behavior and personality.

Both androgyny and gender role strain theorists consider traditional gender roles to be archaic vestiges of history and changing gender roles to be a positive development. Whereas androgyny theorists stress the importance of learning all adaptive behaviors regardless of gender-role definition, gender role strain theorists emphasize being true to one's "inner nature." From the perspective of the gender role strain model, it is acceptable for a man not to be nurturant if he is not naturally nurturant, whereas the androgyny model suggests that innate differences in such characteristics are either nonexistent or unimportant. In contrast, proponents of the gender-role identity model see advantage in maintaining some aspects of gender roles, although probably very few would argue that current social structures are ideal.

All of these models reflect ideas about human nature and behavior with which personality theorists have wrestled for years. We will examine these ideas in more depth in Part Two. First, let's look at some of the attempts to construct measures of gender roles and some of the research that has employed these measures.

Measuring Gender Roles

As gender has become more and more of an object of inquiry, researchers have attempted to construct measures of gender-role characteristics and behaviors. As we shall see, the way that they have gone about constructing these measures has depended critically on the endorsement of the gender-role models just described.

Gender-Identity Measures

The earliest psychological measures of masculinity and femininity were based on a bipolar, unidimensional model of gender (see Figure 2.4). Masculinity was assumed to be the opposite of femininity. It was also assumed that femininity in males or masculinity in females was an undesirable state that reflected psychological problems in the person (Derlega, Winstead, & Jones, 1991).

Terman and Miles (1936) published a scale that reflected these biases. Morawski (1985) described the characteristics of this scale:

> Masculinity scores are gained by replying that you dislike foreigners, religious men, women cleverer than you are, dancing, guessing games, being alone, and thin women. Femininity points are accrued by indicating dislike for sideshow freaks, bashful men, riding bicycles, giving advice, bald-headed men, and very cautious people. (p. 206)

This scale became a prototype for other early attempts at gender measurement. The Minnesota Multiphasic Personality Inventory (MMPI) (Hathaway & McKinley, 1951) is a questionnaire containing 557 statements to which the person answers "true" or "false" in relation to the self. The MMPI yields scores on various scales that were designed to measure depression, odd or unusual thought processes, antisocial tendencies, some aspects of anxiety, and other attributes, including gender characteristics.

The MMPI yields a score on a scale labeled "Mf." This scale was originally designed to differentiate male heterosexuals from homosexuals (Aiken, 1989). Questionnaire items from this scale were based on sex-typed patterns of occupational preference, preferred activities, and emotional responses. A "feminine" man would report not liking mechanics magazines or adventure stories and liking to cook or sew.

A few other scales based on a similar conception of gender roles followed. Among these were the California Psychological Inventory (CPI) "Fe" scale (Gough, 1957) and the Feminine Gender Identity Scale (Freund, Nagler, Langevin, Zajac, & Steiner, 1974). It is important to examine the assumptions behind such measurement techniques:

1. *Masculinity-femininity is a bipolar, unidimensional construct.* Many researchers have demonstrated that these constructs are complex and multidimensional (Cook, 1985; Constantinople, 1973).
2. *Failure to accept the "masculine role" is a sign of psychopathology.* As we have already seen, this is highly questionable. Many authors (O'Neil, 1981b, 1982; Brannon, 1976; Friend, 1991; Goldberg, 1977; and many others) have noted that the refusal to accept some aspects of traditional masculinity may be a sign of vigorous health.
3. *The personality components of femininity and homosexuality are the same.* This assumption would seem to be based on stereotypes of gay men. There have been no successful attempts to differentiate gays from heterosexuals on the basis of personality, probably

because the personalities of gay people are as diverse as those of heterosexuals (Paul, Weinrich, Gonsiorek, & Hotvedt, 1982).

One of the major criticisms of the MMPI and the CPI was that they used relatively insignificant aspects of personality (e.g., liking mechanics magazines) to make inferences about characteristics of central importance such as erotic preference, level of aggressiveness, and gender identity (Pleck, 1975). Reporting traditionally feminine interests such as cooking resulted in interpretations of poor adjustment and lack of masculinity.

For its original purpose, the MMPI "Mf" scale was a total failure, probably because of the flaws in theory. Currently, this scale is considered to be a measure of breadth and stereotypy of interest. College-educated men tend to score more "feminine" on this scale compared with the general population of men (Groth-Marnat, 1990). Under the original intent of the scale, this would mean that college men tend to be disturbed with gender-identity problems. The reality is that college men tend to be broader and less stereotypic than the general population of men in their preferences for activities, perhaps as a consequence of higher than average intelligence and being exposed to a rich variety of ideas. However, some MMPI interpretations continue to make claims based on the original intent of the scale (see Box 2.5).

Box 2.5
The MMPI "Mf" Scale

While the MMPI "Mf" scale has never been useful for describing any kind of gender-related problems, interpretation of scores to this effect persist.

Following is an excerpt from a computer service (*The Minnesota Report*: Butcher, 1987) that scores and provides interpretations for MMPI questionnaires. Presumably, these interpretations are written by an "expert." The testing subject is a 33-year-old, heterosexual, psychologically healthy man whose "Mf" score was about average for a male college student (but higher than the average male in the general population).

"He is rather insecure in the masculine role. Effeminate in both manner and dress and quite passive, he tends to be dependent on others. He may display a feminine identification pattern."

It is interesting to note that a test interpreter could make statements about a person's dress and mannerisms without having ever seen the person.

Androgyny Measures

Beginning in the 1960s, the changing roles of women and the emphasis in psychology on the sociocultural determinants of behavior fueled a resurgence of interest in the concept of androgyny. The conception of masculinity and femininity as independent dimensions (see Figure 2.5) created a need for new measures.

By far the most popular of these measures is the Bem Sex Role Inventory (BSRI) (Bem, 1974). The BSRI is a list of 60 adjectives. Twenty of these are descriptive of traditional masculinity (e.g., "self-reliant," "analytical"), 20 are descriptive of traditional femininity (e.g., "warm," "gentle"), and 20 others are gender neutral (e.g., "conscientious," "likable"). All adjectives reflect the socially desirable aspects of each gender role due to the theory that the combination of positive traits of both roles is the ideal. The person rates himself or herself on each adjective using a seven-point scale ranging from "never or almost never true" to "always or almost always true."

The BSRI yields two scores: one for Masculinity and one for Femininity. People who score high on one scale and low on the other are classified according to gender type. Thus, someone who scores high in masculinity and low in femininity is labeled "masculine." While most people with this kind of pattern would be biological males, this is not always so. Gender-role orientation can be separate from biological sex, and is the case with a feminine man or a masculine woman.

Persons who score high on femininity and high on masculinity are labeled "androgynous." Those who score low on both scales are labeled "undifferentiated." In theory, androgynous people should be the most psychologically healthy of the four types because they have a wider repertoire of adaptive behaviors. Undifferentiated people are thought to be the least adaptable due to the relative absence of the positive characteristics associated with either sex.

A number of other androgyny measures followed the BSRI, including the Personal Attributes Questionnaire (PAQ) (Spence, Helmreich & Stapp, 1974), the ANDRO Scale (Berzins, Welling & Wetter, 1978), and the Sex Role Behavior Scale (SRBS) (Orlofsky, Ramsden & Cohen, 1982). There are, of course, some differences among the BSRI and these other measures. However, Cook (1985), in an extensive review of methods of androgyny measurement, concluded that these differences are relatively minor, indicating that highly related aspects of gender roles are being described by all of these measures. Correlations between these measures and measures such as the MMPI "Mf" scale are low, indicating that androgyny measures are tapping some construct that is relatively independent of what is being assessed by the older gender-identity measures. In addition, masculinity and femininity dimensions on androgyny measures are statistically independent from each other (Marsh, Antill, & Cunningham, 1989), providing some support for Bem's (1974) conception of masculinity and femininity as independent dimensions.

There is strong evidence that sex-typed persons are *gender schematic,* meaning that they tend to process information about themselves and others using gender explanations (Frable, 1989; Frable & Bem, 1978; Bem, 1981b). For example, a gender-schematic person given a list of words to memorize tends to organize the words into "feminine" and "masculine" categories (Bem, 1981b; Markus, Crane, Bernstein & Siladi, 1982). The effects of gender-schematic processing on other behaviors are not yet fully understood.

The 1970s and 1980s witnessed an explosion of research on androgyny. Beere's (1990) literature search produced over 900 references to studies in which the BSRI was utilized. An excellent description and commentary of much of this literature was provided by Cook (1985). She reviewed research on the correspondence of gender role to behavioral flexibility, adjustment, emotional stability, assertiveness, achievement motivation, and psychological health, among other dimensions. Some of this research is reviewed in Chapter Fourteen.

Gender Role Strain Measures

Because the gender role strain model is relatively new, there are fewer measures and a smaller body of research in this area. James O'Neil and his colleagues have developed two versions of the Gender-Role Conflict Scale (GRCS) (O'Neil, Helms, Gable, David, & Wrightsman, 1986). These scales were developed for use with male subjects only and were designed to assess the degree to which a man endorses attitudes, behaviors, and values that have been associated with negative psychological effects. O'Neil proposed four categories of conflict (derived from factor analyses of the GRCS):

1. *Success, Power, and Competition.* The pressure to gain wealth, obtain authority, and be a winner.
2. *Restrictive Emotionality.* Difficulty in expressing one's feelings or allowing others to do so.
3. *Restrictive Affectionate Behavior between Men.* Limiting the expression of warm feelings for other men.
4. *Conflict between Work and Family Relations.* Difficulty balancing these sometimes conflicting demands.

The GRCS-I is a set of 37 statements to which the person responds on a six-point scale ranging from "strongly agree" to "strongly disagree." Some examples of items from each area include:

I worry about failing and how it affects my doing well as a man. (Success, Power, and Competition)

Strong emotions are difficult for me to understand. (Restrictive Emotionality)

Men who touch other men make me uncomfortable. (Restrictive Affectionate Behavior between Men)

My career, job, or school affects the quality of my leisure or family life (Conflicts between Work and Family Relations)

The GRCS-II is a series of 16 brief stories that describe situations in which conflict might be experienced. Respondents report the degree to which they would feel discomfort or conflict in such situations, ranging from "very much conflict–very uncomfortable" to "no conflict–very comfortable." Following are two examples:

1. Your best friend has just lost his job at the factory where you work. He is obviously upset, afraid, and angry but he has these emotions hidden. How comfortable/uncomfortable are you to responding to your friend's intense emotions and fear about unemployment?
2. There's a guy you've idolized since grade school. He's three years older than you are. In high school he was the star quarterback, valedictorian, and very active in the Young Methodist Fellowship. Last year he graduated from college. You have just learned he is a homosexual. How much conflict do you feel between your admiration for this person and the fact that he is a homosexual? (O'Neil, Helms, Gable, David & Wrightsman, 1986, p. 341)

Stillson, O'Neil, and Owen (1991) reported that men with physical problems experienced high gender-role conflict. They also reported that men from varying socioeconomic strata and ethnic backgrounds are similar in patterns of gender-role strain. More research in this area is forthcoming.

Summary

1. Gender roles contain powerful expectations for behavior that are based on a person's biological sex. They include norms and stereotypes that have emotional, cognitive, behavioral, and unconscious components. Violating gender roles often leads to some sort of negative social sanction.
2. Gender roles are at least partly the result of people's tendencies to

categorize events. Roles affect what is noticed and remembered about a person, how behavior is interpreted, and what is expected for one's own and others' behavior.

3. People tend to overestimate differences and underestimate similarities between men and women. Few reliable sex differences have been demonstrated in psychological research.

4. Sexism is the differential treatment of people based on biological sex. It involves disrespect of individuals. Contrary to popular belief, men are sometimes victims of sexism, although sexism against women is more pervasive and often more intense.

5. New models for understanding masculinity and femininity have been constructed in the last 25 years. Chief among these are the androgyny and gender role strain models, both of which view traditional sex typing as limiting and perhaps damaging to people. These models have influenced the psychological measurement of gender and the course of gender research.

PART TWO

Personality Theory
and Male Development

Phil Borges/Tony Stone Worldwide

CHAPTER THREE

The Male of the Species: Biological Perspectives on Male Development

Parents of large families will often say that their children have differing personalities and that these differences were evident even in the first few days after they were born. Such differences could be due to misperception or memory distortion on the part of the parents or from prenatal events such as difficult pregnancies. It is also possible that what these parents perceive are some real differences that are based in biology.

Developmental psychologists have long known that infants differ in **psychological temperament.** Some babies are relatively quiet and content. Others have higher activity levels or are more disposed toward crankiness. Tempermental differences are thought to be determined largely by infants' genes, hormones, and other biological forces, which continue to affect their behavior all of their lives (Vasta, Haith, & Miller, 1992).

It is clear that males and females have differing biologies. There are differences in genetic and hormonal composition that lead to male/female differences in height, weight, muscularity, genitalia, and secondary sex characteristics such as breasts and facial hair. There is little dispute that biological sex differences produce these physical differences. But, to what extent do they produce *psychological* sex differences as well? The controversy over the relative contributions of nature (biology) and nurture (environment) has raged for centuries. Few modern-day theorists on either side of the issue would deny the importance of the other influence, but definite allegiances for nature or nurture can often be found.

In this chapter, we look at theories and research on the biological bases of male development. The central question concerns the extent to which "boys will be boys" because of their chromosomal composition and the extent to which "boys will be boys" because we socialize them to act in certain ways. First, let's turn to the prenatal biological processes that determine male development.

From Conception to Birth: How a Zygote Develops into a Male

Every human being (except one with genetic abnormalities) has 23 pairs of chromosomes. Each chromosome contains genes, which determine or influence a vast number of physical characteristics, such as hair color, height, and complexion. The sex of the person is determined by one of these pairs of chromosomes. Unless there are genetic abnormalities, females have two X chromosomes (XX) and males have one X and one Y chromosome (XY).

During the reproductive process, each parent contributes one of these chromosomes to the offspring. The mother's ovum always contains an X chromosome, and the father's sperm can contribute either an X or a Y chromosome. If a sperm containing the X chromosome (gynosperm) fertilizes the ovum, the offspring will be a genetic female (XX). If a sperm bearing the Y chromosome (androsperm) fertilizes the ovum, the result is a genetic male (XY). Thus, it is the father's genetic contribution that determines the sex of the embryo.

The composition of the sex-determining chromosome pair sets off a string of prenatal events in which the sexes become **dimorphic**, or different in form. For the first several weeks after conception, the embryo is in an **undifferentiated** state, that is, XX embryos and XY embryos are indistinguishable in appearance from each other. (Note that the use of the biological term *undifferentiated* in this chapter is different from the psychological use of the same term in Chapter Two.) There is a pair of undifferentiated gonads that will develop into testes (XY) or ovaries (XX) and later produce sex-specific hormones.

If the gonads are to develop into testes, this process begins around the seventh week after conception. The testes produce **androgens**, which are sex hormones that "masculinize" the embryo during development (again, the reference to "masculinity" is biological and different from the way the term was used in Chapter Two). The best-known androgen is testosterone, which is largely responsible for the development of the penis, vas deferens, seminal vesicles, and other male reproductive structures. Ovaries in the XX embryo begin to develop about the 12th week after conception and produce estrogens.

Estrogens, however, are not necessary for the production of the vagina, uterus, and fallopian tubes. It appears that the embryo is programmed to become physiologically female *unless* androgens are present in sufficient quantity and at the right time to differentiate the embryo into a male. Money and Tucker (1975) called this the "Adam/Eve principle." Unless "something extra" (androgen) is introduced, the embryo will develop into "Eve" without any other prenatal hormonal events.

The necessity of this "something extra" being added is almost certainly the reason that XY embryos are much more subject to genetic complications than XX embryos. For example, if the body cells of the XY embryo cannot respond to androgen (androgen insensitivity syndrome), the person will look like a normal female despite being genetically male.

Case histories of androgen-insensitive people indicate that, since they have female genitalia, they are raised as females with no clue that they are different until they reach puberty and fail to menstruate, due to the fact that they have no ovaries. Their testes remain inside the body. A penis never develops because the body must respond to androgen in order for this to occur. Of course, they produce no eggs and cannot give birth, but they tend to be satisfied with being women (this is evidence that gender roles are largely learned). They also tend to function well sexually, including the ability to have orgasms (Money & Ehrhardt, 1972).

Other cases produce less fortunate outcomes. If the androgen of the XY embryo is overwhelmed by an excess of estrogen, the invariable result is spontaneous abortion (miscarriage). A number of other genetic and prenatal events can cause variations in the normal pattern of sexual dimorphism (Money & Tucker, 1975).

Because of the Adam/Eve process, normal male prenatal development depends on everything going right, whereas normal female prenatal development depends on nothing going wrong. There are many more XY than XX embryos produced. Estimates of the ratio of XY to XX at conception range from 140:100 (Money & Tucker, 1975) down to 108:100 (Harrison, Chin, & Ficarroto, 1992). At birth, there are only about 103 to 106 male infants born for every 100 females (Harrison et al., 1992). So much for females being the "weaker sex"!

At the 7-to-12-week stage of prenatal development, the embryo has two structures (duct systems). The **Wolffian duct system** will develop into male reproductive structures in the XY embryo under normal circumstances. The **Müllerian duct system** in the normal XX embryo will develop into female reproductive structures. The undifferentiated embryo has a **genital tubercle,** which can develop into either a penis or a clitoris. This structure will develop into a clitoris unless influenced by androgens.

The presence or absence of testes and the androgen produced by these glands determines whether the Wolffian or Mullerian system will develop and whether the genital tubercle will become a penis or a clitoris (see Figure 3.1). Although the clitoris has been described as a miniature penis, it is more accurate to say that the penis is a kind of enlarged clitoris.

The hormone production of the testes during the critical period of prenatal development stimulates the Wolffian structures, which then be-

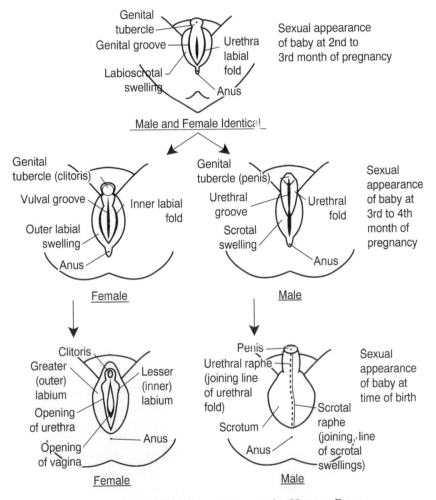

FIGURE 3.1   External Genital Differentiation in the Human Fetus. Three stages in the differentiation of the external genital organs. The male and the female organs have the same beginnings and are homologous with one another.   (From *Man and Woman, Boy and Girl*, by J. Money and A. A. Ehrhardt, 1972, Baltimore, MD: Johns Hopkins University Press. © Johns Hopkins University Press. Reproduced by permission.)

come seminal vesicles, vas deferens, and prostate. At the same time, Müllerian-inhibiting hormone (also produced in the testes) prevents the Müllerian systems from developing into uterus, fallopian tubes, and upper vagina. By the 12th week after conception, the genitals are recognizable as male or female (Rosenzweig & Leinan, 1989).

To summarize, physiological sexual dimorphism proceeds in a sequence beginning with **chromosomal sex** (XX or XY, at conception) and followed by **gonadal sex** (testes or ovaries, determined by the seventh week after conception), **hormonal sex** (dominance of either androgen or estrogen, beginning between 7 and 12 weeks), and then **genital sex** (male or female reproductive structures, which start to develop around week 10) (Rosenzweig & Leinan, 1989). These actions are the result of the *organizational role* of sex differentiation. Later, at puberty, comes the *activational role*, when normal males and females become capable of the only sex-specific behaviors: male impregnation and female menstruation, gestation, and lactation (Money & Tucker, 1975).

Along with these absolute sex differences come some relative differences (secondary sex characteristics). Boys tend to grow facial and chest hair; their bodies get leaner, heavier, taller, and stronger; and their voices deepen. Girls begin to develop breasts and rounder hips. Again, the dominance of androgen or estrogen affects these developments. Keep in mind that these are *relative* differences. There are males with high voices or breast development, just as their are females with facial hair or deep voices.

Evolution and Sociobiology: Sex on the Brain

The rather complex sequence of events just described is necessary in order to ensure that most healthy men and women will have the physiological wherewithal to reproduce. Of course, this is not enough to ensure the survival of the species. Sexual behaviors are also necessary. There is little doubt that hormonal events affect brain structures and pathways, which then have strong influences over these behaviors. But what is the difference in the biological basis of *sexual* behaviors (those necessary for reproduction) on the one hand, and *gender-role* behaviors (social behaviors attributed strongly to either males or females) on the other?

"Not much" would be the answer of those who support the theory of **sociobiology,** the highly controversial belief that both reproductive *and* social behaviors are powerfully influenced by biological forces. These forces, sociobiologists propose, have been put into place through millions of years of human evolution. The position is that if a behavior assists in the survival of an organism, then the gene or gene complex associated with that behavior will be bred into the species through disproportionate representation in subsequent gene pools (Wilson, 1975).

With regard to gender-role behaviors, there may be certain sex-linked social behaviors (like male social dominance) that have survival value for the person, his or her stake in the gene pool, and, ultimately, the survival of the species (Barash, 1982). Critics of this position maintain that it is an ideology disguised as science, and that this ideology is being used to validate male power and privilege by normalizing destructive male behaviors. Box 3.1 invites you to take a critical look at sociobiological proposals.

The sociobiological position is that sex differences in behavior are the result of differences in males' and females' **reproductive investments,** which in turn affect the **reproductive strategies** of each sex. *Reproductive investment* refers to the amount of time and resources that is expended in

---

Box 3.1
Sociobiological Proposals

Highly controversial, biologically based explanations have been offered to account for a wide variety of purported sex-linked phenomena, including:

1. *Male aggression* (Kenrick, 1987). Sociobiologists see men as aggressive in the service of increased breeding opportunities.
2. *All-male groups and "male bonding"* (Tiger, 1969). Because of their aggression, men form groups to protect themselves from harm by other men.
3. *The sexual double standard and male promiscuity* (Wilson, 1975; Daly & Wilson, 1983). Sociobiologists see men as motivated to propagate their genes maximally.
4. *Rape* (Barash, 1979). Sociobiologists see this socially aberrant behavior as an extreme strategy for reproduction.
5. *Female nurturance* (Beach, 1987). Women must protect and feed their young in the service of survival. Men are seen as being more motivated to produce large numbers of offspring than they are to protect the young.
6. *Adult males' preference for younger wives* (Buss & Barnes, 1986). Males prefer younger women because they have more time to reproduce.

What are some alternative (nonsociobiological) explanations of these phenomena? How plausible are these alternative explanations? What kinds of common behaviors have you observed that seem to run counter to sociobiological theory?

producing offspring. *Reproductive strategy* is the behavioral pattern employed in order to ensure that one's genes will be passed on to the succeeding generation (Daly & Wilson, 1983).

Males and females differ markedly in reproductive investment. Physiologically, males need only a few seconds to make their genetic contribution to the reproductive process. Millions of sperm can be deposited into the female in this period of time, and a healthy young male can ejaculate several times a day. Males are capable of impregnating for almost all of their adult lives. Sperm are an abundant resource.

In contrast, females usually only produce one ovum per month and have a more limited number of reproductive years. Therefore, they have a greater investment in the physiological part of the reproductive process than do males. In humans, females carry and nourish the fetus for 9 months, during which time they cannot begin another fertilization. Following birth, they must feed and protect children during the period of helpless infancy if the young are to survive. Whereas sperm are abundant resources, eggs are scarce resources.

Because of these differences in reproductive investment, different reproductive strategies are said to have evolved. In order to propagate his genes as much as possible, the male's strategy is to impregnate as many females as possible and prevent other males from occupying potential partners by making them pregnant. The female, on the other hand, must be selective in her choice of sexual partners. She chooses only the "best" genes for the fertilization of her precious egg (Daly & Wilson, 1983). If she can also persuade the male to stick around, she can ensure a steady supply of Grade A genetic material and even get some help with the care and protection of her offspring.

The consideration of this purported difference in reproductive strategies led sociobiologists to propose a great number of "natural" (biologically based) sex differences. As evidence for the veracity of their claims, they mainly used observations of animal behavior and experiments with animal subjects.

For example, sociobiologists have proposed that men are predisposed to seek more sexual partners, engage in sex more casually, and be more easily aroused by visual stimuli than females (Symons, 1987). These are all the result of evolutionary forces that allow men to be less discriminating than women in their choice of sexual partners. Charles Darwin (1871) described evolution as "survival of the fittest." "Fitness," in this sense, is the male's ability to engage in intercourse with as many partners as possible. Thus, the sociobiological ideal is the promiscuous playboy. Note how conveniently this ideal normalizes the sexual double standard, male sexual irresponsibility, noninvolvement with children, and a lack of a human connection with women.

As evidence in support of their claim, sociobiologists offer the fact that many more societies allow polygyny (men having more than one wife or partner) than allow polyandry (women having multiple partners) (Daly & Wilson, 1983). Sociobiologists downplay the effects of social forces, specifically a historical imbalance of power between men and women, that provide highly plausible explanations of this phenomenon.

Sociobiologists have also offered explanations for male aggressiveness, competition, risk taking, and dominance (Daly & Wilson, 1983; Money, 1987a): Just as rams butt horns in order to win the right to reproduce with ewes, so do men fight with each other in the competition to inseminate women. According to these theories, a male has to take a chance on being hurt or killed in competition in order to pass on his genes. Daly and Wilson (1983) described the process using an animal example:

> Imagine a bull elephant seal that has no stomach for the dominance battles of the breeding beach. Very well. He can opt out: remain at sea, never endure the debilitating months of fast and battle, outlive his brothers. But mere survival is no criterion of success. Eventually he will die, and his genes will die with him. The bull seals of the future will be the sons of males that found the ordeal of the beach to be worth the price. (p. 92)

Sociobiologists have even offered explanations for male dominance of women. Since men can never be sure that they are, in fact, the father of the offspring, they tend to be possessive, controlling, and distrustful of females. Daly, Wilson, and Weghorst (1982) noted that male sexual jealousy is given as a major rationale for spousal homicide and battering. It is difficult to see, however, what evolutionary purpose is served by killing or beating a partner whose attentions have gone astray. Again, we see purported biological explanations for men's disrespect of women (here to the point of violence!) when other, socially based explanations are available.

Behavioral Thresholds

Sociobiology has been presented here as if social-environmental events were of little or no consequence in the formation of personality and gender-role behavior. Even the staunchest of sociobiologists would probably not make such a claim. Sociobiology does not assume the lack of influence of cultural forces on behavior. Rather, the theory is that biology puts into motion a set of behavioral predispositions or thresholds. In other words, we are born with tendencies toward certain behaviors, and the environment can act on any tendency by encouraging it, inhibiting it, or leaving it unchanged (Kay & Meikle, 1984).

John Money (1987a), in speaking of masculine and feminine sexual behavior, said, "Whether the one or the other will manifest itself will depend partly on the strength, insistence, timing, or context of the external evoking stimulus, insistence, timing, or context of the external evoking stimulus, and partly on the internal status of the arousal threshold" (p. 25). Money used the example of language acquisition to illustrate the process. There is a device in the brain that predisposes a child to acquire language. However, there is no gene for the acquisition of the child's native language; it is programmed into the brain postnatally.

In the gender-role realm, if sociobiological assumptions are correct, then the male is born with behavioral predispositions toward sexual promiscuity, violence, and misogyny. If he is born into a culture that considers this behavior normal and desirable (such as mainstream U.S. culture), then it will be relatively easy for this biologically set threshold to be crossed. Thus, we could expect many males in the culture to exhibit behaviors in these realms, because the biological tendency and the social cultural influences work together to produce these behaviors.

On the other hand, the boy could be born into a culture that punishes these behaviors. For example, many fundamentalist Christian cultures discourage promiscuity. In this case, the cultural influence would work against the biological tendency, and we would see less of the behavior. It is also possible for the cultural influence to have a relatively minor effect on the behavior, in which case the frequency of promiscuity would be between the two extremes.

It is important to note, however, that sociobiologists would predict that, in a culture that encouraged promiscuity for both sexes equally, we would see more of the behavior in men. The same would be true for a culture that inhibits the same behavior equally for both sexes. The "bottom line" of sociobiology is that there are some behaviors (such as dominance or aggression) that are easier to produce in males and some (such as nurturance) that are easier to produce in females. The differences are proposed to be the result of the person needing more or less of a cultural "push" to cross the biologically determined threshold.

Sociobiology and Masculinity

Sociobiologists temper their claims with the warnings that cultural influences are also important, that no predictions for individuals are possible, and that describing biological influences is different from prescribing how people *should* act (Kay & Meikle, 1984). Nevertheless, a proposed description of a sex-typed "human nature" does emerge, and the picture of "masculine nature" (as well as men's treatment of women) is not a pretty one.

Sociobiology characterizes the man as an aggressive, driven, immoral, impulsive, uncaring, unfaithful, distrustful, jealous, promiscuous, and cruel animal whose core motivation is to fight off other men and impregnate as many women as possible, at any cost. This view serves to normalize many of the most destructive aspects of the male gender role: overcompetitiveness, attention to task and not relationship, the unimportance of emotions other than sexual and aggressive feelings, and the risking of the body in the attempt to prove one's masculinity. The sad fact is, from a sociobiological viewpoint, that the man can never prove his masculinity. There are always more men to fight off and more women to impregnate. The man can never be sure of his own paternity, so he must be on guard against other men at all times. Eventually, he will grow old and be supplanted by younger and stronger men. The picture that emerges is one of a roaming, violent, uncomfortable creature who can never be satisfied.

From the sociobiological point of view, the only hope for a civilized society is to tame the barbaric nature of masculinity. Whereas male nature is seen as antisocial and valueless, female nature is seen as more civilized, positive, and morally superior (Clatterbaugh, 1990). Gilder (1986) argues that a socialized order can only be maintained if male sexual impulses and antisocial tendencies are subordinated to female nature. He assigns the task of civilizing the world to women, who must use their erotic power to keep men in line by demanding monogamy and commitment from them in exchange for sexual access. The idea is that men have no control and that it is women's job to control them (as if women did not have enough to do!). This view disrespects men and is downright frightening for women.

Gilder's ideal society seems to have traditional morals, where women refuse to have sex before marriage and where monogamy is strictly enforced. Many sociobiologists (Wilson, 1975; Barash, 1982; van den Berghe, 1979) do not believe that this will work because of the primacy of biological over social forces. For these theorists, "boys will be boys" forever, and, therefore war, rape, and the adversarial "battle of the sexes" are unavoidable.

Critique of Sociobiology

People may find sociobiological theory to be compelling because it allows them to maintain the sexual status quo. This is especially true for traditional men, who may be motivated to dominate, disrespect, and overpower women. Biology is often viewed as "real" science, whereas the social sciences are viewed with more skepticism. Oppressors can use the relative statuses of the sciences to validate the unequal status of men and women. The theory of evolution is well accepted, and so sociobiologists look for biological correlates of behavior in a quest to prove that sex differences are of "real" nature, not "trivial" nurture (Money, 1987a).

The major bases of the critiques of sociobilogy are that (1) sociobiological methods are simplistic, (2) sociobiological logic is circular and/or faulty, and (3) the inclusion of supporting data is selective. With regard to the first objection, Goldfoot and Neff (1987) are critical of the usual methods used to test hormonal and other physiological mechanisms in animal studies. The typical approach is to hold constant, or to eliminate, social variables that are known to affect the behavior being studied. For example, sexual behavior in primates might be studied by raising a male and a female primate in a cage together and observing some behavior of interest. Such research ignores the effects of known social influences such as dominance hierarchies and coalition formation within the primate troop.

With regard to the second objection, there is often an assumption in biopsychological research that animals (humans included) behave from the "inside out." If there is hormonal variation and change in behavior at the same time, the bias is to see the hormonal change as causing the behavioral change. There is evidence to suggest that a hormonal change may sometimes be an effect, rather than a cause, of behavioral change. For instance, the attainment of dominance results in testosterone surges, both for humans (male *and* female) and animals (Kemper, 1990).

A good demonstration of the influence of an environmental event on physiology can be found in most people's experience. Let's say that you are very attracted to someone. You begin dating this person and become even more attracted to him or her. At some point, you kiss this person for the first time. You can feel some strong emotional changes, and we might be able to measure them. While hormonal and neural fluctuations "caused" your emotional experience, is it not also true that the kiss "caused" the hormonal and neural change?

Fausto-Sterling (1985) points out that a behavior's frequent occurrence does not necessarily mean that it is genetically based. She cites an example of a primate troop that learned a behavior and passed it down to its next generation. Someone who observed the behavior (which had become universal in the troop) in the second generation might wrongly assume that this learned behavior was genetically based. Fausto-Sterling's criticism is that sociobiologists assume that universal behaviors must be genetic and that genetic behaviors must be universal—a circular logic.

The largest body of critical attacks on sociobiology comes from counterexamples of human and animal behavior that do not support the theory of differential reproductive strategies. (The testosterone/aggression hypothesis is addressed in Chapter Twelve.) Several of these counterexamples cause us to question the hypothesis that it is natural for males to lack parental involvement. In some bird species, the male takes the major responsibility for incubating the eggs (Bleier, 1984). Male primates will protect or adopt orphaned infants, and in the pair-bonding marmoset, the father carries the young more often than the mother after the first few weeks of life (Rosenblum, 1987). Hrdy (1981) and Maccoby and Jacklin (1974) cite a number of studies in which sociobiological hypotheses are not supported by sex-dimorphic behavior in animals.

In humans, the greater involvement of females in the care of children can be accounted for largely by cultural factors. In most cultures, girls are encouraged to partake in nurturing behavior from an early age (Whiting & Edwards, 1988). In cultures that encourage boys to take part in caring for children, no sex differences are found in adult parental involvement (Basow, 1992).

We could also construct a list of behaviors that are difficult to explain from a sociobiological perspective. Homosexuality (Futuyma & Risch, 1984) and sexual behaviors other than intercourse are good examples. Bleier (1984) lists a number of theoretically sound sociobiological hypotheses that are not supported by data.

The major criticism of sociobiology is that behaviors that do not fit the model are ignored or explained away. In the search for the universality of sex-dimorphic behavior across different animal species, we may find that animal behavior is much more diverse than it appears to be at first glance. Human behavior is even more diverse, as almost any social scientist will attest.

Despite many valid criticisms of this theory, we should be careful not to "throw the baby out with the bath water." Many researchers who are not identified with sociobiology (e.g., Money, 1987a; Maccoby, 1987) agree that biology probably produces different sensitivities to behavioral influences in males and females. Social influence can exaggerate or modify these sensitivities, and possibly not in a simple, straightforward way. As Goldfoot and Neff (1987) put it, "most, if not all, behavioral sex differences reflect complicated interactions of endocrine, physical, and social variables" (p. 191).

The quest to discover the relative strengths of biological versus social influences and the nature of the interactions between them is ongoing. It seems certain, however, that biology does not constitute a "whole program" (Money, 1987a, p. 15) for behavior. A man is not "destined" to become violent or promiscuous any more than a tall person is "destined" to become a basketball player.

Summary

1. There is little doubt among developmental psychologists that biology affects personality and behavior, although there is no consensus about the extent of these effects. Since there are differences in male and female biology, there is a good deal of speculation and research about the behavioral implications of these differences.

2. Prenatally, sexual dimorphism begins at conception, when chromosomal sex is established, and proceeds through the development of gonadal, hormonal, and genital differentiation in the normal person. Testosterone is needed to "masculinize" the embryo. A fetus will become female in form without any hormonal action.

3. At puberty, sex hormones are activated and people become capable of reproduction. The only four immutably sex-specific behaviors are impregnation, lactation, gestation, and menstruation. All other behaviors exist in varying amounts in both sexes.

4. The controversial theory of sociobiology is that biology profoundly affects personality by establishing predispositions toward certain behaviors. These predispositions are thought to have survival value for the organism and its genes, and thus they were established through the process of evolution.

5. From the sociobiological viewpoint, major behavioral sex differences are thought to reflect different male and female reproductive strategies. Males who impregnate a large number of females are successful from an evolutionary standpoint because they insure maximum and varied reproduction of their genes. Male sperm are plentiful, and males can participate in the reproductive process with a minimum investment of time and resources. Females, on the other hand, invest a great deal of time and scarce resources (eggs) in the process, and so they are motivated to be more careful in mate selection.

6. These differences in reproductive strategies are thought to underlie important differences in male and female "nature." Females are thought to be biologically predisposed toward monogamy and nurturance, whereas males are thought to have tendencies toward jealousy, aggression, risk taking, promiscuity, and antisocial behaviors. The sociobiological argument reinforces many of the destructive aspects of the male gender role and considers women to be morally superior to men.

7. A number of theoretical and methodological criticisms have been leveled against sociobiology. Many critics charge that sociobiologists selectively include data that support their theories while ignoring other data. Few, if any, theorists consider biology to forge an immutable sexual destiny, but there are major disagreements about the relative strengths of nature and nurture. Critics charge that sociobiology is a patriarchal ideology disguised as science.

Susan Lapides/Design Conceptions

60

CHAPTER FOUR

The Child Inside the Man: Psychoanalytic Perspectives on Male Development

It is fitting that a chapter on psychoanalysis follows one on biology; the two are somewhat closely related. As we have seen, the biological perspective emphasizes the role of the instinctual aspects of human behavior. Psychoanalysis is based on the impact of childhood psychological history against the backdrop of instincts. While the biological perspective is that prenatal events set up propensities for behavior, the analytic perspective specifies the interaction of these propensities with the important events of early childhood.

Few thinkers have had as much impact on the world as Sigmund Freud (1856–1939). His prolific works, along with those of the analytic writers that followed him, provide interesting and controversial frameworks for the understanding of men and masculinity.

Psychoanalysis is a psychology of *meaning*. It addresses questions about the deep, underlying sense of the masculine self in the adult man's life, as understood in the context of important childhood events. Many analytic writers view male gender behaviors as the result of the typical early experience of being a boy, one that differs markedly from that of being a girl.

In this chapter, we look at Freud's view of men, followed by two other important analytic approaches, the ego-analytic position and the theory of Carl Jung. You will notice that, although Freud's theory is based on sexuality, that sexual preference is not addressed in this chapter. It has been saved for Chapter Eleven.

Commonalities among Psychoanalytic Theories

We will be examining some conceptions of masculinity from different psychoanalytic viewpoints. A good starting point is to answer the question, what makes a theory psychoanalytic? May (1986) suggested four broad commonalities among these theories.

First, analytic theories emphasize the importance of **unconscious processes.** These are the parts of an individual's mind of which he or she is unaware. Analytic theorists believe that these deeper parts of the psyche are more important in understanding behavior than the conscious sense of self or the person's thought processes. Freud's theory is often referred to as an "iceberg theory." He believed that, just as most of an iceberg lies beneath the surface of the water, most psychological functioning lies beneath the surface of consciousness.

From this perspective, masculinity is a deep process that goes to the core of a man's being and affects a great deal of his behavior. The awareness of the full impact of gender on the man's life can only be discovered, appreciated, and handled through a long process of self-exploration.

Second, analytic theories emphasize a **developmental and historical approach.** The relevance of early childhood experience is considered to be profound, and the adult is seen as replaying childhood's dramas over and over again. Behavior in the gender-role arena is seen mostly as the result of the boy's early relationship with his mother and father.

Third, analytic theories emphasize the importance of **biology and body.** Jung speaks of the human spirit as a biologically programmed entity. Freud's famous dictate, "Anatomy is destiny" (actually, he was paraphrasing Napoleon) (Freud, [1924] 1989, p. 665), reflected his evaluation that the awareness of and feelings about the body are primary in human functioning. When we combine this emphasis with the relevance of early childhood, we see the importance of the child's awareness of self as separate from mother, the awareness of physical sex differences, and the emergence of sexual feelings in the construction of masculinity.

Finally, analytic theories emphasize the inescapability of **internal conflict.** The man is seen as inevitably caught in the middle of at least two forces. He finds himself struggling with the demands of instinct versus social forces, desire for versus the fear of women, dependency needs versus needs for independence, feminine versus masculine feelings, and/or the desire for something that he cannot possess. These conflicts are seen as having a never-ending quality; nobody can ever resolve them totally. The best the man can hope for is to develop a good compromise, such as finding a comfortable way to deal with the need to be connected and the need to be on his own at the same time.

The Freudian Legacy

Freud's perspective on men and masculinity can best be understood in the context of his personality theory. A thumbnail sketch of the relevant parts of this theory is thus provided.

As mentioned, analytic theories emphasize the importance of the impact of the body on the mind. Freud was a physician, and so he was well educated in the workings of the body. He was also strongly influenced by Charles Darwin's theory of evolution (Freud, [1924] 1989), although he did not apply it in the same way as the sociobiologists.

About Instinct

A major tenet of Freud's biological orientation was the importance of instinct in shaping personality. Instincts are innate bodily conditions that give direction to psychological processes (Hall, 1954). Instincts produce tension (discomfort or pain), and this tension motivates the person to deal with the instinct. For Freud, all behavior is aimed toward the service of the instincts. For example, when you are hungry, a tension is produced and this motivates you to eat. Eating is pleasurable because it removes your hunger. You take a rest from eating when you feel full because the tension is gone. After a while, you will get hungry again, and you will eat again.

You will repeat this pattern of tension, tension reduction, and rest all of your life. Freud called this **repetition compulsion.** You are compelled to repeat this cycle over and over again. You are always trying to go back to the resting state. Instinctual behavior is **regressive** in nature, always oriented toward going back to a past (resting) state.

I have used hunger as an example, but there are other instincts. People are motivated to breathe, drink, remove irritants (such as sneezing when there is a particle in the nose), regulate body temperature, aggress, and reproduce. Instinctual behavior involves seeking **instinctual objects,** which are the things that satisfy instinctual needs. If you are hungry, you might take a hamburger as object. For sexual needs, another person might be the object (the term *sex object* originated with Freud). The instinct provides the impetus necessary for object seeking, and the person invests psychic energy in the object. This process is known as **cathexis.** A person is said to cathect an object.

Instincts never go away completely. They always return in time. Objects, however, are quite variable. If you are hungry, you can invest your psychic energy in cathecting a hamburger, a pizza, or a sandwich—three different objects. Psychic energy can be **displaced**, meaning that it can move from one object to another. With regard to the hunger instinct, the options for displacement are relatively narrow. You can cathect any of a variety of foods, but no activity other than eating will reduce the tension.

The sexual and aggressive instincts are a different story. Broadly defined, the *sexual instinct* is the movement toward any pleasurable physical stimulation. At a higher plane, the sexual instinct can be expressed by a love for any kind of thing or activity. You can love a person, or love learning, or love drinking, or conversation, or money, or creative pursuits. Aggression, too, is highly displaceable. You can express animosity toward a person, or an idea, or yourself.

In sharp contrast with other, more basic instincts, you can deal with sexual and aggressive instincts in very indirect ways. For Freud, the personality is largely a result of the person's pattern of displacing the sexual and aggressive instincts. As mentioned before, most of this psychic functioning takes place in the unconscious.

The Structure of Personality

If instinctual gratification were the only problem we ever faced, life might not be easy, but it would be rather uncomplicated. This is not the case. We cannot seek instinctual fulfillment in an indiscriminate way. What would happen if you saw an attractive person walking toward you on the street and you decided to (using Freud's terms) sexually cathect this person regardless of his or her wishes? It would probably not be a positive experience.

Since we live with other people, instinctual needs inevitably come into conflict with the social world. The person must learn how to gratify needs in a socially acceptable way. The process of maturing is one in which primitive, impulse-driven people get transformed into civilized people who are able to delay gratification until the appropriate time and place. A good deal of what we teach children in kindergarten and elementary school is in the service of learning impulse control and social rules: wait your turn, share, consider other people's feelings, and so on.

The ability to make a compromise between our internal instinctual selves and the demands of living in the real world is what allows us to do the two things that characterize the psychoanalytically healthy person: loving and working. The development of these abilities is a lengthy process, but our style of dealing with the two great forces (instinct and society) is established early in life.

When babies are born, they are wholly instinctual. From the Freudian standpoint, babies are nothing more than bundles of biology with storehouses of psychic energy. Infants are helpless, and parents or care-takers work hard at fulfilling the children's instincts. They feed babies, keep them warm enough, and remove irritants by changing their diapers. Babies are incapable of doing these things for themselves because they are too primitive to seek objects. The part of the personality that is prim-itive, instinctual, and present at birth is called the **id.**

Slowly, babies begin to develop another part of personality. They become less and less helpless. Early in life, people have to feed them, but after a while they begin to grab the food themselves and put it into their mouths. In other words, they start to assert their wills by seeking objects. This is the beginning of the formation of a new part of personality, the **ego.** The ego is more organized than the id and can deal with the real world. In the healthy person, the ego gains more and more strength as the person matures. The ego can plan, and it can hold off the id until a suitable object can be found.

Eventually, parents begin to make social demands on their children, and because children are attached to the parents, they begin to internalize these demands. We all carry our parents around with us, for better or worse. The first important imposition of social demand is toilet training, when, for the first time, children are required to exert physical control over an instinctual process.

Robert Bly (1988) is fond of saying, "You came into this world with all kinds of energy, but your parents wanted a 'nice boy' (or a 'nice girl')." Parents care less about instinctual gratification than they care about your being socialized. They want you to be able to handle your instincts and learn how to make something of yourself in the world. Freud called the internalized parent the **superego,** and there are two parts to it. One part, the **ego ideal,** contains your parents' aspirations for you. It is this part of the superego that makes you feel good when you do something your parents value, like reaching a goal. The other part, the **conscience,** causes you to feel badly when you go against parental wishes.

When you are young, you feel good when your parents praise you. As you get older, you don't need them to do this as much. Your mother and father may have praised you if you brought home good grades in elementary school. By the time you reach college, you should be able to have these feelings of satisfaction all by yourself because the parent is internalized in the form of the ego ideal.

Likewise, you get punished for certain behaviors when you are young, sometimes just with your parents' disapproval. When you get older, you are able to punish yourself with guilt. Again, this is due to the internalization of the parent, this time in the form of the conscience.

Besides parents, the superego is also affected by important other people in the child's life and by the culture. People refer to the superego when they say things like, "I never raise my voice; that's just the way I was brought up." Giving in to instinctual aggressive urges would result in very uncomfortable feelings of guilt and shame emanating from the conscience.

After the formation of superego, the ego finds itself in a clash between id, which is always pulling for pleasure, and superego, which is always pushing for perfection. The healthy person has **ego strength,** which allows him or her to balance these two conflicting demands. If the id dominates the personality, the person will be impulsive and antisocial. If the superego dominates, he or she will be tense and uncomfortable, due to the unrelieved tension of the instincts.

Masculinity and the Structure of Personality

What do id, ego, and superego have to do with masculinity? A number of important connections of both the positive and the negative aspects of male gender roles can be made.

The analytic ideal is a paragon of positive masculinity: the person who can love and work. Such a man can achieve a satisfactory balance between his biological side and his social side. He is able to be responsible both in his work and in his dedication to his partner (and his family, if he has one). Note here that the analytic ideal is quite the social conformist, but note also that many men who fit this description are dedicated, principled, hard-working, caring individuals who enjoy life and contribute to the greater good.

In Freudian terms, the man just described has high ego strength, which was built by his being able to deal with problems and assert his will. This is also a person with a strong ego ideal and a reasonable conscience. He can be goal directed and achieving. Socially, the development of these structures in men is encouraged.

Some men are not so fortunate. Destructive masculinity can be conceptualized as being the result of poor superego development; rigid, harsh, or destructive content of the superego; or poor ego strength.

Theoretically, the id is constant. It is biological and innate, so it exerts about the same amount of influence on everybody. Differences among people reflect differences in the way the id is handled and directed. In the case of poor ego and superego development, the id is the most powerful part of the personality, and so it is allowed to run amok. The result is a person who is antisocial and destructive, giving vent to sexual and aggressive impulses without restraint.

Violent criminals can be conceptualized as people with poor ego and superego development. Most of these people are men. In fact, more than 85% of violent crimes in the United States are committed by men (FBI, 1992). If Freud is correct in his assumptions, many men may retain id domination through faulty early socialization.

The major inhibitor of destructive id impulses is the superego, which makes the boy feel guilty when he is destructive and good when he is prosocial. According to Freud, male superego development depends critically on a boy's identification with his father or "father figure." If the father is absent, emotionally distant, or overly punitive, the identification is weakened. Unfortunately, a lot of fathers fit this description. According to psychoanalytic theory, a lack of ego ideal in the boy leaves him aimless and unable to reward or restrain himself appropriately.

It is also possible for id and superego to be strong but the ego to be weak. In this case, the result is a pattern of behavior in which the person does things that are harmful to someone else, feels guilty about it and expresses regret, but then does something else like it later on. Baseball great Babe Ruth fit this pattern. He was well known for his excesses in food, drink, sex, and aggression. Occasionally, he felt guilty about certain behaviors and their effects on people, especially children who looked up to him as a hero and role model. Nevertheless, he would continue these behaviors, not because he was insincere in his apologies, but because he lacked the ego strength to restrain the id.

In other cases, the content of the superego may be especially harsh, rigid, and/or destructive. This may happen if the parents' demands on the children are extreme. If the parent inculcates the demands of destructive masculinity into the boy, he will have a punitive superego that can make him feel chronically unworthy and unmasculine. This is the case for many, many men, for whom the superego demands that they be competitive, wealthy, in control at all times, and dominant over women.

The Oedipus Conflict

Another perspective on masculinity can be seen in Freud's model of psychosexual development. Freud believed that instinctual energy (called **libido**) courses through stages of psychosexual development that are defined in relation to certain parts of the body (called **erogenous zones**). Each stage entails a crisis that must be handled well for healthy psychosexual development.

In the earliest stage, the center of libidinal pleasure is the mouth. The crisis in this oral stage is weaning. If it is not timed well, negative personality effects are believed to result. In the next stage, pleasurable feelings are centered around the anus. The crisis here is toilet training, when the child must assert ego control over an id function. Poorly timed, harsh, or overly lenient toilet training can have deleterious effects. These first two stages are over by the time a child is about 3 years old, and Freud did not think that males and females were much different from each other in these early struggles.

The third stage of development is the phallic stage, and Freud proposed that sex differences are produced in this stage. The phallic period (roughly ages 3 to 6 or 7) is the first primitive emergence of adult sexuality. Children at this age become very aware of and concerned about sex differences. Masturbatory activity and some forms of sexual play among children at this age are not unusual.

Freud believed that sexual interest at this stage centered around the penis for both boys and girls. He also believed that, during this time, the child begins to experience unconscious sexual feelings for the parent of the opposite sex. It is not unusual for the child to express a wish to marry this parent. As a result of the desire for the other-sex parent, the same-sex parent is unconsciously perceived as a rival for the affection of the other parent. This is a dangerous and uncomfortable love triangle, and the child must resolve this crisis. Freud called this the **Oedipus conflict,** after the king of Thebes in Greek mythology who kills his father and marries his mother.

A boy feels this desire for his mother, who is affectionate and caring. Strong sexual feelings are centered in his genitals, and he betrays this fact by touching his penis often. This masturbatory activity is usually punished by the parents, and the boy gets the message that he might get punished by having his penis removed. This **castration anxiety** is also fueled by the rivalry with his big, powerful father, who might punish him for having these feelings toward his mother. When the boy first sees the female genitalia, he perceives the female as a castrated male and realizes that this could happen to him (Freud, [1924] 1989).

At the height of the Oedipal conflict, the boy feels that gratifying his desire for his mother would mean losing his penis, and it's just not worth it. In the normal resolution, he gives up these feelings toward her and displaces them on to a more appropriate object, such as the girl next door. Part of this solution involves the boy's identifying with the father. As the boy begins to see himself as more and more like his father, the feeling of threat is reduced. Identification also allows the son to experience romantic feelings for the mother vicariously through the father. This is an important step in superego development, as the boy begins to internalize the father's values and characteristics. The sexual love for the mother is converted into feelings of tender affection.

Freud's view of the female Oedipal conflict is different from his view of the male conflict. He thought that girls, too, experienced themselves as castrated males. While girls desire their fathers and see their mothers as rivals, their desire is mixed with bitter feelings because they want a protruding sex organ like their fathers'. While boys suffer from castration anxiety, girls suffer from **penis envy.** The resolution to the conflict is similar: The girl gives up her desire for her father and displaces it. Freud thought that penis envy was converted into the desire to bear a child. He also thought that, because girls do not experience the powerful motivator of castration threat, they do not give up their father desire as easily and they do not identify with their mothers as fully. As a result, they have less well developed superegos. Freud considered women to be morally inferior to men for this reason.

Freud has been roundly criticized for this view of women. The great feminist analyst Karen Horney (1932) counterargued that what women envy is men's social positions and not their penises. In support of this hypothesis, Nathan's (1981) cross-cultural research found that penis-envy dreams among women are more common in cultures where women have low social status. Horney's view is that a girl's psychosexual development centers around her own genitalia and not the male's. Freud himself felt unsatisfied with this part of his theory, and at one point stated that it was the task of women analysts to describe the female psyche (Freud, 1925).

Oedipus and Masculinity

Theoretically, the childhood Oedipal crisis colors the adult man's approach to relationships with women (originally represented by mother) and authority figures (represented by father). Fine's (1987) view of the Oedipal situation is that confusion results when the boy's sexual expression is punished. He loves his mother, but he cannot approach her sexually, and an early split between sex and affection can result. These are the roots of the so-called "Madonna/whore complex" (the religious Madonna, not the singer). The man feels that virtuous women, those whom he respects, are not sexual (the Madonna was conceived without original sin—absolutely pure). Sexual women ("whores") are not worthy of respect. Thus, the man has a tendency to degrade a woman if she is sexual with him. This sexuality/love contradiction causes extreme problems in the man's relationships with women and perhaps in his sexual functioning. The boy who successfully resolves the Oedipal conflict becomes a man who can love and be sexual with the same woman. The boy who does not may grow up to be misogynist, promiscuous, or sexually dysfunctional as he plays out the Oedipal drama again and again. As Freud ([1924] 1989) said, "The finding of an object is in fact a refinding of it" (p. 288).

In the Oedipal situation, fathering may again have an important effect. If the father is caring and attentive to the boy, he will facilitate positive identification and mitigate castration anxiety. If, however, the father is hard on the boy, the identification process will cause the boy to become hard on himself, and castration anxiety may be exaggerated. The boy grows up fearful and without a strong sense of himself as masculine. He may act "macho" to cover up his insecurity. He may be aggressive to defend against the unconscious threat of castration (Tyson, 1986). He may derogate women in order to feel better about his masculinity.

The view of the man as seen through Freud's lenses is a rather pessimistic one (as was his view of women). As with sociobiological theory, the picture that emerges is one of an animal nature that is only controlled through socialization. We do begin to see the troubling effects of conflict within the man, but Freud's view is that this conflict is part and parcel of the human condition. The best that can be expected is an uneasy compromise that leaves us with a manageable level of anxiety. We get the feeling that development is like going through a mine field and that nobody escapes without some battle scars.

Critique of Freud

Many criticisms of Freud are leveled at his assumption that sexual instinct is the primary determinant of personality. Even some of his closest followers abandoned the sexual theory, although most maintained their belief in the importance of the unconscious and early childhood. If we look at the parent-child attachment as not primarily sexual, very different conclusions about male functioning become possible.

Even if sexuality were the basis of human personality, some of Freud's conclusions are open to debate. The description of castration anxiety as being fairly resolvable is one of the most questionable.

Freud's position is that the Oedipal crisis in the boy is touched off by his realization that he could lose something valuable. In the girl, it is stimulated by her imagining that she has already lost it. If you have lost something valuable, it is greatly disappointing at first. After a while, you accept that you have lost it and move on. If, however, you have a deep fear of losing something, you are obligated to anxiously protect it all of your life. The penis is also in somewhat of a vulnerable place, being outside of the body. It seems that castration anxiety would follow many more men into adulthood than penis envy would follow women (if it exists at all, which is doubtful).

In 1932, Karen Horney published a classic essay on male psychology entitled, "The Dread of Women," in which she argues that the male process of psychosexual development produces in the boy a deep-seated fear of the feminine and that much typical male behavior in adulthood is a reflection of this dread. Horney argued that, while castration is fearful, the vagina, with its ability to engulf the penis, is frightening to the male.

Early in the phallic stage, as the boy's sexual feelings begin to center in his penis, there is also the beginning of the urge to penetrate with his penis. After all, that is the sexual function of that organ. Deeply buried in his biology, and thus in his unconscious fantasy life, is the desire for the vagina, the organ that is complementary to his own. The vagina is dark, mysterious, and unfamiliar, yet he has the desire to put the most precious part of himself into it. The threat of castration by the father does not approach the threat of engulfment from the mother. Horney illustrated this in metaphor: "Sampson, whom no man could conquer, is robbed of his strength by Delilah" (Horney, [1932]).

If, as Freud believed, the other-sex parent is the love object in this stage, then the size difference between parent and child leads to a difference in how boys and girls experience themselves. Girls, Horney believed, begin to have sexual desires to take in the penis. If the father is the love object, then her vagina is too small for him, and so she fears that he could hurt her. The boy, with his mother as love object, intuitively senses that his penis is much too small for her and reacts with feelings of inadequacy. He anticipates that his mother (and later other love objects) will ridicule and deride him. Again, these feelings are buried deep in the unconscious.

The implications for masculine psychology are far reaching. Every man, Horney proposed, has a deep sense of apprehension that a woman can destroy his self-respect and that his penis (and thus his manhood) is not large enough. Masculinity, then, is never on very solid ground. Rather it is fraught with dread, and the man must make extreme efforts to manage his anxiety around his masculine adequacy. Basically, he has two options: He can withdraw from women or compensate for these uncomfortable feelings.

Withdrawal solutions include staying away from women either physically or emotionally. Compensation solutions involve a man going to extremes to prove his manhood over and over again. Part of this strategy may involve debasing and controlling women. By doing so, the man can deny the power of the woman to hurt him. At the extreme of masculine inadequacy, we see desperate behaviors such as rape and domestic violence, which can be seen as aggressive reactions to the extreme dread of women.

A number of what might be considered more typical male behaviors could be construed as reaction to the fear of women's derision. Going to great lengths to please women may be one strategy. Staying emotionally distant from his partner may be another. Objectifying women may be a third. When a man reduces a woman to an object, he denies her power. If she hurts him, it softens the blow to feel that she is not a real person. Horney goes so far as to suggest that the institutional male oppression of women is the result of the reaction to deep-seated inadequacy in the collective male psyche.

Speaking to the primal fear of the inadequacy of penis size, we could also make some guesses about what might be compensatory masculine behavior in the culture. More than a few women have complained about how much men talk about and seem to think about penises. Consider how many nicknames there are for the penis, the number of jokes about penises, the huge penises of "actors" in hard-core erotic movies, and the reluctance to depict an erect penis in mainstream movies and magazines.

Horney's essay is an undisguised account of the power of the feminine and is a possible explanation of the core attitude of antifemininity that characterizes traditional masculinity.

Identifying with Mom: Ego Psychology and Masculinity

Many of the theorists who followed Freud disagreed with him on one major point. They believed that some aspects of ego functioning were independent of the id. For these theorists, the ego is not something that merely serves to direct and control the instincts, it also serves to drive the person to deal with some basic psychological tasks: developing a sense of self, relating to other people, learning to work, and developing values.

These theorists are sometimes referred to as Neo-Freudians because of their revisions of Freud's basic framework. They are more often called ego analysts or ego psychologists because of their emphasis on the independent functions of the ego. Implicit in their viewpoints is the rejection of sexuality (instinct) as the major motivator. Various other core motivations are offered in its place by different theorists. Many of their theories center around the person's motivation to develop an identity or sense of self.

Identity is a sense of "who I am" as a unique individual. Identity involves a feeling of being the same person even though one's behavior varies across different situations and roles. The formation of identity is a long process. It starts in infancy with the child's realization that he or she is separate from the mother. From that point on, the definition of self gets more and more elaborate. As the individual progresses through adolescence and adulthood, the formation of identity involves a variety of decisions around relationships, work, sexuality, values, and preferences.

Gender identity is the part of overall identity that defines for the person what it means to be male or female. After children learn that they are not a part of their mothers, boys learn that they are similar to their fathers and different from their mothers in a basic way, and girls learn the converse. Children as young as 2 to 4 years of age become very upset if someone says to them, "What a nice girl (or boy) you are," using the incorrect sex label. This is evidence that gender identity is learned very early and that it has a strong emotional component (Lewis, 1987). The strength of the emotion associated with gender identity attests to its central place in overall identity.

Although there is some disagreement with their position, most analytic theorists think that it is important for a child to establish a strong gender identity. Because of sex differences in child rearing, the formation of gender identity is thought to proceed very differently for males and females, with important implications for the personalities of adult men and women.

Gender identity is formed mainly through the child's interactions with his or her parents. The primary caretakers of infants in most cultures are female. The amount of time a typical mother spends with the infant far outweighs the typical father's time. Thus, the most striking sex difference in early parent-child interactions is that girls are raised by a same-sex parent, boys by an opposite-sex parent.

Hartley (1959) first proposed that the impact of this sex difference in early experience is considerable. In the formation of gender identity, girls learn "I am what mom is." They experience themselves as continuous with their mothers and define themselves through the process of attachment. Boys, on the other hand, do not learn "I am what dad is" so much as they learn "I am what mom is not." Boys experience themselves as different from their mother and define themselves through the process of separation. "I am what mom is not" defines the content of gender identity in a negative way. Rather that starting out with some sense of masculinity, the boy starts out with a sense of antifemininity.

Before sex differences are perceived in early childhood, children of both sexes feel continuous with their mothers, and the identification process has already begun. For girls, it is a process that continues on the same track when gender differences are perceived. For boys, however, gender-identity development depends on switching tracks. There is an interesting parallel here with the prenatal physiological process in which the male needs "something extra" (Money & Tucker, 1975) to diverge from the programming to be female.

From this view, boys must put rigid boundaries between themselves and their mothers in order to define themselves as masculine. If we believe that some identification with the mother has already taken place, then the separation process entails a repression of the mother identification.

These dramas get played out again and again, according to analytic theory. The result of this separation process is that the boy's gender identity rests on his putting psychological barriers not just between himself and mother, but between himself and anything feminine. Included are "feminine activities" and, of course, girls and women themselves. Having already identified with the mother, the boy must also repress the feminine parts of himself, usually represented by his emotional experiences and feelings of relatedness to others. Girls are under no such pressure. They do not have to deny the masculine in order to define themselves as feminine (Chodorow, 1978). This is one possible explanation for the tolerance of "tomboys" but not "sissies."

The feminine parts of the boy are relegated to the unconscious because they pose a threat to the ego. When "feminine" experiences, such as sentimental feelings, surface from the unconscious, they are associated with anxiety, which must then be defended against. In a typical scenario, a man may go to a movie, begin to identify with a character, and feel some strong emotions. He may experience this as a threat to his masculinity and detach himself from emotion by putting his mind on something else. Eventually, he may begin to avoid certain types of movies.

The early childhood, sex-typed mix of separation and attachment is considered by some to result in an enduring, sex-typed approach to the world. Chodorow (1978) described women as "selves in communion," meaning that women tend to experience themselves in the context of relationships. Gilligan (1982) applied this to women's moral reasoning that is centered on concern for the people involved in a situation, rather than the masculine concern for the correct application of abstract principles. Chodorow's (1978) description of men is as "selves in separation" oriented toward independence and task completion.

Similar categories of approach to the world were proposed by Bakan (1966), who described femininity as mainly "communal" and masculinity as mainly "agentic." Communion is involved with attachment, cooperation, and expressiveness. Agency is associated with separation, individuality, assertion, mastery, and the repression of feeling. In the U.S. population of adolescents, sex differences in self-reported agentic and communal characteristics have been stable since the 1960s, despite social changes in gender roles (Galambos, Almeida, & Peterson, 1990).

An individual needs to be both agentic and communal in order to function fully. Sometimes it is important to cooperate, value relationships, and express the self. Other times, it is important to go off by oneself and get something done. In many cases, it is important to do both simultaneously. Obviously this conceptualization values androgyny.

Bakan (1966) warns of the danger of an agentic approach that is not tempered by the consideration of relationship. **"Unmitigated agency,"** which is more often found in men, is responsible for many destructive behaviors, such as dominating a partner or a subordinate or hurting someone who gets in the way. War, in which people's lives are subjugated to a political task, is the ultimate in unmitigated agency.

Unmitigated communion, a trait found more often in women than men, is a situation in which the person subordinates the needs of the self to that of others (Buss, 1990), such as when a person fails to complain when his or her rights are being violated or when he or she consistently defers to others' opinions and wishes.

While unmitigated communion may lead the person to feel powerless and depressed (Stewart & Salt, 1981), unmitigated agency could result in the destruction of the planet. There is also some evidence that unmitigated agency may be associated with physical illness and that an agentic-communal orientation is associated with fewer physical and mental health problems (Buss, 1990).

Heinz Kohut and the Psychology of the Self

Another relevant ego psychology perspective was provided by Heinz Kohut (1971), who theorized about the role of the parents in building two important aspects of personality: ambition and the ability to manage anxiety. The trait of ambition rests on the child's feeling worthwhile and valuable. The ability to manage anxiety depends upon feeling competent to do so. Both characteristics have roots in childhood.

Since the self is unformed at birth, its development depends on feedback from the parents. When a child is very young, parents provide need fulfillment and praise in very generous amounts. A minimum effort on the child's part results in a maximum response from the parents, and the child can be very grandiose. Parents and other adults make children feel like they are the center of the universe.

From Kohut's point of view, young children need two things from parents: someone to admire and someone to soothe them when they are upset. These two needs are the bases of what Kohut called the **bipolar self.**

On the admiration pole, children need their parents to approve their natural grandiosity and exhibition of the self. Children get approval from all kinds of exhibitions. Parents react with a good deal of approval to infants who merely smile. Later on, when a child walks, or talks, or does anything positively self-assertive, the parents express pleasure in the child. Kohut calls this approval **mirroring.** When parents mirror, the child feels powerful and worthwhile.

Sometimes children get hungry, cold, scared, or cranky, and they feel vulnerable and uncomfortable. At these times, the child needs the calming, self-confident parent for soothing and quieting. When the world is harsh, the parent softens its impact on the child and "makes it better."

As children grow, parents expect more and more from them. A smile from a 5-year-old does not always get the same response it got when he or she was an infant. At some point, children have to get their own sweaters when they are cold rather than having the parent do it. Good parents continue to mirror and soothe, but they get more and more stingy and selective about it.

This, of course, is not a bad thing when the doses are right, because children will eventually become adults, when they will have to depend on their own resources. Parents build physical and psychological independence in children by forcing them to do things for themselves. Parents cannot "approve all grandiosities, nor can they soothe all distress" (Sawrie, Watson & Biderman, 1991, p. 145). These **empathic failures** frustrate the child. If the frustration and anxiety from these events are manageable, then the child will be able to deal with the events. Kohut called this **optimal frustration.** These kinds of experiences strengthen the ego by forcing the child to develop his or her own emotional resources.

An example will illustrate Kohut's theory. When newborn infants cry, it is good parenting to pick them up, hold them, and do what is necessary to quiet them. When they get older, you sometimes hear parents say things like, "It's good to let them cry for just a little while; sometimes they stop on their own." As the child gets to each new developmental level, the parent allows a reasonable amount of frustration to force the child to develop inner resources. It is the same with mirroring. The parent cannot praise the child for every display or the child's grandiosity will get out of hand.

The process in which these inner resources develop is one in which the child takes the mirroring and soothing parts of the parent and internalizes them. Kohut called this the **introjection** of the parent. It is similar to Freud's theory of identification. Introjection is the process by which we come to carry our parents around with us.

If optimal frustration is not present, problems develop. Too much mirroring may cause child to become so grandiose that he or she expects special treatment all of the time. Too little causes the child to grow up hungry for mirroring. He or she will tend to become enraged at not receiving enough admiration (Kohut, 1977). In either case, the person will always be dependent on others because his or her emotional resources have not been developed.

The person who does not receive enough mirroring in childhood compulsively seeks it from others in adulthood. People who experience this **mirror hunger** may be quite talented, but underneath they do not feel valued. Because they need a steady supply of admiration and approval from others, they tend to be self-absorbed and not very capable of loving. They often exploit others to indulge their own desires. Such people are called **narcissists,** after the mythological character Narcissus, who fell in love with his own reflection and could not bring himself to look away.

Narcissists, who tend to be unhappy, emotionally unstable, and prone to depression and substance abuse, are disproportionately represented among men (Sue, Sue, & Sue, 1990). Many athletes and performers fall into this category. Culturally, the masculine emphasis on performance may encourage the development of narcissism. The man who receives admiration for what he does (rather than who he is) is driven toward defining the self by accomplishment and display.

A series of research studies by Watson and colleagues (Watson, Taylor, & Morris, 1987; Watson, Biderman, & Boyd, 1989; Sawrie, Watson, & Biderman, 1991) demonstrated some connections between masculine gender roles and internal narcissism, which is described as the repeated effort to get others into one's "orbit."

When grandiosity is able to develop positively, it evolves into mature ambitiousness, a deep belief in the power of the self. If it remains in its infantile state, it becomes arrogance, destructive aggressiveness, and compulsive attempts to seek applause from others. Androgynous men did not exhibit these traits in the studies described, providing support for the view that internal femininity in men mitigates destructive masculinity.

One further note is relevant. Kohut believed that, throughout life, we modify parental introjects by incorporating parts of other people into the self. We become more mature this way. This makes it hopeful for males with poorly developed identities to profit from meaningful contact with more mature people. In U.S. society, there are few opportunities for young men to do so at present. The male gender role, with its emphasis on the avoidance of introspection and emotional expression, hinders these kinds of exchanges.

Archetypal Expression: Carl Jung

Carl Gustav Jung (1875–1961) was a protegé of Freud who, like many others, disagreed with Freud's emphasis on sexuality. Jung developed highly original concepts in personality and related them to mythology, religion, ritual, art, and culture. His ideas about masculinity are the major basis for the mythopoetic men's movement (see Chapter Fifteen), currently the most popular of men's gender-related activities in the United States. Like Freud, Jung enjoyed a long, distinguished career and wrote extensively. His personality theory is intricate and complex and only the barest summary is included here.

For Jung, the personality is a set of raw components that must be refined and interwoven in order for the person to function (Maddi, 1989). Psychological growth is the process of putting these various components of the psyche together into an integrated whole that is greater than the sum of its parts. This is a long and arduous task that consumes most of the person's life. Jung likened the process to that of medieval alchemy, which was an attempt to combine base metals into gold (Jung, [1963] 1989). Another analogy is to cooking, where raw ingredients are transformed into an appealing dish.

The Unconscious

Like all analytic theorists, Jung believed that a great deal of the psyche is not in awareness. Deeply buried in the unconscious are complex forces that impel behavior. As the healthy person grows, he or she begins to understand and express the psyche more fully.

Jung's conception of the unconscious may well be his most original and important contribution. Like Freud, he believed that the unconscious contained emotionally charged material from personal history. Unlike Freud, he also believed that it contained an accumulation of the psychological experiences of the human race. This part of the psyche, called the **collective unconscious,** predisposes a person toward certain behaviors. While the personal unconscious is highly individual, the collective unconscious is about the same in all humans.

The collective unconscious contains a variety of images that are activated by experience. Jung called these images **archetypes.** You have an archetypal structure of the Father that is activated when you see or think of your father. This archetype is also activated by "father figures" such as older men or authorities. Your behaviors and emotional reactions are caused by the interaction of your conscious experience of the person with your unconscious experience of the archetype.

Archetypes have the power to distort experience. For example, if you have a male professor who is older and activates your Father archetype, you might be very disappointed if he does not show a special interest in you. Your reaction to a younger male professor might be different even if his behavior is similar. People tend to project their archetypes onto others, sometimes with disastrous results. To carry the example further, you might respond to your disappointment with your professor by criticizing him inappropriately. However, if you are aware of your tendency toward projection and distortion, you may be able to resist this behavior (Jung, [1959] 1989). Thus, one of the paths to integration is through self-awareness.

Jung and Masculinity

Jung believed that there are countless archetypes. He attempted to describe the most important ones. Some of these archetypes are especially relevant to masculine psychology: anima, animus, and hero.

The **anima** and **animus** are the complementary feminine and masculine components of the collective unconscious. Jung saw the anima as the part of the psyche that is connected and nurturant and the animus as the analytical, logical part. Young men tend to repress the anima in their emphasis on developing masculine identification (Wong, 1982). Because the man is not aware of this part of himself, he tends to project it onto women. There may be a good deal of trouble when he reacts to his anima instead of to the woman. For instance, he may expect her to comfort him (as a doting mother would) when he experiences failure, such as losing in an athletic contest. She might be indifferent to sports and tell him, "Forget it; it's only a silly game." His reaction to this might be anger and disappointment. He might criticize her for not being a good girlfriend. Conflicts and misunderstandings follow.

The developmental tasks for the man in this example are to incorporate his anima into his personality and to understand what he unconsciously wants, needs, and expects from women. This long process of insight and integration is usually not substantially complete until well into adulthood, if at all. Jung saw the first half of life as an adaptation to the outside world. In middle age, the person begins the process of understanding the inner, archetypal world (Hall & Lindzey, 1985).

One of the most frequently stimulated archetypes in the young man is the **hero**, the part of the person that has control of the self and the world (Beebe, 1989). The hero does not want to acknowledge the unconscious or the feminine, as these are the parts of self that are antithetical to power and control. A man who overvalues the hero relative to other parts of the self may deny his emotional experience, dependency needs, and vulnerability. At the same time, he may be quite ambitious and achieving. In short, he exhibits both the positive and negative qualities of traditional masculinity.

As the "heroic" man enters middle age, he finds it more difficult and less desirable to deny that he has limitations and that he yearns for deep attachments to others. Giving up the archetypal fantasies of unlimited power, success, and control allows him to attain more comfort in interpersonal relationships (Satinover, 1986), while he still retains his positive ambitions. He may be able to better appreciate himself rather than compulsively pushing for dominance.

Healthy middle-aged men become more integrated by balancing the anima and the hero. As a result, they become less emotionally constricted and more relationship oriented without giving up the healthy masculine parts of psyche that are already well developed by this time.

Unhealthy men tend to cling to narrower visions of youthful and heroic masculinity, such as physical strength, power for power's sake, and sexual prowess. Jung called this kind of man the **puer aeturnus** (eternal boy). The image is of a man in the midst of the so-called "midlife crisis" who seeks young women, adventure, and other trappings of masculine youth. He continues to project his anima in the search for the ideal woman, and he is destined to be disappointed. He has a difficult time separating reality from archetypal fantasy. As a result, his psychological growth is arrested, at least temporarily.

Mainstream U.S. culture, with its emphasis on the display of the heroic masculine image, discourages the expression of the anima in men. The process of integration, with its emphasis on self-awareness, is surely inhibited by the sanction against introspection ("looking inside") for men. Jung ([1977] 1989) thought that many American men were inhibited in their marital relationships, and we could surmise that this is the result of

their difficulty in accessing anima. Still, we find many healthy and integrated men despite a cultural climate that discourages the process.

Jung's emphasis on the spiritual and higher human aspects of the
person stands in contrast to other analytic ideas. He seems to believe in
the positive power of the man to create himself by integrating disparate
aspects of the primitive psyche. Jung is somewhat optimistic that the
natural path is toward health and growth. For the man, the process is one
of freeing himself from constricting cultural prescriptions of masculinity
by reorienting himself toward his inner life.

Summary

1. Psychoanalytic approaches to the understanding of masculinity emphasize biological, unconscious, and early-childhood determinants of
   behavior.
2. Freud emphasized the role of sexual instinct and its conflict with social
   forces. He viewed psychological health as an individual's ability to
   meet his or her instinctual needs in a socially acceptable way. If a
   young boy does not develop a strong social structure (superego), he
   will become impulsive, destructive, self-absorbed, and antisocial. This
   may result from being overwhelmed by the mother and/or underin-
   volvement with a strong father.
3. According to Freudian theory, the most important period for the development of masculine gender identity is the phallic stage, in which
   the boy experiences strong sexual feelings for the mother and views
   his father as a rival. He fears that he will be castrated for these desires,
   and so he transfers his sexual feelings onto a more appropriate object.
   If the Oedipal crisis is resolved poorly, the boy may later have sexual
   problems and/or problems relating to women.
4. Karen Horney viewed the Oedipal period as a time when males developed deep feelings of insecurity associated with the feminine. She
   thought that misogyny and even violence toward women are desperate attempts to compensate for masculine inadequacy.
5. Ego psychology theories emphasize the processes of attachment and
   separation in early childhood. Because boys are usually raised mainly
   by their mothers, the tendency is to define masculinity through a process of separation. Boys must put rigid boundaries between themselves and the feminine in order to attain a strong sense of masculinity.
   Males tend to avoid "feminine" behaviors because they are accompanied by anxiety. This causes difficulty when situations call for such
   behavior.

6. Heinz Kohut theorized that the process of healthy personality development involves introjecting the soothing and mirroring part of the
   parents into the self. Introjection may be inhibited by the process of
   separation from the mother and/or the emphasis on masculine independence.

7. Carl Jung's view is that all people are born with masculine and feminine aspects. In the healthy person, these become integrated into a
   strong sense of self. In the unhealthy person, the unacceptable parts of
   self are projected onto others, and the person has difficulty distinguishing reality from fantasy. Healthy male development involves the
   progressive balancing of the masculine and feminine aspects of the
   self.

Joel Gordon Photography

CHAPTER FIVE

When in Rome, Do as the Romans Do: Social Learning Perspectives on Masculinity

Why is it that relatively few men know how to sew and relatively few women know how to do car repairs? The simple answer is, of course, that a lot of women and men learned these behaviors as they grew up. But what influenced their learning? For many, it was a parent, older sibling, or family friend. Common stories involve young boys watching their fathers work on a car or young girls watching their mothers sew. Gradually, the child takes an interest and begins to learn the skills with the guidance and encouragement of the parent.

What happens if a boy takes an interest in his mother's sewing? The same kind of process might occur, but other scenarios are also possible. The mother and/or father might say, "You don't want to learn that; sewing is for girls." The boy's playmates might ridicule him if they find out that he likes to do such a "sissy" thing. The mother might not be as encouraging to a son as to a daughter, making it more likely that the son would gradually lose interest. The most common scenario is that the boy would not pursue his interest in the first place, because he perceives himself as male and perceives sewing as something that females do.

At a deeper level of analysis, the answer to our original question is that, while the social environment encourages sex-typed activities, it does not encourage (and often discourages) cross-gender activities. If the boy has a strong interest in sewing, he may pursue it in spite of the social forces that work against it, but the pursuit of more sex-typed activities surely offers less resistance.

The basic assumption of social learning theory is that the major influences on behavior are learning processes. The preceding example illustrates many of these processes: reward, punishment, observation, imitation, and schematic thinking. From this position, gendered behavior is produced by **differential treatment,** the systematic, though sometimes unintentional, provision of sex-specific environmental influences. Social learning theory provides a picture of how males and females are socialized by families, peer groups, schools, and cultures.

Reward and Punishment

Many behavioral patterns are built through the experience of reward and punishment. Behaviors that are followed by pleasant states of affairs tend to be repeated, while those followed by unpleasant consequences tend not to be repeated (Hull, 1943). We are motivated to recognize situations in which rewards or punishments are available and act accordingly.

We also tend to make generalizations based on similarities among situations and discriminations based on differences among situations (Skinner, 1974). For instance, you might receive social approval (a reward) for telling a joke to one group of friends, and so you tell it to another group of friends. In this case, your behavior has generalized because the situations are similar. On the other hand, if you were to refrain from telling the joke in class, you would have discriminated or shown a change in behavior based on the differences between situations.

We find ourselves in a variety of situations during our lives. Some are quite similar to one another; others are more unique. We acquire behavioral habits by operating in varied environments. Over time, these habits become part of us—so ingrained that they are difficult to change without considerable effort.

Some research has focused on the sex-specific application of reward and punishment by various socializing agents: parents, schools, and peer groups. Certain behaviors are typically rewarded or punished in males, and this gender-typed socialization process creates dispositions toward masculine behaviors and away from feminine ones.

Childhood Environments

The experience of the rewarding or punishing aspects of environments depends on being exposed to those environments, and there is evidence that boys sometimes find themselves in markedly different settings than girls. If you were to look at most middle-class children's bedrooms, you would probably have little difficulty guessing the sex of the child. Girls' bedrooms often contain dolls (Snow, Jacklin, & Maccoby, 1981) and are often decorated with flowers, lace, or other stereotypically feminine design. Boys' bedrooms often contain sports equipment and transportation toys (Pomerleau, Bolduc, Malcuit, & Cossette, 1990).

Parents tend to communicate gender stereotypes in children's play and household chores (Lytton & Romney, 1991). Parents in Western cultures (especially fathers) play with boys more roughly, perhaps as a result of the perception that boys are stronger and tougher (Culp, Cook, & Housley, 1983). Children who choose sex-typed toys tend to get more positive responses from their parents than those who do not (Antill, 1987).

Play and family activity can be viewed as a rehearsal for later social roles. For instance, putting puzzles together is rehearsal for task completion and problem solving. "Playing house" is a rehearsal for relationships and domestic work. Here again, parents tend to be sex typed in their treatment of children. Boys are taught to develop structures, to experiment with new approaches to solving problems, to attend to task and performance, and to master the situation. Girls are encouraged to be cooperative and compliant (Block, 1984; Frankel & Rollins, 1983).

In household chores, boys are often assigned activities that take them away from the residence, such as yard work, animal care, or taking out the garbage, whereas girls are assigned more domestic chores such as baby sitting, cooking, or doing dishes (Lytton & Romney, 1991; Burns & Homel, 1989). Whiting and Edwards (1973) reported that these gender differences are seen in a variety of cultures.

The net result of children's play and household chore activity, according to Block (1984), is that we give boys "wings" and give girls "roots." From a social learning perspective, typically masculine (agentic) and feminine (communal) approaches to the world are a result of ingrained habits and reinforcement patterns that continue into adulthood.

Gendered Behavioral Patterns

Another consistent research finding is that boys get punished for out-role behavior earlier in life and more harshly than girls (Maccoby & Jacklin, 1974; Payne, 1981; Stericker & Kurdek, 1982; J. Archer, 1984). Girls can associate with a male group without fearing a loss of status. Boys who play with girls, however, are ridiculed by and ostracized from the male social group (Maccoby, 1987). Parents do not worry about "tomboys" until they reach puberty, but parents show concern about "sissies" before kindergarten (Nelson, 1985). Because of punishment for "feminine" behaviors, boys may begin to view femininity and females with contempt.

Comparisons of fathers' and mothers' sex typing of children reveal that fathers are more stereotypic in their definitions of gender-appropriate activities, especially with their sons (MacDonald & Parke, 1986; Lytton & Romney, 1991). Perhaps as a consequence of their less frequent contact with children, they embellish a lack of information with the use of stereotypes (Basow, 1992). Not surprisingly, the level of the son's gender stereotyping is strongly related to the father's level (Emihovich, Gaier, & Cromin, 1984).

Boys are also encouraged to control their feelings and conform their behavior to external standards, whereas girls are encouraged to "look inside" and think about their lives (Block, 1984). Early in life, the boy is taught not to attend to his emotional life, but rather to look outside of himself in evaluating his behavior. In adulthood, this may transfer into definitions of masculinity that emphasize the external: job status, money, material possessions, power over others, and even the attractiveness of his partner. It is important to note that this style is not only a remnant of childhood rewards for evaluating externally; the encouragement is ongoing. Many social and other rewards are given to men who fit masculine images.

While the encouragement to look outside of the self may cause problems such as an impoverished emotional life, it is also responsible for some of the most positive aspects of traditional masculinity. Boys are rewarded from an early age for going out into the world, solving problems, achieving, and competing. While competition and ambition can get out of hand, at moderate levels this orientation to the world is associated with good occupational functioning and enhanced self-esteem.

Boys are generally rewarded for controlling their emotions, but they are sometimes discouraged from controlling their behavior (see Chapter Twelve for an analysis of masculinity and aggression). Girls are taught to stay close to adults, at home and at school, while boys are rewarded for independence and being active (Aries & Oliver, 1985; Maccoby & Jacklin, 1974). This can cause problems for boys in school settings that emphasize behaviors such as sitting still and listening, which are contradictory to these earlier expectations (Richardson, 1981). Kagan (1964) described school as a "girl's world" in which behavior control and conformity, which are taught to girls at an early age, are rewarded. These contradictory demands for boys may contribute to their higher incidences of behavior and academic problems (Richardson, 1981).

Sex typing of children is greatly accelerated by typical early educational experiences, which Luria and Herzog (cited in Maccoby, 1987) refer to as "gender school." The gender role of boys is largely shaped by two forces: the male peer culture and the differential treatment of boys and girls by teachers.

Children usually segregate themselves into same-sex play groups. They will mix when adults reward them for doing so or punish them for not doing so, but will quickly resegregate when adult sanctions are removed (Maccoby, 1987). Sex segregation has been observed in many different cultures (Whiting & Edwards, 1988). In boys' play groups, we see a great deal of reward for aggression and toughness (Chaze, 1981). Boys' groups tend to demand rigid conformity to masculine behavior by punishing cross-gender behavior very harshly (Maccoby, 1987; Lynn, 1979). Thus, the peer culture strongly reinforces what has been learned at home.

Despite teachers' efforts to treat boys and girls the same, there is ample evidence that they sometimes fail to do so. Boys receive more positive and more negative attention in the classroom than girls (Fagot, 1984; Sadker & Sadker, 1985; Cherry, 1975). Boys' behavior is more likely to be taken seriously than that of girls, and they learn that what they do has consequences.

Parents also tend to give boys more praise and more punishment than girls (Maccoby & Jacklin, 1974; Block, 1984; Lytton & Romney, 1991). One of the reasons for greater frequencies of punishment is that boys get into more mischief than girls, perhaps as a result of a relatively higher activity level (Anderson, Lytton, & Romney, 1986; Maccoby, 1988a).

The punishment of boys is relevant to men's studies for several reasons. First, it is often used to enforce masculine gender-role behaviors, some of which are associated with a number of personal and social problems. Second, boys are more likely to be punished physically, while girls are more likely to be punished with social disapproval (Lytton & Romney, 1991). Physical punishment has the effect of actually increasing aggression in children (Weiten, 1992). This may be somewhat of a vicious cycle for the acting-out boy. He is active and undercontrolled as a result of temperament and socialization. He is physically punished for his behaviors, and the punishments are likely to result in further aggression.

Third, fathers, more often than mothers, do the punishing (Block, 1984; Maccoby & Jacklin, 1974). The boy's experience of physical pain in the presence of the father may inhibit positive feelings and identification, especially if the father is not around much (Goldberg, 1977). In the worst-case scenario, the mother spends much more time with the son, but the punishment duties are relegated to the father. The son who is told, "Wait until your father gets home," does not learn that he gets punished when he does something inappropriate. Rather, he learns that he gets punished when his father gets home, and he may well develop feelings of fear, anger, and resentment toward his father.

Observation, Imitation, and Cognition

A person does not need to perform a behavior and be reinforced or punished in order for learning to take place. A good deal of behavior is learned through observing others and imitating them. Moreover, a person is not merely a passive recipient of behavioral consequences. He or she makes cognitive judgments about situations, categories, and values. What a person thinks about a situation may be as important in determining behavior as the actual reward or punishment contingencies (Rotter, 1954).

It is not unusual to see people behaving like their parents without being aware of it. Parents often reward children for imitative behavior. For example, a father who says, "That's my boy," after his son emulates something the father has done, has provided a social reward. Although the provision of such a reward serves to strengthen the behavior, the child may spontaneously imitate the parent or other model without being rewarded (Bandura & Walters, 1963).

Bandura, Ross, and Ross (1961) described several factors that influence whether or not a behavior will be imitated. First is the amount of exposure to the model: The more time a person spends with the model, the more likely he or she is to imitate the model's behavior. As we shall see, this is an important factor in male development because of the historically small amounts of time that boys usually spend with their fathers. Movies and television can also provide models, and behavior can be affected by frequent exposure to characters portrayed in these media. In fact, children who spend large amounts of time watching television tend to be more sex typed than other children (Zuckerman, Singer, & Singer, 1980; McGhee & Frueh, 1980).

Second, imitation is increased when the person perceives himself or herself as sharing characteristics with the model. In other words, you are more likely to imitate someone if you see yourself as being like that person in an important way. The person's sex is probably the first thing you notice about him or her, and there is evidence that children can make distinctions between the sexes as early as the first year of life (Maccoby, 1988b; DelBoca & Ashmore, 1980; Lewis & Weinraub, 1979). As sex is the most basic division among human beings, it is not surprising to find that children imitate same-sex models more readily than models of the other sex, and this process begins to occur as early as 3 years of age. Boys imitate females less often than girls imitate males (Bussey & Bandura, 1984). This may be due to a number of factors, including punishment for out-role behavior, the antifemininity bias in male gender roles, and the higher social status of males in most cultures.

Third, observing whether or not a model is reinforced for the behavior affects whether or not the behavior will be imitated. For example, if you were to see someone put money into a vending machine and not receive any goods, you would be less likely to put your money into the machine. Boys who observe men being rewarded for gender-typed behavior are more likely to imitate the behavior.

Finally, the performance of behaviors is affected by cognition. As people grow, they become increasingly adept at seeing similarities among models and among situations. They learn how to put behaviors into categories and apply these categories to new situations. A child may notice that males perform certain behaviors more often than females in similar settings. The child may then abstract a model of masculine behavior (Perry & Bussey, 1979). If the child is male, he is then more likely to imitate these behaviors. Because of this abstraction, however, he is less likely to imitate a male whom he perceives as behaving in a feminine way (Eisenstock, 1984).

From a social learning perspective, "gender identity" is formed through the abstraction of masculine and feminine categories of behavior, together with the understanding of physical sex differences and the imitation of same-sex models. As the boy increasingly behaves like his father and other males, his identification as masculine becomes more and more stable (Lips, 1988; Basow, 1992). This view contrasts with psychoanalytic theory, which views gender-typed behavior as following, rather than preceding, gender identification.

David Lynn (1959, 1966, 1969) theorized about the implications of the historical inaccessibility of fathers as role models. When they are young, children spend much more time with mothers than with fathers. When they enter school, the most salient adult models are teachers, most of whom are also female. Therefore, girls get a good deal of exposure to same-sex models. In constructing ideas about femininity, they have a lot of information on which to base their imitation.

In sharp contrast, boys do not get nearly as much of an opportunity to observe their fathers and other adult males. Therefore, they must extrapolate a good deal in constructing a sense of what masculinity is. Boys must fill in large gaps of information, and they tend to do so by using other, more available male models such as peers, older boys, and males in the media. These are not usually good sources of realistic, secure, positively defined masculinity. There is also the tendency to be masculine by avoiding feminine behaviors. When males do so in rigid and extreme ways, they cut themselves off from a large collection of potentially adaptive and satisfying experiences.

Goldberg's (1977) description of gender-identity development is that girls identify with a real person, whereas boys identify largely with a fantasy. This fantasy may be heavily laden with unrealistic, hypertrophied aspects of stereotypical male gender roles. There is some evidence that daughters are more similar in personality to mothers than sons are to fathers, providing support for this view (Lynn, 1979).

Hartley (1959) first noted that this lack of male models, together with harsh, early demands to "be a man," creates a volatile combination of social forces for the boy. He learns that behaving in a masculine way is important, because male gender-role demands are sometimes backed up with threats of punishment. At the same time, he does not have much information about how to do so. Thus, he experiences a good deal of anxiety and inadequacy about his masculinity. To make matters worse, he is supposed to be certain of what to do. Asking for help or even expressing feelings of doubt is considered feminine.

Lynn (1969) theorized that boys' typical reaction to this anxiety is to adhere to stereotypical male gender roles in a very rigid way. There is ample empirical support for his claim. Boys reject feminine behaviors and objects associated with females more often than girls reject male behaviors and objects. Boys are more likely than girls to attend to and imitate same-sex models (Bussey & Bandura, 1984; Bussey & Perry, 1982; Raskin & Israel, 1981).

Since boys often identify with a hypermasculine fantasy, they often feel compelled to become that fantasy. Boys tend to role play occupations that are highly unlikely for them (Greif, 1976), such as astronaut or professional athlete, whereas girls' play is more likely to be around more realistic and universal roles such as mother or caretaker. As a result, the transition from boyhood to adult roles may be somewhat discontinuous for most males (Archer, 1984). Perhaps this is one reason why many adult men place such importance on professional sports or "macho" media figures who provide an avenue for vicarious fulfillment of hypermasculine fantasy.

Another part of the unrealistic fantasy involves masculine invulnerability. If the boy identifies with a fantasy of his father (as most boys do), and if his father is inexpressive of feelings such as fear (as many fathers are), then it is easy for the boy to have a image of his father as invulnerable. Of course, the father does experience fear like any other human being, but he may hide his reactions. The son is likely to figure that fearful feelings do not exist in "real men" (Lynch, 1992). Inevitably, the boy experiences fear, as everyone does from time to time, and may feel unmasculine and inadequate at these times.

Information-Processing Models

Theories based on reinforcement/punishment and observation/imitation have been criticized for their view of the person as a passive recipient of behavioral influence. It would seem that people do not mechanistically reproduce behaviors that have been rewarded or modeled. People, even young children, are more active than that. We think about, categorize, and cognitively transform our experience. We strive to make sense out of the tremendous barrage of information that confronts us every day.

Some of this information is ignored. Some of it is dealt with in very automatic ways. And, we work very hard, consciously and actively, to "take in" other data. Information-processing theories of gender are attempts to describe how we attend to, transform, think about, assimilate, and respond to information about males and females.

Cognitive-Developmental Theory

Kohlberg (1966) theorized that gender-identity development parallels cognitive development. As children grow, they acquire new abilities to understand the world and themselves. Gender becomes a central part of the way in which they deal with information.

We have already seen that children learn the distinction between male and female at a surprisingly early age. At some point in their cognitive development, children acquire the concepts of gender **constancy** and **conservation;** then they understand that the essence of something does not change even if its appearance does. For example, if you pour water from a short, wide glass into a tall, thin one, very young children will say that there is more water in the tall glass. After conservation is established, however, children know that the amount of water does not change with the shape of the container (Piaget, 1954).

Once children become postconservational (sometime between ages 4 and 7), they understand that a person's sex does not change in different situations or over time. A male remains a male even if you put a dress on him or find him in a women's bathroom, and he will always be a male.

This realization clears the way for gender-role development. When the child knows what sex he or she is and knows that it will not change, he or she begins to value behaviors and characteristics associated with his or her sex and devalues behaviors associated with the other sex. Gender-typed preferences seem to be related to these levels of cognitive development (Basow, 1992).

Gender identity is thus established, and there are several consequences. First, the child performs "sex-appropriate" behavior because he or she finds these behaviors reinforcing, and avoids "sex inappropriate" behaviors because they are either aversive or not reinforcing. The reinforcement is internal and automatic; a boy feels good when he does "boy" things. Second, the child begins to seek out same-sex models in order to acquire information about gender-appropriate behavior. Third, the child may identify with and imitate the same-sex parent because of the parent's salience as a model. In this view, gender identity precedes identification, in contrast to the observation/imitation view, in which gender identity is seen as a consequence of identification.

In the early stages (ages 6–8) following the understanding of gender constancy, children have very rigid conceptualizations of masculinity and femininity. This may be a result of their tenuous gender identity (Lips, 1988), their relative lack of experience in gender categorization, and a generally low level of cognitive sophistication. Children at this age tend to have a hard time understanding cross-gender behavior. Later on, they become more secure in their gender identities and become better able to tolerate cognitive ambiguities. As a result, they become slightly less rigid in their gender stereotyping.

Stoddart and Turiel (1985) reported that kindergarten children rated gender-role violations (such as a boy wearing nail polish or a girl having a crew cut) as more "wrong" than breaking school rules or even hurting another person. Third- and fifth-graders viewed these cross-gender violations as less serious than the other transgressions. However, eighth-graders' ratings closely resembled the ratings of the kindergarten children. This would seem to indicate that puberty-aged children recapture the sex typing of early childhood, a phenomenon that cognitive developmental theory cannot account for.

Other studies have also produced data that are somewhat inconsistent with cognitive developmental theory. Some researchers (Bussey & Bandura, 1984; Smetana & Letourneau, 1984; Urberg, 1982; and others) report that a significant amount of gender typing occurs before sex constancy is established, a finding that is more supportive of modeling theory. Basow (1992) suggests that imitation and gender-typed cognitive development may constitute two pathways in which the child learns various aspects of gender roles. Perhaps very early gender typing results from modeling and reinforcement, and then children begin to actively pursue same-sex modeling after gender identity is established.

From the perspective of cognitive developmental theory, it is important for males to have positive role models. In this regard, it is not much different from observation/imitation theory. If the categorization of biological sex is such an important organizing feature of children's thinking, then the more a boy is exposed to positive masculinity, the more adaptive and healthy he will become. Relegating this rather complicated information-processing task to peer groups and media images would surely result in a distorted view of what it means to be a man.

Gender Schema Theory

Sandra Bem (1981b; 1985; 1987) constructed a theory of gender-dependent information processing that is similar to cognitive developmental theory, but with an important emphasis on cultural factors. Similarly to Kohlberg, Bem believes that cognitive development and gender-role development are parallel in some regards. However, Bem also believes that the gender-typed processing of information is not the only natural course of cognitive development. She argues that gender-typed processing is taught to children by a culture that emphasizes sex differences for virtually every domain of behavior. If our culture were not so sex typed, children would learn to use other categories to organize their experiences.

Because we deal with so much information, we must categorize and organize it in order to avoid a sensory overload. To do this, we develop **schemata,** which are cognitive structures that allow us to anticipate and understand events. As a child observes males and females in a sex-typed environment, he or she gathers information about gender. The child makes associations among different aspects of masculinity and femininity and uses these resulting associations to organize new information. The structure and meaning of events is stored in gender-schematic terms. In addition, the person applies the gender schema to the self and behaves in sex-typed ways.

According to Bem, children categorize events according to sex because they live in a culture that communicates to people that sex is important in dress, occupation, clothing, hobbies, children's toys, and other areas where it need not be viewed as important. For instance, I attended a kindergarten graduation ceremony in which the children wore home-made mortar boards and tassels. The girls wore pink tassels and the boys wore blue ones. Bem would say that drawing a distinction between the sexes in such a non-sex-dependent activity as an educational ceremony encourages children to use sex as a cognitive guide for understanding the world. It is not unlike having African-American children wear black tassels and Caucasians white ones, which few people would consider appropriate.

Thorne (1992) described several elementary school situations in which teachers and other adults needlessly called attention to students' sexes. These included statements like "The girls are ready and the boys aren't" (p. 110) or classroom contests in which a team of all boys competes against a team of all girls. In these situations, adults model the use of gender schemata and make it more likely that children will also acquire them. Thorne also described various aspects of children's play that maintain gender boundaries, including teasing for playing with other-sex children, "cooties," and "invasion" of same-sex play groups by other-sex children.

We see many examples of gender schemata in the English language. For instance, work titles differ depending on the sex of the person who occupies the role. The linguistic distinctions between waiters and waitresses, policewomen and policemen, actors and actresses, and comedians and comediennes may lead people to believe that the sex of the role occupant is an important distinction to make when they think about human beings at work. The increased use of nonsexist terms should encourage people to use different, nongendered ways to categorize.

Gender schemata also communicate other schemata. For instance, boys learn to attend to strong versus weak and girls to "sweet" versus "not sweet." Few people ever comment that a girl is strong or a boy is "sweet," and so children learn to organize their thinking along such dimensions.

Bem (1987) describes gender schemata as a "nonconscious ideology." Most people are not aware that they organize their perceptions on the basis of gender, nor are they aware that alternative conceptualizations are possible. "Look through the lens of gender and you perceive the world as falling into masculine and feminine categories. Put on a different pair of lenses, however, and you perceive the world as falling into other categories" (Bem, 1987, p. 309).

The only time it makes sense to be gender schematic is in the realm of biology, and yet gender schema is extrapolated into many other domains. Bem (1985) tells an amusing story of her 4-year-old son wearing a barrette to nursery school. A schoolmate told him that he must be a girl because he was wearing a barrette. Four-year-old Jeremy informed his classmate that being male meant "having a penis and testicles," and he "finally pulled down his pants as a way of making his point more convincingly" (p. 216).

Bem (1985) suggests that some of the destructive aspects of gender stereotyping could be alleviated by providing people with alternative ways of thinking about the world and the self. She suggests an "individual difference" schema (that people within any group vary widely) and a "cultural relativism" schema (that different people believe different things). In this way, sex can be understood as a biological category that is not always important in every setting. Bem clearly emphasizes the role of education in social change, and her theory can be applied to men's studies.

It is often said that "the fish is unaware of the water" because it has never experienced anything else. Because many aspects of culture have long considered masculinity as a normative referent for experience, many men have not been aware of the gender-schematic nature of their approach to the world. Men have remained unaware of the culture of patriarchy because it benefits them, just as a fish benefits from water. Women and other marginalized groups of people are usually more aware of sexism and racism, because they usually suffer its adverse effects on a daily basis. A fish has the luxury to remain unaware of the water. A drowning mammal does not.

Becoming conscious of one's ideologies would seem to require psychological mindedness, nondefensiveness, introspection, and a willingness to listen to another's point of view. Males have been socialized away from every one of these. As femininity has long been associated with loss of power and status for men, there has been a good deal of reward for men's attending to the world in gender-schematic fashion. Men who begin to break out of this stereotyped information processing are finding that they can evaluate themselves with standards that are less punitive and more reasonable. If Bem is correct that gender-schematic processing is destructive and unessential to human development, then we ought to support countervailing educational and therapeutic activities such as consciousness raising, gender-awareness curricula, women's studies, and, yes, men's studies.

Summary

1. The basic assumption of social learning theory is that the major influences on behavior are learning processes such as reward, punishment, imitation, and information processing. From this perspective, gender typing is produced through the differential treatment of males and females by various socializing agents.

2. There is evidence of differential treatment in childhood bedroom decor, toys, assignment of household chores, encouragement of sex-typed behaviors, and discouragement of cross-gender activities.

3. Boys receive more praise, punishment, and attention than girls. They learn that their behavior has definite consequences. On the other hand, they may be reinforced for destructive masculine behaviors and/or suffer harsher punishment than girls for out-role behaviors.

4. Observation and limitation are important factors in behavior acquisition. The understanding of gender constancy, together with the cognitive abstraction of sex as a category, sets the stage for gender identity and the imitation of same-sex models.

5. Historically, many males have suffered from a lack of exposure to positive masculine models. Some theorists believe that boys identify largely with hypermasculine fantasies rather than with real persons. As a result, they often strive to reach unrealistic standards of manliness.

6. Bem argues that gender typing is a result of an overuse of sex categorization in the culture. The inappropriate use of gender schema encourages people to see the world in masculine and feminine terms. The use of other schemata draws attention away from sex categorization in settings where sex distinctions are relatively unimportant.

Grant LeDuc/Monkmeyer Press Photo Service

CHAPTER SIX

The Inner Reality:
Phenomenological Perspectives on
Male Development

Every man lives in two worlds. One is the physical, external world with which he interacts. The other is a unique, private, inner world where he feels, thinks, perceives, and interprets and where he gives meaning to his life. It is here that he experiences the self as nobody else can, and it is here that he constructs his own reality. His self-awareness and private world are unique; he is a phenomenon.

Phenomenological psychologists emphasize the importance of the person's subjective psychological environment. At any given moment, an individual may experience perceptions, sensations, interpretations, and feelings about himself or herself, others, or objects. For the phenomenologist, the subject of study is the totality of the subjective, immediate experience of the individual, termed the **phenomenal field,** and its effect on behavior. For men, the application of phenomenological theory provides a rich avenue for the enhancement of gender awareness and self-understanding.

Phenomenological theories stress the ability of the person to create and fulfill the self by following his or her inner nature and making choices that affect his or her life in a positive way. In this chapter, we will apply two phenomenological theories to the understanding of men: the humanistic approach of Carl Rogers and the existential theories of Rollo May and others.

Humanistic Theory

As we have seen, biological and psychoanalytic theories emphasize the primitive, survival aspects of the person. These theories often characterize human nature as animalistic and selfish. Social learning theories emphasize the aspects of the person that are shaped by the environment. These theories tend to describe human nature as essentially neutral.

In contrast, humanistic theory emphasizes the person's ability to create and express the self. Humanists are unabashedly optimistic about human nature. They believe that the most powerful force in a person's life is **self-actualization,** the fulfillment of one's positive, unique, human potential. In other words, the human being's core motivation is to become whatever his or her nature is to become.

Carl Rogers (1961) believed that all living things, if given the right environmental conditions, would grow and thrive. He termed this the **actualizing tendency** and theorized that it is biologically based. A plant will flourish if provided with a minimum amount of light, water, and other nutrients. There is a genetic blueprint, not only to survive and reproduce (as analytic and biological theories stress), but also to grow, develop, and extend.

Self-actualization is the psychological outgrowth of the actualizing tendency (Rogers, 1959). Just as a healthy plant grows larger and extends itself, a healthy person progressively and vigorously expresses a unique self. Just as a plant will grow on its own, so will a human being. You do not have to control a plant or a person in order for growth to occur. Providing the right conditions is enough (note the contrast with other theories in this regard).

All organisms need physical nutrients in order to display the actualizing tendency, and people need a "psychological nutrient" in order to become self-actualized. The approval of important people early in the person's life allows him or her to develop approval of the self, or **self-esteem.** The person who has a solid, positive sense of self is able to be aware of and fulfill his or her potential.

When children first come into the world, they get a lot of approval. Parents and others hold them, attend to their needs, smile at them, and communicate joy about their existence. Rogers called this **positive regard.** It is roughly equivalent to a nonpossessive love. The child who experiences positive regard feels valued. Later in life, this child internalizes the parents' attitudes and values the self. In other words, he or she develops **positive self-regard.**

As a child grows, he or she acquires a larger behavioral repertoire as a result of the actualizing tendency that causes the body and the brain to develop. Behaviors are a way of expressing the self, but some of these expressions may not be particularly pleasing to others. For instance, a 2-year-old boy who expresses his curiosity about some expensive object may grab and inadvertently break it. If parents or caretakers respond by communicating disapproval of the child (not merely the child's behavior, but his personhood), they have, in effect, withdrawn their love from the child because of his behavior. They can do this by striking the child, by saying "Bad boy" (which says "You are a bad person"), or by saying something like, "Daddy doesn't like you when you do that." These expressions of disapproval can also be indirect or nonverbal, as when the parent gives the child a "dirty look" or becomes emotionally cold.

Rogers called this **conditional positive regard,** or placing **conditions of worth** on the child. It is a communication to the child that he or she is not worthwhile under certain conditions. As a result, the child begins to construct the self in terms of actions, thoughts, and feelings that have been approved. If events like this were to happen repeatedly, the boy in the example would come to deny the parts of himself that are associated with curiosity.

A healthier environment is one in which the child experiences **unconditional positive regard,** which is a warmth, respect, and acceptance that does not depend on his or her behavior. It is possible to communicate disapproval of a behavior while communicating approval of the person. In effect, the parent is saying, "You are valuable no matter what you do" (without conditions). The child is worthwhile for the mere reason that he or she has shown up on the planet.

There are several negative consequences for the person who experiences conditions of worth in large doses. First, feelings of inadequacy result in anxiety and defensiveness as the person denies and rejects the disapproved parts of the self. Second, self-actualization is blocked because the self-concept is narrowed. Rogers believed that the full experience of the self provides the vital information needed to strive toward human potential. It is difficult to fully express the self when a person has lost touch with parts of who he or she is. Third, defensiveness and rejection of these parts of the self leaves the individual less able to appreciate others, and misunderstandings in relationships often ensue.

The net result of conditional regard is that the self-actualizing tendency becomes misguided and full functioning is inhibited. The following example will serve to illustrate Rogers' theory: A child who grows up with an overprotective parent receives disapproval for any minor risk taking, such as going outside if it is a little cold or trying something for the first time. This child denies the parts of the self that are associated with exploring new environments and with self-efficacy. When this person becomes an adult, he or she does not develop a satisfying career or relationships outside the family (despite having the resources to do so), because the parent who disapproved of the independent parts of the self has been internalized. The person feels an undue amount of anxiety around what most people find to be reasonable risks, and thus a good deal of potential is not realized.

Humanistic Theory and Masculinity

The application of Rogers' theory to male development provides an excellent framework for understanding the negative aspects of male gender roles. Typically, boys are socialized in a way that is fraught with conditional positive regard. As a result, a great many men have hidden away large parts of themselves, sometimes with dire consequences.

The gender role strain model (Pleck, 1975; O'Neil, 1982) presented in Chapter Two is based on humanistic theory. A gender role is a set of social demands for behavior that are based on the person's sex. Gender-role strain occurs when these demands conflict with naturally occurring tendencies in the person (Kamarovsky, 1976). This creates a discrepancy between the "real self" and the "ideal self-concept" (Garnets & Pleck, 1979). In other words, gender-role strain occurs when "who I am" is not consistent with "who I should be."

In Rogerian terms, gender-role demands are enforced by conditional positive regard. Boys' "masculine" behavior meets with approval; other behavior results in the withdrawal of approval. The boy learns that he is valued when he acts masculine and that he loses some of his worth when he does not. He may cry when he is sad and be told, "Don't be a sissy; big boys don't cry." He then withdraws value from this emotion.

The boy begins to deny the part of the real self that is "unmasculine." He attempts to match his behavior to the gender-role demands that allow him to gain the positive regard of significant others in his life, and later, himself. The price he pays is in self-alienation. Because the full experience of the true self is necessary for self-actualization, the attempt to live up to gender-role demands that are not a part of the self limits the potential for full functioning (Leafgren, 1990).

The gender-role strain position is that, for the most part, a man often cannot be himself and "be a man" (as traditionally defined) at the same time. The more a man comes to value traditional masculinity, the more he will lose his individuality and his path to fulfillment. Loss of significant parts of the self results in behavior that is destructive to the self and/or others (O'Neil, 1990).

Because every man is unique, and because some men are raised with harsher gender demands than others, the degree to which an individual man experiences gender-role strain will vary. For example, there is generally a demand for boys to participate in athletics. For a boy who is naturally athletic and drawn to sports, this demand would not create much strain. However, a boy who is not athletic or interested in sports would experience a high degree of strain, which would be accompanied by feelings of low self-esteem and misgivings about his masculinity. If his parents and other important people in his life are especially harsh in their demands for the boy to be athletic, he experiences even more strain. Therefore, the level of gender-role strain is a function of the level of gender-role demand together with the congruence of the real self with the gender-role.

An extreme example of the conflict between the real self and gender-role demands can be seen in some transvestites. Many cross-dressers report that they experience "feminine" parts of the self such as gentleness, passivity, and emotional sensitivity. They feel compelled to express these aspects of personality, but feel they can only do so when dressed as a woman (Renaissance Education Association, 1987). These are people who feel a good deal of gender-role strain due to lack of congruence between gender role and naturally occurring tendencies.

Pleck (1981b) advanced the theory that gender-role strain can lead a male to exaggerate his masculinity. Unable to gain approval because he does not naturally fit the cultural ideal, he tries to overcompensate by forcing himself into the gender role. This high level of gender-role strain and the hypermasculine reaction to it result in an extreme degree of self-alienation.

Even though the level of gender-role strain varies from person to person, certain gender-role demands conflict with naturally occurring tendencies in every man. It is impossible for a real self to be congruent with certain aspects of traditional masculinity. Certain gender-role demands also conflict with naturally occurring tendencies in many, though perhaps not all, men.

The experience of emotion is universal across the human race. In Rogerian terms, feelings are a part of the "true self" for everyone. It is natural to express them, as it is every part of the self. Strong emotion is accompanied by strong physical sensations. A person can feel emotions virtually demanding expression from the most primal part of his or her organism. For many young boys, however, the expression of emotion is met with disapproval, and the boy denies the parts of the self connected with emotion. As he incorporates gender-role demands into his ideal self-concept, the experience of emotion becomes associated with lowered self-esteem, and he is motivated to move away from his feelings.

As a result of this undervaluing of the emotional self, many men report difficulties in expressing their feelings (Moore, 1990). The extent of this difficulty is described by Joyce Johnson (quoted in Naifeh & Smith, 1984): "I'd learned myself by the age of 16 that just as girls guarded their virginity, boys guarded something less tangible which they called Themselves. They seemed to believe they had a mission in life, from which they could easily be deflected by being exposed to too much emotion" (p. 1).

Emotion is a huge part of human experience. Denying this primal aspect of the self requires a great deal of psychological effort, and the amount of strain and self-alienation that results can be considerable (O'Neil, 1990). In fact, the problems associated with restricted emotionality require an entire chapter (Chapter Eight) to detail. For now, it will suffice to say that this issue pervades virtually every aspect of a man's life. As O'Neil (1982) put it, "The capacity for accurate recognition and communication of feelings is a prerequisite for coping with life's problems" (p. 24).

A second universal human need is for safety. Part of the actualizing tendency is to protect the self from physical harm. Many males, however, are taught to deny this basic human need in the service of striving to meet standards of masculinity (Jourard, 1971). The conflict here is between the self-protective aspects of the real self and the male gender-role demand to "take it like a man." This eschewal of safety needs is related to the earlier issue of emotion. Fear is the emotional experience that tells us that we are in a situation where our safety is threatened. If the male's self-worth is undermined when he feels fearful, then he is motivated to deny or suppress that fear.

The denial of safety needs shows its effects on the man's physical health (see Chapter Nine). The fact that a man can be reluctant to acknowledge a physical symptom, even a life-threatening one (Solomon, 1982b), attests to the degree to which masculine conditional positive regard has moved him away from his real (self-preservative) self. He would rather die than be unmanly. It is quite common for men to ignore other physiological needs in the areas of sleep, diet, exercise, and alcohol intake (Meth, 1990).

Many a man has risked physical harm in order to preserve his sense of masculinity. You can see gender-role strain in a typical school or neighborhood situation where a bigger, stronger boy challenges a smaller, weaker one to fight. The human part of the smaller boy tells him to run away, but the masculine part tells him to stay and defend his "honor" even though he is sure to get hurt.

Julius Lester (1974) described his boyhood role: "I was the neighborhood champion at getting beat up. 'That Julius can take it, man,' the boys used to say, almost in admiration" (p. 32). It is not uncommon for the boy who runs away or loses a fight to be beaten by his father when he gets home, a communication of conditional positive regard if ever there was one.

Contact sports and war are two arenas where men have traditionally tested their masculinity. Football is dangerous and it hurts. Playing this game requires that a person suppress the self-protective and pain-avoiding parts of the self. Even as young boys, athletes are encouraged to play in spite of pain and to risk their bodies in order to win games. Winners receive a great deal of approval, whereas losers are often shamed or ignored. Again, this is conditional regard.

War, of course, is the ultimate suppression of the self-preservation instinct. Although there may be more reasons to fight in a war than just to prove one's masculinity, men who have refused to do so have historically been branded as cowards and shamed as unmanly (Levy, 1992). Over 50,000 men died in the Vietnam War. It is probably not a coincidence that modern men's movements began near the end of the Vietnam era, in which thousands of men experienced the ultimate in gender-role strain.

A third universal human need is for some degree of dependence on others (Jourard, 1971). Here again there is a conflict between the human and the masculine, and again we find a connection to emotionality. A man cannot be totally independent (as the male gender role demands), and thus he will sometimes feel helpless and alone. Gender-role strain results from these feelings, which are then denied. Brian Allen (1974) described how he learned about masculinity from his "Uncle Macho": "You must never ask anyone for help, or even let anyone know that you are confused or frightened. That's part of learning to be a man" (p. 6).

Many men find it nearly impossible to ask for help when they need it, even when it is readily available. People often laugh at some men's reluctance to ask for directions when they are lost. It seems like such a simple thing to do, yet the power of early prohibitions against dependence prevents it. Being lost on a trip is somewhat trivial, but the reluctance to ask for help in some other areas may have important implications for the man's functioning. These areas include sexuality information (Rappaport, 1981), mental health (O'Neil, 1981a), and relationships (Gordon & Allen, 1990).

Goldberg (1979) illustrated the aspects of gender-role strain discussed above:

> The less sleep I need,
> The more pain I can take,
> The more alcohol I can hold,
> The less I concern myself with what I eat,
> The less I ask anybody for help or depend on them,
> The more I control and repress my emotions,
> The less attention I pay to myself physically,
> **The more masculine I am.** (p. 52)

There are several other areas in which gender-role strain is evident for many men:

1. *Power, control, and competition:* The socialized tendency is to dominate and compare oneself with others. To do so requires a man to bury the parts of the self that are associated with empathy, mutuality, and cooperation. Many theorists believe that this orientation leads to damaged interpersonal relationships (Messner, 1992), role strain (O'Neil, 1990), and sexual conflicts (Gross, 1992).

2. *Homophobia.* The role demand for men to restrict interpersonal closeness to males due to the risk of being labeled homosexual requires a man to deny naturally affectionate feelings toward other men (May, 1988). Many theorists believe that homophobia has the effect of severely limiting the intimacy of male-male relationships (see Chapter Thirteen).

3. *Achievement, success, and money.* Personal value is associated with a man's accomplishments and social standing. At the extreme, this involves a denial of the parts of self associated with pleasure, relaxation, and family life (Skovholt, 1990). Validation of masculinity from this source depends on economic conditions, social position, and talent, as well as education and access to resources (Pleck, 1981a).

4. *"Femiphobia".* Any behavior that might be considered feminine is avoided. This requires the man to suppress any parts of his personality that are culturally associated with women's characteristics. O'Neil (1990) believes that fear of femininity is at the root of all other role strain.

5. *Athletic prowess.* Boys are often shamed and ridiculed if they do not play sports or do not play them well. Athletic participation is the most important factor in boys' high school social status (a form of positive regard), and nonathletic boys are more likely than athletic ones to doubt their masculinity (Richardson, 1981).

6. *Sexual initiative and performance.* Men are expected to seek sex actively and to be insatiable, promiscuous, and sexually goal oriented. This involves denial of the parts of self that make affectional ties to others (Nelson, 1985) and the more sensual aspects of the man. Sexually aggressive men, who are considered to be under a great deal of role strain (Pleck, 1981a), tend to set nearly impossible sexual expectations for themselves and feel chronically unsatisfied with their amount of sexual experience (Kanin, 1970).

The bottom line of male gender-role strain is that conditional positive regard leaves the male out of touch with his "inner world" and overconcerned with the external world (Leafgren, 1990). His socialization has impaired his ability to deal with psychological conflicts, except by denying that they exist.

The self-actualizing tendency, however, is a potent human force. Going back to the comparison between humans and plants, Rogers (1980) says:

I remember that in my boyhood the bin in which we stored our winter's supply of potatoes was in the basement, several feet below a small window.

The conditions were unfavorable, but the potatoes would begin to sprout—pale white sprouts, so unlike the healthy green shoots they sent up when planted in the soil in the spring. But these sad, spindly sprouts would grow two or three feet in length as they reached toward the distant light of the window. The sprouts were, in their bizarre, futile growth, a sort of desperate expression of the directional tendency I have been describing. . . . In dealing with clients . . . I often think of these potato sprouts. . . . The clue to understanding their behavior is that they are striving, in the only ways that they perceive as available to them, to move toward growth, toward becoming. . . . They are life's desperate attempt to become itself . . . this potent constructive tendency. . . . (pp. 118–119)

Despite unfavorable conditions, most men strive, in the only ways that they perceive as available to them, to achieve some degree of emotional expression, intimacy, self-care, and sexual satisfaction. Most men put their power, status, and competitive needs into some kind of perspective with the rest of their lives. In other words, most men cling to their humanness in spite of the forces that seek to wrest it away and turn them into machines. This, Rogers would say, is the manifestation of the self-actualizing tendency.

Rogers is also optimistic with regard to men's ability to deal with the effects of their harsh socialization. Because he believes that the self-actualizing tendency exists in every man, he also believes that it will emerge under the right conditions, just as the potato shoots he described would turn healthy if deposited in rich soil. Given an environment in which men can discover and express their true selves, they can drop their masculine façades and make the transition from "seeming" to "being."

At least two factors work against this happening. First, the emotional "scar tissue" from childhood and adolescence is considerable for most men, making it difficult for them to feel safe in dealing with this inner world that has become so alien. Second, we live in a sexist culture that continues to base approval on traditional masculine characteristics and behavior. Nevertheless, the primacy of this psychological work has encouraged many men to deal with these obstacles.

Existential Theory

Existential theory of personality is based on the writings of existentialist philosophers such as Sartre, Kierkegaard, Heidegger, and Nietzsche. It bears a strong resemblance to humanistic theory in many regards, but it departs in others. The existential view of the person provides an interesting perspective on men, particularly with regard to the positive attributes of traditional masculinity.

The major similarities between humanistic and existential theories are the emphases on self-awareness and self-determination. Like humanistic theorists, existentialists believe in the importance of being in touch with the inner life and using it as a guide to action.

The major difference in these two theories is in the area of conflict within the person. For the humanist, the self-actualizing tendency is only stifled by conditional positive regard, a force that originates from outside of the person. If the environment supports the real self, then the person can move unencumbered toward fulfillment. Growth only entails risk if positive regard is conditional. In contrast, existential theorists see conflict within the person as an inevitable feature of the human condition. For them, growth always entails risk.

Existentialists such as Rollo May (1958) believe that moving toward fulfillment is not just a matter of a person following his or her actualizing tendency. It requires more effort than that. Because the person has many different possibilities and potentials for growth, he or she must decide which ones to pursue and which ones to leave by the wayside.

This is where the conflict emerges. At every moment, the person is forced to make choices that involve giving something up (Boss, 1963; Keen, 1970). If you decide to go to class, you cannot stay in bed. If you decide to stay in bed, you cannot go to class. If you decide to spend an afternoon with other people, you cannot spend it by yourself.

Although these are relatively trivial choices, other decisions are more profound in their effect on our lives. If you decide to marry, you cannot stay single, and vice versa. Maybe you can experience the other alternative later on, but maybe there will not be a "later on." Since we have a limited amount of time to spend in this world, our choices are finite and vitally important.

For the existentialist, it is the pattern of choice that determines the personality, and the person is wholly responsible for his or her choices. This means that you are what you do and that you create who you are.

By making choices, a person ascribes purpose and meaning to life. It is an intensely personal meaning, not some meaning that is bestowed by outside forces such as biology or other people. The decisions that a person makes defines his or her values and individuality.

Life is frightening, because we must continually make choices without having all the necessary information (May, 1958). When you chose a college to attend, you probably gathered information about aspects of several schools, but you could not know everything about every school and be able to perfectly predict the outcome of attending one or the other. You made your best educated guess and you lived with it. For the existentialist, life is a series of such guesses; hopefully, they are educated ones. These choices are made every day and at every moment. Not only did you choose to attend a college, you choose to be in school every day that you stay. If you choose to marry, you will also opt to stay with your partner (or not) every day.

Decisions are satisfying when we make good ones, although we can never know if we have made the best one. To do so, we would need to see into the future. Even when you make a choice that turns out well, you may be left with a lingering feeling that perhaps another alternative might have been better. When you make a poor decision, you are left with the negative feeling that you had a chance but did not take advantage of it.

Every choice involves two basic alternatives: You can choose to face the unknown future or you can stick with the routine, predictable past. For example, you can face the problems of going out on your own and defining your world (future), or you can define your world by what your parents or other people tell you is important (past).

Choosing the future is frightening because it always involves risk. You might make a decision that does not turn out right, and this could result in your losing something valuable. If you left home to go to college, you probably felt apprehensive when you first arrived there. After all, you might not like it, you might not do well, and you might lose touch with your friends at home. You had to risk the loss of peace of mind, self-esteem, and people whom you value. Existential psychologists call this feeling of apprehension **ontological anxiety,** or fear of the unknown (Maddi, 1989).

Choosing the routine, predictable past is not frightening, but it is boring. When you merely stick with what you know, you get the feeling that you are missing out on something and that the routine does not seem to have any meaning in life. In the movie *The Godfather,* aging Mafia kingpin Don Corleone laments, "I could have been somebody—I could have been Senator Corleone; I could have been Governor Corleone." But, instead, he chose to become a criminal. He found that his life had become unsatisfying and meaningless. Existentialists call this feeling of boredom and regret **ontological guilt.** It is the stifling sense of missed opportunity. Don Corleone no longer had the time to develop these other potentials. His choices were limited by the inevitability of his death, as they are for all of us.

Ontological anxiety and guilt are the painful and inescapable realities of the human condition (May, 1958). Ontological anxiety will always be with us because we are faced with the necessity of making new choices every moment, and our prediction of the outcomes of our decisions is always imperfect. Ontological guilt is inescapable because we have too many potentials to be fulfilled in one lifetime. Choosing one thing always involves giving up another, and we are always left with the sense that we might have missed something important.

Although it never goes away completely, we can minimize ontological guilt by making wise choices and vigorously participating in our lives (Tillich, 1952). If you are pursuing a rewarding and interesting career, you do not feel so badly about the other things you could have done. If you are courageous enough to assert your being in the face of ontological anxiety, then ontological guilt will not rear its ugly head very often.

Courage is the hallmark of psychological health for the existentialist (Frankl, 1960). Choosing to grow despite the uncertainty of his or her decisions is what allows a person to be most fully human and fulfilled. It is "daring to be great."

Existential values should not be misconstrued as a prescription for recklessness. Existential psychology places value on the willingness to make your best guess and go with it, not the willingness to make a random guess or to fail to consider the consequences of your actions. Spontaneity is not the same as impulsivity, and making an educated guess is much more than merely "rolling the dice."

But where does the "educated" in "educated guess" come from? If his or her being is so unique and individual, what information can a person use to guide decision making? The answer to these questions comes back to the humanistic theory discussed earlier. If a person's being is unique and individual, then he or she must use it as a guide for decision making. The full experiencing of the self involves a vigorous sense of body, emotions, thoughts, sensations, an appreciation of the physical world, and an ability to examine the self undefensively. The person who has a full experience of self is said to be living an "authentic" life.

Authenticity helps point the way to existential choice. Intentionality and courage actualize the choice. For instance, occasionally people leave high-paying jobs, even if they are good at what they do. When asked why they left, they often say, "That job just wasn't me." Their self-awareness told them that their job no longer had a place in their lives, and they were courageous enough to search for something more important.

Existentialism and Masculinity

From the existential perspective, traditional masculinity has a number of marked advantages and disadvantages (as does traditional femininity). Men are socialized in some ways that help them assert their existential selves. Other influences get in the way of this process. Because responsibility for the self is inescapable, each man is charged with the struggle for overcoming these negative influences and living an authentic life.

These negative influences are conceptualized much in the same way as they are in the application of humanistic theory. If the vigorous experience of the self provides the data on which to base existential decisions, then many men are basing their decisions on limited information. The socialization of boys to not attend to emotion leaves a large gap in the experience of the self. This allows men to see emotional situations only in intellectual terms and may often force them to wallow in emotional problems.

In the movie *Play It Again, Sam,* Alan's (played by Woody Allen), wife has left him and filed for divorce. His businessman friend is trying to console him. The friend seems to think that, since the problem is that the woman has gone away, the solution is to find another woman. He explains it to Alan as follows: "A man makes an investment. It doesn't pay off. What are his options? Reinvest!" Clearly this intellectual, problem-solving, action-oriented approach is not helpful for someone who is dealing with the emotional pain of loss and rejection.

Male gender roles contain a wide variety of prescriptions for behaviors that emphasize the outward appearance of the man: stoicism, job status, wealth, material possessions, control, dominance, achievement, and independence. Traditional masculinity is defined by how the man looks, not by his inner experience.

Many men who chase the masculine dream find it to be disillusioning and self-alienating. This is especially true for men who have reached middle adulthood. Some have exerted considerable effort in attempting to live up to the masculine mystique, and they may have done fairly well at it. Others have given up on trying to meet the harsh standards of masculinity.

In middle adulthood, the body begins to decline and the man must acknowledge his mortality and vulnerability. At the same time, he may have become tired of holding up the heavy burden of the masculine façade in his work and social life. Whether gradually or abruptly, through the so-called "midlife crisis," many men move away from traditional masculine values. One of Vaillant's (1977) middle-aged interviewees described his crisis: "One part of me wants power, prestige, recognition, success; the other part feels all of this is nonsense and chasing the wind" (p. 228).

Many men choose to emphasize family and leisure roles at midlife (May, 1988) or otherwise reevaluate their lives (Levinson, Darrow, Klein, Levinson, & McKee, 1978). In existential terms, their experience of themselves tells them that they need to make adjustments in their choices in order for their lives to remain meaningful. Choosing to define himself by gender-role standards precludes a man from pursuing options in many areas such as work, leisure, relationships, and sexuality. Some men gather the courage to break out of the narrow definition of self and exercise options that were previously avoided.

There are a number of positive aspects to traditional masculinity from the existential perspective. Courage is surely one of them. Throughout history, men have been willing to face challenges and overcome obstacles. Courage is a central part of the masculine value system.

Men have also been raised to believe in the necessity of decision making and action, which are also existential ideals. Sometimes, the most courageous thing a person can do is to get to work and do what must be done. Farrell (1990) goes so far as to define problem solving and the offering of solutions as "male nurturance."

Risk taking is another masculine and existential value. Men have poured themselves into physically and psychologically dangerous ventures and pushed the limits of their capabilities, because they believed that what they were doing was worthwhile. To do so is to risk failure in order to attain fulfillment.

Many men's accomplishments required them to tolerate a good deal of discomfort, which the existential person must do in order to carry out difficult decisions. Millions of working men have suffered horrible physical conditions in order to support their families. From an existential standpoint, these men made the choice to stay in these circumstances, moment after moment and day after day, because they defined their purpose as the role of provider and breadwinner.

The truly creative person is a person with vision, one who can imagine possibilities and future. In boys' play, problem solving, and other aspects of their socialization, the culture often encourages this kind of imagination (Block, 1984). The fact that males are encouraged to go out into the world independently and deal with it helps them to see and choose from a wide variety of options.

An existential men's studies perspective would argue for an expansion not an eradication, of traditional masculinity. Wong, Davey, and Conroe (1976) suggested this approach in counseling men. From a base of independence, courage, and risk taking, men can expand to becoming independent from unreasonable gender-role demands, having the courage to enter the realm of the feminine, and taking emotional risks.

Summary

1. Phenomenological psychology emphasizes the importance of the individual's sense of self and the ability of the human being to attain personal fulfillment. Carl Rogers believed that all living things have an actualizing tendency, which propels the organism toward growth. Self-actualization is the psychological outgrowth of the actualizing tendency in human beings. Under the right environmental conditions, self-actualization allows a person to fulfill his or her unique potential.

2. The healthiest psychological environment is one in which loving and valuing are communicated to the person in all circumstances. Rogers called this unconditional positive regard. When a person gets messages that he or she is not valued because of some behavior, then conditional positive regard is experienced.

3. Because feedback from others is critical in shaping the personality, the person who receives a great deal of unconditional positive regard will internalize this attitude and come to value the self. Large doses of conditional regard cause the person to deny the parts of the self associated with disapproval. Because vigorous experiencing of all parts of the self is necessary for self-actualization, conditional regard inhibits the fulfillment of human potential.

4. The application of Rogers' theory to masculine socialization reveals that many males grow up with a good deal of conditional regard. "Masculine" behaviors often meet with approval and "feminine" behaviors with disapproval. Boys begin to value the masculine parts of the self and deny the feminine parts. This denial leads to self-alienation.

5. The gender role strain model is based in humanistic theory. Boys whose naturally occurring personalities contradict social standards of masculinity tend to experience many negative consequences. They may become hypermasculine in order to force themselves into the cultural ideal.

6. The denial of emotion is central to many male gender roles and creates a good deal of strain for many men. Other areas of strain include safety needs, the avoidance of physical pain, dependence, power needs, homophobia, femiphobia, achievement, athletics, and sexuality. Despite this strain, most men are able to assert their unique human selves. Carl Rogers would be optimistic about men's healing.

7. Existential theory resembles humanistic theory in its emphases on self-awareness and self-determination, but it departs in its emphases on personal responsibility, conflict, and risk. Self-definition is a matter of individual choice, which always involves the possibility of losing something valuable. The human condition is one of ontological anxiety, or fear of the unknown, and ontological guilt, the sense of missed opportunity. While both are unavoidable, an individual can minimize the latter by choosing to push the self forward despite fear. The authentic person is attuned to the self and courageous enough to make difficult choices.

8. From the existential viewpoint, traditional masculinity contains positive and negative influences. The negative influences are the encouragement to deny the emotional parts of self, and the emphasis on the outward appearance of the man. The positive aspects include the masculine willingness to face challenges, overcome obstacles, take action, make decisions, take risks, endure discomfort, and push the limits of one's potential.

Janet Century Photography

CHAPTER SEVEN

Diversity among American Men: The Impact of Aging, Ethnicity, and Race

Bruce Rybarczyk, Ph.D.

Linton's Law:
In some ways each man is like all men;
in some ways each man is like some other men;
and in some ways each man is like no other men.

Kardiner and Linton (1945)

Other chapters of this book mainly focus on the first level of what I refer to as Linton's Law (cited in Gutmann, 1987, p. 10): the developmental and psychological issues that are nearly universal for males in Western culture. The focus of this chapter is the second level of Linton's Law: the common features of masculinities within specific subgroups. I will describe ways in which men are alike and different as a product of three crucial factors affecting gender identity: aging, ethnicity, and race.

In the process of exploring the unique aspects of gender identity among older men, men of various races, and ethnic men, we should not minimize the importance of individual differences and thereby contribute to the process of stereotyping. On the contrary, it is important to address these factors so that we understand the rich complexity and diversity within masculinity. Linton's third level, the uniqueness of each individual, will be left for books and courses dealing with the psychology of the individual.

We begin with a description of some of the demographic factors that shape the different forms that masculinity takes within American cultures. First, changes in male gender roles that emerge in the second half of the life span are discussed. Then, we turn to a general discussion of the impact of race and ethnicity on gender. Finally, we explore gender-role characteristics of one group of men within each of these two categories: African-American men and Mexican-American men.

The Second Half of Life: Male Gender-Role Changes

How does the gender identity of young men change as they become older men? This is a complex issue that has been given only limited consideration in the literature. In fact, there is limited theory and research addressing *general* psychological and personality development during the "adult" years. The only exception is a collection of longitudinal studies showing that most "core" personality traits remain stable over the life course (e.g., McCrae & Costa, 1984; Eichorn, Clausen, Haan, Honzik, & Mussen, 1981). By contrast, the research and writings on development are extensive on the stages of childhood, adolescence, and old age. This lack of continuity in the behavioral sciences gives the false impression that adult men and women do not change in any appreciable way until they reach old age, when they suddenly transform into "elderly" persons.

In reality, the changes that take place among men occur gradually. In contrast to early development, these changes do not seem to be based on the physiological processes of aging. Rather, they are driven by significant changes in family status, social position, career, or health. There is no major physiological change during the middle years of life that parallels the physiological events of puberty. Instead, there are a few *relatively* universal psychological events, such as the death of one's parents, retirement, changes in parental status, and adjustments in relationships.

There are some misunderstandings about the effects of aging on men. For instance, the concept of a male "midlife crisis" was proposed and popularized in the 1970s (Levinson et al., 1978; Sheehy, 1976). These writings implied that this "crisis" is universal and based on chronological age. In other words, one could expect a man to make profound changes in his life around age 40 because most normal men do this. However, several authors have found that no such crisis occurs in most men (Costa & McCrae, 1978; Neugarten, 1973; Vaillant, 1977). If there is a crisis during the middle years, it seems to be brought on by a crisis in the job situation, family life, and/or marriage and not by aging. Moreover, my own experience as a psychologist is that men who are psychologically "hardy" are able to adapt to a crisis in one area of their lives without causing a crisis in other areas. The concept of "midlife crisis" implies sweeping changes in many areas, which is unusual.

For many U.S. men, several changes that may affect gender identity occur in their 40s or 50s. These often include the first markers of inevitable physical decline (e.g., minor hearing loss, graying hair), changes in work-place status (e.g., becoming a "mentor" or "senior partner"), or children moving out of the house (the "empty nest"). They may realize that goals set earlier in life, which would signify "success" when achieved, will not be achieved. The consequences of these changes can be positive (e.g., new roles, new goals) and negative (e.g., feelings of disappointment). For men whose self-concepts rely heavily on youth-oriented masculine traits, these changes undoubtedly force a redefinition of their gender identities.

Two cautions should be made with regard to generalizations about older men in the developmental literature. First, the distinction needs to be made between generation (also known as **cohort**) and age. Most of the research and writing has been based on cross-sectional comparisons between the current generation of older adults and the current generation of younger adults. Research findings can only document age and cohort differences as they occur together. We can only speculate on the relative contributions of each factor from these data. For example, we might assume that older men rarely use illicit drugs, because this is currently true. However, it is possible that this could change in a later generation of older men who will have grown up during an era when the use of these drugs was more socially acceptable. Cohort effects and age effects are inevitably confounded.

A second caution is that the research on development in the second half of life is often limited to white, middle-class, U.S. males (e.g., Levinson et al., 1978; Vaillant, 1977). It may be that nonmajority men experience aging in a very different manner. For example, many working-class men do not have the resources to enjoy a retirement that involves new adventures and activities (e.g., travel, golf). Thus, retirement may afford fewer opportunities for personal growth.

It is easy to fall into the stereotypical belief that, as men lose or surrender their competitive and aggressive "instincts," they become less productive. In fact, many older men continue to base their self-esteem on the success ethic (i.e., you are what you produce or achieve). While many men divest themselves emotionally from their careers as they approach retirement, others are hitting their career peaks as they reach "old age."

Elderly men have made significant achievements in our culture. For example, while in their 80s, Edison invented the dictaphone and Benjamin Franklin helped write the Constitution. Many older U.S. men continue to hold powerful positions well past the age of 65. We have recently witnessed an 8-year presidential term by a man in his 70s followed by a 4-year term by a man in his 60s (a virtual gerontocracy!). Leadership and power by elderly men is common in many cultures (Solomon, 1982b).

Is There a Midlife Gender Shift?

One change that has been hypothesized by several adult developmental theorists (Gutmann, 1987; Jung, 1933; Levinson et al., 1978; Neugarten, 1968) is a movement toward androgyny for both men and women as they pass middle age. Many of these theorists believe that everyone has coexisting masculine and feminine components in their personalities, and that one component (usually the cross-gender component) remains repressed during the first half of life. This repressed component is thought to emerge in midlife.

Gutmann (1987) hypothesized that the minimization of gender-role differentiation is a universal phenomenon, not specific to U.S. culture. He based his conclusions on studies of several different cultures, including the Navajo Indians of Arizona, the Mayans of Mexico, and the Galilean and Syrian Druze. He asserted that there is much anthropological evidence from more "primitive" cultures that, as women pass the postparental years, they assume more informal power and demonstrate an open assertiveness not seen earlier in life. Men, for their part, are more likely to become passive, getting more involved in domestic and religious activities. Gutmann (1977a) also posited that these dimorphic gender roles are an evolutionary adaptation to the requirements of raising offspring, which places his theory in the sociobiological category (see Chapter Three).

The evidence for a gender shift comes from a variety of different sources. Several "projective test" studies have found that, when asked to interpret ambiguous pictures, older men often tell stories that involve a more passive-accommodative (traditionally feminine) orientation to the world (Ames, 1975; Gutmann, 1977a; Neugarten & Gutmann, 1968). Another group of studies indicates that older men and women hold less gender-stereotyped self-concepts compared to middle-aged or younger adults (Fitzgerald, 1978; Hyde & Phyllis, 1979). Although the overall self-concept usually remains gender typed, older men were more likely to view themselves as having more stereotypically feminine characteristics than younger men.

Anecdotal evidence supporting this theory includes qualitative studies of the lives of well-known men (e.g., Gandhi) as well as analyses of later-life changes in the work of writers and artists. Gutmann (1987) points out that the work of Andrew Wyeth progresses from paintings of industrial scenes (in his youth), to houses being observed from a cold distance (at midlife), to representations of the warmth found within a house (in his old age).

A number of studies do *not* support the theory of midlife gender transformation. A longitudinal study by Peskin (1992), which employed a gender self-concept measure, found no significant gender shift among a small sample of college graduates followed for more than 25 years. Huyck (1992) used similar measures and found that gender changes appeared only in the context of the marital relationship, with men and women over time becoming more alike in their marital roles. This study also matched the finding in a previous study (Feldman, Biringen & Nash, 1981) that changes in gender self-concept were more correlated to parenting status than to actual chronological age. In addition, studies that used personality measures to assess life-span differences in gender-stereotyped traits failed to support the theory (Reedy, 1977; Siegler, George & Okun, 1979). For instance, Reedy (1977) found that older men and women were actually *more* stereotypical in their need for autonomy, affiliation, dominance, and nurturance compared to younger men and women.

These contradictory findings led some authors to conclude that observed shifts in gender-typed behavior over time are the result of changes in the social roles available to older men, and not to changes in gender identity, per se (O'Rand, 1987; Solomon, 1982b). For example, as men acquire more free time as a result of retirement, they may assume various domestic roles for the first time (e.g., doing laundry, cooking, gardening). Older men may also view themselves as equally masculine, but they may have less concern about maintaining the outward appearance, or they may choose to express their masculinity in a different manner (e.g., by acting more "gentlemanly"). Similarly, it has been suggested that there are less rigid gender-role expectations for very young males and very old males, resulting in less social pressure on older men to behave in a gender-stereotyped manner (O'Rand, 1987). For example, older men may feel more free to share physical affection with others because it is more socially acceptable than it was when they were younger.

Mental Health Problems of Older Men

The current population of older adults has been socialized not to acknowledge mental health problems. Seeking mental health treatment carries an even greater stigma. This is especially true for older men, who were socialized to suppress strong negative emotions. When psychological problems surface, men often view it as shameful to burden others with these feelings. Emotional "self-containment" is seen as an ideal way of coping with problems.

Typically, an older male brings an emotional problem to the attention of a medical person, either as a part of the picture of a stress-related illness (e.g., high blood pressure, ulcer) or through the process of **soma-**

tization (Busse, 1986), the conversion of psychological distress into physical concerns or complaints. In many cases, these worries or complaints involve real and chronic medical problems (e.g., shortness of breath from emphysema, pain from arthritis), but the somatizing individual becomes completely preoccupied with the illness and its symptoms. Hence, mental health professionals who specialize in working with older adults most often work in medical settings rather than in mental health clinics.

In spite of the fact that depression is the most common mental health problem of older adults (Blazer & Williams, 1980), it often goes undiagnosed and untreated. Part of this problem is attributed to the more insidious form that depression takes in the later years of life, sometimes referred to as **masked depression.** Depression in old age is less characterized by a conscious experience of sadness (a more typically central symptom for younger adults) and more by apathy, a diminished experience of pleasure, sleep, and appetite problems, and a negative view of the future and the world (Klerman, 1983; Trezona, 1991). For older men, this depression is more likely to emerge in the context of an illness or following surgery. Moreover, even when an older person's "classic" depressive symptoms are presented, physicians are less likely to make the correct diagnosis than they are with younger patients (Rapp, Parisi & Walsh, 1988; Waxman & Carner, 1984). This is probably related to a pervasive bias that all of the problems of older adults are medical rather than emotional in nature.

Older men rarely use psychological services and often view these services as being for "crazy people only." There is also a somewhat accurate perception that psychological services are designed to serve the needs of younger adults (Gatz, Smyer & Lawton, 1980). This bias on the part of older adults is mirrored by the biases of health care professionals. Mental health professionals and physicians tend to believe that treatments for depression are less effective with older adults (Rapp & Davis, 1989). Physicians are less likely to refer older adults for treatment (Rabins, Lucas, Teitelbaum, Mark & Folstein, 1983; Waxman & Carner, 1984). This is unfortunate since older men who have mental health problems are most likely to visit a physician. One study reported that 70% of a sample of (mostly male) older adults who committed suicide visited their physicians within one month of the suicide (Clarke, 1992).

Depression in older men should not be confused with a generally negative world view: "Today's world is corrupt. Back when I was young, we did things the right way." Older men sometimes develop this viewpoint but still manage to enjoy and value their individual lives. Idealizing the past reinforces self-esteem by associating the self with a unique and special historical period. Similarly, the personality characteristics of eccentric older men, sometimes referred to as "geezers," should not be confused with depressive characteristics (Pankratz & Kofoed, 1988).

Several theorists assert that depression in older men is often caused by increased gender-role strain. As a man ages, he finds it more and more difficult to live up to the masculine demands for work, success, physical strength, independence, and invulnerability. If he retains these values and tries to live up to these demands, he inevitably comes up short.

Indeed, depression in older men is often linked to the loss of either of two important social roles that are crucial to the traditional masculine identity: husband and breadwinner. Although many adults experience great distress for a period of months following bereavement (Holmes & Rahe, 1967), it often evolves into a chronic depression for older men (Walsh, 1980). This is frequently due to the loss of social support, since a man's wife often maintains his connection with other family members and social contacts, especially after retirement (McGadney, Goldberg-Glen, & Pinkston, 1987).

Depression often follows retirement and is linked to several key factors: mandatory retirement (Solomon, 1981), retirement from either a white-collar or professional job (Sheppard, 1976), the lack of planning for the postretirement years (Friedmann & Orbach, 1974), and financial difficulties following retirement (Kart, 1981). The comments of an older man epitomize the "rolelessness" and loss of meaning in life that contribute to postretirement depression: "I was born a plumber. What else am I? Who else am I? There's nothing I can do. No one will want to have anything to do with me. I'm useless. There's nothing lower than a plumber who isn't working" (cited in Solomon, 1982b, p. 217).

Other mental health problems may also be linked to midlife gender transformation. In the case of somatization, men who find their increased emotional neediness unacceptable may unconsciously resort to physical complaints. By becoming medical patients, they can be dependent and obtain emotional nurturance through the more acceptable means of being in the "sick role."

Suicide is another significant mental health issue for older men. Data spanning several decades of research indicate that men older than age 60 are four times more likely to commit suicide than men or women in any other age group (National Center for Health Statistics, 1987). The high rate of suicide is found among white males only. By contrast, rates of suicide among nonwhite men peak in young adulthood and rates for women peak in middle age, with both groups showing a decline in old age (National Center for Health Statistics, 1987).

Explanations for this shocking phenomenon are difficult to come by because these older men rarely seek mental health treatment for their problems prior to taking their own lives. The best demographic predictors of suicide among older men are health problems (Copeland, 1987), social isolation (Osgood & Thielman, 1990), and the recent death of a spouse (Kaprio, Koskenvuo, & Rita, 1987). It seems quite plausible that gender-role stress would be a key factor, since older men who have chronic medical problems are least likely to have access to opportunities for social achievement and prestige. Depressed older men with chronic medical problems who do participate in psychotherapy often make statements that illustrate these issues: "If I can't *do* anything, what good am I?", "Since my wife has to do everything for me, I feel like a wimp," or "I'm nothing but a burden to my family" (Rybarczyk, Gallagher-Thompson, Rodman, Zeiss, Gantz, & Yesavage, 1992).

Late-life alcoholism among men can also be seen as a dysfunctional response to an inability to live up to the increasingly impossible demands of traditional masculinity. When the male alcoholic is drinking, he is allowed to express both hypermasculine and dependency needs without having to take responsibility for either ("it was the liquor talking"). Gutmann (1977b) describes how this process occurs:

> On the one hand . . . strong drink is instant machismo. Because it releases inhibitions on aggression, it is . . . a liquid metaphor for masculinity. On the other hand, drinking is an oral activity, a re-capitulation of infantile sucking. . . . Within the course of the same drinking bout, the alcoholic is both god and helpless infant. He starts the evening by saying he "can lick anybody in the house," but ends it impotent, like an infant, unable to walk and submerged in his own mess. (p. 513)

It should be noted that most older men adjust well to changes in gender identity. They find new roles that grow out of the opportunities created by retirement, disability, and widowerhood. They often come to appreciate aspects of life that were previously "off limits." For some, the "feminine" pleasures of tenderness and sensuality and an interest in the aesthetics of everyday life are experienced for the first time (Gutmann, 1987). New activities, which are not based on aggression or sexuality (e.g., cooking, gardening, religion), are undertaken. Older men often experience a freedom from some of the gender-role taboos encountered in the first half of life.

Reminiscence and Older Men

Reminiscence is the process of thinking or telling about past experience. Until the 1970s, older adults who reminisced more frequently were seen as being somewhat maladjusted, as persons who were showing signs of "senility" or who were living in the past. We now have a much better understanding of the various positive functions and benefits of reminiscence in old age, as well as a greater interest in the oral history of family members as a means of learning about our own "roots."

Although gender differences have not been studied systematically, older men appear to reminisce for different reasons than women (Habegger & Blieszner, 1990; Merriam, 1980). Based on my experience with two reminiscence intervention studies (Rybarczyk & Auerbach, 1990; Rybarczyk 1992), I hypothesize that older men most often reminisce for two primary purposes. First, aging men tell stories about the past as a means of making an emotional connection with other men. An example of this type of reminiscence would be two men discussing the 1947 American League Championship for the purpose of reexperiencing the positive memories they have in common. Second, older men who continue to hold onto a traditional masculine identity use reminiscence to validate their self-concepts by retelling stories of lifetime successes and achievements. By telling a story of how, as a volunteer soldier, he miraculously survived a World War II battle, an older man would be reinforcing his self-concept as someone who remained brave in the face of danger and was willing to risk his life for justice in the world.

One of the most overlooked facts regarding old age is the preeminence of past events in the identity of older adults (i.e., "I am who I was" or "I am who I remember myself to be"). In fact, the process of "constructing a life story and reconstructing the self in that story" may be one of the most important undertakings of old age (Sherman, 1991). At least one gerontologist has hypothesized that this process is more important to most older adults than finding happiness in the present (Kaufman, 1986). This process may be more important for older men who maintain a more traditional gender identity as compared to an older woman or man with a more androgynous identity.

Ethnic Identity and Masculinity

Ethnic identity is defined by the culture(s) of an individual's ancestors, and it includes the associated characteristics of that culture or cultures (e.g., Polish, German-Italian). The most apparent cultural characteristics are language, customs, food, religion, dress, and history. The more subtle characteristics are "psychological" in nature, such as world view, values, and rules about appropriate behavior. These types of cultural characteristics are passed from one generation to the next within family systems.

Ethnic identity patterns thinking, feeling, and behaving in profound yet subtle ways. "Cultural filters" seem to operate at an unconscious level. Historically, behavioral scientists have overlooked the impact of ethnicity on development, probably due to pervasiveness of the belief that all immigrant groups rapidly assimilate into the mainstream culture (i.e., the "melting pot" myth, McGoldrick, 1982). However, there is evidence that ethnic psychological characteristics are retained for many generations after immigration (Greely, 1981) and emerge during different phases in the life cycle (Gelfand & Kutzik, 1979).

"*Actually, Lou, I think it was more than just my being in the right place at the right time. I think it was my being the right race, the right religion, the right sex, the right socioeconomic group, having the right accent, the right clothes, going to the right schools...*"

(Drawing by W. Miller; © 1992 The New Yorker Magazine, Inc.)

Rules that guide gender behavior are important components of ethnic identity. Greek-American men, for instance, tend to value extreme individualism and individual achievement, leading to a strong belief against working for others, especially non-Greeks. To violate this rule for any length of time is to risk losing self-esteem and pride. This emphasis on pride and honor are reinforced by **philotimo** (literally "love of honor"), a driving force for men in Greek culture as well as other Mediterranean cultures (Welts, 1982).

By contrast, Polish-American men have generally been willing to work for others, at low-paying and low-status jobs, to "bide their time" for a better future. These values derived from the peasant identity of their forebearers (Kuniczak, 1978), who developed an intricate system for coping with domination and oppression by foreign powers. Another adaptation that has been repeated by Polish-American immigrants is an emphasis on contribution and status within their tight-knit Polish community rather than in the larger U.S. culture (Mondykowski, 1982). There is also a common disdain for being "stuck up," which is measured by the degree to which the ways of the U.S. "gentry" class have been adopted (Mondykowski, 1982). This deemphasis on "fitting in" with the larger culture has played a significant part in the stereotypes contained in the many ethnic jokes about Polish-American men (i.e., implying that they are ignorant or lacking in good taste).

Similar gender issues may also be *expressed* in different ways across different ethnic groups. For example, the fear of same-sex attraction may be expressed in the lack of physical contact between men of British descent (a.k.a. WASPs), while Portuguese-American men may feel comfortable embracing each other (Moitoza, 1982). However, Portuguese-American men may express homophobia by bragging among themselves about sexual exploits with women. The expression of a certain quality of masculinity will also vary across generations. For instance, the son of a first-generation Greek immigrant who goes to medical school and marries a German woman is likely to express his sense of honor and pride differently than his father.

To illustrate the effect that ethnic identity has on masculinity, I will briefly review the psychosocial literature on Mexican-American men, who have both a prominent racial identity and ethnic identity. Within the Hispanic racial category, there are as many as 20 distinct ethnic groups in the United States (Valdes, Baron, & Ponce, 1987). Mexican-Americans view themselves as having a very different ethnic identity than other Hispanic groups, such as Cuban-Americans and Puerto Rican-Americans. Because many Mexican-American men are recent immigrants, the influence of ethnicity on their gender identity is pervasive. This ethnic identity is further reinforced by the proximity of Mexico: "Trips to and from the native land help renew the ties, maintain a group of reference, activate a support system, and reaffirm ethnic identity" (Falicov, 1982, p. 145).

Mexican-American Men

Most Mexican Americans can trace their lineage back to peoples of both Spanish and native Central American ancestry, referred to as **mestizos.** Mexican culture has thus been a mixture of elements transported by the Spaniards in the process of colonization with those of the indigenous Central American cultures (Falicov, 1982). It was estimated that there were 8.7 million Mexican Americans in the United States as of 1985 (Comas-Diaz, 1990). Although some communities have existed since the United States took over what is now the southwestern states, the majority of Mexican Americans were either born in Mexico or have parents who were born in Mexico (Falicov, 1982). There is also a group of uncounted Mexican Americans who are so-called "illegals" or "undocumented workers." Most have settled in ethnic ghettos within the larger cities of the United States.

Box 7.1
A Personal Glimpse

I am currently living and working in the city of Chicago, which serves as an ideal backdrop for writing about male gender roles. Chicago is a place where masculinity reigns supreme, the "City of Big Shoulders." It is a city known by its "tough guy" male characters, like gangster Al Capone, actor Mr. T, and, more recently, football coach Mike Ditka. The hypermasculine characters portrayed in the popular "Saturday Night Live" skit, "da sports fans," are caricatures of typical Chicago men. For decades, this city has spawned gritty writers, such as Studs Terkel, Mike Royko, Pulitzer Prize winner Nelson Algren, and the entire genre of the hard-boiled detective story. It is the home of the Playboy empire, the ubiquitous steak restaurant, the "sports bar," and a popular version of softball played without gloves (leading to the peculiar custom of showing off previously broken fingers while "out with the guys").

Chicago is also home to what is probably the largest variety of ethnic enclaves anywhere in this country. Within these communities, many of the ways and customs of the "old country" have been preserved. The city is often referred to as a "patchwork quilt" comprised of cohesive communities of Indians, Ukranians, Bohemians, Guatemalans, and Swedes, to name a few. It is a city where the concept of **pluralism** has challenged the notion of the United States being a **melting pot,** with all immigrant groups rapidly assimilating into a single mainstream culture.

Thus, Chicago affords a great opportunity to observe the diversity in masculinity among different ethnic groups. These differences are striking even to the casual observer who is participating in a favorite Chicago pastime, dining in ethnic restaurants. For example, if you eat in any Greek or Indian restaurant in the city, you are likely to encounter only male employees working on the floor, whereas Polish and Ethiopian eateries usually have only women managing the floor and working the tables. These differences in business practices hint at dramatic variations in gender roles across ethnic groups. Undoubtedly, these rules and roles brought from the "old country" are included in the scripts of more ethnically mixed men who are several generations removed from immigration.

Mexican-American men have been greatly influenced by the fact that most came to this country for employment rather than for permanent immigration as well as by their frequent "undocumented" status. They often accept jobs with very poor working conditions or ones that are "off the books" and, therefore, not subject to the labor protections enjoyed by other men. Due to fears of detection, the "illegals" have also been forced to live a somewhat low-key existence. However, these exigencies are difficult to separate from masculine traits that are present in Mexican culture, such as an emphasis on courtesy, formality, submission to authority, and dissimulation in social situations. Some authors have even traced these qualities to an "oppressed servant" mentality that grew out of centuries of foreign domination in Mexico (Falicov, 1982).

The stereotypical Latino male has an attitude and behavior pattern known as **machismo.** The literal translation of this term is "to display masculine characteristics." In U.S. society, the term *machismo* has come to embody the relatively negative qualities of physical aggression, sexual promiscuity, dominance of women, and excessive use of alcohol (Gutierrez, 1990). In contrast, the traditional connotation of *machismo* in Latin culture includes the positive qualities of courage, generosity, dignity, respect for others, and love for family (Ruiz, 1981; Valdes et al., 1987). Since Mexican-American men have been subject to discrimination and denied access to economic and political power, it may be that many have compensated through an emphasis on machismo (Baca Zinn, 1980). This may be part of the more universal tendency for relatively powerless men to overemphasize the more obvious aspects of masculinity (Pleck, 1981a; O'Neil, 1990).

The stereotype of the macho Mexican-American male has been challenged in recent years by a number of behavioral scientists. When a gender-role questionnaire was given to 524 undergraduates in California, Mexican-American males demonstrated less of a traditional gender-role orientation than Anglo males (Gonzalez, 1982). Contrary to the dominant male stereotype, numerous studies show that Mexican-American wives play an egalitarian part in almost all aspects of the marital relationship including decision making. The majority of Mexican-American males also prefer to participate in social and recreational activities with their wives and children (Baca Zinn, 1992). Therefore, it seems likely that many of the positive qualities of machismo have gone unnoticed in U.S. culture and that the exaggerated aspects of machismo that do appear in some men are more of a function of *class* than *culture* (Baca Zinn, 1992).

Race and Masculinity

Racial identity refers to membership in one of the major groups that are distinguished in U.S. society by their physical characteristics (e.g., Asian,

Hispanic, African American, Native American, Caucasian). Racial identity is based on immutable physical characteristics such as skin color. Because racial characteristics are visible, race often plays a prominent role in social relations. In contrast, ethnicity can be changed over the life span (e.g., through acculturation), expressed in selective situations only (e.g., family get-togethers, religious ceremonies), or concealed (e.g., by adopting a spouse's name or changing a surname).

The impact of race on personality development stems primarily from the fact that persons of a "minority" race are often perceived as being different by those in the "majority" racial group (creating a "we and they" mentality). This perception of difference can take on an even more insidious form in **racism,** the belief in the innate superiority of one's own race. Racism has direct social consequences such as discrimination, stigmatization, and alienation, all of which have a profound impact on psychological development.

In the 1990s, race continues to be a divisive force in U.S. society, and it has been characterized as an "American obsession" (Terkel, 1992). The 1992 Rodney King incident and the subsequent riot in poverty-stricken South Central Los Angeles gave testimony to the intensity of racial tensions. Moreover, the tensions between African-American and Korean communities in the inner city and recent violence perpetrated against Asian Americans demonstrate that racial tensions go beyond a simple "black and white" issue.

It can be argued that race has an even greater impact on gender development than ethnicity, because it involves both *social forces* and the *psychological responses* to those forces. The social forces that shape male gender identity and expression include racism and the consequent social conditions (e.g., isolation from "mainstream" culture, joblessness, poverty). Due to barriers in the job world, for example, men of color are often forced to achieve status through alternative means (e.g., music, sports, criminal activity, the gang subculture). Psychological responses to racism that have been described in the literature include internalized oppression, low self-esteem, and anger (Boyd-Franklin, 1989; Pinderhughes, 1982).

To illustrate the influence of the factors associated with race, consider the case of African-American men. Although they also comprise several ethnic groups, the identity of African-American men has been dramatically shaped by race.

African-American Men

While there is a great deal of diversity among African-American men, those who have not been able to climb into the ranks of the middle class are in the midst of what could easily be described as a national crisis. African-American men are beset by the highest rates of unemployment, marriage failure, drug and alcohol abuse, premature death by violence and preventable diseases, crime victimization, and incarceration for criminal offenses (Taylor Gibbs, 1991). Tragically, about one in four (23%) of all African-American males in their 20s are in the criminal justice system (The Sentencing Project, 1990).

The social forces that have affected today's African-American men date back to slavery. In *The Promised Land,* Lemann (1991) describes how the lack of employment opportunity has created a cycle of poverty and powerlessness. The cycle began with a lack of real opportunity following emancipation from slavery, which led to a great many African Americans earning a living via the exploitive system of share cropping. This became an obsolete way of life when the quantum leap in farm technology took place in the 1940s. The loss of farming employment, together with other factors, led to the mass migration of African Americans from the rural South to the industrialized northern cities (the largest migration in U.S. history). Eighty-one percent of the African-American population still reside in large urban areas (Moore Hines & Boyd-Franklin, 1982). The eventual collapse of the industrial base in most cities has created mass unemployment and underemployment among African Americans and the subsequent "culture of poverty" in the inner-city ghetto (Wilson, 1987).

Needless to say, there is a great deal of debate in academic and political circles as to the social causes and solutions for the current crisis within African-American urban communities. During the Reagan/Bush years, the popular wisdom preached by conservatives was that an open-ended welfare system has created a "culture of poverty," sapping the initiative of African-American men. Hence, welfare reform was the proposed solution. An alternative point of view presented in *The Declining Significance of Race* (Wilson, 1978) is that lack of economic opportunity is a much greater problem than race-driven discrimination in education, housing, or employment. President Bill Clinton campaigned on the promise that job training and job creation would alleviate inner-city problems. Critics charged that these two viewpoints "blame the victim" and/or ignore the 400-year history of racism in the United States. A more balanced point of view is that all three factors make a contribution: racism, economic dynamics, and social factors within ghetto communities.

The lack of older male role models for boys growing up in African-American families is another social factor that has been given much attention in the past few years. Although the notion of African-American fathers being "peripheral" family members has been challenged (McAdoo, 1981), more than half of all African-American children do not have a father permanently residing in their home (Blum, 1992). The 1991 movie by African-American writer/director John Singleton, *Boyz 'n the Hood,* dramatized the importance of having a father in the home to establish discipline and set an example of how to express anger in constructive ways. In cities around the country, various community programs have been started to provide more contact between African-American males of different generations (McLarin, 1992).

Psychological responses to social forces are more difficult to document, although few would doubt the profound impact of these factors on the collective psyche of African-American men. Anger and despair are obvious responses. The large amount of anger and rage continually processed by African-American men may account in part for the high rate of physical ailments, such as high blood pressure and heart disease (Pinderhughes, 1982). Despair also has its severe consequences. Since 1960, the suicide rate for young African-American males has nearly tripled to become the third leading cause of death in this age group (Terkel, 1992). The rampant hopelessness among African-American males was exemplified in a statement made by a man being interviewed for a recent study: "I think the Black man is the last one that's going to get anything" (Reynolds, 1992, p. 83).

By necessity, the development of a masculine gender identity among African-American males takes a different path. Unlike their Euro-American counterparts, African-American males have been denied the message from family, school, and the larger society that "power and control are their birthright" (Lee, 1990, p. 126). Within current social conditions, it is difficult to imagine young African-American males developing a belief that they are masters of their own destiny. Moreover, even the most basic requirements for fulfilling the masculine role are often unavailable: being able to earn enough money for survival and being able to support a family.

One response to being denied access to masculine power or privilege in this country has been the formation of an alternative "masculine style," termed the *cool pose* (Majors & Billson, 1992). This concept includes a range of ritualized behaviors, such as looking tough, hustling, and "playing the dozens" (i.e., the rapid exchange of insults). It also includes behaviors of African-American men who are prominent in the popular media:

> Black athletes, with their stylish dunking of the basketball, spontaneous dancing in the end zone, and high-five handshakes, are cool. The twenty-year-old pimp, with his cadillac and "stable of lace" (prostitutes), is cool. Celebrities such as Miles Davis, Eddie Murphy, and the late Adam Clayton Powell, Jr. are cool. (Majors & Billson, 1992, p. 4)

Majors and Billson summarize the function of cool pose as follows:

> The purpose of posing and posturing—being cool—is to enhance social competence, pride, dignity, self-esteem, and respect. Cool enhances masculinity. Being cool also expresses bitterness, anger, and distrust toward the

dominant society for many years of hostile mistreatment and discrimination. Cool pose helps keep the dominant society off balance and puzzled and accentuates the expressive self. (p. 105)

Cool pose is a way of continually communicating essential elements of the masculine identity: pride, strength, and control. Unlike Euro-American men, many African-American men appear to need to express these qualities at all times, a sort of "compulsive masculinity" (Majors & Billson, 1992). Paradoxically, this response also serves as a kind of "restrained masculinity," since it involves portraying emotional toughness and invulnerability in the face of the injustices of everyday life. Again, this can be viewed as an adaptive response to the chronic lack of fairness or justice in society for African-American males. For example, the report of an older African-American man traces the survival value of being able to "play the dozens" back to the days of slavery:

> It was a game slaves used to play, only they wasn't just playing for fun. They was playing to teach themselves and their sons how to stay alive. The whole idea was to learn to take whatever the master said to you without answering back or hitting him 'cause that was the way a slave had to be, so's he could go on living. (Guffy, 1971, cited in Majors & Billson, 1992, p. 101)

Needless to say, this masculine response has both a positive side and a negative side. It may be at the root of reckless violence and criminal activity as well as stress-related medical problems and substance abuse. This self-destructive aspect of cool pose is vividly portrayed by a contemporary African-American poet:

> We real cool. We
> Left school. We
> Lurk late. We
> Strike straight. We
> Sing sin. We
> Thin gin. We
> Jazz June. We
> Die soon.
> —Gwendolyn Brooks

There are a number of stereotypes of African-American males, even within the social science literature. A recent sociological research book entitled *Slim's Table* (Duneier, 1992) has challenged the stereotypes regarding inner-city African American males. One reviewer summarized the impact of the book:

> A quietly devastating attack on misguided social analysts and black and white journalists in search of sensational sound bites on the ghetto, who

replace traditional racist stereotypes of the black man with patronizing caricatures of a demoralized and utterly marginalized race of men hopelessly wrecked by white racism. Rejecting this homogenized travesty, Duneier gives voice, dignity and meaning to the lives of the majority of working class black men who pay their bills, fear their god, respect their women, and cherish their friendships. (Patterson, 1992, cited in Duneier, 1992).

Rather than exhibiting a moral impoverishment, the older blue-collar men who frequent a cafeteria on the edge of a Chicago ghetto embody a high level of personal responsibility and social respectability. Duneier argues that the media and social scientists have ignored the significance of this large category of men in the inner-city neighborhoods. Moreover, inner-city African-American communities have also failed to look to these individuals as "role models," due in large part to a de-emphasis on conventional morality in the larger context of U.S. culture. In other words, the moral problems that are present in the ghetto are a reflection and magnification of the moral problems present in society as a whole.

Summary

1. While some developmental and psychological issues are nearly universal for males, others are associated with specific age, ethnic, and racial groups.

2. A number of problems in the social science literature on aging have been identified. These include a paucity of theories and research studies, myths such as a universal "midlife crisis" among men, and difficulty separating age from cohort effects.

3. Several studies, along with anecdotal evidence, support the theory that midlife entails a shift in gender patterns. However, other research has either failed to identify such a shift, or it has tied gender changes to marital/family changes or social-role changes.

4. Older men with mental health problems face considerable difficulties. The stigma associated with having such problems can prevent them from seeking services. They often present complaints to medical personnel rather than to mental health practitioners. Due to the "masked" nature of these problems, physicians sometimes misdiagnose or fail to notice mental health problems in older adults.

5. Typical mental health problems in older men include depression, suicide, and alcoholism. These may be associated with declines in the

work role and other traditionally masculine areas. However, many older men benefit from a freedom from traditional gender demands.

6. For aging men, reminiscence seems to serve the important functions of emotional connecting and maintaining masculine self-esteem.

7. Ethnic identity has a powerful effect on how masculinity is expressed. Mexican-American men are often stereotyped as having "machismo," but this concept appears to have different meanings in minority and majority cultures. The social oppression of Mexican Americans may have influenced some men to overemphasize its more negative aspects. However, recent research has demonstrated that, in some ways, Mexican-American men are less sex typed than has been portrayed in the literature.

8. Race also has an important impact on the expression of masculinity. African-American men, who are subject to widespread and longstanding racial oppression, experience a variety of unique problems, including high rates of unemployment, premature death, and incarceration. "Cool pose" is one reaction to being denied masculine power and privilege. The majority of working-class African-American men, who are well adjusted in spite of their circumstances, have been ignored by social scientists and the media.

PART THREE

Men's Issues

Jean-Claude Lejeune/Stock Boston

CHAPTER EIGHT

It Never Lies
and It Never Lies Still:
Emotion and Masculinity

There are few human experiences that are as basic and ubiquitous as emotion. A person responds to almost any internal or environmental event with some degree of affect, and the experience of positive feelings is probably one of the most important motivators for many. People seek money, love, knowledge, physical pleasure, relationships, or human service because these things provide some degree of emotional fulfillment. The United States Constitution holds the "pursuit of happiness," an emotion, as an inalienable human right. Just as the brain structures associated with emotion are at the center of the brain, emotion is at the center of human experience.

The following passage about a teenage boy playing softball illustrates a connection between masculinity and emotion:

> I take off at full speed not knowing whether I would reach (the ball) but knowing that this is *my chance*. My cap flies off my head, which must have been pre-ordained, and a second later I one-hand it as cool as can be, still moving at top speed. . . . I hear voices congratulating my mother for having such a good athlete for a son. . . . Everybody on the team pounds my back as they come in from the field, letting me know that I've MADE IT.
>
> But I know enough not to blow my cool so all I do is mumble thanks under a slightly trembling upper lip which is fighting the rest of my face, the rest of my being, from exploding with laughter and tears of joy. I don't even allow myself to smile because I know that it won't be just a smile, that if I let go even a quarter of an inch it will get beyond control, and at the very least I'll giggle, which is unheard of on the ballfield. (Candell, 1974, p. 16)

You can sense how much effort it took for this 14-year-old boy to control his feelings. Strong emotions seem to have a life of their own. You can feel them physically; they seem to cry for expression. If you accept the premise that emotional experience strongly encourages emotional expression, then it must take an even stronger force to suppress emotion. That powerful influence may well be male gender socialization.

Even the casual observer will notice that many men have difficulty understanding, dealing with, and expressing emotions. Restrictive emotionality has been described as the most frequently discussed issue in men's studies (Skovholt & Hansen, 1980). Male gender roles often encourage men to resist the awareness of affect, avoid emotional vulnerability, and hide feelings.

In this chapter, we explore the origins and consequences of restrictive emotionality by addressing the following important questions: (1) Are there demonstrable sex and gender differences in emotional expression and self-disclosure? (2) What typical male socialization experiences lead to restrictive emotionality? (3) What have researchers learned about the effects of emotional constriction on the person? (4) What are the possibilities for helping men to improve the quality of their emotional lives?

Sex and Gender Differences in Emotional Expression

There is little doubt that men tend to be less emotionally expressive than women. Although 7- and 8-year-old boys and girls do not appear to differ in the expression of feelings, distinct sex differences emerge by middle adolescence (Balswick, 1982). High-school-aged females are more expressive of fondness, pleasure, and sadness than males (Balkwell, Balswick, & Balkwell, 1978), while males are more expressive of antipathy (Balswick & Avertt, 1977). Stapley and Haviland (1989) found that adolescent boys were much more likely than girls to deny that they *ever* had emotional experiences. Studies have demonstrated sex differences in expression of feelings for college students (Snell, 1989) and other adults (Saurer & Eisler, 1990). The stereotype is that "feminine" expression involves the disclosure of emotions such as love, joy, and sadness, and that "masculine" feelings are anger, hate, and resentment. Balswick (1982) reported that the available research evidence indicates a strong trend for men and women to behave in accordance with these stereotypes.

Self-disclosure is described as a verbal communication of personal information from one person to another (Cozby, 1973). Theoretically, self-disclosure is basic to mental health and the establishment of close relationships (Lombardo & Fantasia, 1976). The person who is able to reveal himself or herself has the opportunities to express the self, receive support from others, gain insight into the self, understand his or her emotional nuances, and form close relationships (Jourard, 1971). In order to do so, however, the person must tolerate some degree of vulnerability (Lewis & McCarthy, 1988). In other words, the revelation of the self to important others involves some degree of interpersonal risk, but also helps the person to be understood, connected, and in touch with the self. Moreover, being in touch with the self helps a person to better understand others (Jourard, 1971).

Cohn and Strassberg (1983) reported that third- and sixth-grade girls spend significantly more time than their male counterparts in intimate conversation. Davidson, Balswick, and Halverson (1983) reported similar findings for a group of high school students. In an extensive review of child and adolescent self-disclosure studies, Kilmartin (1986) reported no studies where male disclosure exceeded that of females, although there were some studies in which no sex differences were demonstrated. The evidence that this difference carries over into adulthood is fairly clear cut (Williams, 1985; Aries & Johnson, 1983; Caldwell & Peplau, 1982). Adult men are also more likely to reveal negative feelings than positive ones (Saurer & Eisler, 1990).

In a study by Walker and Wright (1976), undergraduates were instructed to talk about intimate topics. Fifty percent of the male subjects refused to cooperate with this direction. Men who did cooperate, however, did not differ from women in the intimacy level of their disclosures. Assuming that these men were less sex typed than those who refused to participate, gender may be a better prediction of self-disclosure than sex. Lavine and Lombardo (1984) and Lombardo and Lavine (1981) found that androgynous individuals of both sexes exhibited equally intimate levels of disclosure. Balswick (1988) reported similar findings.

There also appear to be differences in topics about which males and females disclose as well as the sex of the person who more often receives the disclosure. Mulcahy (1973) found that male adolescents were more likely to disclose about studies, attitudes, and opinions, whereas females tended to disclose more about personality. Stapley and Haviland (1989) reported that adolescent boys disclosed more about their activities and achievements than girls and that they found these areas (where performance is assessed) to be more emotionally charged than other areas. Girls reported relationships with others to be more emotionally charged, and they disclosed more in this area. In general, girls tend to reveal personal information and boys tend to reveal what they are doing or thinking (Kilmartin, 1986).

The *target* of a self-disclosure refers to the person to whom the disclosure is directed. Here the data are unambiguous. People disclose more often to females than to males (Mazur, 1989; Balswick, 1988; Franzoi & Davis, 1985). We could view this as a sex similarity (higher disclosure to females) or a sex difference (same sex versus other-sex target). Sex-typed males tend to reveal very little personal information to other males, although they disclose about the same to females as androgynous men do (Winstead, Derlega, & Wong, 1984).

In summary, there are fairly robust findings to indicate that males, especially sex-typed ones, are less expressive and disclosing than females for emotions other than anger, that they tend to reveal thoughts more than feelings, and that these self-revelations are not often made to other males. A variety of explanations for the roots of these differences have been proposed.

Origins of Restrictive Emotionality

Emotional constrictedness is one of the hallmarks of traditional masculinity. Males are usually socialized to deny and suppress feelings from an early age. The masculine values of toughness, self-reliance, task orientation, logic, fearlessness, and confidence are antithetical to the expression of emotions, especially those that are associated with vulnerability. Anger would seem to be a potentially empowering emotion and, therefore, it is allowable for men.

A number of cultural and social forces encourage men to restrict their emotionality. O'Neil (1981a) believes that the antifemininity norm is at the heart of men's fears of emotional expression. He describes the following four commonly held masculine beliefs:

1. Emotions, feelings, and vulnerabilities are signs of femininity and therefore to be avoided;
2. Men seeking help through emotional expressiveness are immature, weak, dependent, and therefore feminine;
3. Interpersonal communication emphasizing emotions, feelings, and intuitions is considered feminine and to be avoided;
4. Emotional expression may expose inner fears and conflicts that could portray the man as unstable, immature, and unmanly. (p. 206)

Some psychoanalytic interpretations of masculine inexpression appeal to the early childhood denial of mother identification. Because boys are raised by their opposite-sex parent, they must put rigid boundaries between themselves and their mothers in order to define themselves as masculine. If the boy's mother is emotionally expressive and his father is not (a fairly common case), then emotions are experienced as "feminine" and they threaten masculine identification. When the boy feels something, he becomes anxious about his masculinity and learns to deny and devalue feelings.

Girls' gender identity is based on attachment to the mother, whereas that of boys is based on separation from the mother (Chodorow, 1978). As a result, girls tend to become more relationship oriented (communal) and boys more task oriented (agentic).

Relationships do not really have outcomes, per se. They are experiences, just as emotions are, and the maintenance of attached, intimate relationships requires affective self-disclosure (Jourard, 1971). Tasks, on the other hand, are often defined by outcome. They tend to be more cognitive in nature, and the important thing is not to experience the task, but rather to get it done. A task-oriented approach to the world may often involve the view that emotions are a nuisance to be disposed of as soon as possible. The engineering honor society at the General Motors Institute proudly claims the name "The Robots" (Penwell, 1992), reflecting the agentic value on eschewing emotion.

If the boy's father is emotionally inexpressive, then this style may become a part of the boys' identification with the father. Balswick (1988) reports that boys who have expressive fathers are as expressive as girls. In families where both parents are expressive, boys will not tend to view emotional expression as an exclusively female trait and, therefore, the natural tendency to express themselves will emerge, since it is not associated with threats to masculinity.

We could also easily view the finding that expressive fathers tend to have expressive sons as merely a product of imitation. If we look at the availability of male models in U.S. culture, it is easy to see how inexpressiveness perpetuates itself generation after generation. Fathers' inexpressiveness is imitated, and male heroes in popular culture are often paragons of traditional masculinity. More adventure films than ever are being made in the United States at present, and the stars of these movies are almost invariably male, task oriented, tough, inexpressive, and violent.

An interesting research finding is that fathers tend to be more expressive to their daughters than to their sons (Block, 1984), and adult females are more frequent recipients of self-disclosure than males (Balswick, 1988). Therefore, beginning in childhood, women have more opportunities to observe and imitate self-disclosing models.

Rewards and punishments for self-disclosure may also affect the frequency of this behavior. It is clear that "unmasculine" behaviors such as crying often meet with disapproval from parents and peers. Most men have a storehouse of memories of times when their emotionality was punished. The crying little boy whose father says to him threateningly, "I'll give you something to cry about" can quickly extinguish that behavior.

The male peer group can be especially brutal in its enforcement of the restrictive emotionality norm. Skovholt and Hansen (1980) give an example of a man who remembers the message that he got from his male high school friends: "Show any weakness and we'll kill you" (p. 9). Balswick (1982) reports several studies that detail male subcultures that strongly disapprove of gentle, affectionate, or compassionate behavior. In extreme groups, such as street gangs, this norm is rigidly enforced with threats of violence. Besides punishing expressiveness, male subcultures also reward the suppression of emotion. For instance, in some fraternity initiation rites, a group symbol is burned into the arm of the initiate, and he is applauded for remaining stoic and unresponsive.

We can see from these research findings and examples that restrictive emotionality is not only the product of a *history* of these sanctions. Sex-typed reward and punishment contingencies exist in many settings in which adult men find themselves. Not only did men get punished for emoting when they were children, they often get punished for emoting as adults. From blue-collar to corporate work places, for example, emotions other than anger are often not tolerated in men. Goldberg (1977) suggested the following brief exercise as an illustration: Picture a man crying in the work place due to job frustration. Imagine your reaction. Now picture a woman reacting to the same frustrations with the same behavior.

If you found that you had different reactions to the same behavior for different sexes, you are probably not alone. Women's expression of emotion may be tolerated in many of these settings. Derlega and Chaikin (1976) reported that both male and female subjects judged a man who disclosed a personal problem to be more maladjusted than one who kept his troubles to himself. Women were judged to be healthier when they disclosed. People seem more likely to comfort women in distress and avoid men in distress.

Maccoby (1976) noted that "corporate work stimulates and rewards qualities of the head and not the heart" (p. 99). We could probably add the rewarding of qualities of the body and have a good picture of the blue-collar world.

Women in the corporate world sometimes find that expression of weakness is disadvantageous to their careers. A female banking executive relates that, among her female colleagues, the rule is, "You die before you cry." I suspect that, for males in these settings (and blue-collar settings), this goes without saying. My experience of the corporate culture is that, for women executives, emotional restriction is situation specific. They practice emotional restriction in the work place because it is defined as inappropriate there, but it is seen as appropriate elsewhere. For men, however, emotional constriction is more cross-situational. There are precious few settings in which they feel safe enough to disclose. For women, "die before you cry" is a hyperbole that stresses the career importance of avoiding the display of weakness in a male-dominated setting. For men, it may be literally what they are doing. (See Chapter Nine on physical health.)

Role Theory

As noted in Chapter Two, social roles are powerful determinants of behavior. It is in this theoretical area that we find one of the most convincing explanations of male inexpressiveness. People tend to assume roles in organizing their behavior, and they tend to avoid out-role behavior (Turner, 1970). As we have seen, masculine and feminine roles are generalized social roles that function to influence a wide variety of social behaviors. This may be especially true for gender-schematic people, who tend to rigidly organize their worlds into male and female categories (Bem, 1981b).

Masculine roles involve a set of expectations for task-oriented behaviors that emphasize logic and rationality and deemphasize emotional experience. From early childhood, boys come to value masculine traits and behaviors and devalue feminine ones. The ideals of masculinity are courage, toughness, risk taking, competitiveness, and aggression (Balswick, 1988). Emotional expression is not compatible with these traits. For example, men are socialized to view all other men as competitors. One does not exhibit vulnerability to a competitor (Skovholt & Hansen, 1980). Since self-disclosure often involves vulnerability, it is avoided.

Besides being incompatible with the masculine role, emotional expression is defined as part of the feminine role. Men are less likely to disclose because out-role behavior is to be avoided. In addition, masculine gender demands are applied earlier in life and more intensely for boys than feminine ones are for girls (Basow, 1992). Thus, behavioral role sanctions are stronger for men than for women. Consider what your reaction might be if you overheard the following conversation:

> "Mike, I've been so upset since we had that argument, I could hardly sleep last night. Are you *sure* you're really not mad at me?"
> "Heck, Jim, I'm so relieved. . . . I was just afraid that you'd be mad at me!"
> (Brannon, 1985, p. 307)

Because of the social dominance of men, out-role behavior is viewed as a loss of masculine power and privilege, and this is not tolerated. Hence, pejorative terms such as *sissy* or *wimp* are applied to men who exhibit emotionality, submissiveness, or dependence. Masculine privilege not only devalues and restricts women, it devalues and restricts the feminine-defined parts of men.

Emotional expression can also be understood in the context of relationships. One broad social expectation is for **reciprocity.** We tend to respond to other people as they behave toward us (Brehm & Kassin, 1993). For example, when someone expresses anger toward you, you tend to respond with anger. When haggling over the price of something, a salesperson who reduces an asking price influences a buyer to increase an offer.

With regard to self-disclosure, people are influenced by the reciprocity norm to disclose at a level similar to that which they receive (Cohn & Strassberg, 1983). Herbert (1976) found that adolescents' perceptions of their own levels of disclosure matched their perceptions of their parents' levels, although males disclosed less than females. Other studies (Norrell, 1984; Cohn & Strassberg, 1983) have supported the hypothesis that reciprocity operates in self-disclosure. Since males are less often the targets of disclosure than females (Balswick, 1988), it is not surprising that they tend to disclose less themselves.

The other side of the coin from reciprocity is **complementarity**, the tendency to balance the expression of the other person. If one person in the relationship is dominant, he or she influences the other person to be submissive (Strong, 1986). L'Abate (1980) argued that male inexpressiveness is a complementary reaction to female overexpressiveness. While current evidence indicates that complementarity may operate in certain circumstances, it is influenced by complicated interactions among many setting and relationship variables (Kilmartin, 1988).

Sattel's (1976) explanation of male inexpressiveness is very different from those presented thus far. He argues that men are inexpressive simply because they want to maintain power. By being emotionally withholding, men force women to "draw them out" and do the emotional work in the relationship. As evidence, Sattel offers that men are often expressive early in relationships with women as a way of seducing them. Later on, they become inexpressive as a way of asserting control, since masculinity and male privilege demand control. Sattel goes so far as to suggest that inexpressiveness is directly related to the power of a person's role.

In summary, it seems that a variety of social and cultural forces influence men to be inexpressive. The available evidence is that these forces do a pretty good job of inhibiting what seems to be a natural, healthy inclination to disclose and express feelings. Since emotion is pervasive, the results of compulsively restricting it may also be pervasive.

Consequences of Restrictive Emotionality

It is said that "emotion never lies, and emotion never lies still." Affective experience is central to human experience, regardless of whether or not an individual attempts to deny its existence. Feelings that are not expressed directly are handled indirectly. Many men deal with emotions by placing feelings outside of themselves, through externalizing defenses, by "acting out" emotional conflicts, and/or through physical symptoms.

We have seen that, from early childhood, girls are encouraged to look inside of themselves and think about how they feel, and boys are encouraged to look outside of themselves and think about what they do (Block, 1984). Strong "feminine emotions are experienced as threats to masculinity, and these threats are difficult to ignore. The traditional male deals with these feelings with strategies that allow him to perceive them as nonexistent. In this way, he preserves his masculinity by defending against the feminine.

Lobel and Winch (1986) measured defensive styles in male college students. They found that masculine men prefer defenses that allow them to avoid emotional expression. Men showed a tendency to deal with anxiety by finding an object to attack (acting out) or by splitting affect off from content and suppressing the emotion.

Some examples will help to clarify these styles. Let's look at the painful experience of being rejected by a romantic partner. This kind of event can precipitate feelings of sadness due to the loss of the valued person and anxiety due to doubts about your adequacy. There are several ways to deal with these feelings. You could talk about them with a close friend and gain support, express the sadness through "having a good cry," convert these feelings into anger and engage in some aggressive behavior, or deal with the feelings as though they were an intellectual problem. The latter two strategies are preferred by masculine men. The former two are feminine styles which, despite their effectiveness, cannot be accessed by these men, since doing so would constitute a threat to masculinity.

Because of the overwhelming quality of these emotions, the man might punch a wall, drink heavily or compulsively, and desperately seek a new partner. In all of these strategies, solutions come from outside of the self. The man can take out his frustrations on an object or find something (alcohol or another person) that will hopefully soothe him, as he is not good at soothing himself.

There are several negative consequences to this external style. First, if the soothing person or object is not available, the man cannot deal. Second, little new learning can take place. He does not have the skills to introspect and think about himself, and thus he has difficulty in learning what caused the troubling situation and how he might behave differently. If he always deals with emotions externally, he can learn little about what is inside. Third, these kinds of behavior may have a tendency to alienate other people. It is frightening to be around someone whose aggression is not in control; drunks do not make good company, and people who are desperate in seeking a lover may not be comfortable to be around.

Alexithymia

Inexpressiveness begins as part of a social role, but continuous participation in a role over time can have an enduring effect on the person. Actors who play the same stage role for long periods of time report that they incorporate some aspects of the role into their personalities (Brannon, 1985). The man who continually acts like he has no feelings over many years may virtually lose his ability to experience emotion.

Sifneos (1972) first coined the word **alexithymia** to describe this trait. It comes from the Greek (*a* = lack, *lexis* = words, as in *lexicon,* and *thymos* = emotions). Literally, the word *alexithymia* means "no words for feelings." Alexithymic persons have such an impoverished emotional life that they cannot even identify feelings, much less express them.

Nemiah, Fryberger, and Sifneos (1976) described alexithymia as having four features: "(a) difficulty identifying and describing feelings; (b) difficulty distinguishing feelings from bodily sensations; (c) reduction or absence of symbolic thinking (lack of imaginative ability); (d) an external, operative cognitive style" (pp. 227–228).

Consider what it would be like to be unfeeling and unimaginative. It would be very difficult to experience satisfaction or fulfillment, connections with other people, or the creative aspects of the self. The picture of the alexithymic is one of a person "going through the motions" in a life devoid of rich experiences.

There has been a good deal of research interest in alexithymia in recent years, including attempts at the measurement of this construct and its connection to other psychological and physical states. Hendryx, Haviland, and Shaw (1991) demonstrated that the alexithymic dimensions of poor identification and expression of feelings were strongly related to symptoms of anxiety and depression in medical students. Bagby, Taylor, and Ryan (1986) reported similar findings in a sample of college students. Haviland, Shaw, Cummings, and MacMurray (1988) found a depression-alexithymia relationship in a group of newly abstinent alcoholics. A number of researchers have also discovered that alexithymia is related to a variety of physical problems (Kleiger & Jones, 1980; Heiberg, 1980; Cooper & Holmstrom, 1984; Taylor, 1984; and many others), as well as to narcotics abuse (Solomon, 1982a).

This large body of research provides strong support for the hypothesis that "emotion never lies still." People who do not deal with feelings directly do not make them go away. The alexithymic style often becomes destructive to the person either physically, psychologically, or both. Although only a small percentage of men are truly alexithymic, and some women also suffer from this problem, the connections between alexithymia and masculinity can hardly be denied. Although the origins of alexithymia are complex (Taylor, 1984), harsh male gender socialization can only encourage its development.

Other Consequences

A variety of other consequences for restrictive emotionality has been proposed. Many of these are in the realm of interpersonal relationships, where self-disclosure is a crucial factor in building trust and connectedness. Not surprisingly, much of the available data come from studies of heterosexual married couples.

Jourard's (1971) contention is that disclosing the private self is one of the primary functions in marriage. Several studies (Chelune, Waring, Vosk, Sultan, & Ogden, 1984; Schumm, Barnes, Bollman, Jurich, & Bregaighis, 1986; Hansen & Schuldt, 1984; and others) have demonstrated a link between positive self-disclosure and partners' reported marital satisfaction.

Men tend to disclose less than their wives (Notarius & Johnson, 1982; Pascoe, 1981), and inequality of disclosure is related to lowered levels of marital satisfaction (Balswick, 1988; Davidson, Balswick, & Halverson, 1983). It appears, then, that two of the factors in having a good marriage are that partners disclose a good deal and that they disclose approximately the same amount. It is quite common for a wife to complain that her husband won't "let her in" and that this is a source of frustration for her. We will return to this issue, as well as to men's difficulties in relationships with other men, in Chapter Thirteen.

Emotional restrictedness may also affect sexual enjoyment and/or functioning (O'Neil, 1981a). Since emotions and physical sensations are associated with each other, the man who suppresses emotion also loses touch with his sensuality. It is difficult for traditional men to see sex as something to be experienced, rather than as a task with a goal (orgasm). At its best, sex is an expression of positive emotion and, therefore, an inexpressive style limits the enjoyment of the man and his partner.

Fathering is another area affected by male inexpressiveness. In order to be a good father, a man must sometimes go against gender demands that require him to be unemotional, unconnected, and task oriented. He finds himself in situations that call for expressiveness in the form of nurturing, play, giving comfort, and being affectionate (Balswick, 1982). The inexpressive man may feel inadequate in doing these things for which he has had very little practice (more on this in Chapter Thirteen).

Male inexpressiveness has been hypothesized to be a major contributing factor to the reluctance of men to seek medical (Kinder & Curtiss, 1990) or psychological help (Good, Dell, & Mintz, 1989). Only one in seven men seek mental health services at some point in their lives, compared to one in three women (Collier, 1982). There are no indications that men need these services less often than women (see Chapter Fourteen).

There are also societal consequences for restrictive emotionality. **Compassion** is the sympathetic awareness of another person's distress. It is impossible to understand someone else's feelings if you do not understand your own. Men who have embraced task-oriented and inexpressive gender-role characteristics may find it easy to perceive people as if they were things and subordinate human welfare to a task that they define as more important. When such men are in power, their potential for destruction is great. War, racism, sexism, violence, exploitive business practices, the pollution of the planet, and other forms of victimization are all at least partly the result of a failure of compassion and empathy. Men have not been the exclusive perpetrators of these human wrongs, but they have certainly contributed more than their share. Social encouragement to become unfeeling machines, together with the disproportionate allotment of power to males, shoulders some of responsibility for this state of affairs.

Toward Solutions

We have seen that restrictive emotionality has many psychological, physical, interpersonal, and societal consequences. The good news is that we are not doomed to live with them. A number of therapeutic, educational, and social interventions have been designed to help men become more comfortable with affect. Since feelings such as satisfaction, love, and emotional connectedness are critical to quality of life, and because restrictive emotionality has negative consequences, it is not surprising that many men desire to become more expressive (Dosser, 1982).

We have already seen that inexpressiveness arises, at least in part, from situations in which males are discouraged from being emotional. The solution is to create environments that give men permission to break the social norm of nondisclosure, thus allowing the natural human propensity for expression of feeling to emerge.

One popular method for creating such settings is men's consciousness-raising groups. In these groups, men who want to learn expressive skills come together into an unusual all-male situation. Rather than having the common men's group norms of competition, task orientation, and macho rigidity, group members strive to create an atmosphere of cooperation, empathy, and self-disclosure. It is important for groups such as this to critically examine the effects of the male gender-role demands on their lives as part of their activities (Farrell, 1974; Moore & Haverkamp, 1989; Kilmartin, 1987).

Since these groups are usually formed outside of academic or therapeutic settings, not much research evidence of their effectiveness has been accumulated (Balswick, 1988). Many men, however, appear to find these experiences meaningful and helpful. Considering that social roles are powerful influences on behavior, it stands to reason that establishing expressiveness as a role expectation has some real potential. Whether consciousness-raising groups are able to establish this role norm and whether behavior changes generalize to settings outside of the group remains to be seen.

Other interventions have been designed by therapists and researchers, and some evidence of effectiveness has been accumulated. Moore and Haverkamp (1989) designed a structured group approach for increasing emotional expressiveness in 30- to 50-year-old men. Group activities included training in listening skills, reading assignments, and general discussion around male gender-role issues such as competition, power, control, and relationships.

Many men exhibited strong emotional reactions within the context of the group, and participants showed significant gains in emotional expressiveness, according to several measures. Although we cannot be sure how long the changes endured or whether they generalized to other settings, the evidence is clear that men can change affectively, at least in the short term. Moore and Haverkamp also noted that many of the group members continued to meet informally as of 6 months after the formal group ended. Many group members reported that their new skills were helpful in their marriages, careers, families, and the management of their health concerns. These reports provide anecdotal evidence that participation in nontraditional groups has significance for motivated men.

Dosser (1982) also designed an intervention program for increasing male expressiveness. He suggests that, in addition to communication-skills training and consciousness-raising activities, assertiveness training is also helpful. We do not usually think of traditional men as lacking assertive skills, but the expression of feeling is a type of assertion (Lange & Jackubowski, 1976) men often lack. *Assertiveness* refers to the ability of the person to claim his or her rights as a human being. Men have the right, and often the desire, to say, "I love you," "I feel close to you," or "I need your help and support," but the confines of male gender roles make this difficult. Many men also have problems with the appropriate expression of anger.

Balswick (1982, 1988) adds that increases in male expressiveness can also be realized through societal changes. We have seen some movement in this direction in the United States in recent years. As women increasingly share the involvement in economic activities, many men are increasing their family involvement, with its emphasis on expressive activities. Balswick (1988) suggests that, in the traditional structure of the family, women are economically dependent on men, while men are emotionally dependent on women. Just as some women are beginning to attain economic independence, some men are beginning to work toward emotional independence. This kind of "emotional independence" does not mean disconnectedness or stoicism, but rather the man's expressive management of his emotions in the context of relationships and self-awareness.

Summary

1. Even though emotion is at the center of human experience, male gender roles define it as feminine and discourage it in men, with the exception of the expression of anger.

2. There is a great deal of evidence that men, especially sex-typed men, tend to be less self-disclosing than women. This difference is first evident in adolescence. Differences in topic of disclosure also emerge at this time, with boys more focused on thinking and performance and girls more focused on feeling and relationships. Both sexes show a greater willingness to disclose to females.

3. The origins of restrictive male emotionality are in the gender-role definitions of vulnerability, inner conflict, dependence, and feeling as unmasculine. These norms are often enforced by family and peers, as well as by media images of masculinity. Boys with expressive fathers, however, tend to be expressive themselves. Norms for adult male inexpression are enforced in many work and interpersonal settings. Men who exhibit cross-gender behavior may suffer negative consequences in these settings.

4. The reciprocal nature of role behavior also encourages men toward low levels of self-disclosure, as they are less often the targets of disclosure than women. There have been suggestions that low male disclosure is a balancing reaction to women's overexpressiveness, and that low disclosure is merely a power maneuver in relationships.

5. Emotional constriction may have a number of negative consequences for men and those around them. Men who are uncomfortable with their feelings are prone to using external defenses and acting out. These methods of coping are often less effective and efficient than self-disclosing and asking for help.

6. The extreme of inexpressiveness is alexithymia, which involves a poor awareness of and ability to describe feeling states. Alexithymia has been associated with a wide variety of physical and mental health problems. The hypothesis that "emotion never lies and emotion never lies still" is supported by the research in this area.

7. Restrictive emotionality also appears to have negative effects on relationships in general and marriages in particular. Low levels of disclosure and partner inequity in disclosure are associated with a lack of marital satisfaction. Sexual dissatisfaction and dysfunction may also be linked to restrictive emotionality. The role of father sometimes calls for expressive skills in which many men are lacking.

8. Many men have expressed a desire to improve their abilities to express and disclose. Interventions for this purpose include consciousness rais-

ing, structured group activities, and assertiveness training. There is good evidence that these interventions are effective, although more research in this area is needed.

9. Male inexpressiveness should also increase as a function of more liberal gender roles. Since restrictive emotionality is strongly influenced by the expectations of social settings, the creation of nontraditional settings with alternative expectations holds a great deal of promise for improving the quality of men's emotional lives.

Ulrike Welsch Photography

CHAPTER NINE

Surviving and Thriving:
Men and Physical Health

There are sex differences in the statistical incidences of many physical problems. For example, males are more likely than females to contract heart disease, emphysema, and most forms of cancer. On the average, men die at a significantly earlier age than women. Many researchers believe that sex differences in disease and longevity cannot be explained solely by biological differences between males and females.

A good deal of evidence has led theorists to suggest that certain aspects of traditional masculinity are at least partially responsible for men's problems with disease and longevity. In this chapter, we describe some of these problems and review the relevant psychological literature on physical health as it relates to gender.

Sex Differences in Longevity

In 1991, the United States Bureau of the Census (USBC) reported that the average life expectancy for African-American males born in the United States in 1988 was 64.9 years, compared with 73.4 years for African-American females. For whites, the expectancies were 72.3 years and 78.9 years for males and females, respectively. As you can see from these data, minority men are especially at risk for early death. They are more likely

TABLE 9.1   Ratio of Male to Female Deaths
(1988 U.S. Data)

AGE IN YEARS	MALE : FEMALE
under 15	134:100
15–24	297:100
25–34	265:100
35–44	210:100
45–54	169:100
55–64	158:100
65–74	139:100
75–84	96:100
over 85	49:100

Note: Calculated from data in United States
Bureau of the Census, *Statistical Abstract of the
United States: 1991* (111th ed.). Washington, DC:
U.S. Government Printing Office, 1991.

than majority men to live in hazardous and stressful environments, as well as to lack access to health care.

Table 9.1 details sex ratios for United States deaths in 1988. As you can see, males are more likely to die than females at every stage of life until age 75 (the ratios change direction at that point because so many more women than men have survived to that age). At ages 15 to 24, the ratio of male to female deaths is a staggering 297:100! *At best,* U.S. males die "before their time" at about a 5 to 4 ratio to females. At worst, the ratio is almost 3 to 1. Contrary to the social belief that males are heartier and more resistant to disease, the evidence is indisputable that males are more vulnerable than females at every age.

At birth, there is a slight imbalance in the ratio of males to females. Conception favors males because Y-chromosome-bearing sperm (androsperm) are more motile than X-chromosome-bearing sperm (gynosperm), and thus are more likely to fertilize the ovum. Despite the fact that male fetuses are more likely to have problems in utero, leading to spontaneous abortion (miscarriage), there are between 103 and 106 male births for every 100 female births (Harrison, Chin, & Ficarrotto, 1992). But, because males die at higher rates than females, parity (an equal number of males and females in the age-group population) is reached somewhere between the ages of 25 and 34 (Basow, 1992). From this age range and up, women outnumber men. Twice as many women as men survive beyond age 80, and 11 out of 12 U.S. wives outlive their husbands (Dolnick, 1991).

Sex Differences in Disease

There is some evidence to suggest that women get ill more often than men do. Women report feeling sicker than men on a day-to-day basis. For instance, women are more likely than men to report being bothered by headaches, bladder infections, arthritis, corns and calluses, constipation, hemorrhoids, and varicose veins. We cannot be sure to what extent these differences are real and to what extent they reflect the social permission that women have to report illness. When it comes to serious (life-threatening) diseases, which are, of course, hard to ignore, men outnumber women in almost every category (USBC, 1991).

The two diseases that most often cause death are heart disease and cancer. About 35% of all people eventually die of heart disease. The male:female ratio for cause of death by heart disease is about 101:100 (USBC, 1991), a very small sex difference. When we look at these data *by age group*, however, a very different picture emerges. Between the ages of 25 and 44, the ratio of male to female deaths from heart disease in 1988 was 283:100 (USBC, 1991). Although many people die of heart disease, males tend to die much earlier than females.

With regard to cancer, sex ratios differ depending on the location of the cancerous tumor in the body. As a cause of death, men lead women in every category except breast cancer. The greatest differences are in mouth and throat cancer (250:100), lung and respiratory cancer (263:100), and cancer of the urinary organs (201:100) (Harrison, et al., 1992).

Other diseases (e.g., influenza, liver disease, and diabetes) kill men in greater numbers than women in almost every category. Some of these differences are relatively large (e.g., respiratory diseases, 191:100), others are smaller (e.g., pneumonia and influenza, 113:100), and women lead men in a few categories, such as cerebrovascular accident (stroke), in which the male to female ratio is 66:100 (USBC, 1991).

In the United States in 1989, Acquired Immunodeficiency Syndrome (AIDS) killed 19,499 males and 2,176 females, a ratio of almost 9:1. In 1986 this ratio was 12:1 (USBC, 1991). Sex ratios from AIDS deaths will probably continue to change. As with many other causes of death, AIDS strikes minority men disproportionately (Priest, 1993).

Other Causes of Death

There are sex differences in the incidence of accidents, suicide, and homicide, and they are very large ones. Males are much more likely than females to die in motor vehicle or other accidents (210:100), to commit suicide (382:100), or to be victims of homicide (315:100) (USBC, 1991).

Thus, a staggering number of physically healthy men die "before their time" from causes that are somewhat preventable. In fact, homicide is the leading cause of death for African-American men between the ages of 15 and 24 (Kimbrell, 1991).

Why Do Men Live Less Long than Women?

The preceding might strike you as an awkwardly worded title. It would be smoother to ask "Why do women live longer than men?" However, it appears that the difference in life span may be due more to men's lives being shortened rather than women's lives being lengthened.

Around the beginning of the 20th century, men's and women's lives, on the average, were about the same length. In modern industrial nations such as the United States, there has been a dramatic reduction in the risk of death from pregnancy and childbirth, which were relatively dangerous at the beginning of the 20th century. The decrease of this risk resulted in the life-span sex differential. It could be said that both women's and men's lives were shortened 100 years ago, and that we have found ways to stop shortening women's lives. Hopefully, the same can be done for men. However, it may become apparent to you that this is a complicated process.

There are two basic types of explanations for the sex difference in average life span. The first is a *biogenic* explanation. From this viewpoint, men die earlier because of genetic, hormonal, or other biological differences between the sexes. The second type of explanation is a *psychogenic* one in which sex differences in life span are attributed to gender differences in psychological and social areas such as behaviors, socialization, and ways of dealing with the self.

It should be noted that these two types of explanations are not necessarily competitive with each other. It is possible for there to be both biogenic and psychogenic reasons for sex differences. In fact, there is good evidence to suggest that both factors are operating. The question is one of the relative contribution of each factor. There has been a trend among researchers in recent years to speak of *biopsychosocial* models that take biology, individual psychology, and the effects of other people and social systems into account in constructing comprehensive pictures of phenomena.

It is also possible for biogenic and psychogenic factors to interact with one another. For instance, a man who is at high risk for heart disease because of his physiology (biogenic factor) might be less likely than a woman to see a physician for regular checkups because to do so would be an admission of weakness and vulnerability, which he views as being unmasculine (psychogenic factor). The man in this example might have a shorter life than would be the case if either factor were operating in isolation.

In the preceding example, the biogenic factor might be the major contribution. It would also be possible for a psychogenic factor to make a major contribution while still interacting with a biogenic factor. For instance, a man might drink alcohol heavily in response to the pressure of meeting masculine gender-role demands, thus damaging his body and shortening his life, or he might use tobacco to enhance his masculine image, with a similar result.

Biogenic Explanations

As mentioned earlier, male fetuses are more vulnerable in utero than female fetuses, and the death rate for males aged 1 to 4 exceeds that of females. These data are ample evidence that biological factors operate in the life-span sex differential, as it would be difficult to argue that male socialization could have a profound effect on mortality at such an early age. Explanations of biological factors include genetic and hormonal sex differences.

Genetic Differences

The difference in males' and females' genetic makeup is that females have two X chromosomes and males have one X and one Y chromosome. When recessive disease genes are found on the X chromosome, having a second X chromosome turns out to be quite a genetic advantage. The second X chromosome often contains a dominant corresponding gene that protects the female from contracting the genetic disease. For example, if there is a gene for hemophilia on one X chromosome, the female will not contract the disease unless there is also a hemophilia gene on the other X chromosome.

Because the form of the Y chromosome does not correspond exactly to that of the X chromosome, the male is not always afforded such protection. Genetic abnormalities on the X chromosome are much more likely to appear in the male because of the absence of a second (corrective) X chromosome. Some "X-linked" abnormalities such as color blindness or baldness are relatively innocuous. Some are more serious. For instance, there is some speculation that dyslexia (a learning disability) and hyperactivity might be X-linked. A few genetic abnormalities, such as hemophilia, can be life threatening.

In the search for explanations of the life-span sex differential, genetic differences make a very small contribution because of the rarity of life-threatening, X-linked diseases. As Waldron (cited in Dolnick, 1991) stated, "Most of the common X-linked diseases aren't fatal, and most of the fatal X-linked diseases aren't common" (p. 12).

Hormonal Differences

The major sex difference in hormones is in males' higher levels of testosterone and females' higher levels of estrogen. These two hormones account for physiological sex differences such as muscle size, body fat percentage, and metabolic speed. There is evidence to suggest that testosterone may render men somewhat more physiologically vulnerable to certain diseases, and that estrogen may have some protective effect.

The most demonstrable effect of these two hormones is in the area of heart disease. In recent years, the effect of cholesterol on heart disease has been the subject of much research and discussion. There are two kinds of cholesterol: high-density lipoprotein (HDL), called "good cholesterol" because it protects against heart disease, and low-density lipoprotein (LDL), called "bad cholesterol" because of its damaging effects.

In prepubescent males and females, HDL levels are about equal. At puberty, HDL levels drop rapidly in boys, but they hold steady in girls. This change coincides with the large surge of testosterone in boys and estrogen in girls. It is assumed that adolescent testosterone production is responsible for the reduction of HDL cholesterol, while estrogen has little or no effect on HDL levels (Dolnick, 1991).

LDL ("bad") cholesterol begins to rise in both males and females after puberty. Males show a more rapid rise, however, leaving them more susceptible to heart disease. After menopause, when women's estrogen level is greatly reduced, LDL levels show this same kind of sharp increase. It is assumed, therefore, that estrogen has a protective effect against LDL cholesterol, while testosterone probably has little effect (Dolnick, 1991).

These hormonal effects are important because heart disease is the leading cause of death. However, there is also some evidence that testosterone may shorten men's lives in other ways that are not fully understood.

Male cats who are neutered (which drastically lowers testosterone) live a good deal longer than those who are not (there is no corresponding effect for spayed female cats). Part of this difference is due to the fact that unneutered cats are more likely to fight, as testosterone is related to aggression. Thus, these cats are more likely to die in fights. When cats who died in fights are eliminated from the data, however, a large lifespan difference between neutered and unneutered cats remains (Hamilton, Hamilton, & Mestler, 1969). Still, we cannot be sure of the possible life-shortening effects of fighting, even if the cat does not actually die in a fight. Human boxers and football players do not live as long as most men, but we can't necessarily attribute this difference solely to participation in the sport.

If we wanted to make a true experimental study of the effects of testosterone on human longevity, we could take a group of males, castrate them, and see if they live as long as their counterparts. This kind of experimentation is obviously not possible for ethical reasons. However, there have been times in history when castrations were performed on humans for various reasons, as recently as 1950! In China and the Ottoman Empire, castrated males (eunuchs) were employed as palace guards. They could guard harems of women without the possibility of sexual liaisons. In Europe, boy singers were castrated in order to keep their singing voices in prepubescent ranges (Daly & Wilson, 1983). In Kansas, mentally ill and retarded men were sometimes castrated in order to reduce their aggressiveness (Hamilton & Mestler, 1969).

Historical anecdotes tell us that Chinese, Turkish, and Italian eunuchs seemed to live longer than other men, but no data on life span were collected. However, a research team did study 297 men who had been castrated at a Kansas institution for the mentally retarded. When compared with a matched group of inmates, the eunuchs' lives were an average of 14 years longer (Hawke, 1950)!

What is the relative contribution of biogenic factors to sex differences in longevity? Estimates range from two-thirds of the approximate 7-year difference (Dolnick, 1991) down to one-quarter (Waldron, 1976), and, because of the aforementioned interactions with psychogenic factors, apportioning fractions to either type of cause may be difficult and misleading. Almost all researchers would agree that biogenic factors are in operation. However, almost no researchers would say that these are the *only* factors.

Psychogenic Explanations

There are at least four ways in which psychological processes can contribute to illness, injury, and/or the shortening of a man's life. First, behaviors can be directly self-destructive. Suicide is obviously the best example of this type of psychogenic factor, but we might also consider the use of tobacco products or the excessive use of alcohol and other drugs in this category. These behaviors involve a man's active harm of his own body. It is also possible for a man to passively harm his health by neglecting to perform behaviors that maintain health. For example, a man with high blood pressure who refuses to take the medication to control it or someone who does not see a physician even though he has detected a symptom of cancer (when he has medical resources available to him) adversely affects his health through his behavior.

Third, some behaviors involve physical risk of illness, injury, or death. These behaviors include sharing needles in intravenous drug use, drunk driving, and contact sports. Fourth, some psychological processes seem to have adverse effects on the body. For instance, the effects of stress on physical health are well documented, and certain personality characteristics are also predictive of some physical conditions. These four categories of psychogenic factors will be separated for purposes of discussion.

Self-Destructive Behaviors

Suicide. Suicide is, of course, the ultimate self-destructive behavior. Although females in the United States are more likely than males to make suicidal gestures or attempts, males make "successful" (a strange use of the word) attempts over three times more often than females (Robins, 1985). Among older people, the ratio of male to female suicides approaches a staggering 10:1, and elderly suicide is on the rise (Ritter, 1991).

There is some conjecture that more women than men use suicide attempts to "cry for help" rather than as determined efforts to die, which are more common in men (Harrison, 1978). Women are also more likely to use suicide methods that have relatively low potential for death, such as overdose or wrist slashing, whereas men are more likely to use violent and highly lethal methods such as firearms or motor vehicles (Carson & Butcher, 1992). In 1988, males committed suicides with firearms six times more often than females. Firearm suicides accounted for 65% of all male suicides, compared to 39% of all female suicides (USBC, 1991).

What connections does traditional masculinity have to suicide? There are several. Foremost among these is a differential gender-role socialization for dealing with psychological pain. Whereas women have been socialized to think about and express feelings, gain social support, and take care of themselves, men are socialized to act on problems, be hyperindependent, and disdain emotional self-care. The hypermasculine man in severe emotional distress is often alone with his pain. He cannot express it, and he cannot ask for help with it. If the pain becomes great enough, he may feel that suicide is his only option.

The sex differential in suicide for older people is a powerful clue to the effects of traditional masculinity on suicide. Men are culturally defined by physical abilities and the work role. The older man must face the facts that his body is declining and, after he retires, that he is no longer a valued contributor in the working world. If his sense of self is overly consumed by this narrow and distorted standard of masculinity, body and work-role decline can seriously undermine his sense of self-worth. Additionally, the man may also be faced with a loss of independence at some point during his physical decline, which is also antithetical to the traditional male role.

Use of Tobacco.   Tobacco products are the only commodities legally sold in the United States that, when used as intended, will kill the user. The most common results of extended tobacco use are bronchitis, emphysema, asthma, and cancers of the respiratory system, mouth, and throat. In 1982, men outnumbered women in deaths by a 3½ to 1 ratio for bronchitis, emphysema, and asthma, and a 2½ to 1 ratio for lung, mouth, and throat cancer (Harrison et al., 1992).

In 1976, Waldron estimated that one-third of the sex difference in longevity was attributable to the sex difference in smoking. Deaths from bronchitis, emphysema, and asthma are proportional to the number of cigarettes smoked (Harrison, 1978). The use of "smokeless" tobacco (chewing tobacco and snuff) has also been linked to mouth and throat cancer, and these kinds of tobacco are used almost exclusively by males. Because the sex difference in smoking has been shrinking steadily since 1960, we might expect some of the disease proportions to also change (Harrison et al., 1992).

Socialization of destructive male behaviors can certainly be implicated in tobacco use. Advertisers have long used masculine mystique approaches (e.g., The Marlboro Man) to sell their products by associating tobacco with desirable images of masculinity (self-assuredness, independence, and adventurousness). Advertisers know that they can sell a great deal by playing on people's insecurities. When he is asked to live up to vague and impossible standards of masculinity, what man would not feel insecure? This advertising is both reflective and encouraging of certain cultural values for men: Do whatever you want; don't worry about dying.

Neglectful Behaviors

Men sometimes shorten their lives or become ill because they fail to perform the behaviors necessary to maintain their health. For example, 30 to 50% of hypertension (high blood pressure) patients stop taking their medication, leaving them at increased risk for heart attack (Hackett, Rosenbaum, & Cassen, 1985). Men are disproportionately represented in this group.

Men can also create problems by failing to seek help or take time off from work when it is indicated, such as when they are injured, sick, emotionally distraught, or when they have not had a physical examination for a long time. Taking necessary medication and seeking help are admissions of weakness, vulnerability, and dependence, which go against the masculine cultural prescriptions to handle problems on one's own, focus outside of the self, be strong and invulnerable, and "take it like a man." Negative or extreme masculinity is related to poor health practices (Helgeson, 1990).

In a recent national survey conducted by the American Medical

Association and the Gallup Poll, 40% of doctors endorsed the belief that over 50% of men aged 50 or older undermine potential lifesaving treatment for prostate or colorectal cancer (which kill an estimated 200,000 men per year in the United States) by ignoring symptoms, delaying treatment, or refusing to discuss symptoms. Embarrassment was cited as the major reason for failing to discuss medical problems (Royner, 1992). Fifty percent of the male population does not know the symptoms of these cancers or those of prostate enlargement, which affects 75% of men over 50 (Friend, 1991).

Risk Behaviors

Men sometimes choose to engage in behaviors that involve the risk of injury, death, or legal sanction. For instance, habitual drinking to excess puts a man at increased risk for liver disease and accidents. Drunk driving, high-speed driving, drug dealing, sharing hypodermic needles, using firearms, engaging in gang violence, and working in dangerous jobs are other risky behaviors. Again, these are all engaged in by many more men than women. For instance, more than 90% of those arrested for alcohol and drug-abuse violations are men (Kimbrell, 1991). Our discussion will focus on three areas of risk: dangerous sports, war, and unsafe sexual practices.

Dangerous Sports.   To say that sports and masculinity are strongly connected in U.S. culture is an understatement. The almost religious fervor with which many men approach athletics is evidence that sports have more importance to men than mere physical fitness. An unfortunate minority of men and boys has suffered debilitating injuries and even death as a result of overexertion, physical contact, or accidents in sporting events. The most dangerous sports would seem to be auto racing and professional boxing. The object of the latter is to pummel one's opponent into unconsciousness. Some (like Korean boxer Du Koo Kim) have died from blows to the head. (Kim was killed by U.S. fighter Ray Mancini.) Others—such as former heavyweight champion Muhammad Ali, who now suffers from Parkinsonian symptoms and general intellectual decline—have suffered irreparable brain damage.

Few men participate in auto racing and boxing relative to other violent sports such as ice hockey and football. In one research study (cited by Bock, 1991), it was reported that an average of 13 U.S. high school football players die every year. Approximately half die from injury and half from overexertion. Other estimates of the number of fatalities range as high as 40 (Kupferberg, 1986). There are approximately 30 catastrophic injuries (such as permanent brain injuries or paralysis) per year (Bock, 1991), and an estimated 600,000 other injuries (Kupferberg, 1986). At least one professional or college football player has suffered paralysis in each of the last several years.

Football is one of the ultimate expressions of hypermasculinity in the United States. It involves sacrifice of the body for a task and denial of basic instincts for self-preservation and safety. Television commentary of football injuries (and sports injuries in general) almost always involves reference to the task: "Will he return in the second half?"; "How will they contain the pass rush without their best blocker?"; "Will the other team exploit the substitute?" Imagine a television commentator reacting to an injury with, "I wonder how he feels about that?"

The U.S. Army does a great deal of advertising during televised professional football games. One Army commercial depicted a football player who acted as a "wedge cracker" on kickoff plays. (This player's job is to throw his body into as many opposing players as possible.) The commentary on the commercial said the following about this man: "He's always willing to sacrifice his body for the greater cause of victory"! Is there any better statement that epitomizes self-destructive masculinity?

War.   Generation after generation, we have marched young men off to be killed in wars. In U.S. society, dying or being maimed in war is considered an act of heroism rather than the victimization of a young man. While participating in the defense of their country might be considered to be a loving thing to do, only recently have men been given a choice as to whether or not they would serve in the armed forces.

Goldberg (1977) compared the men's issue of the military draft to the women's issue of reproductive rights. In both cases, the individual's control over his or her own body has been restricted by the law. Although there is currently no mandatory draft, and the legal right to abortion still exists, mechanisms are in place that can remove what many consider to be basic human freedoms.

The wars of the 20th century have been described as "holocausts of young men" in which millions of men were killed and over 100 million men were injured. The average age of World War I and II casualties was 18.5 years (Kimbrell, 1991). Thus, the victims of war tend to be the youngest men, who feel (and often are) less powerful and who feel the strongest need to establish a sense of masculinity. Men of color, who are marginalized by mainstream U.S. culture, have also been disproportionately represented among the war dead. Many men who have survived the modern, technological war in Vietnam returned with physical and emotional scars of profound proportions. It is perhaps no coincidence that the modern men's movement began at about this time, when it was becoming obvious that soldiers were finding it difficult to "take it like a man."

The recent war in the Persian Gulf raised the question of whether women should be able to serve in combat. There seemed to be little awareness that perhaps *nobody* should be in combat. A letter to advice columnist Ann Landers (Ziff, 1990) argued against women participating in combat because of its hardships. In this letter, the author states that "combat means sleeping in a muddy foxhole, eating a can of beans for your main meal of the day, urinating and defecating wherever you happen to be, and keeping your toilet paper on your head under your helmet because it's the only dry spot on your entire body when it rains. Combat means watching your buddy step on a land mine and get blown to pieces." It is implicit in this person's letter that it is acceptable to subject men to these hardships.

Unsafe Sexual Practices.   Kimmel and Levine (1992) reported that 93% of U.S. adults with AIDS are men and that AIDS is the leading cause of death for 30- to 44-year-old men who live in New York City. It is only possible to contract AIDS through introduction of the Human Immuno-deficiency Virus (HIV) into the bloodstream. This may happen due to unfortunate accidents such as receiving an HIV-tainted blood transfusion, but the overwhelming majority of HIV infections occur through sharing hypodermic needles by intravenous drug users and through unsafe sexual practices.

It is not difficult to find connections between sexual-risk behaviors and cultural prescriptions for masculinity. Foremost among these are the expectations that males will be sexually promiscuous and adventurous. Condom use reduces the risk of infection, but there is a good deal of resistance to using condoms, perhaps because their use involves an acknowledgement of vulnerability, as well as a caring for the self and the sexual partner. These go against masculine norms. As Kimmel and Levine (1992) put it, "Abstinence, safer sex, and safer drug use compromise manhood. The behaviors required for the confirmation of masculinity and those required to reduce risk are antithetical" (p. 321).

Adverse Physical Effects of Psychological Processes

Only recently has science begun to understand in some detail the connections between psychological and physiological processes. The relatively young field of behavioral medicine is focused on understanding and treating physical disorders that are thought to be strongly influenced by the person's psychological functioning (Gentry, 1984). Masculine socialization may well contribute to some physical disorders that are disproportionately experienced by men (Eisler & Blalock, 1991). Chief among these are cardiovascular disorders and peptic ulcers.

Cardiovascular Disorders.   It has long been suspected that coronary artery disease and hypertension have strong relationships to stressful work environments and certain behavioral patterns of response to those environments. Hypertension is common among workers in highly stressful occupations (e.g., air traffic controllers, policemen). It is also common among those described as projecting an image of being easygoing but at the same time suppressing a good deal of anger (Hackett, Rosenbaum & Cassen, 1985). It is not surprising that many African-American men have problems with hypertension, given the emphasis in many African-American cultures on "cool pose"—an outward appearance of calmness (Freiberg, 1991). At the same time, many of these men experience the anger that is created by membership in an oppressed group and by harsh masculine socialization. These men may experience the powerful internal conflict between these feelings and the demand to be "cool," and this conflict may be partially manifested in high blood pressure.

Several decades ago, cardiologists Meyer Friedman and Ray Rosenhan coined the term *Type A behavior* to describe a personality pattern commonly found in people who had suffered myocardial infarction (heart attack). This pattern described the classic compulsive, hostile, competitive, emotionally inexpressive "workaholic." Friedman (cited in Hackett et al., 1985) defined *Type A* as "a characteristic action-emotion complex which is exhibited by those individuals who are engaged in a relatively chronic struggle to obtain an unlimited number of poorly defined things from their environments in the shortest period of time and, if possible, against the opposing efforts of other things or persons in this same environment" (p. 1154).

Again we see vestiges of the destructive aspects of traditional masculinity in this pattern: the aggressive attempt to measure up to vague standards of achievement and competition. Type A individuals tend to be hyperindependent; they seize authority and dislike sharing responsibility. Contrary to popular belief, they tend to be less successful than those who are more relaxed and less aggressive (Hackett et al., 1985). Type A behaviors are significantly related to masculine sex typing (Grimm & Yarnold, 1985). Negative or extreme masculinity is also related heart-attack severity (Helgeson, 1990).

Peptic Ulcer.   Peptic ulcers are cuts in the lining of the stomach. They are a common condition, affecting about 12% of men at some time in their lives. This is approximately double the rate for women (Oken, 1985). Ulcers may well be the result of hydrochloric acid in the stomach, which is part of the stress response (Greenberg, 1990). There are significant positive correlations between ulcer and chronic feelings of anger, frustration, and resentment. Among middle-class men, there is a subgroup of ulcer sufferers who are described as hyperindependent, striving, ambitious, competitive, having poor diets, and overusing alcohol (Oken, 1985).

Conclusion

It is clear that men are biologically predisposed toward certain physical health problems. This predisposition interacts with certain aspects of masculine socialization, as well as with the negative effects of dangerous, historically male environments. Women who expose themselves to these environments and exhibit traditionally masculine behaviors increase their health risks (Rodin & Ickovics, 1990). Thus, it is hazardous to be male, and it is also hazardous to be negatively masculine.

Sidney Jourard said it best in his landmark 1971 article, "Some Lethal Aspects of the Male Role." Jourard described a set of human needs: to know and be known, to depend and be depended upon, to love and be loved, and to find some purpose and meaning in one's life. The masculine role is poorly designed to fill these human needs. It requires men to "be noncommunicative, competitive and nongiving, and to evaluate life successes in terms of external achievement rather than personal and interpersonal fulfillment" (Harrison, 1978, p. 13). Jourard's belief was that this not only limited the quality of men's emotional lives, but that it also had the effect of slowly destroying them physically.

Summary

1. Many health problems are more common in men than women. Men's average life span is about 7 years shorter than that of women as a result of a number of factors.

2. Biogenic explanations for sex differences in disease and longevity include male chromosomal vulnerability, the damaging effects of testosterone, and the protective effects of estrogen.

3. Psychogenic explanations for sex differences in disease and longevity include the masculine denial of vulnerability, eschewal of self-care, risky sexual behaviors, and the cultural expectation to take part in dangerous sports and in war.

4. Stressful work environments and typical masculine responses to them also take their toll on health and longevity. There is a growing awareness that living up to masculine gender demands involves the denial of some basic human needs and that the results may be illness, injury, and/or premature death.

Joel Gordon Photography

CHAPTER TEN

Men at Work:
Jobs, Careers, and Masculinity

You load sixteen tons; what do you get?
Another day older and deeper in debt.
Saint Peter, don't you call me, 'cause I can't go;
I owe my soul to the Company Store.

Merle Travis

If there is anything that men have been about throughout history, they have been about work. From the assembly-line worker to the chief executive officer, most men define themselves according to their jobs. It has been argued that the masculine socialization process is wholly oriented toward preparing men for the working world.

The working world is changing, however. Women are entering the work force in record numbers and rightfully demanding that they be treated as equals. Many men are having trouble adjusting to increasingly mixed-sex environments. In addition, the character of the work itself is changing. More and more labor-saving devices are becoming available, and the competition-oriented, individualistic working culture is giving way to team building, quality circles, and environments in which cooperation is valued. As a result, there are fewer and fewer places for the physically powerful working man or the hard-nosed manager and more and more places for the technician and the executive with "people skills."

While much of the masculine value system encourages men toward being good workers, it may do so at a considerable cost. Additionally, some aspects of male gender-role socialization are counterproductive to men's functioning in many of the work places of the 1990s. While changing gender roles create considerable stress for many, they also provide exciting opportunities for men in the working world.

In this chapter, we investigate the relationships between masculine gender-role socialization and work. In order to provide a context, we look first at the history of the labor division between the sexes, with particular attention to the historical connections between work and masculinity.

A History of Work and the Sexes

Hunter-Gatherer Societies

For millions of years, human labor chiefly consisted of hunting animals and gathering edible vegetation. Societies based on other forms of labor are a relatively recent phenomenon, comprising only about 2% of the history of the human race (Collins, 1979).

Theoretically, the division of labor between the sexes in these societies was based on two biological facts: that men tend to be bigger and stronger than women and that women's reproductive role made their movement away from the home or camp problematic compared to men. In most of these societies, men did the hunting, where physical strength and the ability to roam were assets, and women did the gathering, an activity compatible with child care (Neilsen, 1990).

Basow (1992) notes a couple of variations to this pattern. In some societies, game is available nearby the home or camp, and both men and women hunt. In others, hunting provides all of the food because there is nothing to gather, and men do all of the hunting. Eskimo societies are an example of this pattern, which is quite rare.

Although there were variations in the sexual labor division, man the hunter and woman the gatherer was probably the most common pattern. Basow (1992) points out some interesting features of cultures that currently retain the hunting-gathering pattern. First, it is typical for gathering to produce 60 to 80% of the food. Thus, women contribute more to the family economy than men. Second, family roles are different. Gender roles are more egalitarian and cooperative, and fathers tend to be involved with their children.

The picture of these societies that emerges is one in which men and women share the provider and nurturer roles. At the same time, we see that hunting and masculinity may have a long-standing historical connection. Keen (1991) wrote about the association between the spear and the penis in prehistoric art. Here, perhaps, is the earliest connection between violence and sexuality, a theme we return to in Chapter Twelve.

We also see some early connections between masculinity and adventure, roaming, and predation.

Agricultural Societies

When people learned to plow, plant, and domesticate animals, some 6,000 years ago, the character of labor changed. Plowing required the person to be relatively far from home, thus it largely became the man's job. Producing offspring meant more help in the fields, and thus there was an economic advantage to control women's sexuality and reproduction.

Another important change characterized agrarian societies. There was no longer a need for people to be nomadic. In hunter-gatherer societies, survival depended on moving to where vegetation and game were available. In agrarian societies, people could stay in one place and produce food with a little cooperation from nature. There was a certain harmony with the earth, and husbandry, the cultivation and respect of nature, became a dominant value (Keen, 1991). Sons spent a good deal of time working with and learning from their fathers. Thus, there was a sense of intergenerational continuity (Stearns, 1991). Civilizations and communities took on a relatively permanent and, therefore, more elaborate character.

Land was now useful and valuable for long periods of time, generation after generation. It became something a person owned, bought, sold, protected, and willed to his or her heirs. Land meant food, and food meant wealth. Institutions were created to deal with land transactions. The most notable institution was **patriarchy,** the system by which males inherited property from their fathers and passed it on to their sons. This system established male social and economic dominance, as well as the control of women's sexuality by men (Neilsen, 1990).

Basow (1992) describes changes in the !Kung society of Africa, a foraging society that has moved to the agrarian way of life during the last 30 years. She noted that women's mobility is more restricted and that they contribute less to the food supply than before. Children's play groups are becoming more sex segregated, and aggression has increased. Basow argues that agrarian society is historically responsible for gender inequity and that these types of societies are the bases for every industrialized society in the world.

Property ownership and patriarchy changed masculinity in important ways. Men created institutional laws to protect their land, but physical force also came to be used, hence the transition of man the planter to man the warrior. In hunter-gatherer societies, men bonded together in order to share resources in the hunt, and the kill was shared by the whole community. After property ownership, men's bonds were in the service

---

Box 10.1
The Gods Must Be Crazy

The Gods Must Be Crazy illustrates the social changes that resulted from property ownership. This movie describes a civilization of bush people in the Kalahari Desert of South Central Africa. In their community, there are no scarce resources to compete for and, therefore, no ownership. In the movie, a scarce resource (humorously, a Coca-Cola bottle discarded from a small airplane) is introduced into the culture, which results in competition and aggression. This movie provides an interesting commentary on modern societies.

---

of killing other men. Therefore, organized violence became a hallmark of masculinity. Keen (1991) speculated that the masculine ethic of cooperation gave way to an ethic of conquest at this time and that the quest for harmony became a quest for control. He also noted that men from victorious armies routinely raped the women of the conquered territories. Thus, we see in these societies the origins of negative masculinity: violence, overcompetitiveness, physical risk, and failures of empathy.

Patriarchy also dictated that men should control their children's (especially their male children's) lives. Fathers had to see that their sons learned to act properly, since they would someday control the family wealth. In Western cultures, this gave rise to an ethic of discipline, which was sometimes administered physically. The punitive nature of this relationship created a tension between affection and resentment for both father and son (Stearns, 1991).

Industrial Societies

The turn of the 19th century witnessed the dawn of the Industrial Revolution in Europe. Hand tools were increasingly replaced by machines, and production became larger scale and centralized. Industrialization continues to spread throughout the world.

Since patriarchy was firmly established by this time, the vast majority of industrial work was at a distance from the home, and a good deal of this labor required physical strength, factory work became largely men's work. The sex-based division of labor became sharper than ever. Women typically assumed domestic duties, and men obtained paid employment outside of the home. In times of labor shortages, more women worked outside of the home, but their work was devalued, and they were pushed aside by men when jobs became scarce.

The development of many male gender-role norms can be laid at the doorstep of industrialization. First and foremost is the establishment of the breadwinner role. Gould (1974) described this as the beginning of "measuring masculinity by the size of a paycheck." Socially, masculine attractiveness is based largely on economic power. Many men attempt to project a masculine image through external success, not internal fulfillment. Gould noted that if a man "flashed a roll of bills, no one would see how little else there was of him" (p. 97).

The Industrial Revolution ushered in the age of specialization. In agrarian societies, a man plants, reaps, takes care of animals, and is able to see the fruits of his labor. In contrast, the industrial worker may spend the better part of a lifetime putting a single bolt on a million machines. Karl Marx first described the dehumanizing character of such a job. The person cannot take pride in the *process* of planting, growing, and harvesting. Industrial man is focused on *outcome,* the amount of money produced.

For most men, this was not a lot of money, as the few powerful men exploited the many less powerful men. Most men became (and still are) "work objects" (the term *object* in reference to a person was first coined by Marx). Objectification is the denial of the person's humanness. Just as many women have historically been treated as sex objects, men have been exploited as work objects.

Men have also been war objects. When the work of the wealthy and powerful involves organized violence, it often becomes the task of poor young men. Most victims of World War II and the Vietnam War were teenaged boys, the least powerful males in the society. A disproportionate number of victims were men of color. The more privileged men were often allowed to opt out.

The stereotype of men as socially and economically powerful does not fit the experience of most men. While men as a group retain more economic power than women, the vast majority of men have jobs, not careers. They sacrifice and labor day after day, under the pressure to be good providers for their families. The necessity of doing so makes many men vulnerable to exploitive employers. Emotional expression is also of little value to the factory worker.

Perhaps the most profound effects of industrialization on masculinity were that it *effectively banished men from their homes* (Keen, 1991) and devalued domestic work. It is no surprise that many men are not very relationship oriented. They spend the vast majority of their time on tasks away from their families. When the father returns home at the end of the day, he finds it difficult to flip the switch that turns on all of the emotional and relationship attitudes that he has suppressed all day at work. As Robert Bly (1990) put it, "When a father, absent during the day, returns home at six, his children receive only his temperament, and not his teaching." The result is the disconnection of father and son (Keen, 1991) and an intergenerational pattern of masculine alienation.

The ethic of paternal discipline carried over from agrarian societies, but now fathers had to assert this role after coming home from the industrial work place. This may have involved more physical punishment both as a function of diminished contact with children (Stearns, 1991) and work strain on the father (Stearns, 1990). Many sons now had to deal with fewer positive contacts with fathers in addition to harsher negative contacts.

Postindustrial Societies

While many people throughout the world continue to be employed in industrial and preindustrial settings, large segments of the population are involved in work that is characterized as postindustrial. This recent trend is a movement away from the production of goods and toward the provision of information and services. In these settings, physical strength is all but valueless, and thus men have no biologically based advantage over women. Because a single income is no longer sufficient for most families, and because many women want to claim their right to be full economic partners in society, these settings are becoming increasingly heterogeneous.

Work outside the home is no longer the exclusive province of men, and thus social changes are taking place. We will return to a discussion of these changes later in this chapter. Before doing so, a description of men's issues around work seems appropriate.

Net Worth Equals Self-Worth: The Socialization to Work

Male gender socialization is oriented toward preparing boys for work. Boys are asked at a young age, "What do you want to be when you grow up?" They learn that the right answer is not "a husband, father, and friend," but rather a worker of some kind. Males tend to develop an occupational "dream" in childhood and strive to attain it in adulthood (Levinson et al., 1978). Boys are impressed very early in life with the idea that gainful employment is manly. The masculine values of competition, task completion, and independence serve to provide attitudes conducive to functioning in a wide variety of work settings.

Sports and play are the training ground for the world of work. Boys' sports usually have elaborate sets of rules, score keeping, and clear-cut winners and losers (Pasick, 1990). Sports results are quantifiable in terms of wins and losses, batting averages, and other statistics that invite comparisons between players and teams. The amount of adulation a boy receives for being an athletic success is matched by the amount of adulation a man receives for being a career success. We see connections between sports and work in the language of the business world: "Who are the players?"; "They have a good batting average"; "Let's see if we can get them to play ball with us." An easy business deal is sometimes referred to as a "slam dunk."

The messages are clear. In the athletic world, you are a valued person if you are a winner. Later, being a winner translates into being a *bread*winner—a vocational success. In fact, a man's very definition of himself depends on occupational status. As Pasick (1990) points out, "For males in our culture, simply passing through puberty is not sufficient to enter adulthood" (p. 39). A man cannot "be a man" without masculine (economic) power. The important factor is the outcome, not the process. Success for men is often defined in terms of being "better" by getting promotions, having high job status, and making more money. Women tend to be more oriented toward providing a helpful service (Bridges, 1989).

The historical association of masculinity with work and money can hardly be denied. Anybody that works knows that it is a two-edged sword with both advantages and disadvantages. The work tradition has gotten men where they are today, in both a positive and a negative sense. We will look briefly at the positive masculine aspects of work and then more fully at the negative aspects. The reason for this difference in emphasis is that the positive components are more obvious and more frequently discussed than the negative ones.

Positive Masculinity and Work

Ruth Hartley's classic 1959 essay on male gender-role socialization includes the statement that, "on the positive side, men mostly do what they want and are very important" (p. 463). The social status that men have enjoyed from work is unmistakable. The fact that men are less often the victims of job discrimination than women has given many men opportunities for self-determination. Of course, this is not often the case for minority men, who have been occupationally marginalized throughout U.S. history. There is also evidence that men who choose traditional female occupations lose social status and are perceived as less likeable, attractive, and mentally healthy than women who enter occupations that are considered gender inappropriate (Shinar, 1978). At the same time, they tend to be comfortable with themselves and their masculine sexuality (Chusmir, 1990). Thus, men who are gender-role transcendent may tend to be strong enough to cope with the social stigma of being considered unmasculine.

Work can be quite satisfying. Men who are fortunate enough to have careers may find the challenge and satisfaction of their work to be one of the most important aspects of their lives. It also goes without saying that money goes a long way toward making life easier and more enjoyable. Traditionally, men's orientation toward task completion and self-reliance, together with work opportunity, have made economic and career success a strong possibility for many men. The "winners" may get some of the best that life has to offer: status, material wealth, and the opportunity to make a difference.

Men who have not been able to enjoy satisfying work have been able to take pride in fulfilling the breadwinner role, a traditional expression of masculine love. Historically, many men have felt a deeply emotional investment toward this role, which has also been valued socially (Stearns, 1991).

Negative Masculinity and Work

Although vocational success carries great rewards, they can come at a cost to the man's relationships, leisure life, and health. It is also important to note that many, perhaps most, men do not feel successful, and the association of success and masculinity for these men may lead to chronic feelings of masculine inadequacy. Following is a list of some potentially damaging effects of the male gender role in the world of work:

1. *You only hurt the ones you love.* Many men work in frustrating environments, for example, the assembly-line worker who is bored and unable to find much job satisfaction, the mechanic who faces difficult problems and time pressure, or the middle manager who faces pressure from both his subordinates and his superiors. Some have not learned how to deal with the emotional aspects of work frustration. They have been raised to ignore emotion, especially if it is connected to feelings of weakness or powerlessness. As discussed in Chapter Eight, these men frequently deal with feelings by projecting them outside of the self. Since spouses and other family members are most available for these projections, they may bear the brunt of these negative emotions, and this can lead to strained family relationships. A spouse interviewed for Weiss's (1990) study illustrates the effects of "bringing work home":

> He is so proud, telling people that he works things out for himself and he doesn't worry his family. . . . Well, that really isn't the case. Because what happens is, (if) he has a problem, whatever it is, whether it's a business slowdown or a difficult supplier or whatever, he is just a *bear* . . . to live with until he has worked it out. . . . If we say, "What is the problem?" he will say, "What do you mean, what is the problem?" (p. 99)

Box 10.2 illustrates an interaction between a man's work and family life.

Box 10.2
Work, Family, and Masculinity

A television commercial for a bank's financial planning services shows a middle-aged man standing in a nicely appointed suburban kitchen and speaking to the camera:

> For years, I worked my fingers to the bone, going to the office nights and weekends, so that Beth and the girls could have what we wanted. Then one day it hit me: I've made it! Now I want for all of us, especially the girls, to enjoy all that we have for a long time to come.

There are several interesting aspects to this 30-second commercial. First, there is the man's satisfaction of having achieved some vocational success. This is one of the most fulfilling aspects of the traditional male role. Second is his commitment to the good-provider role, which is traditionally the way that men have expressed love for their families. The caring that being a provider expresses should not be devalued.

A few other messages are beneath the surface. First, making money is not enough. This is an advertisement for financial management services. A "real man" must know what to do with money after he has earned it. This is another role demand that entails the acquisition of a variety of skills. These may or may not be compatible with the man's job skills. Second, and most importantly, "Beth and the girls" may not know who this man is. If he has been working nights and weekends, he probably has not had much time to maintain a close relationship with his wife, and he has probably missed the chance to be closely involved with his daughters as they grow. The former opportunity may be recoverable; the latter will never be.

As an aside, the phrase, "especially the girls" is puzzling. For some reason, their welfare supersedes that of his wife.

2. *What price glory?* The competitive, pressure-packed nature of masculine occupational striving is associated with a wide variety of physical and mental health problems such as heart disease, ulcers, back pain, alcoholism, and suicide (Crites & Fitzgerald, 1978; Harris, 1992). Chapters Nine and Fourteen detail some of these problems.

3. *The burden of proof.* Skovholt and Hansen (1980) described the masculine working world as one in which "there is only one game. That game is king of the hill" (p. 11). A man proves his masculinity by succeeding in work and being "number one." A success, however, does not last. There is always another goal to set and accomplish (Pleck, 1976). If

a man is fortunate enough to become "number one" at something, he can only remain in this position by continuing to compete with and vanquish his opponents. Thus, the validation of masculinity involves attempting to prove something that is essentially unprovable. Satisfaction, for many men, becomes a dangerous feeling, since it may inhibit further competition. In the world of sports (the metaphor for work), we hear sportscasters lauding players and coaches who can never be satisfied. We hear sports figures talking about next year an hour after they have *won* the championship! Box 10.3 illustrates the cultural expectation that men should not be satisfied.

4. *You've got to break a few eggs to make an omelet.* A man who wishes to "work his way up" in an organization may have to subjugate his behavior to the wishes of his superiors. Of course, nearly everybody alters their behavior to adapt to social situations, so it is a matter of degree. To what extent are men willing to move against their naturally occurring personalities in order to "fit in" at work?

Several studies have indicated that business organizations expect sex-stereotypical behavior from men, and that men who do not display such behavior often forfeit the opportunity for advancement (Rosen & Jerdee, 1973, 1974; Kanter, 1977). Therefore, the man who refuses to act like "one of the boys" may not succeed, regardless of his level of competence. If he plays the masculine role in order to gain approval, he may experience a high level of gender-role strain. In corporate culture, a large part of this strain is based in the organization's encouragement for men to emphasize the work role over the family role (Bowen & Orthner, 1991).

Box 10.3
Masculinity, Work, and Satisfaction

A television commercial for a corporation depicts a football coach berating his team at half time for its performance. After several highly critical statements, one of the players looks up and says, "Coach, aren't we ahead by 21 points?" The coach replies, "That's what I mean . . . the moment you're satisfied as a football player, we're finished as a football team."

This commercial is trying to communicate that the corporation's people are never satisfied. It is no mistake that the advertiser chose football, the most hypermasculine of pursuits, to illustrate the corporate ethic. What a statement about masculinity! You must never be satisfied with what you do. It will never be enough. Moreover, satisfaction is sometimes defined as *dangerous*. A satisfied person is thought to lose the competitive "edge."

The extent to which a man will compromise his behavior to fit the work environment involves a decision that each individual must make. Is he willing to engage in derogatory humor, wear ties and white dress shirts, and lie to customers? Because men are socialized against introspective skills, they may have difficulty in accessing the information necessary to make these decisions.

Crites and Fitzgerald (1978) described the constriction of human qualities in order to meet organizational demand as a "straitjacket of success" that requires the man to "be able to obey rules and follow orders, regardless of how silly and unnecessary they may seem ... to control and hide true feelings when faced with an incompetent superior ... (to be) intensely loyal to an employer, yet able to transfer that loyalty when you change jobs" (p. 44). These prescriptions produce men who are "expedient, shallow, conforming but competitive, and ultimately ruthless" (Crites & Fitzgerald, 1978, p. 44).

According to humanistic theory, extreme conformity to outside demands leaves an individual feeling alienated and out of touch with the self-actualizing tendency. The man may sacrifice some of his human potential in order to strive for external success. This conflict is common among working men.

5. *Standing on one leg.* The man who submerges his entire human identity in his work role has a rather tenuous basis for his self-esteem (Gould, 1974), yet society teaches males from an early age that their competence as a person depends on their earnings and/or job status (Berger & Wright, 1980). Several researchers have reported that men's senses of self-esteem are directly related to their job status and income (Sekeran, 1986; Morgan, Skovholt, & Orr, 1978; Tavris & Offrir, 1977).

6. *Cast your fate to the wind.* Job of career success often depends on factors that are beyond the man's control and, perhaps, his understanding. The American myth that working hard enough always brings success may be a reality for the talented and privileged, but the "average Joe" depends at least partly on opportunity and the vicissitudes of the market. The combination of subscribing to the American myth and equating economic success with masculinity leaves the average man feeling emasculated.

7. *You can't win if you don't play.* Equating masculinity with vocational accomplishment has especially damaging effects on men who encounter significant boundaries to meaningful employment. In many poor segments of society, few opportunities for work, education, or training are provided, yet the men in these subcultures tend to subscribe to the "money equals masculinity" value (Liebow, 1980). Is it any wonder that some of these men turn to illegal activities such as drug dealing? They may see such activities as their only opportunity to validate their masculinity.

Skovholt and Hansen (1980) also noted that young, disadvantaged men are especially prone to translating their feelings of hopelessness and despair into angry and violent behavior. In the "king of the hill" game, "the real losers are the men at the bottom of the hill looking straight up" (p. 12). Pasick (1990) noted that the unemployment figures for Hispanic and African-American men are consistently 5 to 10% above the national average, and that unemployed men are more likely than employed men to turn to drugs and crime. The high rates of incarceration, violence, and drug use among men of color are not the result of negative influences in ethnic subculture. Rather, they are the result of the oppressive nature of mainstream U.S. culture, which imparts its masculine values to these men without providing any avenues for them to participate in the American Dream.

Employed men who lose their jobs through economic downturn, injury, or even retirement face a battle to retain their masculine self-esteem. Kamarovsky ([1940]/1971) published a classic study of 59 unemployed men and their families. Many of these men were ridiculed, blamed, and rejected by their families for failing to fulfill the provider role. They also tended to blame themselves and to suffer from symptoms of depression.

Retirement presents a difficult transition for many men, as they must leave the activity through which they have defined themselves for most of their lives. Although most men report a satisfactory adjustment to retirement, as many as 15 to 20% report being unhappy (Parnes & Nestel, 1981). Box 10.4 depicts the tragic story of an unsuccessful man at retirement.

8. *What have you done for me lately?* As we pointed out in Chapter Four, early masculine socialization shapes behavior, but ongoing social contingencies maintain it. Successful men have their masculinity affirmed frequently across many social settings. Conversely, less than successful men are socially devalued. Fogel and Paludi (1984) reported that unsuccessful men are viewed less favorably than unsuccessful women.

Socially, successful men are defined as the most desirable partners for dating and marriage. It is not surprising that men learn to connect sexuality with money. It is said that "power is an aphrodisiac." A business deal is sometimes referred to as "getting into bed with" the partner.

Gould (1974) remarked on the association of money and desirability:

> Women have been taught that men who achieve success are the best "catch-es" in the marriage market. Women have also been taught that the right motives for marriage are love and sexual attraction. Thus, if a woman wants to marry a man with money, she has to believe she loves him; that he is sexually appealing—even if the real appeal is his money. . . . Many women

Box 10.4
Death of a Salesman

Arthur Miller's classic (1949) play is a brilliantly insightful examination of the relationship between masculinity, work, and family. Willy Loman, the lead character, is a salesman in his 60s. His job skills are deteriorating, and thus his value to his employer is decreasingly rapidly.

Because Willy is relatively poor, and because his self-esteem is almost wholly invested in his identity as a salesman, he is suffering emotionally. He is a traditional man who refuses to admit vulnerability, and so he tries to delude himself into believing that the best is yet to come. He frequently fantasizes about his brother Ben, a successful and adventurous man who reminds Willy of his wealth: "When I was seventeen I walked into the jungle, and when I was twenty-one I walked out. And by God I was rich."

Willy Loman wholly subscribes to the value that wealth equals masculinity and self-worth. Underneath, he has the painful feeling that he has not been courageous or industrious (masculine) enough. He says, "The world is an oyster, but you don't crack it open on a mattress." To make matters worse, Willy's two sons, Biff and Happy, are also not successful. Because Willy cannot deal with his feeling of failure, he deals with it indirectly through his sons, alternately berating them for their irresponsibility and pumping them up with unrealistic dreams of instant success. Biff occasionally tries to fight through his father's denial, but the effect is to flood Willy with overwhelming pain.

Willy's feelings of emasculation and depression peak in intensity when he loses his job and realizes that his sons are also not on the path to success. He takes the provider role so seriously that he contemplates suicide in order to bequeath $20,000 in insurance money to his family. In an imaginary conversation with Ben, Willy says, "A man can't go out the way he came in, Ben, a man has got to add up to something." Willy has come to feel that he has only added up to an insurance policy, and thus he is worth more dead than alive.

Because of his sense of loss and hopelessness, his feelings of failure as a father and worker, and his ardent desire to live up to the masculine ideal of the good provider, Willy finally does commit suicide by intentionally having a car accident. Ironically, he does so in the same week that the final payment on the family house is made, a joyous occasion for most couples. In some ways, Willy was a success: He provided an acceptable standard of living for years and purchased a house "free and clear." But traditional standards of masculine success are much more than this, and Willy did not feel free or clear. *Death of a Salesman* details the tragedy of a man who dies in order to preserve his masculinity.

learn to make this emotional jump: to feel genuinely attracted to the man who makes it big, and to accept the equation of moneymaking power with sexual power. There are many phenomenally wealthy men in the public eye who are physically unattractive by traditional criteria; yet they are surrounded by beautiful women and an aura of sexiness and virility. (p. 97)

9. *When enough is never enough.* Men who overemphasize the work role sometimes fall prey to what are commonly referred to as workaholism and success addiction. A **workaholic** is someone who works because it provides a feeling of self-worth that he or she cannot find anywhere else (Wilson-Schaef & Fassel, 1988). Pasick (1990) described two major negative outcomes for workaholics. First, their families and other relationships suffer, if only from a lack of time in interpersonal contact. Second is the constant tension and worry that workaholics tend to experience around their job performance. Box 10.5 describes the relationship of a workaholic and his wife.

Success-addicted people crave achievement, but each success is enjoyed for only a very short time, and they quickly set a new goal (Berglass, 1986). They make their goals the total focus of their lives and concentrate so much on the future that they lose touch with the present. These men often suffer from exhaustion (burnout), anxiety, and chronic disappointment (Pasick, 1990). Both workaholics and success-addicted men lose the capacity to enjoy themselves outside of the working environment.

10. *The lonely hunter.* Striving for success is often incompatible with forming relationships. We have already pointed out the negative effects of the success-masculinity connection on the family. This connection also inhibits the formation of close relationships with other men.

Ochberg (1988) described an interesting pair of role demands on a group of career men he interviewed. He investigated aspects of these men's relationships with male coworkers and concluded that men are encouraged to present the *illusion* that they are personal with each other without going overboard. Friendliness is expected, but men who get too close are seen as losing control of their situations. According to Ochberg, "Striking this balance between detachment and the appearance of friendliness is actually more of a strain than being either genuinely personal or

---

Box 10.5
The Blue-Collar Workaholic

A therapist related the story of a woman who "dragged" her husband into marital therapy under threat of divorce. He was an automobile mechanic who worked a 40-hour-per-week job and had a free-lance business in his home garage on evenings and weekends. His side business provided more than enough work and a good deal of money, but the man rarely spent more than a few minutes with his wife or family before the phone would ring or someone would pull into the driveway in need of repairs.

When asked why he worked so hard, the man said, "I don't want to retire at 65 like my father; I'm going to retire at 45." It was clear that this man was chasing a quantifiable and probably mythical definition of success, to the detriment of his family. One has to question the rationality of extreme overwork in reaching a goal of *not working.*

---

genuinely indifferent" (p. 11). Although most men Ochberg interviewed reported a desire for personal relationships with their colleagues, they work hard to resist them because the man who is a colleague today may be a subordinate tomorrow. It is difficult to discipline or give orders to a friend.

Thus, men want to be close to their coworkers, but they are uncomfortable with this prospect at the same time. Ochberg reported studies indicating that "successful executives show that they have an unusual ability to cultivate friendships with those who are ahead of them on the corporate ladder, and disentangle themselves from attachments to people who once were their peers, but whom they have since left behind" (p. 11).

Working in the 1990s

The world of work in the United States has undergone many changes in recent years. One of the most salient developments is the demise of the single-earner family. Only about 10% of families maintain the traditional arrangement whereby the husband works outside of the home and the wife attends to household and child-care duties (Astrachan, 1992). There are increases in women's participation in nearly every segment of the work force, and these increases are accompanied by slight decreases in men's participation. Several men's issues have arisen in response to these changes.

Probably the most important development in the work arena for men is that breadwinning and providing can no longer be considered exclusively masculine. Traditionally, most men have not gained much satisfaction from their work. They validated their masculinity through the *results* of their work, money and providing. As women begin to earn money as well, men find that they need to turn elsewhere for this validation, although many do not know where to turn. As Bernard (1981) put it, "The good-provider role may be on its way out, but its legitimate successor has not appeared on the scene" (p. 12). Men who have been marginalized (e.g., men of color and older men) have experienced the greatest difficulty living up to the breadwinner role demand (Wilkie, 1991).

Male-Female Relationships in the Work Place

The dominance and antifemininity norms of the traditional male gender role can cause men difficulty when their work peers, superiors, or subordinates are women. Sex-typed men tend to react to a woman in a "man's job" with some mixture of anger, fear, confusion, and anxiety (Astrachan, 1992). The traditional view of woman as underling and sex object is dysfunctional in a number of increasingly common work situations, a few of which are detailed here:

1. When a man and woman are required to work together cooperatively, unreasonable dominance by the man is damaging to employee relationships and the quality of the work.
2. When a man and woman are competing for promotion, he may feel emasculated if she wins.
3. When hiring, promotion, and pay-increase decisions discriminate against women, the male supervisor may open himself and the company to litigation or job action. Even if these things do not happen, he is failing to maximize the potential of the company's human resources and victimizing a human being.
4. When a man's supervisor is a woman, he may be uncooperative, anxious, resentful, or disrespectful if he persists at retaining sexist values. This can be damaging to the man's job performance and to the organization.
5. Incidences of sexual harassment in the work place are pervasive (Pryor, 1987). The man who sexually objectifies women at work and acts on this attitude is committing a crime, harming other human beings, and damaging his own potential for vocational success (see Chapter Thirteen).

Although a large majority of victims are women, sexual harassment also happens to men. A survey of federal workers by the U.S. Merit

Systems Protection Board (1981) revealed that 42% of female and 15% of male federal employees stated that they had experienced unwanted sexual attention on the job at some point within the previous 2 years. In another study (Gutek & Nakamura, 1983), 17.3% of women and 4.8% of men said they had resigned from a job because of sexual harassment. We can see from these figures that the ratio of female to male victims is around 3:1. Although about one in four victims is male, these victims are largely ignored.

The lack of attention to male victims may be a reflection of widely held sexist attitudes toward men. First, people believe that there is no such thing as "unwanted sexual attention" for a man. He is viewed as sexually indiscriminate. The exception here would be if the harasser is another man, but the stereotype of gay men as powerless and passive and the denial of the existence of homosexuality in mainstream United States culture may preclude people from considering this possibility. One study (Tangri, Burt, & Johnson, 1982) reported that about 22% of the harassers of male employees are other men.

Second, the cultural attitude is that men should be able to take care of themselves. Third, men are viewed as the sexual aggressors. The idea of a woman being aggressive is not very credible. Fourth, there are prevailing social attitudes that men cannot be hurt, that men who are hurt get what they deserve, or that hurting men is acceptable. For example, there are several television programs and commercials in which men are physically abused and it is supposed to be funny. If a woman were depicted in a similar situation, many people would be outraged.

There is a good deal of evidence to suggest that sexual harassment is strongly related to organizational and social power (Loy & Stewart, 1984; DeAngelis, 1991). Whether female-initiated sexual harassment will increase as women gain more positions of power remains to be seen. However, women tend to define sexual harassment more broadly than men, and they tend to be less tolerant of these behaviors (McKinney & Maroules, 1991).

Male-Female Relationships in Dual-Earner Homes

The influx of women into the work place has also changed traditional household arrangements. Women who are equal economic partners usually expect their spouses to become equal domestic partners. However, the easing of breadwinner pressure is accompanied by an increase in household responsibilities for men.

Pasick (1990) points out several problems for men in this area. First, there is often a skill deficit. Many men have little training in cleaning, cooking, and especially in child care. Second, sex-typed men resist learning these skills because they consider them unmanly. Third, wives may be reluctant to relinquish control of what has traditionally been women's domain. The man may feel that he is in a double-bind situation. He feels the demand to contribute, yet he may receive frequent criticism that he is not doing the task "right" or well enough. Finally, many employers do not offer much support to men who are trying to adopt nontraditional roles. For example, a man who leaves work in order to care for a sick child may receive much more disapproval than a woman who does the same thing.

As a result of these difficulties, women tend to do more housework than men, even when both partners work equally long hours (Atkinson & Huston, 1984; Pleck & Rustad, 1980). Most people still consider housework to be primarily a woman's responsibility (Herzog, Bachman, & Johnson, 1983). However, there has not been much research or publicity on women's sharing of men's traditional household work, such as house and car repairs. It is not unusual to see a newspaper article headlined, "Men still not doing their share of work around the house," but you probably won't see one that reads, "Women still not doing their share of vehicle maintenance." The development of this skill for many women may be as difficult as the development of childcare skills for many men.

Traditional men in dual-earner families also tend to feel threatened if their wives earn more money than they do (Pleck, 1978). Clearly, subscribing to the belief that money means power and masculinity would cause problems for the man whose wife outearns him. The incredible power of the gender role is illustrated by some men's reactions to their wives' getting a raise: They feel strong resentment and feelings of being unmanly, and they would rather get along with less money than deal with these feelings and their underlying attitudes.

Although the entry of women into the work force has complicated the lives of men both at home and at work, the benefits of these changes often outweigh the costs. First, the man can share the breadwinner pressure with his partner. Second, since outcome (earning) can no longer be defined as traditionally masculine, men can pay more attention to process and seek satisfaction from the work itself. Third, egalitarian roles at work and home enhance the appreciation of women as human beings. Fourth, men may have opportunities to enter new realms of rich experience as they give up the view of themselves as functional work machines.

In the traditional heterosexual relationship, the woman experiences success vicariously through the man, who experiences emotions vicariously through the woman. Now that women are succeeding for themselves, men are slowly learning to express emotions for themselves.

Summary

1. Work has defined men's identities throughout history, and the masculine socialization process is strongly oriented toward producing workers. The character of work and the sexual division of labor has changed throughout human history.

2. Men did most of the hunting in primitive societies, the plowing in agrarian societies, and the factory work in industrial societies. Women's participation as economic partners decreased with each evolution of work, and some researchers believe that the oppression of women is tied to this decrease.

3. As a consequence of industrial demands, most men were effectively removed from their homes and often specialized in some small part of the production process. As a result, they were alienated from both their work and their families, and they had to rely on the financial outcome of work for the validation of masculinity. The good-provider role requires sacrifice and emotional restrictiveness. These aspects of masculinity continue to live on in many men.

4. The masculine values of task orientation, competition, and independence are conducive to a wide variety of work settings. Boys' sports and play, with their emphasis on outcome and quantification, socialize males toward work.

5. The advantages of this socialization for men are social status, opportunity, and work satisfaction, but many men who lose jobs or do not succeed feel emasculated. Even men who do well at work may encounter difficulties in relating to family and coworkers, maintaining physical and mental health, dealing with the pressures of competition, and coping with gender-role strain.

6. In recent times, economic and social conditions have led to changes in the traditional single-earner family. Men who adhere to sex-typed attitudes may encounter significant problems at work and at home, as they find it necessary to adjust to newer, more egalitarian gender roles. Issues around the loss of the masculine breadwinner role, sexual harassment, and the sharing of domestic duties have come to the fore. Although the result is a more complicated life for working men, the benefits may outweigh the costs, as many men are expanding their senses of self beyond their occupational roles.

Joel Gordon Photography

CHAPTER ELEVEN

Pleasure and Performance:
Male Sexuality

Few areas of human behavior are as fraught with emotion as sexuality. Dealing with oneself as a sexual person often involves a wide array of experiences, including pleasure, mystery, wonder, lust, love, anxiety, guilt, repression, and confusion. During socialization, males (and females) receive quite a few messages about sexual feelings, sexual relationships, differences between male and female sexuality, sexual preference, seduction, intimacy, and sexual communication. Many of these messages are highly value laden. Some involve misinformation, half-truths, or unhealthy ways of thinking about the self. All of them influence the shaping of biological sexual tendencies into sexual behaviors and feelings, as well as the place in the total personality that is given to sexuality.

Masculine socialization experiences pervade every area of experience, and sexuality is no exception. The traditional male gender role contains many prescriptions for sexual behavior and experiencing, and these are embedded in the larger context of masculine values. Being a "real man" has often included expectations for certain ways of being a sexual man.

In this chapter, we explore the role of sexuality in masculinity, beginning with a discussion of the ways that males have typically been socialized to think about themselves and behave as sexual people. Then, we turn to a few sexual issues for men: circumcision, sexual preference, and sexual problems.

Sexuality and Physical Development

A boy discovers his penis very early in life. Compared with the girl's vagina and clitoris, the penis is more external and visible. It is easily accessible to the boy's hands, and he finds that touching his penis produces very pleasurable sensations. It is not surprising that boys tend to begin masturbating earlier in life than girls, and that males tend to masturbate more frequently than females throughout life (Hunt, 1974; Kinsey, Pomeroy, Martin, & Gebhard, 1953). The stronger social prohibition of sexual expression for females in Western cultures may also contribute to this difference.

Since the boy's genitals are so obvious to him and touching them is so pleasurable, there is a tendency in males to focus sexual feelings solely on the penis. In contrast, girls' sexuality may be experienced as more diffuse, internal, and mysterious (Nelson, 1988). This "genitalization" of sex may dissuade males from developing a sensuality—an appreciation of pleasurable sensations in other parts of the body. Adult heterosexual women frequently complain that their male partners are only interested in the "main event" (intercourse), and that they do not value caressing, intimate conversation, or other forms of sensuality.

When a boy reaches puberty, his genitals increase in size, and he begins to experience very strong sexual feelings. Erections occur frequently and without warning, sometimes at the most inappropriate times. Occasionally, the boy wakes up to find that he has ejaculated in his sleep (a nocturnal emission, or "wet dream"). These events may give the boy a sense that he has no control over his penis. It seems to have a "mind of its own." Although he is obviously aware that it is a part of him, he may also experience his penis as somewhat extrinsic to the self. The large number of slang terms for male genitalia may be a cultural reflection of the male sense that a penis has its own identity and personality.

Sexuality and Masculinity

While the physical sex differences just described contribute to the distinct quality of male sexuality, they probably pale in comparison to the social forces that shape sexual expression in the male. Sexuality is central to gender identity, and thus we find prescriptions for sexual experiencing deeply embedded in traditional masculine forms.

Brannon's (1976) description of the four themes of traditional masculinity (summarized in Chapter One) provides a useful framework for understanding masculine sexual demands in the context of general male gender-role demands:

1. *Antifemininity* ("No Sissy Stuff"): The avoidance of "feminine" behaviors, interests, and personality traits. Sexually, women are seen as gentle, sensual, tender, submissive, passive, relationship oriented, and sexually desirous toward males. In order to define the self as masculine, the male may feel pulled toward expressing his sexuality with the opposites of these qualities.

Heterosexual men find themselves in somewhat of a quandary when they try to relate to women sexually. On the one hand, they have been raised to be separate from women. On the other hand, they naturally feel drawn toward women. Intimacy is threatening for many men because it involves connecting, being vulnerable, and sharing power, all of which have been labeled feminine.

Men employ a few typical strategies to deal with this contradiction between naturally occurring desires for intimacy and role demands for separation. First, they may learn to equate sex with intimacy. In fact, one euphemism for intercourse is "being intimate with" someone. However, sex and intimacy are not the same thing, and physical intimacy is not the same as psychological intimacy. True intimacy involves letting someone in to some of the most private parts of the self. While some of these parts may be physical, it is certainly possible to be sexual with someone in a very impersonal or detached way. Likewise, it is possible to be intimate without being sexual, through shared communication and experience.

Equating sex with intimacy creates a number of problems for men and women. While women tend to see sex in the context of psychological closeness and affection, many men experience sex in a more isolated way, as a physical release or an adventure (Blumstein & Schwartz, 1983). The antifemininity norm inhibits men from establishing true intimacy, which is considered a basic human need (Jourard, 1971). Women may feel deprived in their intimacy needs and become frustrated with male partners who seem overly focused on sex.

Some men encounter a different problem: the sense that love and sex are contradictory. Raised to believe that "good girls" do not have sexual feelings, men may degrade women who express their sexuality. The sexual "double standard" is alive and well. Women who engage in frequent sex with multiple partners are called "sluts" or described with the pejorative term "promiscuous," but men who engage in the same behaviors are "studs" or heroes.

Men who embrace the double standard fall victim to what has been termed the Madonna/whore complex: they cannot love someone if they are sexual with her, and they cannot be sexual with someone if they love her. Sexual expression is relegated to "one night stands," short-term affairs, or perhaps hiring prostitutes. Most men prefer to have sex and love together (Pietropinto & Simenauer, 1977), but some find this to be impossible. They must separate sex from other aspects of relationships

(Gross, 1992) in order to define themselves as masculine (Fasteau, 1974). Many studies have shown that men are much more comfortable than women with viewing sex as a physical activity that is relatively unconnected to relationships (Carroll, Volk, & Hyde, 1985).

2. *Status and achievement* ("The Big Wheel"): The masculine expectation for success and power. This norm is expressed in a set of demands for sexual competence, conquest, and performance. Traditional men view the sexual arena as one in which they can prove their masculinity by being successful competitors.

For many men, "success" is an outcome, not a process. The traditional masculine emphasis has been on getting something *done*, rather than on *the experience* of doing something. Masculine achievements are, by definition, things that have happened in the past that contribute to the sense of masculine identity. They are also *quantifiable*: Masculine success means "putting up numbers." Carrying this orientation over into sexual behaviors has often created problems for traditional men and those around them.

Sexual success can be described in a number of ways. First, it can be defined as "scoring"—having sex with as many partners as possible. This goal-oriented attitude toward sex focuses the man on the good feelings that come from having "conquered" someone and leads to a focus away from enjoying the sexual experience. Some men even want to hurry sex so that they can go and tell their friends about having "scored" and thus gain admiration and respect. The sexual partner, however, is a victim of disrespect. She (or he) is seen as merely an avenue to achievement and status (Gross, 1992) for the "playboy." This mentality dehumanizes the sexual partner.

Another way to succeed is through sexual performance, which is defined as being able to produce erections at will and repeated orgasms in one's partner, as well as having sexual stamina. Of course, "real men" are also described as having huge penises (another quantification). In fact, the penis is sometimes described as "his manhood." The message is that having less of a penis means being less of a man. Worse yet are equations of the penis with personhood: "He put *himself* inside her," or the parental admonition, "Don't play with *yourself*." The masculine norms for performance, size, and stamina are summarized in what Zilbergeld (1992) calls "the fantasy model of sex . . . it's two feet long, hard as steel, always ready, and will knock your socks off" (p. 37).

These masculine demands are impossible to fulfill for most men. First, despite numerous attempts, nobody has created a penis enlargement technique (an interesting development is described in Box 11.1). Despite reassurances from women and sexuality experts that genital size bears no relationship to sexual pleasure, many a man feels inadequate about the size of his penis (Nelson, 1988). Statements like, "It's not the size of the wand, it's the magic in the magician" or "It's not the size of the ship, it's the motion of the ocean" provide little comfort to these men.

Second, penile erection is affected by a variety of factors besides sexual arousal. Among these are hormonal fluctuation, fatigue, anxiety, drug use, distraction, or physiological problems (Luria, Friedman, & Rose, 1987). Very few men have not had at least an occasional transient erectile problem (Zilbergeld, 1992). Because of the social connection between sexual performance and masculinity, these experiences can lead to confusion, anxiety, self-doubt, or depression.

Third, men do not "give" women orgasms. Women experience orgasms, sometimes with the man's help. If the man takes responsibility for the woman's orgasm, he may be risking his masculine self-esteem on a process over which he has little control. Many men ask, "Did you come?" and "How many times?", not out of concern for their partners, but in order to validate their masculinity through success and quantification. Many women report having faked orgasms in order to soothe the man's worries about his masculinity (Basow, 1986).

Fourth, sexual interest wanes on occasion. Many who equate manliness with ubiquitous sexual impulse may feel inadequate at these times. In fact, a surprising number of men report having faked orgasms in order to maintain a façade of perpetual masculine arousal (Levine & Barbach, 1984). The popularly held belief that men have biologically stronger sex drives than women is not supported by any available scientific evidence (Byrne, 1977).

The performance orientation toward sex also downplays the pleasure orientation for the man. Zilbergeld (1992) points out that fictional accounts of sex nearly always emphasize male *action* and female *feeling*: his performance and her pleasure. Zilbergeld notes that, with regard to male characters in novels, "it is rarely clear what he feels and experiences. It's as if his feelings and pleasure are beside the point" (p. 49).

The image that emerges from this view is of the man as a sexual machine with his penis as the main component of that machine. Some slang terms for penis ("tool," "rod") convey this connotation. Of course, the man has to know how to run the machine, and there is a tendency for men to see sex as a set of technical skills rather than as a human connection. Gross (1992) notes that "sex manuals" reflect this orientation. Success involves mastering sexual technique.

3. *Inexpressiveness and independence* ("The Sturdy Oak"): The maintaining of emotional control and self-reliance. In nearly every arena of male gender-role behavior, men are expected to know what to do without being told. It is considered unmanly to be unsure of oneself or to ask someone else for help. Many adolescent boys receive relatively little information about sex from parents or the school (Petrie, 1986). Thus, they rely on the peer group, a source notorious for an atmosphere of boasting,

Box 11.1
Penis Size and Masculinity

A wide variety of penis-size-enhancing products are available from adult book stores and mail-order catalogs. They include creams, ointments, stretchers, and vacuum pumps. All have one thing in common: They do not work.

Long Daochou (sometimes called "Professor Penis"), a plastic surgeon from Wuhan, China, has been using surgery to increase penis size, apparently with some success. His procedure involves cutting two ligaments that attach the penis to the pubic bone. This, Long says, allows a portion of the penis which is normally internal to extend to the outside of the body. The surgery, which Long has been performing since 1984, takes about 90 minutes. Although the procedure costs five to seven times the average monthly salary of a Chinese man, Long's services are in high demand (Sun, 1991).

The men who seek this surgical intervention claim that their small penises are destroying their marriages, damaging their self-esteem, and preventing them from reproducing. In reality, sexual intercourse is possible with all but the very smallest of penises, and the vagina easily accommodates itself to a penis of any size or shape (Luria, Friedman, & Rose, 1987).

With regard to being large enough to "satisfy" a woman, the most sensitive female sexual structure is the clitoris, which is located outside of the body, within easy reach. Men can stimulate their female partners using their fingers or mouths. Thus, a penis is not necessary for female sexual pleasure, and intercourse is not a particularly effective way of producing a female orgasm.

Small penises are adequate for reproduction, and penis size bears no relationship to fertility. In fact, impregnation can occur without sexual intercourse, through artificial insemination. This procedure does not require state-of-the-art medical technology. There are techniques that can be used at home (Boston Women's Health Book Collective, 1992).

There is one rare condition in which medical attention may be indicated. If the penis lacks the necessary hormone receptors, it will not enlarge at puberty, and the adult male will have a *congenital microphallus*. This is a condition in which the penis is less than ¾-inch long unerect (Luria, Friedman, & Rose, 1987). In other cases, an injury to the penis might warrant medical intervention.

Women seem much less concerned about penis size than men (Wade & Cirese, 1991). Despite the fact that the vast majority of penises are adequate for reproduction and the sexual pleasure of both the man and his partner, many men experience a great deal of anxiety about the size of their genitals. Part of this anxiety may come from ignorance or misinformation about sexual functioning. Most of it, however, probably stems from the typically masculine orientation that "more is better" and that men with small penises are not as manly as men with large ones. Zilbergeld (1992) says that "penises in fantasyland come in only three sizes: large, extra large, and so big you can't get them through the door" (p. 50).

Men may also have unrealistic notions about what constitutes an average penis size. Men often view other men in locker rooms or bathrooms. A man with a large flaccid penis may be no larger when erect than a man who is smaller when flaccid. Still, there is an almost inevitable anxiety because of the traditional masculine values of comparison and competition.

As long as men continue to equate penis size with masculinity, they will continue to feel unnecessary sexual anxiety. The man with a small- to average-size penis will feel that he cannot "measure up" as a man, and even the man with a large penis may worry that other men are larger. Medical interventions like Long Daochou's are physiologically unnecessary for most men, expensive, and possibly dangerous. As long as men perceive themselves as having a catastrophic physical shortage, the surgeon will have no shortage of patients.

---

lying, and transmitting misinformation, for education around this very important topic. In order to be accepted by his peers, the boy must act like he is "getting it" (from females, of course) and that he knows what to do sexually. In other words, he must display an aura of competence and knowledge while he often feels incompetent and ignorant.

The gender-role demand for inexpression encourages men to approach sexuality as if it were a job to do rather than a pleasurable encounter. Sexuality is a highly emotional and self-expressive area of human experience, but men who are oversocialized into their gender role feel compelled to approach it in a machinelike way. Zilbergeld (1992) reports that an astonishing number of men say that they do not enjoy sex.

For many men, sex is the only area of experience where they can express some positive feeling and desire for emotional attachment to another person. When sex and connectedness are compartmentalized, any feelings of tender emotion or attachment become associated with sex. As Nelson (1988) puts it, "If a man feels intense emotion, sex seems called for" (p. 40). But it is clearly possible and also desirable to be emotional and connected to people in nonsexual ways. The association between emotion and sexuality, together with the cultural prescription for the sexual objectification of women, makes it very difficult for some men to relate to women as friends or coworkers (see Chapter Thirteen). These factors are related to a variety of social problems such as sexual assault and harassment (see Chapter Twelve).

The sexualization of feelings of attachment causes considerable consternation when men begin to feel close to other men. Because a woman's connectedness is not defined as exclusively sexual, she may feel quite comfortable in touching, sharing feelings, or even sleeping in the same bed with another woman. Men's relationships with each other, however, are often limited by the threat of feeling too close (see Chapter Thirteen). The fear of same-sex attraction is termed *homophobia*. Increasingly, homophobia is being identified as related to a variety of social issues (Blumenfeld, 1992).

4. *Adventurousness and aggression* ("Give 'em Hell"): The expectation to be daring, fearless, and self-assertive. This masculine norm encourages men to view sexuality as yet another area in which to exercise dominance and control. "Real men" want to get down to the business of intercourse. Fasteau (1974) notes that "for most men, courting and seduction are nuisances" (p. 32). Feelings and communication are "sissy stuff" (Zilbergeld, 1992). At the extreme, there are implications here for coercive sexuality (see Chapter Twelve). The cultural myth, portrayed in movie after movie and novel after novel, is that women are reluctant participants in sex and that they respond to "forceful" men.

Traditional gender roles dictate that men take every sexual initiative. Farrell (1986) describes the following social message to the male: "Be prepared to risk rejection about 150 times between eye contact and sexual contact. Start all 150 over again with each girl" (p. 126). Because men are expected to be tough and strong, rejection is not supposed to hurt. While the sexual initiator has a kind of power, the ability to reject is also powerful. Neither role in the sexual script seems very comfortable: She must wait somewhat passively for him to approach, signaling her availability without being "too forward"; he must gather his courage and risk his masculinity despite his anxiety and feelings of inadequacy.

The pressure of being responsible for all sexual initiative may lead a man into a variety of dysfunctional and harmful behaviors. Treating women as sex objects and inferiors is one way to defend against the pain of rejection. If a man reduces a woman to a less than human status, he can more easily attribute her disinterest to stupidity or deny that, being nothing more than a "piece of ass," she has little power over his feelings. There may also be the tendency to deny the emotional component of sex or to develop anger and resentment toward women in general (Farrell, 1982).

If the man is "successful" at living up to the masculine ideal of promiscuity, then he is *really* taking risks. The very real threats of AIDS and other sexually transmitted diseases are more serious than ever, and unwanted pregnancies also present as much of a possibility as they ever did. Once again, being a "real man" is hazardous to one's health. "Studs" don't spend their time taking precautions to avoid disease or pregnancy, talking to partners about sexual histories and birth control, or turning down sex because it is risky to be promiscuous.

In conclusion, sex has traditionally been a major way for men to demonstrate their masculinity. Male gender-role values require men to be sure of themselves sexually, to be perpetually ready to perform, to retain a genital focus and goal orientation, to separate sex from love, and to obtain as many partners as possible. On the one hand, males are encouraged to freely express and enjoy their sexuality. In another sense, however, male sexuality may often be fraught with high anxiety, emotional constrictedness, and a strong sense of inadequacy.

Male Sexual Issues

Circumcision

The cutting and removal of the penile foreskin of the male infant is the most common surgery performed in the United States (Goldman, 1992). Despite the statement by the American Academy of Pediatrics Task Force (quoted in Milos, 1992) that "there is no absolute medical indication for routine circumcision of the newborn" (p. 16), over a million male infants undergo this procedure every year. Only 20% of boys in the United States escape the knife, and the cost of this routine procedure is estimated to be over $50 million annually (Hussey, 1989).

Elsewhere in the world, 85% of men are not circumcised (Goldman, 1992). A century ago, circumcised men were also a small minority in the United States. The rise to the current 80% rate was fueled by beliefs about the value of circumcision for hygiene, disease avoidance, reduction of cancer risks, and other concerns (Hussey, 1989). For some religious groups, circumcision has ritual meaning (Luria, Friedman, & Rose, 1987).

Following is a description of the circumcision procedure:

> The baby's arms and legs are strapped to a board to prevent movement. The genitals are scrubbed to prepare for surgery. The foreskin is torn from the glans and slit lengthwise to allow for the insertion of the circumcision instrument. Then, the foreskin is cut off. This is usually done without an anesthetic because of the risk to the infant." (National Organization of Circumcision Information Resource Centers, 1991)

A number of researchers believe that circumcision is quite painful (Goldman, 1992; Chamberlain, 1989; Tyler, 1988). Sometimes, a local anesthetic, lidocaine, is used. However, the baby is thought to suffer whenever he urinates during the 7 to 10 days it takes the wound to heal (Milos, 1992). Surgical complications can also occur, and 1 in 500 circumcisions involves a serious complication such as hemhorrage, infection, mutilation, or even death (NOCIRC, 1991).

Why is this seemingly painful and unnecessary surgery performed so routinely? Milos (1992) cites several persistent myths about the value of circumcision:

- *Myth*: A circumcised penis is cleaner.
  Although circumcision may reduce the frequency of urinary tract and other kinds of infections (Wiswell & Geschke, 1989), an uncircumcised penis is easy to care for. Infections can easily be avoided by simple hygiene procedures, which most men around the world use routinely.
- *Myth*: Circumcision prevents penile cancer.
  There are more deaths from circumcision than from penile cancer.
- *Myth*: Babies don't remember the pain.
  Many experts disagree.
- *Myth*: A boy needs to look like his dad or the other boys in the locker room.
  This did not appear to be a concern when, from 1870 to 1900, most boys in the United States were circumcised and their fathers were not (Hussey, 1989). It has been suggested that boys readily accept the explanation that "when I was a boy, they thought circumcision was necessary for health, but now we know better" (Milos, 1992, p. 15).

Most U.S. parents seem to circumcise their baby boys as a matter of course, without much thought to the implications of this procedure for the child. As you can see, some writers believe that the potential for psychological and physical harm far outweighs most rationales for circumcision.

Sexual Preference

Imagine that you are in a movie theater watching a first-run feature. The hero of the film is a detective who cleverly figures out who has committed a murder, outduels the criminal in a gun battle, and returns home triumphantly to his boyfriend. Imagine parents telling their young son, "Someday you'll meet the right woman or man, and you'll settle down." Imagine a male presidential candidate proudly accepting his party's nomination and calling for his gay lover to join him at the podium.

Obviously, these three scenes are highly unlikely. Heterosexuality is so ingrained in Western culture that people tend to assume that everyone is attracted exclusively to members of the other sex unless something is wrong with them. Yet a significant portion of the world's population is homosexual or bisexual, and the available evidence suggests that this has been the case throughout human history.

What percentage of the population is homosexual or bisexual? It depends on how these terms are defined. Do we define them with regard to current sexual practices, sexual history, fantasy content, or the identification of the self as being homosexual or bisexual?

Kinsey and his colleagues (1948, 1953) were the first to recognize that homosexuality and heterosexuality are not neat categories with clearly identifiable boundaries. They proposed a behavioral scale of 0 to 6 to describe "sexual orientation," ranging from an extreme of 0 (exclusively heterosexual) to a midpoint of 3 (equally homosexual and heterosexual) to an extreme of 6 (exclusively homosexual). Bell and Weinberg (1978) later recognized that the content of erotic fantasies was also important in describing the sexual self. It is not unusual for a person with little or no history of homosexual contact to nonetheless be aroused by fantasies involving sexual contact with persons of the same sex. Coleman (1990) expanded the description of sexual orientation to include nine dimensions, including behaviors, fantasies, emotional attachments, idealized sexual orientation, identity, and life style.

Kinsey and his colleagues (1948, 1953) estimated that 4% of males and 2 to 3% of females were exclusively homosexual as adults. Other estimates range as high as 10 to 15% (Anctil, 1992). Kinsey, Pomeroy, and Martin (1948) estimated that 37% of adult men had a history of at least one sexual experience with another man that involved orgasm. Clearly, homosexual behavior is not unusual, and millions of people identify themselves as predominantly or exclusively homosexual.

Origins of Homosexuality.   What causes homosexuality? Even asking this question reveals a heterosexist bias. Rochlin (1982) published a "heterosexual questionnaire" that contained questions like, "What do you think caused your heterosexuality?" and "If you have never slept with a person of the same sex, is it possible that all you need is a good gay lover?" These are questions that heterosexuals would probably never ask themselves. Culturally, exclusive heterosexuality is assumed to be normal and natural, and homosexuality is assumed to be some sort of deviation. John Money (1987a), one of the world's foremost experts on sexuality, considers homosexuality to be a *typological distinction*, not a *syndrome*. He likens the characteristic of same-sex erotic preference to left-handedness: It exists in a minority within the population, but it is not pathological. Many gay and lesbian people enjoy healthy, satisfying lives.

The origins of homosexuality seem to be quite complex. They possibly involve genes (Adler, 1992), brain structure (Angier, 1991), hormones (Moses & Hawkins, 1982), and environmental factors (Wade & Cirese, 1991). There have been theories that dominant mothers, weak or absent fathers, modeling of homosexual behavior, or inappropriate gender-role socialization lead a male toward homosexuality, but these theories have not received much scientific support. In fact, homosexuality cannot (or at least has not yet) been strongly associated with any single origin or family pattern (Money, 1987b; Bell, Weinberg, & Hammersmith, 1981).

There is strong evidence that gay adults have histories of same-sex erotic arousal and feelings of being different from others, both of which date back to childhood (Bell & Weinberg, 1978). Surprisingly, most homosexual adults are not lacking in heterosexual experience. About one-fifth of gay men have been married, and many are fathers (Raymond, 1992). Contrary to popular belief, gay identification does not usually begin through enjoyable homosexual experience as often as it does from ungratifying heterosexual experience (Bell & Weinberg, 1978; Hill, 1986). Indeed, many heterosexually identified people have had homosexual experiences but prefer heterosexual ones. Thus, sexual *experiences* are not the critical determinant of sexual preference. The *feelings* that precede the experiences are, and adult homosexuality is a continuation of childhood same-sex erotic arousal.

Attitudes toward Homosexuality.   The social acceptance or nonacceptance of homosexuality varies from culture to culture and from one historical era to another (Gregersen, 1982). There is a long history of antihomosexual sentiment in the United States. The attitude that gays are mentally ill, immoral, vulgar, or dangerous is probably connected to Americans' strong Christian roots. Early Catholic theologians, most notably Augustine, pronounced that sexual activity had procreation as its purpose, not pleasure or self-expression (Nelson, 1988). Since homosexual behavior could not possibly produce offspring, it was seen as immoral. The Victorian ethic of repressed sexuality led one to ask, "Why would a person have sex if he or she did not 'have to'?" There is no good answer, from the perspectives of these values, except to vilify the homosexual.

There have been some fluctuations in U.S. attitudes toward gays. In the 1970s, support for gay legal rights increased, perhaps as a function of more liberal political and sexual attitudes. The 1980s witnessed a resurgence of negative attitudes toward gays. AIDS struck the gay male community first, and some people believed that this was a result of gays' lack of morality. Some prominent fundamentalist Christian leaders publicly stated that AIDS was a punishment from God for homosexuals' sins. People tend to believe in a "just world"—that bad things happen to bad people (Lerner, 1980)—and gays became a convenient scapegoat for this deadly disease.

Strongly negative attitudes toward homosexuality have always been present in the United States, and gays have long been victims of various forms of oppression, such as violence, interpersonal insult, the outlawing of homosexual behavior, and discrimination in housing, insurance, and employment (Blumenfeld, 1992). The U.S. military discharged a number of gay soldiers after they returned from the Persian Gulf War in 1991 (Lambert & Simon, 1991) (see Box 11.2). In 1992, the State of Colorado passed a law preventing its municipalities from passing antidiscrimination laws that protect gays and lesbians. The Vatican recently reaffirmed its stance that homosexuality is a mental illness and supported discrimination against gay people (Stepp, 1992). The city charter of Springfield, Oregon, not only allows, but actually *requires*, discrimination on the basis of sexual preference (NGLTF, 1993). Gays who openly display affection for their partners risk being assaulted.

Some people seem to believe that same-sex erotic preference is a "choice." In light of the kinds of phenomena just described, who would choose a life in which they encounter threats of physical, psychological, and institutional violence on a daily basis? It is remarkably insensitive to believe that gay people can and should change their sexual preference.

Homophobia and the Male Gender Role.   **Homophobia** is the irrational fear and intolerance of homosexuality and homosexual persons (Smith, 1971). Homophobia is a widespread phenomenon that manifests itself in a variety of ways, including the avoidance of nonsexual intimate behaviors between men, derogatory terms and jokes about gays, societal bigotry against homosexuals, and even unprovoked violence against persons perceived as gay.

Sexual attraction between people of the same sex carries a powerful taboo in most Western societies, especially if the two people involved happen to be male. Morin and Garfinkle (1978) reported that male homosexuality is subject to much greater intolerance than female homosexuality. Males are more disapproving and fearful than females of any homosexuality (Herek, 1986; Astin, 1985). In other words, men tend to be more homophobic than women, and gay male behavior is especially disapproved.

Homophobia seems clearly related to the acceptance of stereotypical gender roles. Heterosexual men and women who hold positive attitudes toward egalitarian gender roles tend to be more accepting of homosexuals (Kurdek, 1988; Whitley, 1987). People who hold more traditional attitudes often feel threatened by gender-role deviance, and an alternative sexual life style is viewed as one of the most extreme forms of this deviance.

Box 11.2
Gay Soldiers

When Bill Clinton was elected President of the United States in 1992, he spoke in favor of allowing homosexual people into the military. While gays and lesbians have always been in the service, they have had to hide their sexual preferences or risk being discharged. Various arguments for and against Clinton's position have been proposed. A few of these are listed here for thought and discussion. Which ones are convincing to you? What is your position?

Arguments for Allowing Gays in the Military

1. The military is a work place. A worker should be judged by job performance. Sexual preference has nothing to do with being a good serviceperson, as evidenced by the thousands of gay men and women who have served well in the military.
2. Many other countries allow self-acknowledged gay men and lesbian women to serve in the armed services. This has not seemed to have an adverse effect on the functioning of the military.

Arguments against Allowing Gays in the Military

1. Gays in the military make heterosexual soldiers uncomfortable, and this affects their job performance.
2. Being a good soldier in life-and-death situations involves "bonding" with fellow soldiers. People with different sexual preferences cannot "bond" effectively with one another. This puts many military personnel and, in fact, the entire nation in danger.

Box 11.3 illustrates a few extreme reactions to homophobic feelings. These descriptions attest to the deep levels of anxiety that tend to arise when men consider the possibility of same-sex erotic feelings. One method of dealing with this anxiety is to defend against it by placing very rigid boundaries between the self and other men. The man who claims to have absolutely no clue about male attractiveness or who becomes violent when dealing with gay men wants it to be absolutely clear to everyone (including himself) that he does not have an ounce of homosexuality in his body.

Why would men go to such great lengths to deny even the slightest possibility of homosexual feeling and thought? After all, it's not like we have been given a huge sexual partner "menu" in this life. You can love

---

Box 11.3
Homophobic Behavior

Homophobia reaches almost incredible proportions in many men. Consider the following true stories:

1. A teenaged boy received disapproval from the male peer group because he revealed that he had kissed his girlfriend after she had performed oral sex on him. The message was that you do not want any connection between your mouth and a penis, even if the contact is indirect and even if the penis is your own!
2. A businesswoman having lunch with a colleague (in his 30s) pointed out a man in the restaurant and commented that he was attractive. Her male colleague replied, "I wouldn't know."
3. Many men, especially young men, have been heard to comment that they would become violent if approached by a gay man.
4. During the 1992 controversy around allowing gays and lesbians into the military, a military man wrote a letter to the editor of a small town newspaper. He spoke against integrating the military with persons of alternate sexual preferences, saying, "Military personnel have the right to live in a nonthreatening environment." He seems to have forgotten that a large part of the military mission is to face threat. Perhaps being on a battlefield is experienced as less threatening than being in the same room with a gay man.

Preston and Stanley (1987) found that, among college students, labeling a man homosexual is the worst possible insult one could use. What other events in the media or everyday life attest to the depth of homophobia?

---

men, women, or both. It would make sense that the possibility has at least crossed the minds of even the most heterosexual of men. Yet these experiences are so disturbing to many men that they feel compelled to use somewhat desperate measures to protect the self.

Homophobia is both the *substance* and the *enforcer* of the traditional male gender role (Lehne, 1976), patriarchy, and sexism (Pharr, 1988). Recall from Chapter Two that one of the central messages of masculine socialization is "don't be like a girl." A male proves his masculinity by behaving in opposite ways from females. Any "feminine" behavior casts

doubts on his masculinity, and what could be more feminine (in a heterosexist culture) than loving a male?

The childhood male peer group uses homophobia to enforce gender
conformity (De Cecco, 1984). The male who behaves in stereotypically
unmasculine ways is often labeled a "queer," "fag," or "pansy" and is
ostracized from the social group. He may be given these pejorative homosexual labels for sexual behavior such as getting an erection in the
boys' locker room, but more commonly he is labeled for failing to live up
to masculine role norms. Regardless of the boy's sexual preference, his
heterosexuality may be called into question if he refuses to be violent,
express a love of sports, or participate in the derogation of females. Males
who want to maintain the approval of other males often find it necessary
to display rigid, defensive attitudes toward homosexuality and homosexuals.

On a personal level, homophobia functions to trap men into rigid
gender roles and limit their friendships with other men (see Chapter
Thirteen). Gay men are not immune to homophobia, and the anxiety
created by these feelings sometimes compounds an already difficult process of understanding the sexual self in the context of a heterosexist
culture. The gay man who has learned to hate homosexuality in his
childhood may find himself dealing with feelings of self-hatred in adulthood. On one level, he knows that these feelings are irrational. On another, they seem quite real and difficult to ignore.

Many people believe that intolerance of homosexuality is a way of
projecting unacceptable feelings about the self onto others. Vague feelings
of same-sex attraction threaten the sense of masculinity and, ultimately,
self-esteem. If the man can psychologically place these unacceptable feelings outside of the self, then he can hate the feelings without hating
himself. Herek (1986) reported that people who hold defensive attitudes
toward gays also showed a generalized tendency toward this externalizing defensive style. It is not surprising that we often see this style in
males, who are usually socialized to deal with the world rather than to
"look inside" and think about how they feel.

The external defensive style prevents the man from learning anything about himself and encourages him to react to the pressure of masculine insecurity by overconforming to the male gender role (Pleck,
1981a). This hyperconformity is dehumanizing and has serious negative
implications for physical health, psychological health, and relationships
with other people. When men lower their defenses against homophobia,
they often find that homosexuality is not the huge threat that they perceived, and they feel somewhat freed from the pressure of constantly
proving to themselves and others that they are masculine (heterosexual)
men. Homophobia is highly emotional and deeply rooted (see Box 11.4).
Some suggestions for dealing with homophobic feelings are presented in
Box 11.5.

Box 11.4
Are You Homophobic?

Like any form of prejudice, homophobia has cognitive, emotional, and behavioral components. These sometimes conflict with one another. For example, you might believe that gay people should not be treated any differently from others, but at the same time, you might feel uncomfortable around openly gay people and avoid them. A parallel in racial prejudice would be a white person's discomfort around people of color. Although a person may be very egalitarian in his or her ideology, racism, sexism, and heterosexism often operate at emotional and/or unconscious levels.

Most, if not all, of us were raised in a heterosexist, homophobic environment. Therefore, we should not be ashamed for having emotional reactions to gay people. On the contrary, the openness to these reactions reveals a willingness to be honest with the self, to learn something about the self and about others who are perceived as different, and to work toward dealing with homophobic anxiety.

My most memorable personal experience with homophobia occurred a few years ago after I had given a lecture on men's issues. During a subsequent question-and-answer period, one of the students said, "You have said that men who step outside of the traditional masculine role are often perceived as homosexual. You also said that talking about male emotion and experience is outside of the role. Since you do just that in your lectures, do your audiences tend to think you're gay?" She stopped just short of simply asking, "Are you gay?" While I thought that I understood and had dealt with my homophobia, I recall a strong wave of anxiety coming from the deepest part of my gut. This feeling alerted me that I had more personal emotional work to do on this problem.

In assessing your own feelings and attitudes toward sexual preference, think about the following:

1. How and when did you first learn about homosexuality? What attitudes toward gays were conveyed by your family and your peer group? What nicknames for gays did you learn when you were growing up? What connotations for these names did you perceive? How did you feel about homosexuality when you were a child?
2. Imagine that you are having a conversation with several friends and someone tells a disrespectful joke about gays. How do you react, emotionally and behaviorally? Do you feel pressured to join in, to confront the person, to withdraw?

3. Imagine that a family member or close friend has just revealed to you that he or she is gay. How do you react? Will
your relationship change and, if so, in what ways? Does your
reaction differ depending on whether you imagine a male or
a female?

4. If you are heterosexual, role play or imagine that you are gay
or bisexual and "coming out" (revealing your sexual preference) to a close friend. How do you go about the task? What
feelings are present? If you are gay or bisexual, you may
have had this experience or at least thought about it. What
feelings come up? How would (or did) you deal with the
emotions and with the task?

Sexual Problems

Sexual problems are difficulties with sexual desire, functioning, or enjoyment. Clinically, the terms *sexual dysfunction* or *sexual disorder* are sometimes used. The former term seems to imply that the "equipment" is not
working, the latter that there is some pathology. Since male sexuality is
not only in the penis (the "equipment") and since sexual difficulties do
not necessarily mean that there is something "wrong," the term *problem*
seems more appropriate.

Montague (1988) suggests three dimensions for describing male
sexual problems. The first is the etiology (source or origin) of the problem, which may be biological, psychological, or mixed. The second is
whether the problem is primary (lifelong) or secondary (acquired). The
third is whether the problem is global (generalized) or situational (specific to certain times, settings, or partners).

These considerations are important with regard to the treatment of
the problem. If a condition is longstanding and global, it usually presents
a more serious problem than transient or situational difficulties. A problem that is largely biogenic usually points to different interventions than
a problem of psychological origin.

The overall incidence of sexual problems is difficult to estimate
because sex is usually such a private matter, but it is probably the case
that most people have, at sometime in their lives, experienced sexual
disinterest, arousal difficulties, and/or sexual performance problems
(Wade & Cirese, 1991).

Inhibited Sexual Desire

Inhibited sexual desire is a lack of interest in sex. It only becomes a
problem if it is distressing to the man and/or his partner. The male

---

**Box 11.5
Dealing with Homophobic Feelings**

What can an individual do to work against homophobia at a personal level and against heterosexism (the cultural-institutional manifestation of homophobia)? Following are several suggestions:

1. If you are heterosexual, do not avoid contact with gay people. We call them "homosexuals," but like everybody else, they are also students, sons and daughters, athletes, workers, friends, and so on. You may find that you have something in common with a gay person. Direct interpersonal contact with feared people tends to reduce that fear (May, 1990). Homophobia encourages people to avoid gays (Schneider & Lewis, 1984). Don't wait for your homophobia to go away before having contact with a gay person. Do it *despite* these uncomfortable feelings.
2. Work toward understanding that occasional same-sex erotic feelings are probably more a rule than an exception, and that homophobic feelings are a consequence of growing up in a heterosexist culture.
3. Support gay rights.
4. Refuse to participate in interpersonal or institutional gay bashing.
5. Learn about the gay rights movement and gay people's struggles.
6. Participate in an antiheterosexism workshop (see Blumenfeld, 1992).
7. Work to understand the freeing effects of breaking out of homophobia and rigid gender roles.

---

gender-role prescription that a man should always want, need, and be ready for sex may produce negative feelings in the man when he experiences even a normal ebb in his sexual appetite.

Inhibited sexual desire can stem from physiological causes, such as fatigue, drug use, or illness, and/or from psychological/interpersonal causes. For example, the man who suffers from the so-called Madonna/whore complex (a felt contradiction between love and lust) may experience low sexual desire for his wife and high desire for other women. Sexual desire might also wane as a consequence of other problems, such as work stress or conflicts in the relationship with the man's sexual partner.

Erectile Problems

Transient or longstanding difficulties in achieving or maintaining erection are relatively common in men, and few problems produce as much distress as these. The term *impotent* is often used to refer to these men. Literally, this word means "powerless." What greater blow to a man's self-esteem can there be than the loss of masculine power? Clearly, the erection is culturally symbolic of a man's strength.

Clinically, these problems are now referred to as erectile *problems* or *erectile dysfunctions* in order to avoid negative connotations about the man's personality (just as the term *frigid* is no longer used to describe a woman with orgasmic difficulty). However, the use of the word *impotence* continues in many circles.

A number of physical and psychological factors are associated with erectile difficulties. Although the exact proportion of physical and psychological causes is not known, the estimate of physical origin has increased in recent years, and some researchers believe that close to half of erectile problems are biologically based (Shabsigh, Fishman, & Scott, 1988). Physical causes include illness, disease, high blood pressure, the use of some types of prescription and nonprescription drugs, injury, hormonal imbalance, or vascular problems (Wade & Cirese, 1991).

Emotional factors can also play a role in erectile difficulty. Anxiety is probably the most common (Zilbergeld, 1992). Many men feel a good deal of pressure to perform sexually. Paradoxically, the fear of losing his erection can result in erectile problems for a man. Men who think of intercourse as the only mode of sexual expression often think that they must get an erection in order for sexual pleasure to occur for the self and the partner. Something of a viscious cycle may result: He feels self-induced pressure to get an erection and perform, which leads to anxiety, which leads to erectile difficulty, which results in more pressure, more anxiety, and so on. Nelson (1988) describes the ubiquity of performance anxiety: "Impotence is a man's threat, always waiting in the wings while he is on stage" (p. 33).

There are several treatments for erectile problems. Men with intractable physiological barriers to erection often opt for penile implants, which produce erections by pumping liquid into a cylinder that has been surgically implanted in the penis.

Psychological treatments for erectile problems usually involve turning attention away from penis, intercourse, and performance and toward sensuality, the partner's pleasure, and sexual communication. Most men can achieve erections when the pressure to do so is removed.

Premature Ejaculation

Many experts believe that premature ejaculation is the most common sexual problem for men (Zilbergeld, 1992; Wade & Cirese, 1991). A premature ejaculation occurs very shortly after, or even before, the man's penis enters his partner. It is difficult to define the problem in absolute terms. How soon is too soon? A subjective criterion is probably useful: If the man and/or his partner is unhappy with the man's level of ejaculatory control, some attention may be warranted.

The cause or causes of premature ejaculation are not well understood, but we might guess at some. First, the reproductive function of intercourse requires only that the penis be inside the vagina at ejaculation. Animals are somewhat vulnerable to predators during sexual activity, so quick ejaculation has some evolutionary utility for survival. Of course, human beings are quite different from animals in many respects, so this sociobiological explanation might not be very convincing.

Another possible explanation is that early male sexual experiences are often rushed. Many times, a pubescent boy might masturbate or have intercourse quickly because his privacy could easily be disturbed in his bedroom or in the back seat of a car. However, this explanation does not tell the whole story either, because many men who have had these kinds of boyhood experiences do not experience problems with ejaculatory control (Luria, Friedman, & Rose, 1987).

Although the exact nature of the origins of premature ejaculation is not known, sex therapists have developed reliable treatments for this problem. These techniques involve the starting, stopping, and restarting of stimulation at various points of arousal, the squeezing of the base or glans of the penis, and a number of other exercises that the man can do alone or with a partner. These treatments are highly effective. Various estimates put their success rates at between 80 and 98% (Zilbergeld, 1992; Arentewicz & Schmidt, 1983; Masters & Johnson, 1970).

Retarded Ejaculation

Some men experience an opposite problem: the inability to ejaculate during a reasonable period of time (or sometimes not at all). This problem is thought to be anxiety based, perhaps related to a fear of impregnating the partner or a discomfort with one's own erotic pleasure. A number of techniques for increasing arousal have been prescribed by sex therapists.

Summary

1. The sexual self is obviously shaped by biological forces, but it is also strongly influenced by gender-role socialization. Males are often encouraged to be promiscuous and perpetually ready for sex, to take sexual risks, to quantify sexual experience as if it were an achievement, to be performance oriented, and to focus sexual feelings in the penis.

2. Masculine socialization can create problems for men and their partners in the areas of sexually transmitted diseases, intimacy, interpersonal exploitation, and sexual satisfaction. The traditional male role of sexual initiator is fraught with anxiety and may create resentment toward women.

3. Because men sometimes confuse sexual and intimate feelings, they may feel very anxious when natural feelings of closeness to other men arise. Homophobia, the irrational fear of homosexuality and homosexuals, results in a number of negative personal and social consequences, including gay bashing, institutional bigotry toward gays, and the limiting of male-male friendships. The threat of being labeled homosexual enforces conformity to traditional male gender-role prescriptions under the threat of ostracization from the male peer group. Because we live in a heterosexist culture, most people experience some degree of homophobia.

4. Many men experience at least occasional difficulty with sexual desire, enjoyment, or functioning, including inhibited desire and erectile or ejaculatory problems. The origins of these difficulties can be physiological, psychological, or mixed. Sometimes, these problems are transient. In other cases, some intervention may be warranted. Sex therapists have developed a number of treatments for various male sexual difficulties.

D. Chidester/The Image Works

CHAPTER TWELVE

Boys Will Be Boys:
Men and Violence

In the United States, we hate violence. We think that people who commit violent crimes should go to jail for a long time. We wallow in shame at "senseless" violence like the My Lai massacre of Vietnam in the 1960s and the killing of college student protesters at Kent State University in 1970.

In the United States, we love violence. We spend large amounts of time and money watching exhibitions of football, boxing, and "professional wrestling," in which men inflict pain on other men. We love to see heroes in "adventure" films who get the job done with their guns and their fists. We experienced an almost druglike "high" during the Persian Gulf War, when high-tech, sophisticated warfare devices allowed us to do violence in video-game fashion, where we were spared the inconvenience of having to watch victims suffer.

There may be no other place in the world where the culture has such a powerful love-hate relationship with aggression. Although we abhor "senseless" violence, we often feel or think that there are times when violence makes a lot of sense. We seem comfortable with destructive acts as long as they are performed for the "right" reasons, against those that "deserve" to be victimized. We glorify those who are willing to "fight the good fight."

It is a well-documented fact that the vast majority of violent acts are committed by males. It seems that masculinity and aggression sometimes go hand in hand. While the traditional male gender role leads many men to become disturbed, it also leads many to become disturbing. One of the central issues in the study of men is the link between masculinity and violence.

We explore this link in this chapter, beginning with a brief description of the extent of male violence, followed by a summary of theories about its origins. Then, two specific issues, domestic violence and rape, are examined with regard to origin and potential solutions.

Origins of Male Violence

Almost 90% of violent crimes in the United States are committed by men (FBI, 1992). Three to four million U.S. women are physically beaten by their male partners every year (Pellegrini, 1992). Sexual assaults are almost exclusively perpetrated by males. Although sex-comparison research has demonstrated small or nonexistent differences between males and females in most areas, violence is a glaring exception.

The search for the connections between masculinity and violence leads us back to the old nature-nurture question. Many people believe that men are biologically predisposed toward aggression. It is certainly also true that males are socialized toward these kinds of behaviors more than females are. We probably will never know the relative contributions of nature and nurture to violence, but it is important to consider the roles of each of these types of forces.

The Biological Perspective

Sociobiologists argue that male aggression is tied to reproductive competition. In many different animal species, males engage in violent, confrontational, and sometimes mortal competition for breeding access to females (Daly & Wilson, 1985). Dominant males overcome other males through ritualized violence (such as rams butting horns), and these dominant males mate with more females. The submissive males sometimes do not mate at all.

Of course, all animals are motivated to breed, according to the theory of evolution. The males who breed most often have the greatest chance of propagating their genes. Because they must compete with other males for breeding opportunities, they are motivated to be more aggressive toward males. As a group, men are by far more violent than women, and men are also victimized more often by extreme violence. In the United States, men are three times more likely than women to be victims of murder, usually at the hands of other men (USBC, 1991).

Daly and Wilson (1985) argue that violence between human males can be explained by this evolutionary pattern of ritualized competition. As evidence, they cite a 1958 study in which it was judged that 37% of the cases in which a male murdered another male were precipitated by "trivial" (ritual) events, such as the killer's "saving face" when another man had insulted him. Daly and Wilson's contention is that these types of killings are the result of the competition for dominance, and that this competition is fiercest among young, poor men who have little status. Men with higher socioeconomic status, they say, tend to be less violent because they are higher on the dominance hierarchy and thus able to attract suitable mates.

Daly and Wilson are accurate in their description of the population of men who are most at risk of being involved in violence—young, poor men. And, in fact, they are probably also correct in describing much of this violence as taking place for reasons that most people would consider trivial. However, to say that this kind of behavior is a result of breeding competition seems to be quite a leap. In fact, even in animals, male aggression is not always associated with increased breeding opportunities, nor is it universal (Basow, 1986). Would there be so many angry, aggressive young men if we took better care of their emotional and material needs? If we ceased to expose them to so many violent models? If we stopped holding them to impossible standards of masculinity? As we shall see, other explanations of male violence (and young, poor men's violence) are at least as plausible as the sociobiological one.

Researchers who study biological influences on behavior are often interested in hormonal factors. Since males and females differ greatly in levels of sex hormones and in levels of violence, it would make sense to look to these hormones for a possible link.

Some researchers speculate that the male sex hormone testosterone may be related to aggression, and there is some evidence in support of this hypothesis. For example, in some animal species, males with high positions in social dominance hierarchies (which are established by fighting) have higher testosterone levels than lower status males. In fact, rhesus monkey dominance hierarchies have been known to change when low-status monkeys are injected with testosterone (Rose, Gordon, & Bernstein, 1972).

While this study provides compelling evidence for the role of testosterone in aggression, there are complicating data. First, testosterone levels drop when a monkey falls in the hierarchy. Therefore, while testosterone level may be a cause of aggression, it may also be an effect. Second, the excretion of high levels of testosterone in the monkey's urine may stimulate other monkeys to aggress toward him, and he must then fight back in order to protect himself. This evidence comes from a study in which male rats were more likely to attack a castrated male rat after it had been coated with the urine of a dominant male (Pleck, 1981a).

The extent which testosterone is a cause, effect, or simply a marker of aggression is a continuing subject of inquiry. Of course, the degree to which animal studies relate to human behavior is always a matter of debate. In a classic study by Kreuz and Rose (1972), testosterone levels were measured in prison inmates who were labeled as either "fighters" or "nonfighters" on the basis of prison records of aggressive incidents. There were no significant differences in testosterone levels between these two groups of men, casting considerable doubt on the straightforward testosterone-aggression hypothesis.

Kemper (1990) reviewed the extensive literature on testosterone and concluded that, in animals and in humans, there exists a "socio-bio-social chain" in the effects of testosterone on behavior. When dominance is gained, testosterone levels increase, and the male is, in turn, affected by these hormonal surges in various ways. In other words, the social affects the biological, which in turn affects the social. Kemper described a complicated causal chain that included connections between testosterone, dominance, social structure, sexual behavior, and aggression. Mazur (1983) contended that dominance, not aggression, is the primary motive. Aggression is an avenue for dominance. Therefore, aggression and testosterone may be linked, but only if aggression produces dominance.

Recent research has implicated another endogenous chemical, the neurotransmitter seratonin, in levels of aggression. In contrast to testosterone, which is thought to stimulate aggression, seratonin is thought to inhibit it. This hypothesis comes out of studies that revealed that violent monkeys have low levels of seratonin compared with other monkeys (Rensberger, 1992). This research is very preliminary, and again there is the same question: Are these differences causes, effects, or byproducts of the behavior?

In evaluating the biological bases for male aggression, we return to the conclusion of Money (1987a) and many others that biology does not determine behavior, but it does appear to set thresholds. Possibly because of higher activity levels, hormones, neurotransmitters, or some yet undiscovered biological force, it may take less stimulation to push the average male over the aggression threshold than it does the average female. We turn now to an examination of how these "pushes" are created through socialization and culture.

Psychosocial Perspectives

A variety of male socialization experiences encourages violence. If we look at male gender-role norms, we see the seeds of aggression at every turn. Brannon's (1976) description of the structure of traditional masculinity is useful in understanding male violence:

1. *Antifemininity* ("No Sissy Stuff"): The avoidance of stereotypically feminine behaviors. Women are often viewed as the very antithesis of aggression. They are seen as caring, nurturing, and

vulnerable. The hallmark of the "sissy" (the feminine man, as traditionally defined) is backing down from a fight.

2. *Achievement* ("The Big Wheel"): Success and status. Two factors operate here. First, dominance through aggression is one way of increasing status in some male social groups. Second, the male who does not succeed often suffers from doubts about his masculinity, and violence is both a way of proving to himself that he is a "real man" and a way of venting his anger at having to live up to masculine norms. Poor and oppressed men tend to be more violent than other men. This is not surprising, given that they feel the pressure to be a "big wheel" while at the same time being prevented from many of the avenues for status attainment that privileged men enjoy.

3. *Self-Reliance* ("The Sturdy Oak"): The masculine expectation to be tough and unemotional. In a fight, men try their best. If they are beaten, they "take it like a man."

4. *Aggression* ("Give 'em Hell"): Physical risk taking and violence. These are primary defining features of traditional masculinity.

Despite the fact that aggression is deeply embedded within traditional masculinity, it is important to remember that most men are not violent. Even if there is a biological propensity toward aggression, we should keep in mind that there is also a biological propensity against aggression—the instinct to protect and preserve oneself.

Just as there are biological forces that work against violence and those that work toward it, there are psychosocial forces that work in both directions. Aggression, then, is a behavior that can be either encouraged or inhibited in various ways. We can look at violent men as men who have experienced encouragement and/or a lack of discouragement for aggressive behavior.

This approach should not be construed as absolving men from responsibility for their own behavior. As a man matures, he becomes increasingly capable of providing his own inhibitors and of resisting the encouragement to be violent. Still, a look at how male socialization sets the stage for violence helps us in constructing solutions. Simply put, solutions to male violence involve reducing encouragers and increasing inhibitors. In practice, of course, this is not so easily done.

Violence-Encouraging Factors

1. *Separation.* Chodorow's (1978) analysis of masculine and feminine orientations (discussed in Chapter Four) is useful here. According to this theory, girls' early experiences involve connection and attachment, while boys' experiences involve the construction of a "self in sep-

aration." The more one experiences oneself as being unconnected to another person, the more likely it is that one can tolerate the other's being hurt.

2. *Objectification.* Male privilege and the masculine mystique encourage men to see other people as objects. This is especially true of women and gay men. It is easier to aggress against someone if he or she is not accorded the status of being a real person. Rape, domestic violence, and gay bashing are fueled by this kind of insensitivity.

3. *Externalizing defensive style.* Males are not socialized to "look inside" and think about how they feel. Instead, they are taught to deal with what is "out there" in the world. Therefore, when bad feelings about the self arise, they are sometimes dealt with in an external way. For example, a man's female partner leaves him, and he feels unlovable and worthless. Experiencing himself like this threatens his masculinity, so he projects all of his bad feelings onto the woman and deals with these feelings symbolically by being violent toward her.

4. *Overattention to task.* Men are raised to view the world as competitive and hierarchical (Messner, 1992). They are taught to get the job done regardless of the consequences for others. Bakan (1966) called this orientation *unmitigated agency.* When tasks become more important than people, violence is sometimes a problem solving measure. Examples of this are not hard to find: the football player who intentionally hurts the other team's star player to put him out of the game, the gangster who has his rival killed in order to eliminate the competition, the man who rapes his date in order to "score," and the armed services commander who allows many men to be killed in order to secure a strategic position. War is the intentional sacrifice of human lives in the service of some task. While the rationale for doing so is often that other lives are being saved, women are more likely than men to want to explore nonviolent solutions to problems (Colburn, 1991).

5. *Reinforcement.* Simply, behaviors that are rewarded tend to increase in frequency. More than one boy has returned home from beating up another boy to receive the glowing approval of his father. Classroom aggression by boys often meets with loud reprimands from the teacher. All of the action in the room stops, and all attention (which has a strong social-reward quality) focuses on the boy. Girls' aggression is usually reprimanded more quietly (Maccoby, 1988b). In some circles, especially sports and war, highly aggressive men reap social and material rewards. Culturally, male violence maintains patriarchal privilege through overpowering and intimidation.

6. *Violent models and vicarious reinforcement.* Males may pattern their behavior after violent male models, who are not hard to find. Sons of aggressive fathers tend to become aggressive themselves. When they grow up, they tend to produce aggressive sons of their own (Olweus,

1979; Huesman, Eron, Lefkowitz, & Walder, 1984). Modeling accounts for this intergenerational pattern of violence.

You do not have to be a keen social observer to see that many U.S. media idols are violent. In the movies, actors like Arnold Schwartzenegger, Sylvester Stallone, Charles Bronson, Chuck Norris, and Jean-Claude Van Damme have built incredibly lucrative careers portraying extremely violent characters. The depiction of male violence in sports, cartoons, western and war movies, and "cop shows" is a longstanding tradition of the glorification of masculine aggression. Boys who imitate these characters in their play are engaging in rehearsal for later violence. Toy companies that manufacture toy guns and other play representations of violence encourage such rehearsal.

Bandura and Walters (1963) demonstrated that behaviors were more likely to be acquired from a model if the person observed that the model was rewarded for the behaviors. In movies and television, aggressive men (who engage in what is perceived as "legitimate" violence) get the love of women, the admiration of others, and a feeling of self-righteous satisfaction.

In other research by Bandura (1973), girls and boys were compared with regard to their willingness to imitate an aggressive model. Boys were more likely to do so. However, when the researchers provided rewards for imitating the model, there was no sex differences. It would not be unreasonable to speculate, then, that the higher incidence of male aggression is at least partly the product of the differential reinforcement of aggression for males and females. People are also more likely to imitate models who are perceived as being similar to the self (Bandura & Walters, 1963). It is indisputable that there are vastly more violent male models than female ones.

7. *Drug use.* Some drugs have the effect of reducing the inhibition toward violence. The most notable of these is alcohol. Intoxicated people tend to overestimate threats to the self, to choose aggressive solutions when they are frustrated, and to be more sensitive to social pressure both to increase or to decrease aggression (Gustafson, 1986). Drinking is a cultural symbol of masculinity (Lemle & Mishkind, 1989), and male social groups are almost certainly more likely to encourage aggression compared with female social groups.

8. *Social expectations.* We expect males to be aggressive and we communicate these expectations to young males. The phrase "boys will be boys" captures it well. Sometimes a baby boy who is aggressive will elicit the comment, "He's all boy."

These social-cognitive links between aggression and masculinity carry over into the evaluation of adult men. Miedzian (1991) argues that political leaders are often willing to engage in war in order to affirm masculinity and gain the approval of the populace. Former President

George Bush's popularity rating rose to an all time high during the Persian Gulf War (despite gloomy economic conditions), but then plummeted after the homecoming parades had faded from memory. The bodies of U.S. servicemen killed during the war were quietly buried with little media coverage or government ceremony. As a result, Americans were able to revel in the "glory" of war without experiencing its human tragedy or grieving for loss.

Political observers were quick to note that Bush's reelection would have been a foregone conclusion had the war been "timed better." In the U.S. political system, traditional masculinity is valued in leaders. As Miedzian (1991) put it, "Being compassionate and concerned about human life can cause a man to lose his job" (p. 27).

A great deal of Ronald Reagan's popularity rested on his machismo. He presented an image of being self-assured and unemotional, except for occasional anger. He often threatened other world leaders who crossed him, and he was not afraid to back up his threats with military violence. After being shot in an assassination attempt, Reagan "took it like a man," publicly expressing no fear for his safety. Later, in answering questions about why his wife, Nancy, had consulted astrologers, Reagan explained that she had worried a great deal after he had been shot. He never said that *he* had worried at all. It was clear that Nancy's job was to emote for Ron so that *he* could focus on more masculine concerns.

9. *Low masculine self-esteem.* The man who is unsure of his status or identity is prone toward violence as a compensation for feelings of worthlessness (Toch, 1992). The more powerless a man feels, the more likely he is to make attempts to seize power, thus preserving his masculinity through desperate means. This type of violent man is like the stereotypical schoolyard bully who beats up other kids in order to cover his insecurity and vent his anger toward those who will not love him.

The traditional male gender role emphasizes that a man is valued for what he does, not for who he is. Therefore, many men feel that they must prove their masculinity, to themselves and to others, over and over again. Men who are unsuccessful by traditional social standards, who succeed but feel empty inside, and who are enraged by a sense that they are not valued are more likely to be violent. The diminishment of others draws attention away from feelings of a diminished self. In the "big picture," the relegation of women, gays, poor men, and men of color to a social underclass serves the precarious sense of masculinity in majority men.

Violence-Inhibiting Factors.   Several social forces may have the effect of preventing violence. It is, therefore, important to look at these factors in the context of masculine socialization.

1. *Empathy.* Some of the foremost inhibitors of aggression are the abilities to be sensitive to, identify with, and be concerned about the pain

of the potential victim. Girls are often socialized to think about how other people feel and to be connected to others. For example, playing with dolls is a rehearsal for being attuned to another's needs and caring for that person.

Culturally, there seems to be less concern for building these violence-inhibiting qualities in boys. To begin with, boys are socialized away from the emotional life. It is nearly impossible to understand and experience someone else's emotions when an individual does not understand his or her own. The masculine emphasis on competition and task completion does not emphasize the consideration of others. In team sports, players often feel for and protect their teammates, but it is a byproduct of the task of winning, which is always defined as the most important outcome.

2. *Modeling.* Just as aggressive models can be imitated, control of aggression can also be imitated. It is vital for fathers to model this control for their sons. Many fathers do. Boys from father-absent families tend to be more aggressive (Hetherington, Cox, & Cox, 1985), perhaps partly because of their decreased exposure to a model of aggression control.

3. *Punishment.* Behaviors that are punished tend to decrease in frequency. Appropriate and consistent punishment of aggression clearly communicates that this type of behavior is unacceptable. In some social systems, this is done well.

4. *Social and political systems.* Increasingly, people are speaking out against the institutional violence of war. Educational efforts have been launched to sensitize people to the effects of various forms of violence (see Box 12.1).

5. *Therapeutic interventions.* Individual men who have problems with control of violent behaviors can learn how to inhibit explosive urges through a variety of techniques.

The elimination of male violence involves reducing the needs and incentives for this kind of behavior and providing alternative ways for dealing with the feelings that precede the aggression (Toch, 1992). Violence is deeply ingrained in the traditional male gender role and in the culture. Therefore, efforts in this direction must cover a broad range of settings, including parenting practices, education, the legal system, politics, and therapeutic settings. Since violence is so much a part of the male gender role, the very fabric of masculinity must change if violence is to be reduced.

Domestic Violence

Sad to say, perhaps the most frequent site of male violence is the home. Estimates of at least mild physical violence taking place between partners

---

Box 12.1
The White Ribbon Campaign

For a week in December 1991, tens of thousands of Canadian men wore small white ribbons pinned to their clothing. The occasion was the anniversary of the 1990 "Montreal Massacre," when Mark Lepine murdered 14 women at the University of Montreal before committing suicide. The White Ribbon Campaign was an effort to get men to show their support for ending men's violence against women. It was the first large-scale initiative ever developed by men to speak out on a subject usually considered to be a "women's issue."

Supporters of the campaign distributed the ribbons at schools, churches, shops, and places of employment. The prime minister, several celebrities, and some corporate heads were among the men who participated. As the campaign became highly visible, men's violence against women became a subject for publicity, discussion, and debate. Many men across Canada were talking seriously about the problem for the first time.

One of the goals of the campaign organizers was to break the silence on the issue. In that regard, the effort was an unqualified success. A larger goal is to build a permanent national men's anti-violence organization. That effort is now well underway.

The White Ribbon Campaign is significant in that it is a grassroots movement by men in the direction of dealing with a central men's social issue. It provides a stimulus for men to begin to understand the impact of gender socialization and sexist culture on their lives.

Source: Sluser & Kaufman (1992).

---

range as high as 60% for married couples (Pagelow, 1984) and 22 to 28% for people in dating relationships (Makepeace, 1981; Thompson, 1990).

Surprisingly, some research indicates that women use physical violence against their partners as much as or even more than men (Thompson, 1990; O'Leary, Barling, Arias, Rosenbaum, Malone, & Tyree, 1989; Straus & Gelles, 1986). However, women's aggression usually results in less fear (O'Leary & Curley, 1986) and less physical damage (Berk, Berk, Loseke, & Rauma, 1983) than men's domestic violence. Therefore, while female domestic physical aggression is common and should not be ignored, it is male aggression that engenders the highest levels of control, intimidation, and danger. Former U.S. Surgeon General C. Everett Koop described domestic violence as the number-one health problem for women (Hoffman, 1992).

Men's violence in the home has a long history. For many years, a man's exercising his authority over his family via physical abuse was accepted and tolerated (MacLeod, 1980). The patriarchal tradition of woman as property allowed the man to do whatever he wanted with his wife. This tradition has yet to die, as evidenced by the size of the populations in battered women's shelters and the need for more such facilities.

Research into the characteristics of male batterers reveals that, in general, they tend to be overconforming to the traditional gender role and the masculine culture of violence (Gondolf, 1988). They have a high need for power (Mason & Blankenship, 1987) and control and tend to blame their partners for their own violent behavior (Lips, 1988). Thus, they tend to think that they beat their wives, not because they have trouble controlling their tempers or feel threatened by their partners' independence, but because their wives behaved wrongly or "don't know how to listen." Blaming the victim allows men to abdicate responsibility for and downplay the impact of their violent behavior.

Male batterers also tend to have low self-esteem (Gondolf & Hanneken, 1987) and low socioeconomic status (Sugarman & Hotaling, 1989). These data support the hypothesis that violence is a compensatory measure for feelings of masculine failure (Gondolf, 1988). It is also true that low socioeconomic status involves higher levels of life stress, fewer resources to cope with that stress, and sometimes a more exaggerated subculture of violence (Sugarman & Hotaling, 1989).

One of the most striking (but not surprising) risk markers of male domestic violence is the presence of a physically aggressive father in the family of origin. Sugarman and Hotaling (1989) described the following childhood experience of the typical male batterer: "Essentially, the individual not only witnessed his father physically aggress against his mother and be reinforced for this behavior (the individual's mother gave in to the father's demands), but his own violent behavior goes unpunished and is reinforced by his partner's surrendering to his will" (p. 1035).

In summary, male batterers tend to be angry, hypermasculine, and disenfranchised men who often see male domestic violence as natural and normal. They also have learned that engaging in this kind of behavior gets them what they want: dominance, power, control, and a vent for their anger.

Toward Solutions

The reduction of such a widespread problem as domestic violence would seem to require a comprehensive, coordinated effort. The city of Duluth, Minnesota, launched such a program in 1982. It involved the establishment of a woman's shelter, stricter criminal penalties for spousal assault, and mandatory participation in rehabilitation programs for offenders. Police officers who have probable cause that an assault has taken place are required to make an arrest (Hoffman, 1992). Seminars, training, and resource materials are offered for prosecutors, human services providers, community leaders, and educators (Duluth Domestic Abuse Intervention Project, undated).

The Duluth project has met with some degree of success, particularly in the citywide reduction of domestic homicide, and it has been used as a model in many other cities. At the same time, recidivism in offenders is high (about 40%), and even the director of the program doubts that it has a strong deterrent effect on men as they consider engaging in violence (Hoffman, 1992). Gondolf (1988) noted that a substantial proportion of battering men, perhaps nearly half, have antisocial personality tendencies or full-blown sociopathic disorders. These men do not respond well to the kind of self-control treatment approaches that batterer programs often use. Unfortunately, many do not respond at all to any psychological interventions, and these men must be controlled through the legal system.

Many male batterers, however, are treatable, and a number of strategies for intervention have emerged in recent years. Among these are anger-control therapies, social skills training, therapy groups, and educational programs. The goals of these programs are to sensitize men to the personal and interpersonal consequences of their violence and to teach them ways of changing their thinking, emotional responses, and behaviors in conflict situations.

Rape

Rape is sexual penetration without consent. It is a violent crime that is alarmingly common. Large-scale research studies have revealed that about one in four women in the United States is the victim of actual or attempted rape at some point in her lifetime (Russell & Howell, 1983; Koss, Gidycz, & Wisniewski, 1987; Koss, 1983).

Some men are also victims of rape. It is estimated that 1 in 10,000 men is a victim of rape or attempted rape in the U.S. general population every year (Struckman-Johnson, 1991) and the incidence of a prison rape is much higher (Lockwood, 1980). In one large-scale survey, a startling 7.2% of men reported that they had experienced pressured or forced sexual contact at least once in their adult lives (Sorenson, Stein, Siegel, Golding, & Burnam, 1987). Contrary to popular belief, these experiences are usually traumatic, even if they involve heterosexual men being assaulted by women (Struckman-Johnson & Struckman-Johnson, 1992).

The stereotypical rapist is the evil stranger that lurks in the bushes, but, in fact, more than three-quarters of rapes occur in cases where the victim knows the attacker (Harney & Muehlenhard, 1991; Parrot & Bechofer, 1991). These *acquaintance rapes* have been the subject of increased research and publicity within the past 10 to 15 years. Acquaintance rape occurs at incredibly high rates on college campuses. Koss (1990) estimated that about 50 out of every 1,000 college women are victims of rape or attempted rape in any given year!

One common misconception about rape is that it is primarily motivated by sexuality. For some people, the image of the rapist is one of a lusty, sex-starved man whose frustrated urges get the best of him. However, most experts believe that the primary motivation for rape is not sexual, but aggressive (Groth, 1979; Brownmiller, 1975; Burt, 1991). Rape is the use of sex in the expression of power, control, anger, and hate. Groth (1979) referred to rape as a "pseudosexual act." In describing the relationship between rape and sex, one (unknown) speaker (quoted by Hawks, 1986) put it this way: "If I hit you over the head with a rolling pin, would you call it cooking?"

Rape and Masculinity

Sexual aggression is part and parcel of the socialization of males. In the search for an understanding of why men rape, it is useful to identify the rape-supporting cultural messages that boys receive as they grow up:

1. *Femiphobia and misogyny.* Males are raised to be separate from women and the feminine in themselves. The result is a fear of femininity. One way of dealing with this fear is to overpower and control the woman. From this perspective, derogatory nicknames, misogynist jokes, and other behaviors that disrespect women create the social atmosphere that encourages rape. Many feminist theorists believe that rape is a symptom of economic and political systems in which women have been rendered relatively powerless by men (Ellis, 1989). U.S. culture encourages men to dominate women, and victimizing a woman with something so emotional and intimate as sexuality is extreme domination. Sexual aggression in men is related to stereotyped views of gender roles, among them the belief that women and men are sexual adversaries (Hall, 1990).

2. *Emotional denial.* As with any violence, rape is a failure of empathy. The socialized inability to be sensitive to one's own feelings makes it difficult to be sensitive to the feelings of another person.

3. *The two exceptions to emotional control.* While men are raised to deny and control emotions, the expression of anger and sexual feelings is socially condoned. These two emotions, interestingly, are considered to be out of the man's control. It is not unusual to hear that a "man's gotta do what a man's gotta do" when he gets angry, that a "man's gotta have it" sexually, and that an erect penis "has no conscience."

With anger and sexuality being the only two permissible emotions, it is not surprising that they can become combined. In fact, probably the most frequently used slang term for intercourse (*fuck*) is also one of the most frequently used terms for victimization. Violence is sexualized time and time again in movies, television shows, and literature such as detective magazines.

Western culture encourages men to act out emotion rather than deal with it in other ways (Leong, 1986). This may be a partial explanation for the striking difference between East and West in the incidence of rape and other violent crimes (Sue, Bernier, Durran, Feinberg, Pedersen, Smith, & Vasquez-Nattall, 1982).

4. *The "rape myth".* Many men believe that women secretly want to be raped and "ask for it" by dressing or acting provocatively or by putting themselves in rape situations (Burt, 1980). Male undergraduates who viewed films depicting the rape myth were more likely to subscribe to the myth, less likely to identify with the victim, and less likely to agree that the rapist deserves punishment (Briere & Malamuth, 1983; Koss, Leonard, Beezley, & Oros, 1985; Malamuth, 1981). One out of eight Hollywood movies depicts at least one scene with a rape theme in it (Gelman, Springen, Elam, Joseph, Robins, & Hagar (1990). One need not see an actual rape depicted in a movie to accept the rape myth. The sexual domination of the woman, followed by her giving in and becoming aroused, conveys the same message in milder form. In a typical scene, a leading man forcefully kisses an unwilling woman, who then "melts into his arms" and falls in love with him.

There is some question as to whether pornography also encourages violence toward women (See Box 12.2).

5. *Performance and quantification over experience.* U.S. culture emphasizes that a man's worth is measured by deeds and results, not by his emotional satisfaction or feelings about the self. We also tend to judge people by quantity ("more is better"). In the sexual arena, this attitude is played out by the encouragement of men to have intercourse with as many women as possible. *Stud* and *playboy* are complimentary terms, and the "macho mentality" values the man who "goes after what he wants" and "won't take no for an answer."

6. *Poor sexual communication.* One of the questions that Biernbaum and Weinberg (1991) ask men in their campus rape prevention workshops is, "How do you know when your friend wants to kiss on a date?" Most men respond, "It's in her eyes . . . she leans toward me and I lean toward her. . . . It's in the air. . . . I just know. . . . Body language" (p. 22). Few men say, "I ask her," or "I tell her I would like to kiss her and see how she responds."

It is a peculiar part of U.S. culture that engaging in sex is viewed as

Box 12.2
The Question of Pornography

Does pornography cause men to become violent toward women? This question tends to produce strong responses from both sides of the issue. Until the 1960s, few studies examined the effects of pornography on behavior (Walsh, 1987). The report of the U.S. government-sponsored Commission on Obscenity and Pornography (1970) concluded that there was no evidence that pornography is linked to sex crimes. However, a subsequent government-sponsored commission reached the conclusion that violent pornography is causally related to violence against women (Attorney General's Commission on Pornography, 1986). Social scientists have challenged the conclusions of both of these commissions (Walsh, 1987).

One of the difficulties in evaluating the effects of pornography is terminology. When the U.S. Supreme court first considered legal challenges to explicit erotic material, it had a serious problem with constructing the definition of *obscenity.* This difficulty prompted Justice Potter Stewart to say that, "I can't define it, but I know it when I see it" (quoted in Green, 1987, p. 437).

The definition of pornography is a critical factor in research. Explicit photographs and films can depict clothed people in provocative pose and situation, nudity, sensual sexual activity, the dominance of one sex over the other, or the violence and degradation of a person in a sexual situation. In the latter two types of material, it is nearly always women who are depicted as being dominated, objectified, and raped.

Opponents of the pornography-violence hypothesis often cite cross-cultural research that shows a decrease (or lack of increase) in sex crimes in countries such as Denmark and the former West Germany after pornography was legalized. Still, these are correlational data. Two events occurring together does not mean that one has caused the other. Theorists on this side of the issue also point out that violent pornography and depictions of consensual sex (often referred to as *erotica*) produce different effects on viewers (Green, 1987).

On the other side are theorists like Brownmiller (1975), who argued that erotica is degrading by its very nature and that it creates a social climate for the tolerance of sexual assault. MacKinnon (1985) stated that pornography "eroticizes hierarchy, . . . sexualizes inequality . . . institutionalizes the sexuality of male supremacy, fusing the eroticization of dominance and submission with the social construction of male and female" (p. 1).

Some researchers have focused their investigations of erotic material on that which is aggressive in content, and there is evidence to support the hypothesis that violent pornography may have a link to sexual violence. Malamuth and Check (1981) demonstrated that male research subjects who viewed sexually violent films became increasingly accepting of sexual violence against women. More specifically, male subjects who viewed scenes depicting the "rape myth" (that the victim becomes sexually aroused during the rape) tend to respond with increased acceptance of this myth, increased self-reported likelihood of raping (Malamuth, 1981), and increased likelihood of suggesting that rapists should get light prison sentences (Zillmann & Bryant, 1982). Laboratory research by Donnerstein (1983, 1984) demonstrated an increase in men's willingness to aggress against a female after viewing aggressive sexual material.

Thus, the sexualization of violence does seem to have some effect in the direction of producing more callous attitudes toward women's feelings. Donnerstein and Linz (1986) opined that "aggressive images are the issue, not sexual images" (p. 601). They argued that nonpornographic sexualized violence, such as that found in "slasher" films, detective magazines, and many movies, has more of an effect on sexual (and other) violence than does the kind of material one would buy in an "adults only" store (Linz & Donnerstein, 1992).

While nonviolent erotica probably has no direct link to violence against women, there is some evidence that it may have a damaging effect on relationships between men and women. Male research subjects who viewed *Playboy* and *Penthouse* centerfolds tended to give lower ratings of their female partners' attractiveness and individual worth (Malamuth, 1984). Moreover, they reported being less in love with their partners than men who did not view these pictures (Kenrick, Gutierres, & Goldberg, 1989).

"Men's magazines," like these are certainly guilty of the sexual objectification of women. As the preceding evidence suggests, men who view the physical "perfection" (enhanced with lighting and photograph retouching) of these magazine models seem to make comparisons of centerfolds with other women. The fact that they report being less in love reveals that erotica reinforces the patriarchal notion that relationships between men and women depend on the woman's sexual desirability.

Farrell (1986) pointed out that the parallel to these erotic magazines is the "romance novel." Over 98% of these are purchased by women. In these novels, male protagonists are portrayed as powerful, handsome, wealthy, brave, and adventurous. Farrell called these men the "centerfolds" of romance novels, which he considers "women's pornography." Thus, while erotic men's magazines reinforce the limiting aspects of the traditional female gender role, romance novels reinforce the unreasonable demands of the male gender role.

The unequal power between the sexes and the reality of rape make the romance novel less of a concern than erotic men's magazines or, especially, violent pornography. Still, objectification in any form is dehumanizing.

Is pornography harmful? Although, as we have seen, there are some answers, there are probably more questions. The controversy continues, as does the research into this important area.

---

acceptable, but talking about it is not. It is probably rare for two people, especially if they are young, to actually discuss sex before engaging in it. This leaves open a potential for miscommunication. The man who misreads or ignores the woman's signals may be more likely to commit acquaintance rape. Even if the woman verbally refuses intercourse, the man may rape her if he subscribes to the rape myth, thinking that she really wants to have sex and just needs to be forced a little.

7. *Homophobia.* Men see "scoring" as a way of proving to themselves and others that they are not homosexual. Rape may be a desperate way for men who are sexually unsuccessful to affirm their heterosexuality.

Rapist Characteristics

Rape-encouraging attitudes and socialization experiences are rather common and pervasive, yet it is clear that all men do not rape. Recent research and theory have sought to describe the psychology of the rapist. Although rapists are not all alike, some typical characteristics are associated with rape.

Groth (1979) described three basic patterns in incarcerated rapists. The most common one was *power rape,* in which the rapist's major motive seems to be to conquer and control the victim. The power rapist's main goal is to possess the person sexually. Intercourse is taken as evidence of conquest, and the rapist uses whatever force he thinks is necessary to subdue the victim.

For the power rapist, sex is used to compensate for "underlying feelings of inadequacy and serves to express issues of mastery, strength, control, identity, and capability (Groth, 1979, p. 25). In other words, the rapist makes a desperate attempt to prove his masculinity. He is desperate because his underlying feelings are so painful and because he has no emotional resources to use in dealing with his pain. About 55% of convicted offenders are judged to be primarily motivated by power.

The second most common pattern is the *anger rape*, which comprises about 40% of imprisoned rapists. The anger rapist's primary objective is to harm the victim. Sex is his weapon, and he typically uses more force than he needs to overpower the victim. He typically includes verbal abuse in his attack, as he wants to make the victim feel as badly as possible, both psychologically and physically. Typically, the anger rapist feels that he has been wronged and hurt by women. Rape is his revenge and the discharge of his anger. Any woman is a symbol of the source of his pain.

Like the power rapist, the anger rapist is not usually sexually aroused at the time of the attack, nor does he derive much sexual pleasure from his crime. Often, he does not achieve an erection without masturbating or forcing the victim into oral sex. Many anger rapists do not have orgasms during the assault, and some even have trouble identifying whether or not they have ejaculated.

The least frequent pattern is the *sadistic rape*, in which power and violence are eroticized. For this type (about 5% of incarcerated rapists), sexual gratification comes from hurting another person. The sexual motive is more connected to the assault for the sadistic rapist, unlike the other two patterns. Similar to the others, however, are underlying feelings of masculine inadequacy.

Groth's study described men who had been arrested, convicted, and imprisoned as a result of having raped. However, as we have seen, these are a very small minority of rapists. It remains to be seen whether or not unincarcerated rapists are different from convicted rapists in significant ways.

Lisak and Roth (1988) compared questionnaire responses of college men who reported having engaged in sexually aggressive behavior to those who reported that they had not. The sexually aggressive men were more likely to perceive themselves as having been hurt, betrayed, or dominated by women. They were highly sensitive to being teased or manipulated by women, and they often experienced angry feelings in connection with interactions with women. The researchers' conclusion was that the motivations for college men's sexual aggression are similar to those of incarcerated rapists.

As we paint the picture of the rapist as an insecure, hypermasculine man, it seems important to search for the origins of masculine inadequacy in the sexual aggressor. Lisak (1991) collected data from psychological measures and conducted in-depth interviews with 15 men who admitted to acquaintance rape and 15 control subjects in a college population. Although this was neither a large nor a representative sample of the population of men, this study does provide some important clues to the origins of rape.

These data confirm what we have already described. The rapists scored significantly higher than the nonrapists on "standardized measures of hostility toward women, underlying anger motivation, dominance as a motive for sexual interactions, underlying power motivation, and on two indices of hypermasculinity" (Lisak, 1991, p. 248). Hypermasculinity has been found to be related to callous sexual attitudes and misogyny in other studies (see Mosher & Tomkins, 1988; Archer & Rhodes, 1989; Smeaton & Byrne, 1987; Mosher & Anderson, 1986).

In Lisak's (1991) interviews, the most striking finding was that the rapists almost invariably expressed bitter feelings and clear disappointments toward their fathers. They described their fathers as distant, both emotionally and physically. Some of the rapists reported having suffered significant physical violence at the hands of their fathers. While the nonrapists also reported having wanted to be closer to their fathers, the underlying bitter feelings were not there, and they made positive statements about their fathers much more often than the rapists.

The impression carried away from these interview data is that many men feel loved and affirmed by their fathers, but that some feel unvalued. These men, who have not been accepted by the most important male figure in their lives, are most likely to strike out at women.

Without an internal sense of positive masculinity, these men are more likely to be drawn into and contribute to hypermasculine peer groups that are aggressive and misogynist (Koss & Dinero, 1988). They use these groups to protect themselves from their insecurities by identifying with the group and viewing women as an underclass. The street gang is the most common of these in the inner city. It has been argued that fraternities (Sanday, 1990) and athletic teams (O'Sullivan, 1991) serve this function on college campuses. The sense of some college athletes that they are somehow privileged contributes to the atmosphere of victimization, and male college athletes tend to have more traditional gender-role attitudes than nonathletes (Houseworth, Peplow, & Thirer, 1989). The most extreme example of sexual violence in negative cultures of masculinity is the gang rape. Fraternities and athletic teams are disproportionately involved in these crimes (O'Sullivan, 1991).

Sexual violence in the context of hypermasculinity is also thought to be related to patriarchal culture. Whiting (1965) argued that the internal sense of masculinity is only necessary when the culture demands that men be different, more important, and more powerful than women. When the man feels powerless, he denigrates and attacks women in an attempt to affirm this cultural definition of masculinity, an act that Whiting labeled *masculine protest*.

Thus viewed, rape is an extreme compensatory reaction to the gender-role strain created by patriarchy. There would be no motivation to rape if men did not feel the need to prove themselves superior by virtue of being men. Sanday (1981) reports that rape is virtually nonexistent in 44 nonpatriarchal societies.

Toward Solutions

The reduction of rape can involve a variety of strategies, including those that thwart the attempted rapist, prevent the rapist from committing repeated crimes, prevent potential rapists from ever committing the crime, and change the rape-supportive aspects of the culture. These varied interventions may involve legal, educational, family, community, therapeutic, and political systems. To describe all of the possibilities would require several volumes, but we can outline some ideas here.

Preventing a rapist from committing repeated crimes is a matter of vigorous legal enforcement and rehabilitative interventions. Watts and Courtois (1981) described a number of treatment programs that involved facilitating the rapist's acceptance of responsibility for the crime, building the criminal's empathy for the victim, developing social skills, decreasing sexual arousal to rape, and chemotherapy. These programs are only available to a small percentage of incarcerated rapists, who in turn are a small percentage of the total population of rapists.

Attempts to thwart the potential rapist have historically taken the forms of rendering environments less conducive to rape and of educating potential victims. Lighting dark areas, police patrols, and teaching self-defense skills are strategies in this area. On some college campuses, escort services, danger-avoidance education (i.e, don't walk alone at night, make sure windows and doors are locked), alcohol rules, and fraternity policies have been used.

When these kinds of strategies are the sole interventions, there are implicit assumptions that men will rape if given the chance, that there is little we can do to stop them, and that, therefore, we must deal with the problem largely by helping potential victims and environments to be prepared. Corcoran (1992) describes these approaches as "victim-control" strategies. She argues that they subtly place the responsibility for rape prevention on women.

While there is no argument that safety measures can and should be implemented, it is not enough. Broader rape-prevention efforts involve changing the behaviors and underlying motivations of men. Surprisingly, rape-prevention services for men are a relatively recent development.

Men Stopping Rape (MSR), a national coalition of men's groups, was formed in Madison, Wisconsin, in 1983. MSR chapters provide antirape educational resources, publicize the problem, and participate in political action toward their goal of increasing the awareness of rape as a men's problem. This effort is supportive of men's attempts to understand and mitigate the negative effects of their gender socialization and the rape-tolerant aspects of the culture. The Men's Anti-Rape Resource Center (MARC) is a recent effort to provide and coordinate similar services nationwide.

The alarming estimates of the incidence of acquaintance rape at colleges and universities have stimulated a number of programmatic efforts to decrease violence against women. Services designed specifically for men include rape-awareness programs (Rozee, Batemen, & Gilmore, 1991; Roark, 1987), experiential workshops (Lee, 1987; Ring & Kilmartin, 1991), and fraternity workshops (Kilmartin & Ring, 1991). Other programs offer victim services, rape education for women and coed groups, alcohol and judicial policies, and faculty and staff training (Parrot, 1991).

Some programs are "one-shot" or annual events; others are ongoing, comprehensive, institutional efforts. Fassinger (quoted in Moses, 1991) notes that the latter are, of course, preferable. A model ongoing program for men has been in place for several years at The Ohio State University (Stevens & Gebhardt, 1984).

The goals of all of these rape-prevention efforts include sensitizing men to the negative consequences of sexual violence for the perpetrator, facilitating empathy for victims of sexual assault, and educating men about the rape-encouraging aspects of socialization culture, and patriarchy. Parrot (1991) points out that a major goal is to effect an understanding of the continuum of sexual violence against women. Sexist behavior, objectification, and exploitation of women have the effect of desensitizing men to the seriousness and deep pain of sexual assault.

Rape-prevention efforts have only recently begun to address the broader societal issues around rape. It is obvious that the rapist causes a great deal of pain for the victim. The awareness that the rapist is also in pain himself needs to be addressed as well. If the pain can be alleviated, or the potential rapist can learn to deal with his pain in a different way, then sexual assault should decrease. Thus, efforts to help men understand themselves as gendered beings, to facilitate the improvement of positive relationship skills, and to support attempts for men to change the destructive aspects of masculinity are positive steps. We need to address rape specifically as one of these aspects, but the overall effort of men's gender awareness and change also contributes to dealing with the problem of sexual assault.

Summary

1. Men commit a vast majority of violent crimes, and this fact leads researchers to investigate the origins of violence and the connections between aggression and masculinity.

2. Sociobiologists view male aggression as an evolutionary strategy for propagating one's genes, yet aggression is not always associated with an increase in breeding access, even in animal species.

3. Another possible biological link is the hormone testosterone. While it may set the stage for aggression, implicating testosterone as the cause of male violence ignores the complexity of human behavior and the powerful influence of psychosocial forces.

4. Socioculturally, aggression is a defining feature of the male gender role. A number of factors encourage aggression in men, including the privilege of patriarchy, a socialized external defensive style, unmitigated attention to task, violent modeling, and rewards for aggressing. Violence-inhibiting factors such as empathy, nonaggressive modeling, and consistent punishment for aggression are less socialized into males than females. Male violence is thought by many to be a compensation for the inadequate feelings that sometimes result from male gender-role strain.

5. Men who are violent in the home often show this compensatory pattern. They have exaggerated needs for power and control, as well as the externalizing style of blaming their partners for their own negative feelings and behaviors. Domestic violence often follows an intergenerational pattern against the backdrop of a patriarchal system that tolerates violence against women and even children. A number of interventions are focused on legal, therapeutic, and educational systems.

6. Research and debate about rape has increased dramatically during the past two decades. Most people are alarmed to hear how commonplace this crime is. Many researchers believe that rape is fueled by aggressive, not sexual motivations. The social construction of masculinity, with its emphasis on misogyny, sexual promiscuity, performance, and homophobia, makes for a rape-tolerant social climate.

7. As with other violent behaviors, rape is perpetrated by men who are desperately attempting to compensate for feelings of masculine inadequacy through hypermasculine displays of dominance, anger, and control. For many acquaintance rapists, low masculine self-esteem may be related to poor relationships with (emotionally and/or physically) distant or abusive fathers. Some theorists believe, however, that fathering would not be such a crucial factor if gender roles were more egalitarian and males were not expected to go to such extreme lengths to prove their worth as men.

8. Interventions for decreasing rape include more vigorous enforcement, rehabilitative efforts, safety measures, and the education of potential victims. However, rape is a men's issue and men need to address it. Recent interventions include a focus on potential perpetrators, espe-

cially in college populations, where acquaintance rape is rampant. Men who can understand, at a deep level, the negative consequences of rape, the origins of male violence, the pain of victims, and the continuum of violence against women will be less likely to rape. Positive changes in the male gender role should have a positive impact on rape prevention.

Gary Walts/The Image Works

CHAPTER THIRTEEN

No Man Is an Island:
Men in Relationships with Others

Independence is a central demand of the male gender role. Rather, it might be more accurate to say that the *appearance* of independence is demanded. As members of a variety of social systems, men depend on others for information, resources, and human contact. It is difficult, if not impossible, for a "loner" to be productive or psychologically healthy.

From our earliest childhood interactions, we develop styles of relating to others. A large volume of research indicates that males and females tend to evolve rather distinctive interactional patterns. Describing the effects of these styles on men's relationships with others is the task of this chapter.

Male Social Development

The brilliant developmental psychologist Eleanor Maccoby (1990) has described distinct, sex-typed interactional patterns that emerge early in life. Maccoby contends that these are largely a function of children's preferences for same-sex interaction. By the age of 6½, children spend 11 times more of their time with same-sex than with other-sex children. Children play in sex-integrated groups when adults force them to do so, but return to sex-segregated groups when the adults withdraw (Maccoby, 1988b). This segregation is not limited to sex-typed activities such as playing with dolls or trucks. It also occurs in sex-neutral activities (Maccoby, 1990) such as drawing or playing with clay.

Finding themselves frequently in the company of male peers, boys develop a way of relating to others that is distinctly male. This style involves an orientation toward dominance, competition, and rough-and-tumble play (Humphreys & Smith, 1987). Boys also tend to play in larger, less intimate (Maccoby, 1990), and more publicly visible groups (Thorne & Luria, 1986).

In these all-male groups, we see boys interrupting each other, bragging, telling stories, ridiculing others, and using commands much more frequently than we see these behaviors in girls (Maltz & Borker, 1983). Girls' conversation involves more requests rather than demands, expressions of interest in others, and a general communication of a desire to sustain the relationship. Whereas girls' conversations are more of a give-and-take interaction, boys conversations are more like taking turns, with one boy telling a story, followed by another boy (who often tries to "top" the first boy's story). Maccoby's (1990) view is that, while typical female speech serves the dual purpose of collaboration and self-assertion, typical male conversation is more singularly self-assertive.

These manners of relating to others continue into adulthood (Tannen, 1990). Since interpersonal interactions serve to form and maintain relationships, men's long-established pattern of communication colors the character of their social ties with women, children, and other men.

One of the Boys: Male-Male Friendships

Typically, boys and men have more friends than girls and women. However, women's friendships are characterized by deeper levels of intimacy (Sharabany, Gershoni, & Hofman, 1981). While women often talk about how they feel about their experiences, men's focus is usually on the sharing of activities (Aries & Johnson, 1983; Farr, 1988).

It is sometimes said that men have many "buddies" but few true friends. Buddies are people you do things with; friends are people with whom you are intimate. The formation of warm feelings between men is many times the result of an indirect process of spending time in a mutual pursuit or interest (sometimes referred to as *male bonding*), as opposed to a more direct process of emotional self-disclosure. The expression of closeness between men often takes the form of continuing to spend time with each other and helping each other with tasks, rather than more direct expressions such as touching or saying "I like you," "I'm glad you're my friend," or "I feel close to you."

Men often lack the more collaborative relationship skills that are helpful in the formation of deeper friendships, yet they usually have a desire to be emotionally close to other men. Social structures such as tasks and rituals enable men to affiliate with one another in cooperative ways. For example, men on athletic teams or men who work together often form close ties with one another. Maccoby (1990) argues that males usually need the structure that these settings provide in order to feel comfortable with others. On the other hand, women usually require less structure because they are more readily adaptable to affiliation for its own sake. This social-structure hypothesis provides a partial explanation for the almost religious character of athletics in the lives of many men. Being involved as a sports participant or fan serves to give men something to talk about and do together. These activities mitigate the isolation that comes from hiding oneself behind a façade of masculinity. Still, men tend to experience more loneliness than women, probably because they experience lower levels of social support (Stokes & Levin, 1986).

Several aspects of the masculine gender role inhibit the formation of intimate relationships between male friends. The orientation toward competition and task completion is one. Males are socialized to believe that other men are their competitors. The establishment of intimacy rests partly on revealing one's weakness and vulnerabilities to another (Jourard, 1971). It is not wise to reveal these to a perceived competitor, who might well exploit the weakness. This would be like telling your opponent before a tennis match that your backhand is not very good. Men who feel competitive with other men tend to have friendships that are inhibited by an undercurrent of distrust. Adolescent boys tend to trust their friends less than do girls (Berndt, 1992).

The gender-role demand for independence also inhibits self-disclosure. A "real man" is expected to solve his problems on his own. If he is hurt, he must "take it like a man." The expectations for hyperindependence and pain tolerance result in the devaluing of men who reveal weaknesses or ask for help. Derlega and Chaikin (1976) asked research subjects to read stories about someone who was troubled by a personal problem. They varied the sex of the person in the story as well as the level of intimacy in this person's disclosure. Research subjects rated men who disclosed at a high level as less mentally healthy than men who did not disclose. The opposite judgment was made for women.

Thus, men may face negative social consequences for revealing themselves, yet disclosing oneself to others is a human need (Jourard, 1971). Men who place a high value on traditional masculinity tend to avoid self-disclosure (Winstead, Derlega, & Wong, 1984). When a problem arises, they tend to rely solely on their own resources, even when other people are available and willing to help. The familiar situation in which a man who is on a trip gets lost, but refuses to ask for directions, is a good illustration of how some men solve problems inefficiently in order to protect a fragile sense of masculinity.

Homophobia is perhaps the greatest barrier to friendships between men. Because men frequently have difficulty making a clear distinction between sexual and nonsexual intimacy, getting close to another man may feel similar to being sexual with him. The powerful antifemininity demand of the male gender role then rears its ugly head and near panic sets in. In order to avoid the discomfort of this anxiety, men often keep other men at arm's length, both physically and psychologically. The friendships of highly.homophobic men are significantly less intimate than those of other men (Devlin & Cowan, 1985).

The handshake is symbolic of men's ambivalence around being close to one another. One scholar (Petrie, 1986) asserts that the handshake began as a way of showing the other man that you did not have your hand on a weapon! Young boys whose fathers refuse to kiss, hug, cuddle them, or tell them that they are loved are deprived of the important human needs for touching and valuing. In addition, these fathers model unaffectionate behavior as a distinctive feature of masculinity. As a result, these boys may well grow up to be distant fathers to their own sons.

According to Thorne and Luria (1986), boys in the United States begin to use homophobic labels such as "queer" or "fag" by the fourth grade. These labels are terms of insult for low-status boys, thus they serve to highlight and maintain a masculine hierarchy. Thorne and Luria theorized about the impact of homophobic labeling on boys' physical contact:

> As "fag" talk increases, relaxed and cuddling patterns of touch decrease among boys. Kindergarten and first-grade boys touch one another frequently and with ease, with arms around shoulders, hugs, and holding hands. By fifth grade, touch among boys becomes more constrained, gradually shifting to mock violence and the use of poking, shoving, and ritual gestures like "giving five" (flat hand slaps) to express bonding. (p. 182)

Thus, boys appear to have a strong desire to maintain interpersonal contact with other boys, but the threat of homophobic labeling forces this contact to become highly ritualized and sometimes aggressive.

The desire for true intimate contact with other males sometimes leads men to fight against years of socialization. Male bonding may be a suitable substitute for deeper connections when a man is still young, but there is sometimes a feeling that something important is missing when men reach their 30s and beyond. It is a difficult task to make a friend when one has a decades-long history of entrenched buddyship patterns. Box 13.1 describes techniques for doing so.

"Cross-Cultural" Interactions: Men with Women

As we have already discussed, children spend inordinate amounts of time in same-sex groups, and male and female groups have different interpersonal styles. All-male and all-female groups could be considered gender cultures. When a person interacts with a person of the other sex,

---

Box 13.1
Guerrilla Tactics for Making a Friend

Letich (1991) makes some excellent, step-by-step suggestions for working on deeper friendships:

1. First, you have to want it. Breaking patterns not only cause anxiety, it is hard work. "You have to remind yourself that there's nothing weird or effeminate about wanting a friend" (p. 87).
2. Identify a possible friend. Seek someone who seems to want to question the values of traditional masculinity.
3. Be sneaky. Get involved in a comfortable, nonpressured activity. Get used to spending time with this man.
4. Invite him to stop for a beer or a cup of coffee. Try to make honest, personal conversation at these times.
5. Call just to get together.
6. Sit down and talk about your friendship.

Letich calls these suggestions "guerrilla tactics" because they seem extreme and difficult for traditional men in a culture that discourages male-male intimacy. The last two suggestions are especially antithetical to male gender-role norms. Men who try these "tactics" will feel awkward, but as with any skills, they will improve and become more comfortable with practice.

---

it may be somewhat like meeting a person from another part of the country, another nation, or even a different world. Both men and women often complain that they have difficulty understanding the other sex (Tannen, 1990). This may be due in large part to having grown up in such different social environments. The effects of gender-specific socialization may be most salient in cross-sex interactions.

Male-Female Friendships

Friendships between males and females are rare compared to same-sex friendships (Block, 1980). Several factors operate as barriers to male-female friendships. First, we live in a sex-typed culture that emphasizes differences between the sexes despite the fact that men and women are much more alike than they are different. As friendships are often based on having something in common, people are not likely to pursue friendships with those that are perceived as dissimilar.

Friendships are also based on reciprocity, or mutual influence. In the childhood peer culture of males, influence tends to be exerted through direct demands. Girls are more likely to use polite suggestions. While girls' style works well with adults, it is not very effective with boys. Therefore, girls may find it quite frustrating and unpleasant to interact with boys who will not respond to their influence attempts (Maccoby, 1990).

While the aversive nature of boys' interactional style keeps girls away from them, the antifemininity norm keeps boys away from girls. The boy who acts like a girl in any way, including being friends with girls, risks losing his place in the male peer dominance hierarchy. When a boy falls to a low level in this hierarchy, he finds it difficult to exert any influence on his peers. As a result, his interactions with them may also become aversive.

Thus, the masculine culture does not foster egalitarian relationships with females. Boys are barraged with messages that females are inferior and have value only as sexual objects. It is not surprising, then, that there is a tendency among men to perceive sexual interest in a woman when it is not present. Abbey (1982) demonstrated that men are more likely than women to label a woman "seductive" or "promiscuous." These findings were replicated by Saal, Johnson, and Weber (1989). Abbey speculated that this readiness to sexualize behavior may result in men misperceiving friendliness as flirtation, making it difficult to establish nonsexual, cross-sex relationships. There may also be a connection between this misperception and sexual harassment in the work place (see Box 13.2).

Despite the barriers to male-female friendships, some people do manage to establish them and find them satisfying. Although traditional gender roles emphasize sex differences, it is likely that similarity with a person of the other sex would be perceived on occasion. Not surprisingly, androgynous men and women are more likely to have friends of the other sex (Ickes & Barnes, 1978; Lavine & Lombardo, 1984).

The most common developmental period for cross-sex friendships is young adulthood. This is a time of increased cross-sex interaction for many. Later in adulthood, especially after marriage, it is difficult to establish these types of relationships, perhaps because of the anxiety that the sexual possibility creates in potential friends and in spouses. Cross-sex friendships among married people are often confined to the context of friendships between couples (Fox, Gibbs, & Auerbach, 1985).

Romantic Relationships

Beginning at puberty, most heterosexual males feel a strong urge to approach females. As they attempt to form close relationships, gender demands exert considerable influence over their behavior. Many men feel

Box 13.2
Sexual Harassment

In October of 1991, a United States Senate committee held hearings on the confirmation of Judge Clarence Thomas to the Supreme Court. Anita Hill, a University of Oklahoma law professor, testified that Thomas had pressured her for dates and made frequent lewd comments in the work place while he was her supervisor in the early 1980s. Hill's accusations and the reactions to them by the all-male Senate Judiciary Committee elevated the public awareness of sexual harassment. In 1992, several women reported similar behaviors by Oregon Senator Bob Packwood.

The frequency of sexual harassment is described in Chapter Ten. Tangri, Burt, and Johnson (1982) reported that most harassers are male: 95% of female victims and 22% of male victims said that they had been harassed exclusively by males. The sex difference in perpetrating harassment is tied to various aspects of masculinity.

The Equal Employment Opportunity Commission (EEOC) (1980) defined sexual harassment as:

> Unwelcome sexual advances, requests for sexual favors and other verbal or physical conduct of a sexual nature when submission to such conduct is made either explicitly or implicitly a term or condition of an individual's employment; submission or rejection of such conduct by an individual is used as the basis for employment decisions affecting the individual; or such conduct has the purpose or effect of unreasonably interfering with an individual's work performance or *creating an intimidating, hostile, or offensive working environment.*" (p. 25024, emphasis added)

You can see by this definition that sexual harassment can be a matter of whether or not the person who is the target of the sexual advances feels uncomfortable, attacked, offended, or intimidated. If a person enjoys or is not bothered by sexual comments, flirting, or requests for romantic attention, then there is no sexual harassment in these behaviors.

This "eye of the beholder" criterion has left a lot of men confused about what they can and cannot do and say in the work place. It is clear to most people that saying, "Have sex with me or you're fired" to a subordinate constitutes an illegal act, but most sexual harassment is not so blatant. Many men are wondering, at what point does "normal" flirting, sexual discussion, or complimenting cross the line into harassment? Can a man say, "Let's go have a drink after work," "How are things going with your boyfriend?", "You look especially good today," or "I think you have nice legs"?

We see a gender-role-related problem in the mere understanding of the behavior. Most men are raised with the notion that rules should be clear and unambiguous. Sports, that basic training ground for masculinity, have clear, rigid rules. "Guidelines" like those established by the EEOC tend to make men uncomfortable.

More importantly, the "eye of the beholder" definition means that men have to make *judgments about what another person is feeling.* As we discussed in Chapter Eight, many men have little experience with this sort of interpersonal orientation. Not surprisingly, men (especially traditionally masculine ones) are much less likely to perceive sexual harassment than women (Powell, 1986).

Other aspects of the male gender role contribute to a sexual harassment proclivity. The view of women as subservient sexual objects is a primary one. Men who see women as sexual objects first and human beings (or coworkers) second are at risk for committing harassment. The sense that one has to be dominant in order to be a man is assoicated with the likelihood of sexual harassment (Pryor, 1987).

The traditional sexual roles of man as initiator and woman as sexual gatekeeper also set the stage for sexual harassment. Men who subscribe to the belief that sexual activity is a matter of power and conquest feel that they must persistently pressure women, and the work place provides opportunities to do so. Men who hold adversarial sexual beliefs—that sexual relationships are a matter of exploitation and manipulation—are more likely to harass (Pryor, 1987).

These characteristics of sexual harassers are not unlike those of acquaintance rapists (Pryor, 1987). Again we find evidence that underlying masculine inadequacy may be related to damaging others and perhaps the self. Sexual harassment is a men's issue, and it is intertwined with other issues involving men's power, emotionality, sexuality, relationships with others, antifemininity, and self-definition. The solutions to the problem include holding perpetrators responsible for their actions, education, and prevention programs. They also involve social change in the male gender role and the structure of patriarchy, as well as in the lives of individual men.

caught in a conflict between the masculine values of antifemininity, inexpressiveness, and independence on the one hand, and attraction toward women, natural intimacy needs, and demands for relationship-oriented behaviors on the other.

Beginning early in life, boys are required to put rigid boundaries between themselves and females in order to define themselves as masculine. When they get older, however, they are expected to merge and be intimate with women. Most males have little practice in the skills required for building intimate relationships, including emotional self-disclosure, reciprocity, and empathy for the other person. It is no wonder that they often feel inept in this foreign area. They are aware at some level that females are the relationship experts. Traditionally masculine expressions of love, such as physical affection or helping, are devalued in U.S. culture (Cancian 1986, 1987).

One interesting research finding is that males tend to "fall in love" faster than females (Huston & Ashmore, 1986; Rubin, Peplau, & Hill, 1981), contrary to the popular belief that women are more emotional and love hungry. The origins of this male readiness to fall in love are not known, but we might make some guesses. First, men tend to place more value than women on a partner's physical attractiveness (Deaux & Hanna, 1984). Thus, they may be more likely to report being in love largely on the basis of this attraction, which of course happens early in the relationship (or even from across the room). Second, men have not been socialized to understand and manage their emotional lives except through repression. Feelings that are difficult to squelch may be experienced as a "flood" of emotion.

Third, the level of intimacy in a romantic relationship is likely to be very different from that of a male's other relationships, which are often centered on activities. This level of intimacy is likely to be less different from the intimacy level of the female's other relationships, which are often focused on feeling and disclosure. The man's hunger for intimacy is greater because he has few or no other places to get this need met. The heterosexual relationship becomes the only safe haven from the masculine demands for independence and inexpressiveness, the only place where he can show the "softer" side of himself. A man might well experience the normal feminine style of reciprocity and consideration as love.

One interesting finding is that married men tend to disclose even less to their male friends than single men do (Tschann, 1988). Perhaps men tend to rely almost solely on their wives for filling their intimacy needs. This is a heavy burden for wives, and men often have difficulty filling these needs if the relationship should break up (see Chapter 14).

There is a considerable body of evidence indicating that the skills required to make an intimate relationship work and last are traditionally feminine. The couples that have the longest lasting and happiest relationships are those in which both partners are either androgynous or feminine (Antill, 1983). This is true for gay and lesbian as well as heterosexual couples (Kurdek & Schmitt, 1986). For men, the abilities to be caring and emotionally expressive are strongly related to the longevity of their relationships (Blumstein & Schwartz, 1983).

In contrast, some aspects of traditional masculinity are related to problems in relationships. Women tend to desire high levels of intimacy (McAdams, Lester, Brand, McNamara, & Lensky, 1988), but sex-typed men tend to be emotionally inexpressive and unempathic. Married women often describe their husbands' lack of attention and affection to be a major source of dissatisfaction (Cunningham, Braiker, & Kelley, 1982).

The degree to which partners perceive that the relationship is equitable (i.e., that partners' power in the relationship are roughly equal) is also a predictor of marital satisfaction (Utne, Hatfield, Traupmann, & Greenberger, 1984). A number of factors work against relationship equity. Most notable among these is a cultural climate that confers economic and social status and other types of power disproportionately to men and erotic power disproportionately to women. In addition, most men are physically bigger than their partners, and power differences resulting from this size difference should not be discounted.

The aforementioned difference in interpersonal styles works against women's power in relationships. Males are often not responsive to the typical feminine influence style of polite suggestion. If this unresponsiveness is common in the context of a relationship, the woman may feel somewhat powerless. While men may view direct demands as a natural way of negotiating in a relationship, this style may feel aversive and overpowering to women.

MANKOFF

"*Thanks for coming, Olga—I want you to help me contact my husband.*"

(Drawing by Mankoff;© 1992 The New Yorker Magazine, Inc.)

The masculine demand for dominance may encourage men to ignore even direct-influence attempts by their partners. Women are more likely than men to use unilateral strategies, such as withdrawing by becoming cold or silent or walking out, in order to influence their partner's behavior. These types of strategies are characteristic of people in all types of relationships who perceive themselves as being at a power disadvantage (Falbo & Peplau, 1980).

Men are not always the most interpersonally powerful ones in the relationship. In fact, it is the partner who seems to be more attractive or less in love (the one who "needs the relationship least") who tends to have the most power (Peplau, 1979; Homans, 1974). However, it is safe to say that when partners view a relationship as an adversarial power competition, it will either not last long or it will quickly become unsatisfying for one or both partners. According to Maccoby (1990) successful couples "develop a relationship that is based on communality rather than exchange bargaining. That is, they have many shared goals and work jointly to achieve them. They do not need to argue over turf because they have the same turf" (p. 518).

Sons and Fathers

In his gender-role workshops with men, John Lee (1991) asks participants to do this simple exercise. "Close your eyes and get a good mental picture of your father, then pay attention to your feelings as I say these words: "Father . . . my father . . . Dad . . . Daddy . . . my dad."

The emotional responses of men (and perhaps women) to this simple exercise are incredibly powerful. The experience is one of being flooded with emotions: love, anger, disappointment, grief. It is hard to underestimate the father's role in shaping the personality of the son.

Traditional gender demands emphasize that the father's role is to be the provider and protector. The mother's role is to be the caregiver. While the father's role usually takes him away from the home, the mother's role emphasizes being with the children and taking care of the home.

Of course, these arrangements are changing. Today, most mothers work outside the home (U.S. Department of Labor, 1991), and fathers are more involved in child care than at any time in recent history (Pederson, 1980), albeit still far short of equal participation. Still, the man as breadwinner and woman as caregiver remain the dominant models for parental roles (Pleck, 1987).

Hard work and sacrifice are the traditional ways a man has expressed his love. While these are profoundly significant to the family, they are indirect expressions of love. It is difficult for children to understand and appreciate that their father disappears in the morning and is gone for most of the day because he loves them. It is much easier to feel loved by someone who feeds you, dresses you, comforts you, and says, "I love you."

In my experience, most men say two things about their fathers: "I know he loves me, but he rarely shows it," and "I wish I could be closer to my father." While warm, affectionate feelings for the father predominate for most men, there is also a feeling of deep disappointment for having been deprived of the father's time, affection, and approval (Garfinkel, 1985; Kamarovsky, 1976). This feeling is sometimes referred to as *father hunger* (Bly, 1991) or even as *the wound* (Lee, 1991). It is perhaps the central issue in the lives of most men. Reactions to father hunger include working compulsively at trying to win the father's respect, rebelling against the father by trying hard to be different from him, or acting out the rage at having to earn his love rather than being valued unconditionally.

There are several barriers to fathers' emotional involvement with their children. Sociobiologists would have us believe that it is biologically based—that males have no "maternal instinct" and that they are unmotivated toward attachment to their young. There is a good deal of countervailing evidence to this hypothesis. Pleck (1981a) reviewed a number of studies that showed that male animals are responsive to their young when exposed to them for a sufficient period of time. When human males are allowed to interact with their children shortly after birth, they react similarly to mothers, showing strong emotional reactions and becoming enthralled with the baby (Parke & Tinsley, 1981). In these early interactions, fathers thus form a paternal "bond" that resembles the mother-child attachment (Parke & Sawin, 1976; Greenberg & Morris, 1974). While mothers may be more biologically predisposed to respond to children, this sex difference is almost totally erased by males' early and repeated exposure to the young.

Social forces inhibit men from spending time with children and performing caregiving behaviors. In industrial and postindustrial society, the breadwinner role has been a structural barrier to paternal involvement. This role prescribes that men spend most of their time away from the home and put a greater priority on task and achievement than on relationships (Pleck, 1985; LaRossa, 1989). Many men report feeling strong conflicts between work and family roles (O'Neil, Fishman, & Kinsella-Shaw, 1987), and employers have been slow to accommodate employed fathers who wish to participate more fully in family roles (Bowen & Orthner, 1991; Wellesley College Center for Research on Women, 1984).

Another inhibitor of paternal participation is men's perceived lack of caregiving skill. In contrast to women, men usually have no childhood parentlike experience, such as babysitting or playing with dolls (Chafetz, 1978), nor were they taught the psychological skills of nurturing or empathy (Levant, 1990a). They are not likely to approach tasks that are

associated with feelings of ineptness (especially considering the role demand to always be competent). Fathers who perceive themselves as skillful in child care are usually more involved with their children (McHale &
Huston, 1984). A number of models for training fathers in caregiving
have been proposed (see Moreland & Schwebel, 1979; Resnick, Resnick,
Packer, & Wilson, 1980; Levant, 1988, 1990a).

Some mothers seem to be reluctant to share the control over child-
care duties with their husbands. Palkovitz (1984) found that women's
negative attitudes toward their husbands' involvement were associated
with low levels of paternal involvement. McHale and Huston (1984) suggests that an increase in men's caregiving to children is only possible if
mothers are willing to relinquish some of their child-care duties. Not
surprisingly, husbands of less traditional wives tend to be more involved
in these duties than husbands of sex-typed wives (Nyquist, Slivken,
Spence, & Helmreich, 1985; Baruch & Barnett, 1981). Other variables
known to have a positive effect on paternal involvement are father's
education, mother's education, mother's income, and mother's employment. Father's income is negatively assoicated with paternal involvement
(Erickson & Gecas, 1991).

At one time, men were usually absent during the births of their
children and were only peripherally involved during the first few days of
the baby's life. The father's presence at this time appears to be critical in
the formation of the parent-child bond (Greenberg & Morris, 1974). This
is one barrier to paternal involvement that is breaking down in the United
States. The proportion of men who attend the births of their children was
80% as of 1985, a nearly threefold increase from 1975 (Lewis, 1986).
Clearly, it is also critical for fathers to increase the amount of time they
spend with their children during all phases of development. Frequent
contact with children facilitates the father's psychological involvement
(Hood & Golden, 1979).

Finally, the general character of male gender-role demands inhibits
many of the kinds of behaviors that make for good parenting. Therefore,
better fathering is linked to the process of men breaking out of their rigid
roles. Many men become less sex typed as a result of trying on the
nontraditional role of caregiver (Meredith, 1985), and men also feel freer
to adopt this role as they reduce their sex-typed views of the world.

Summary

1. Children spend a disproportionate amount of their time in same-sex
   groups, and distinct, sex-typed, patterns develop at an early age. Boys'
   orientation is toward dominance and competition, while girls tend to

value relationship-enhancing interactions. The typically male communication style and the male gender role affect the quality and character of men's relationships with other people.

2. Although males tend to have more friends than females, male same-sex friendships are characterized by less intimacy than those of females. While women share activities and feelings, men are much more likely to share only activities.

3. The skills necessary for building a friendship are often lacking in men, and they often need the social structure of settings like work places and sports in order to affiliate. Masculine demands for competition, task orientation, independence, pain tolerance, and homophobia limit male-male friendships. Many men have a lot of "buddies" but few friends.

4. Sex-typed interactional patterns and gender-role demands also make relationships with women difficult for men. Nonsexual friendship between a man and a woman is relatively rare because the cultural climate prescribes nonegalitarian relationships between the sexes. Because of the socialization to view women as sex objects and connect with them only in sexual ways, many men have difficulty in distinguishing friendly behavior from sexual flirtation.

5. In romantic relationships, men feel conflicts between attraction and gender-role demands. They often lack the social skills necessary for building and maintaining an intimate relationship, and the traditional masculine behaviors of emotional inexpression and hyperindependence are antithetical to collaborative interactions. Couples' partnerships can become adversarial power struggles, leading to relationship dissatisfaction or dissolution.

6. Feelings toward their fathers often form a central psychological issue in men's lives. Emotionally and/or physically distant fathers leave sons with feelings of disappointment, neediness, and rage. Fathers are slowly becoming more involved with their children, but at present they must fight social, institutional, and historical forces in order to do so. Nontraditional men who have nontraditional partners and who view themselves as skilled caregivers are most likely to be actively involved in parenting.

Kenneth Chen/SYGMA

CHAPTER FOURTEEN

Coping in a Difficult World:
Men and Mental Health

A middle-aged man gets so distraught after his wife leaves him that he has to be hospitalized. A teenaged boy commits frequent robberies and assaults. A young man cannot resist the urge to expose his genitals to pubescent girls. A senior citizen, pained from loneliness and the decline of his body, contemplates suicide. An alcoholic experiences significant difficulties with his job, relationships, finances, and the law.

The problems these men experience in living their lives have become unmanageable. All of them are experiencing a good deal of psychological discomfort, although some of them might be able to hide it. Many of them would have trouble admitting to themselves or others that they need help or believing that they could benefit from treatment. Even if they come to an awareness that their problems are out of control, they might be very reluctant to ask for assistance.

Throughout this book, I have hinted at the negative psychological effects of adhering to the rigid and unreasonable demands of the male gender role. The other side of the coin, that certain aspects of masculinity may contribute positively to mental health, has been less emphasized. In this chapter, we explore in more depth the relationships between gender role and psychological well-being for men. First, we will look at definitions of mental health and the connections between masculinity and psychological adjustment. Then, the mental health problems of men and their associations with masculinity are investigated. Finally, we explore the special issues around men in counseling and psychotherapy.

Defining Mental Health

Virtually ever abnormal psychology textbook begins with a chapter on the definitions of mental health and mental illness. If these were easy concepts to define, it would not take an entire chapter to cover the territory. Setting forth criteria for mental health and mental illness turns out to be a rather complicated enterprise. Nearly everyone agrees that a person who hallucinates frequently or cannot remember his or her name is suffering from a mental disturbance. On the other hand, when does "normal" sadness become "abnormal" depression? What if a person is satisfied with a life style that others considered "sick"? How about the person who is a member of an oppressed group: if he or she is suspicious of others' motives, is that "paranoia" or is it "accurate reality testing" (Sue et al., 1990)?

Some of the major difficulties are in the culture-bound character and historical context of definitions of mental health. For instance, suppose that you knew nothing about mainstream U.S. culture and you were visiting the United States. You find out that, every Saturday and Sunday in the fall, men get together, run as fast as they can, and knock each other down. Some of these men suffer severe injuries and are carried off on stretchers. Others experience a good deal of lingering pain from these frequent violent collisions. Moreover, tens of thousands of people gather to watch these spectacles, and sometimes they even cheer when someone gets hurt.

As an outside observer, you wonder if the American term for *war* is *football*, yet you see the players shaking hands after the game. You might be likely to go back to your native land and describe these "crazy," self-destructive men who engage in these exhibitions and the sadistic people that observe them. You are making a judgment about the mental health of these people that few Americans would make.

Even the professional community has difficulty in agreeing on standards for mental illness, and in fact these standards change over time. In 1968, the American Psychiatric Association published the second edition of the *Diagnostic and Statistical Manual of Mental Disorders* (DSM-II), a guide for labeling psychological disturbances. In this version of the manual, homosexuality was defined as a mental disorder. When the next revision (DSM-III) (American Psychiatric Association, 1980) was published, the diagnostic category was called "ego-dystonic homosexuality," which meant that, if you were gay, you had a mental disorder only if you wanted to become heterosexual.

This development prompted psychiatrist Thomas Szasz to describe himself as having "ego-dystonic chronological disorder" because he was older than he wanted to be! His point was well taken. All of us have some aspects of ourselves with which we are disappointed. Why have we chosen only sexual preference to pathologize? Perhaps as a result of convincing arguments by Szasz and others, this diagnostic category disappeared in the following edition (DSM-III-R) (American Psychiatric Association, 1987).

Landrine (1988) pointed out the cultural bias in defining health and illness:

> Contemporary concepts of normalcy and psychopathology perpetuate the construction of the behavior of minorities and women as pathological along with the view that culture is peripheral to psychopathology. . . . The term *normal* suggests, among other things, an individual who exhibits abstract and logical thinking, emotional control, independence, delay of gratification, happiness, a concern with developing one's own potential to the fullest, and a sense of self as an autonomous individual who exerts personal control over self and environment. . . . The sense of self described above—from which many other characteristics derive—is not how the poor experience the self . . . how Blacks experience the self . . . how Asian Americans experience the self . . . how women experience the self . . . or how most people throughout the world experience the self. . . . This concept of normalcy, held by U.S. public and professionals alike, . . . is largely synonymous with the characteristics of upper income White men in this country . . . and is firmly rooted in the social meanings shared by middle-class White Americans. (p. 40)

It is clear that gender-role definition is a central feature of culture. Since the definition of mental health is culture bound, it is also strongly tied to gender stereotypes. Children as young as 4 and 5 will say that there is something wrong with people who do not conform to gender roles (Stoddart & Turiel, 1985).

Especially since the publication of DSM-III in 1980, some feminist scholars have argued that the mental health establishment pathologizes women for the way that they have been socialized (e.g., to be dependent, emotional, and self-sacrificing) (Kaplan, 1983). Pantony and Caplan (1991) suggested that a diagnostic category of "delusional dominating personality disorder" be used to describe people who have an "inability to establish and maintain meaningful interpersonal relationships, an inability to identify and express a range of feeling in oneself and others, and difficulty responding empathically to the feelings and needs of close associates and intimates" (p. 120). This is a description of a hypermasculine interpersonal style.

These objections to gender bias in the diagnostic schemes focus on the negative social consequences of being labeled as "disordered." However, we should not overlook the fact that it is not the purpose of diagnosis to stigmatize and blame people for their problems. Stigmatization is an unfortunate byproduct of diagnosis in a society that is prejudiced against the mentally ill.

The purpose of diagnosis is to identify problems that require attention. In many cases, the willingness of health insurance providers to pay for treatment hinges on the diagnosability of the person seeking mental health services. Failing to label the hypermasculine behaviors just described as disturbed, therefore, has at least two consequences. First, it reinforces masculine privilege by tacitly approving the behavior. In other words, it says to the mental health community that it is all right to be emotionally withholding, aggressive, and unempathic. Second, it says that men who behave in such a way merit no attention. There is a denial that such behavior limits the quality of the man's life to a significant enough extent that we should do something for him.

Masculinity, Femininity, and Mental Health

Against the backdrop of the patriarchal culture and the male-dominated mental health profession, we now turn to the research on the connections between gender and psychological well-being.

Many people believe that part of being psychologically "adjusted" is behaving in accordance with one's gender role. In this view, the same behavior could be considered vigorously healthy for a man and unhealthy for a woman, or vice versa. Ambitious women and emotional men are sometimes considered disturbed, but fewer people would give this negative label to an ambitious man or an emotional woman.

If we look at more "objective" criteria than popular opinion (such as life satisfaction, self-esteem, and absence of psychological symptoms), we find little support for the hypothesis that conforming to one's gender role is a consequence, antecedent, or a byproduct of psychological health. This is especially true for women. In most studies, psychological femininity has been found to be unrelated or even negatively related to indices of psychological adjustment (Frank, Towell, & Huyck, 1985; Olds & Shaver, 1980). This is not surprising, as we live in a culture that oppresses women and undervalues femininity.

For both men and women, a great many studies have demonstrated a positive relationship between psychological masculinity and many measures of mental health (Long, 1989; Maffeo, 1982; Frank, McLaughlin, & Crusco, 1984; Whitley, 1984; Cook, 1987; and many others). Most of these studies utilized the Bem Sex Role Inventory (BSRI) (Bem, 1974) and/or the Personal Attributes Questionnaire (PAQ) (Spence, Helmreich, & Stapp, 1974) to measure gender typing. Recall from Chapter Two that the BSRI emphasizes the positive aspects of masculinity and femininity. The PAQ has been similarly described (Adams & Sherer, 1985). It is safe to say that positive masculine traits (e.g., self-efficacy, assertiveness, persistence) are associated with psychological well-being. One should not take this to be a reaffirmation of traditional masculinity. Some typically masculine characteristics such as arrogance, egocentrism (Spence, Helmreich, & Holahan, 1979), and emotional inexpression (Kinder & Curtiss, 1990; Hendryx, Haviland, & Shaw, 1991; Dosser, 1982; Balswick, 1982) are strongly related to psychological and/or physical maladaption. It is clear that research on the association between masculinity and mental health needs to be specifically focused on particular aspects of both of these rather complex and global constructs (Snell, Belk, & Hawkins, 1986).

Androgyny has not panned out as a model of mental health for men, and it is little wonder that it has not. The androgynous man sometimes behaves in a feminine way. Socially, there are very few rewards but quite a few punishments for cross-sex behavior in men. People tend to reach negatively to men who self-disclose (Derlega & Chaikin, 1976), hold sterotypically feminine jobs such as nursing (Shinar, 1978; Fitzgerald & Cherpas, 1985), or otherwise exhibit gender-role-deviant behavior (Silverberg, 1986). The sex-typed characteristic of dominance has been associated with increased attractiveness of men (Sadalla & Kenrick, 1987).

Men who suffer social punishment for their feminine behavior may, as a result, suffer from lowered self-esteem, which is certainly a risk factor for mental illness. As gender-role standards change to allow the expression of femininity in men, the relationships between these traits and men's psychological well-being might also change.

The concepts of gender-role conflict and strain (O'Neil, 1981a, 1981b, 1990) show some promise in the study of gender and adjustment. Gender-role conflict is a negative psychological state that results from the contradictory and/or unrealistic demands of the gender role (O'Neil, 1990). O'Neil et al. (1986) suggested that male gender-role conflict centers around four themes: (1) success, power, and competition, (2) restrictive emotionality, (3) restrictive affectionate behavior between men, and (4) conflict between work and family relations.

The hypothesis of the gender-role conflict and strain model is that men who experience and accept traditional gender-role prescriptions, yet do not feel that they fulfill these prescriptions, will experience the most conflict and negative consequences. For example, a man thinks that being unemotional means being manly, but he finds it difficult to suppress his emotions. This man would experience more role conflict than either (a) a man who accepts unemotionality as manly but has no difficulty suppressing his feelings, or (b) an emotional man who does not experience much pressure from the masculine prescription for emotional restrictedness.

There is a growing body of evidence linking male gender-role conflict with negative psychological states. Davis and Walsh (1988) found that gender-role conflict was negatively correlated with self-esteem and positively correlated with anxiety. Good and Mintz (1990) found a significant positive correlation between depression and gender-role conflict. Sharpe and Heppner (1991) replicated the findings of these two studies.

Sharpe and Heppner (1991) also noted that the concept of psychological well-being has often reflected a traditional masculine bias in the research. When we expand the traditional view of mental health to include an emphasis on intimacy and relationship satisfaction, then femininity adds to the prediction of psychological well-being. Sharpe and Heppner propose a two-factor model in describing the relationship between gender and mental health for men. One factor is "Traditional Masculine Well-Being"—the contributions of positive masculine aspects. The other factor is "Affiliative Well-Being"—intimacy, emotionality, and a lowered emphasis on competition.

The findings of these various research studies would seem to suggest that there are healthy aspects to traditional masculine socialization and that building upon these aspects with new skills may be a benefit to men, although this benefit may not be as great as androgyny theorists once believed.

Sex Differences in Mental Disorders

The proportions of men and women vary significantly in several categories of mental illness. A number of factors are thought to contribute to these sex differences. Gender socialization is one of them. The gendered habits a person acquires may affect how he or she expresses psychological distress. For instance, a sex-typed woman who experiences psychological pain may often become depressed. A sex-typed man might react to the same kind of pain by abusing alcohol. These tendencies may be fueled, at least partly, by the woman's socialization to "look inside" and think about how she feels and the man's gender-typed encouragement to deny vulnerability and look to the environment for solutions to his problems.

A related possibility is that gender socialization sometimes prevents a person from acquiring certain coping skills (O'Neil, 1981b). A highly sex-typed man may not have learned how to deal with emotions and relationships. A highly sex-typed woman may not have learned how to deal with independence. Thus, gender socialization can contribute to *behavioral deficits* as well as to negative patterns of behavior.

The view expressed here is that individuals are predisposed toward certain types of mental disorders because of the way they were raised. While past socialization undoubtedly makes a contribution, we should not forget that, in an important sense, men and women live in "different worlds." There is a tendency for men and women to experience different stressors and to find themselves in different settings and roles (Cook, 1990; Barnett & Baruch, 1987). We saw in Chapter Thirteen that sex-segregated social groups tend to have gender-characteristic interpersonal styles. In the sociocultural context, different behaviors are anticipated, rewarded, and punished on the basis of sex. For example, expressions of sadness and helpless feelings by a woman might be met with sympathy and emotional support. The same behavior in a man might result in social isolation.

As a result of a variety of biological, psychological, and social forces, the following sex differences in mental illness have been observed:

1. Males experience a disproportionate number of many childhood disorders, for example, attention deficit hyperactivity disorder and conduct disorder.
2. Women are much more likely than men to have eating disorders and somewhat more likely to be diagnosed with depression and most anxiety-based disorders.
3. Males constitute a majority of substance abusers, sexual deviates, and people with behavior-control problems such as pyromania, compulsive gambling, and angry outbursts ("intermittent explosive disorder").
4. There are unequal sex proportions for a variety of personality disorders: More men than women are diagnosed as paranoid (67%), antisocial (82%), narcissistic (70%), and schizoid (78%); more women than men are diagnosed as histrionic (85%), "borderline" (62%), and dependent (69%) (Millon, 1986).
5. Men are much more likely than women to commit suicide, although women make more "unsuccessful" suicide attempts (Sue et al., 1990).

Mental Health Issues for Men

The amount of research on the connections between gender and mental disorder is surprisingly sparse (Cook, 1990). There is a great need for further investigation in this area. However, there has been speculation about the relationships between some aspects of masculinity and the disorders just listed. The following discussion will focus on a few areas: personality disorder, suicide, the role of marriage in men's mental health, and the effects of parental divorce on sons.

Personality Disorders

Personality is a relatively stable set of behavioral predispositions that characterize a human being (Maddi, 1989). In the case of the person who is **personality disordered**, the generalized ways in which he or she approaches the world are marked by an inflexible and self-defeating nature that results in poor mental stability (Millon, 1981). The ingrained styles that personality-disordered individuals use almost always cause them problems in their work and social functioning. They also tend to experience a good deal of personal distress.

The DSM-III-R (American Psychiatric Association, 1987) lists 11 of these disorders. According to Millon (1986), four of these affect men more often than women and three affect women more often than men. The remaining four disorders are distributed fairly equally between the sexes. A description of the male-dominated diagnoses follows.

Persons with **paranoid personality disorder** are prone to be overly suspicious and guarded. They tend to view the behavior of others as deceiving or attacking them, and they usually react with hostility on the frequent occasions when these perceptions occur (Millon, 1981). These people are characterized by emotional coldness, no sense of humor, stubbornness, defensiveness, and an unwillingness to compromise. They seem especially on guard against losing their independence (American Psychiatric Association, 1987).

Antisocial personality disorder is characterized by a long history of behaviors that violate the rights of others, such as lying, stealing, and assaulting. Antisocial people feel little remorse for having mistreated people. They are frequently in legal trouble and fail to sustain any close relationships (American Psychiatric Association, 1987). Many antisocials are dangerous criminals.

People with **narcissistic personality disorder** have a grandiose sense of their own importance. They present themselves as exceptionally talented, accomplished, and "special." Narcissists are easily hurt by any kind of criticism. They feel that they are entitled to special favors by virtue of being so wonderful. They feel ashamed and enraged when others react negatively to them and when they do not receive steady admiration and attention (American Psychiatric Association, 1987). Underneath this grandiose exterior is a fragile sense of self-worth. (See Chapter Four for a theoretical view of the concept of narcissism and its relationship to masculinity.)

Schizoid personality disorder is characterized by flat emotionality and interpersonal aloofness. People with this disorder seem to lack the capacity to feel. They lead dull, joyless, and solitary lives.

We could characterize many of the traits described in these four disorders as caricatures of masculinity. All of these personality types are marked by self-absorption, an indifference toward others, and an overemphasis on independence. Narcissistic and antisocial people are interpersonally exploitive, using others to reach their personal goals. All of these styles are characterized by extreme difficulty in relationships, another stereotypically masculine characteristic.

There is also pronounced emotional restrictedness in antisocial, paranoid, and schizoid disorders. Schizoids feel nothing or next to nothing. Antisocials and paranoids express little emotion except for anger, which is stereotypically masculine. The combination of hostility and hyperindependence in antisocial and paranoid disorders is an especially volatile one. These people feel that they must protect themselves at all costs, and thus they are prone to violence.

Although mental illnesses are caused by multiple factors, personality-disordered individuals do tend to come from families with dysfunctional interactional styles (Millon, 1981). If we consider hypermasculinity to result from harsh masculine socialization, we could speculate that men who exhibit the preceding personality disorders may well have received an exaggerated "dose" of overly stern masculine socialization.

Suicide

Although females attempt suicide more often than males, males much more often "succeed" at taking their own lives. Across the life span, the ratio of male to female completed suicide is about three to one (Robins, 1985). For adolescents, females make 90% of the suicide attempts, but males represent 80% of completed suicides (Stillion, McDowell, & May, 1989). Among the elderly (who commit suicide more often than any other age group), the sex ratio is especially alarming. According to 1988 data published by the U.S. Bureau of the Census (1991), the suicide rates for men at ages 65 to 74 were almost five times those of women in the same age group. At ages 75 to 84, men committed suicide at a rate of over eight times that of women, and at ages over 85, the male to female ratio was 12:1 (60.4 male suicides and 5.0 female suicides per 100,000 in population).

Stillion, McDowell, and May (1989) noted that the higher level of male suicide risk exists across cultures and apparently throughout history. These facts may lead to speculation about a possible biological factor. However, the rather stable sex ratio may also reflect the redundancy of masculine socialization practices across cultures and history.

In looking for explanations for this rather large sex ratio, Stillion and her colleagues offer three masculine socialization factors. First, males show higher levels of aggression throughout the life span and, thus, aggression toward the self may also be seen at higher levels. Males tend to use more violent and lethal means of committing suicide, such as firearms or jumping from high places, than females, who more often use methods like wrist slashing or pill taking (Robins, 1985; USBC, 1991). The lethality of method does not account for the whole difference, however. Males complete more suicides with every method (Stillion, 1985).

A second factor is the success, status, and problem-solving orientation in males. The masculine value of "getting the job done" may actually relate to the "job" of taking one's life. Stillion and her colleagues (1989) report anecdotal evidence from emergency room personnel that males who make unsuccessful suicide attempts are often distressed over their failures.

Finally, there is the masculine norm of independence. Needing and requesting aid is antithetical to traditional masculinity. Thus, despondent men often feel alone with problems that seem unsolvable and pain that seems intractable. For these men, suicide may seem like the only alternative. Suicide attempts are sometimes seen as a "cry for help." It is apparent that males, more often than females, are unwilling to ask for help either before their problems escalate to the point of suicide contemplation or through giving messages by the act itself.

The combination of pain and masculine bravado can indeed be quite volatile. In a strongly worded statement, Stillion et al. (1989) describe this association:

> If we wanted to write a prescription for increasing suicide risk, we could not improve on the traditional male socialization pattern. Take one male child, who has higher levels of aggression and activity than his female peers. Put the child into competitive situations. Tell him he must win at all costs. Teach him that to admit fear or doubt is weakness and that weakness is not masculine. Complete the vicious circle by assuring him that his worth is dependent on winning games, then salary and promotion competitions, and you have the perfect recipe for enhanced suicide risk. (p. 243)

It is also interesting to speculate about the two periods of development in which the suicide sex ratio is most unbalanced, adolescence and old age. Adolescence is the most sex-typed time of life, the time in which the boy begins to establish himself as a man, often with few positive clues. In old age, the traditional hallmarks of masculinity fade away. The body breaks down, work productivity wanes, and there is sometimes less money. Suicide in either of these high-risk developmental periods may at least partially be affected by feelings of not measuring up as a man.

The Role of Marriage in Mental Health

Consider this stereotypical scene: A man and a woman have been dating for an extended period of time. The relationship is monogamous and mutually satisfying. They love each other. The woman expresses a desire to marry, and the man shies away. She asks, "Why don't you want to get married?" He doesn't really know. He asks, "Why is getting married so important?" She doesn't really know.

Scenes like this are repeated over and over. For a man, committing to and being intimate with one woman for the rest of his life feels very dangerous. He may lose his independence and freedom, and then he would become very unhappy. For a woman, committing to and being intimate with one man for the rest of her life seems like the "thing to do." Remaining unmarried after extended dating feels dangerous. She may feel very unhappy if she does not marry.

A cultural myth is that marriage fulfills women and restricts men. Cultural sterotypes reflect this bias—the happy and devoted housewife, the lonely spinster or old maid, the carefree bachelor, and the henpecked husband.

In recent years, social scientists have investigated the accuracy of this bias by examining mental illness rates for married men, single men, married women, and single women. If marriage has damaging or beneficial effects for any of these groups, these effects should be reflected by mental illness rates that are at variance with contrasted groups.

In general, the results of this research cast considerable doubt on the accuracy of the cultural myth. Rosenstein and Milazzo-Sayre (1981) conducted an extensive survey of mental hospital patients. They found that single (never married) men were hospitalized at about three times the rate of married men and also at a higher rate than never-married women. Married women were hospitalized at a higher rate than married men. Married people in general were hospitalized less often than single people, but the size of that difference was much greater for men than for women.

Although we cannot say from these data that marriage *causes* better mental health in men, there certainly are relationships between being married and staying out of the hospital (Barnett & Baruch, 1987), avoiding mental illness (Walker, Bettes, Kain, & Harvey, 1985), and avoiding stress-related physical illnesses (Cleary, 1987). These relationships hold for women, but they are much stronger for men (Cleary & Mechanic, 1983; Gove & Tudor, 1973).

If marriage is more protective for men than for women, we should see higher rates of mental illness and hospitalization in divorced and widowed men compared with their female counterparts. This is indeed the case. Divorced men show higher rates of hospitalizations than any of the other groups—nearly eight times the rate for married men (Rosenstein & Milazzo-Sayre, 1981). Men have more psychological difficulties than women in adjusting to divorce and separation (Wallerstein & Kelly, 1980; Bloom & Caldwell, 1981; Siegel & Kuykendall, 1990; Hetherington, Cox, & Cox, 1976). Widowers experience more psychological and physical problems than widows (Stroebe & Stroebe, 1983). And men remarry more quickly than women following divorce or the death of a spouse (Bardwick, 1979).

We can make sense of these data by looking at the functions of marriage for men and women. For both partners, marriage would seem to provide opportunities for intimacy and companionship, as well as fulfilling a social obligation; 90% of people in the United States get married at some time during their lives (Basow, 1992).

We have already discussed elsewhere the gender-role prohibitions against intimacy and self-disclosure for men. Yet these are human needs, and failing to attend to them has adverse effects on the person. Although marriage does not necessarily involve psychological intimacy, it certainly sets the stage for it. For many men, then, marriage is an opportunity to fill a void that has been created by harsh masculine socialization.

Women need intimacy, too, but they often experience it in relationships with other women (see Chapter 13). In the realm of psychological intimacy, marriage is less novel for women than for men. Men may also tend to be less responsive to women's disclosures. As a result, fewer psychological benefits accrue for women.

The social-role aspects of marriages are also worthy of mention. In the traditional Christian marriage ceremony, the celebrant ends by saying, "I now pronounce you man and wife." The man keeps his identity ("Man"), and the woman's identity ("wife") seems to become defined by her relationship to the man. She relinquishes her last name. Sometimes she even gives up her first name ("Mrs. John Smith"). Historically, marriage has been a legal agreement by which the woman becomes the property of the man, and women have usually been expected to adapt to their husbands and take responsibility for the relationship.

This part of the social role is slowly changing. Some marriage ceremonies have become more egalitarian, with language like, "I now pronounce you *husband* and wife", and "You may kiss each other" rather than "You may now kiss the bride" (as if she has no choice in the matter). Today, many women retain their last names, which is symbolic of their having identities apart from their husbands. The social myth that women are incomplete unless they are married is slowly being modified.

Despite men's stereotypical resistance to getting married, it appears that benefits are associated with being a husband. The fact that most men eventually marry (despite gender-role demands for hyperindependence) is good evidence that men want and need intimacy. Pleck (1985) reported that men usually experience their family roles as more important in their lives than their work roles and that satisfaction with family roles is strongly associated with psychological well-being.

Divorce and Father Absence

Marital separation and divorce are becoming more and more prevalent in the United States. Although much research has been done in the context of what Hill (1987) called "Dick and Jane" families (those with a working father, a housewife mother, and two or more children, none of whom are from the parents' previous relationships), these families constitute less than 10% of U.S. households (Hodgkinson, 1985). Social scientists have become interested in how children are affected by parental conflict, divorce, remarriage, and family blending.

The breakup of a marriage is rarely, if ever, easy on any of the people involved. Children of divorce tend to experience psychological difficulties for several years (Hetherington, Stanley-Hagen, & Anderson, 1989). Some researchers have discovered that marital dissolution has an especially negative impact on boys.

Researchers Jeanne and Jack Block began to follow a cohort of young children in the late 1960s in a longitudinal study designed to investigate several developmental hypotheses. As they collected data on these young-sters year after year, some of these children's parents divorced. With another colleague, they investigated the effects of parental conflict and divorce on children (Block, Block, & Gjerde, 1986). This study is espe-cially important because it is *prospective*, meaning that the researchers were able to gather data on these children prior to the marital breakup, often for several years. They did not have to rely on children's memories of what happened to them and how they felt.

Comparisons of 60 intact families with 41 subsequently divorced or separated families revealed that sons are more vulnerable than daughters to the negative effects of parental conflict. Boys from subsequently di-vorcing families showed more aggression, more difficulty in controlling impulses, less cooperation, and higher anxiety in novel situations than boys from intact families. These characteristics also stood in contrast to girls from subsequently divorcing families, who showed different and milder symptoms than boys.

Another important finding from this study was that marital conflict was much more likely to be displayed in the presence of boys than in the presence of girls. If you think about the experience of your mother and father fighting with each other when you were a child, you might recall (or imagine) it to be very frightening indeed. The sex difference in wit-nessing parental conflict may be a critical factor in explaining the signif-icantly more negative impact of marital difficulties on sons. It is also important to note that these impacts are not simply a result of divorce, per se. The researchers observed these sex differences in symptomatology for years prior to the marital separation.

The fact that parents in conflict are much more comfortable with expressing their animosity in front of their sons may reflect the uncon-scious beliefs that boys can "take it" and their emotions are nonexistent, unimportant, or at least less important than those of girls. We can see that childhood gender-role strain in interaction with family stress can have pronounced negative effects on the boy's personality development. Some children carry the wounds of parental conflict well into adulthood (Wallerstein & Blakeslee, 1989).

About 90% of fathers lose custody of their children during the di-vorce process (McKenry & Price, 1990), so boys as well as girls usually find themselves in the custody of the mother. Kelly (1988) found that children who live with their same-sex parent after divorce were better off than those living with other-sex parents, as measured by several indices of psychological health. If parental skills and resources are relatively equal, mounting evidence indicates that it is best for boys to live with their fathers. Perhaps this would not be the case if our culture did not imprint antifemininity on males, but we will not know unless and until patriarchy dies its slow death. The reality is that daughters tend to adjust to divorce better than sons (Hetherington, Cox, & Cox 1985) and that boys in their mothers' custody have strong reactions to diminished contact with their fathers (Kelly, quoted in Buie, 1988).

The effects of father absence on boys are difficult to separate from the effects of parental conflict and other stressors that accompany marital dissolution. Although parental separation is probably the most prevalent cause of father absence, fathers may also be gone from the home because of death, military service, or other work. Additionally, many males have complained about fathers who, although physically present, are psychologically absent because of their emotional unresponsiveness. At the same time, there are physically absent fathers who may be somewhat psychologically present through telephone communication, letters, and visits.

There may well be variant effects of father absence depending on the type of absence (physical, psychological, or both), the circumstances around which the father left the home, the characteristics of the mother or other caretaker, the sex typing of father and son, or other factors. Although there is a widespread societal assumption that father absence is damaging to males (Stevenson, 1991), research on the connections between father absence and mental health has not demonstrated that it is necessary for boys to have same-sex role models in order to develop healthily. On the other hand, it has not been demonstrated that same-sex role models are unnecessary, either (Jones, 1990). A good deal more investigative work in this area remains to be done.

Whatever the effects of father absence on boys are, we can be quite certain that relationships with fathers and feelings about fathers are of profound importance to sons. In an extensive research study of men, Barnett, Marshall, and Pleck (1992) found that the quality of the adult son's relationship with his father was significantly associated with the son's level of mental health. This conclusion supported an earlier finding, from an equally extensive study of Kamarovsky (1976), that male college seniors with psychological adjustment problems tended to report low levels of satisfaction in their relationships with their fathers.

In both of these studies, the relationship to the father was much more predictive of mental health than the son's relationship to his mother. Both studies corroborate a great deal of anecdotal evidence from therapists and men's studies educators that feelings about the father constitute a major psychological issue in men's lives.

Counseling and Psychotherapy with Men

As we have seen, quite a few men are disturbed, and a great many are also disturbing. These men, and the world in general, will be better off if we can alleviate their psychological suffering and help them change their behaviors. The processes for doing so are counseling (psychotherapy), education, and social change. The latter two are saved for the final chapter of this book. The following discussion centers on the treatment of individual men in a psychotherapeutic context.

Men as a Special Population

Carl Rogers (1957) first popularized the idea that a counselor's understanding of the client's subjective psychological environment is a critical first step in the therapeutic process. If the therapist is to be helpful, he or she has got to gain a deep awareness of how the client experiences the self and the world. Rogers was an important early influence in defining the field of **counseling psychology**, which is founded on the appreciation and respect of individual differences.

One of the important ways in which therapy clients differ is in their identifications with, and memberships in, different sociocultural groups. For example, people of color, people with disabilities and gay people have almost always had some different experiences than Caucasians, able-bodied people, and heterosexuals, respectively. Some of these experiences have important effects on people's sense of self and view of the world. When these people see counselors, especially ones who are dissimilar to them, it is important for the counselor to be sensitive to the typical psychological and political issues associated with memberships in various groups.

With this basic assumption in mind, many counselors began to undergo formal and informal training in understanding diversity in the 1960s and 1970s, and this kind of training continues today. One of the basic categories of individual differences is, of course, sex. In 1979, the American Psychological Association's Counseling Psychology division published a list entitled "Principles Concerning the Counseling and Therapy of Women." The preamble to these principles begins: "Although competent counseling/therapy processes are essentially the same for all counselor/therapist interactions, special subgroups require specialized skills, attitudes, and knowledge. Women constitute a special subgroup" (Division 17, 1979, p. 21). The people who drafted this document felt that it was essential for counselors who treat women to be knowledgeable about biological, psychological, and social issues affecting women, to be aware of their own values and biases about women, and to develop skills that are particularly geared toward women.

Around the same time this document was published, therapists were beginning to realize that men, too, had typical styles and psychological issues that they bring to the therapeutic setting. Therapists also began to recognize and examine their values and biases about men, and some realized that a gender-aware perspective on masculine socialization would be helpful in their treatment of male clients.

A number of excellent books and journal articles have been published in the past 10 to 15 years on the subject of men as a special population in psychotherapy. Some of these have integrated men's issues with those of special subpopulations of men such as ethnic, older, divorced, gay, and bisexual men (see Scher, Stevens, Good, & Eichenfield, 1987; Moore & Leafgren, 1990).

Good, Gilbert, and Scher (1990) argued that all counselors should be aware of the impact of gender in the treatments of all clients. They suggested five broad principles of "gender-aware therapy":

1. *Regard conceptions of gender as integral aspects of counseling and mental health.* The counselor needs to understand how gender socialization and sexism affect a person's well-being.

2. *Consider problems within their societal context.* "The personal and political cannot be separated for women or men in society. Thus, the availability of quality child care or an employer's policy with regard to paternity or maternity leave would need to be considered in understanding the experience of personal stresses and conflicts."

3. *Actively seek to change gender injustices experienced by men and women.* Counselors should explore nontraditional options and examine gender stereotypes with their clients.

4. *Emphasize development of collaborative therapeutic relationships.* Counseling relationships should deemphasize power and emphasize cooperation.

5. *Respect client's freedom to choose* despite what is "politically correct," traditional, or nontraditional. (p. 377)

As we move into the 1990s, counselors are becoming increasingly aware that men constitute a special subgroup of clients. A number of psychotherapeutic men's issues have been identified, and some specialized treatments have been developed.

Men's Issues in Counseling and Psychotherapy

Traditional one-to-one psychotherapy is a set of methods that were developed by mostly male therapists in order to treat mostly female clients. If we look closely at the counseling relationship, we see that very little of traditional masculinity is conducive to requesting treatment, sustaining the therapeutic effort, or performing the activities required of clients.

Help-Seeking

People who request psychotherapeutic services have often been stereotyped as "crazy," weak, or out of control. This stigma makes it difficult for almost anyone to come to counseling, but it is especially difficult for men, who often place a special value on being rational, strong, and in control. The act of telephoning or walking into a counseling center and asking for an appointment may feel like the equivalent of declaring, "I am weak, afraid, dependent, and vulnerable. I don't know what is going on with me, even though I should, and I can't handle my problems on my own. I need help."

We would be hard pressed to find statements that better reflect masculine failure than these. Given the social expectations to "work it out for yourself," "take it like a man," and "control your feelings," it is not surprising that men utilize psychological services considerably less often than women (Levant, 1990b; Collier, 1982). Good, Dell, and Mintz (1989) found that traditional attitudes about the male gender role were significantly associated with men's negative attitudes toward help-seeking. Clearly, if you cannot ask for directions when you are lost, you will have difficulty asking for help in other areas.

Since entering counseling is a threat to masculine self-esteem, men often resist asking for services until they experience a very deep level of psychological pain and until their problems reach crisis proportions. If they do begin treatment, they may drop out when their discomfort reaches a barely manageable level. After dropping out, their pain may worsen. At that time, it may be even more difficult for them to return and ask for help, because they now admit two failures by doing so: the one that brought them to counseling in the first place and the failure of the first attempt as a therapy client.

Because of the incompatibility of help-seeking with masculinity (as well as other reasons detailed next), the average length of treatment for male clients is about half that for female clients. At college and university counseling centers, many more men than women request short-term counseling, despite the fact that counselors judged the therapy needs of the two sexes to be similar (Prosser-Gelwick & Garni, 1988).

Counseling Activities

Counseling is an activity in which clients are usually expected to perform certain behaviors thought to be helpful in solving emotional problems. These behaviors often include emotional self-disclosure, exploration of feelings, nondefensive introspection ("looking inside" of oneself), and emphasizing interpersonal material. Men usually have little experience in these areas, which are traditionally feminine. Therefore, the counseling setting tends to be a rather poor match of person and environment for men (Bruch, 1980). In other words, asking a man to do these things may make him feel like a fish out of water, and this may well be another factor that contributes to the high male dropout rate.

Because many counseling activities are uncomfortable for them, men often ask for masculine kinds of help, such as a logical analysis of the problem, an emphasis on thinking over feeling, or help with defending against rather than experiencing the problem. For instance, typically masculine strategies for dealing with the breakup of a romantic relationship might be to find a substitute lover, to use thoughts to master feelings, or to learn how to not think about the former partner.

In the preceding scenario, the counselor might think that it is more important for the man to deal with powerful feelings and go through the process of grieving for the lost lover. This would not fit very well with a client who expects directive, analytical, problem solving. Thus, counselors find themselves in quandaries when these kinds of situations arise. They do not want to reinforce a maladaptive masculine strategy, yet they also do not want their client to terminate treatment. In these cases, counselors should address the client's needs and expectations in the context of feelings about control, independence, and vulnerability. To do so requires a sensitivity to men's issues.

Men's skill levels in these emotionally focused activities is another consideration. Many have had their emotional experience systematically removed from their lives. Not only are they uncomfortable with the expression of feeling, they are understandably not very good at it. Asked how he feels, a man might often reply, "About what?" The counselor might then say, "About your girlfriend breaking up with you." The man tells the counselor what he *thinks*: "I feel she shouldn't have done it." He may feel sad, disappointed, angry, and so on, but these feeling words are not in his working vocabulary.

For counselors, it is an extraordinary challenge to reach a man in the context of questions like, "How do you feel?", when the man has been socially manipulated to the point that the question does not even make sense. The good news is that men who can learn emotion-focused coping in the therapeutic setting may gain a skill that will be helpful to them in virtually every area of their lives.

Counselor Sex and Gender Issues

If a man is considering entering therapy, should he choose a male or a female therapist? The answer to this question involves a wide variety of factors. It is usually more important that he choose a good therapist of either sex who is a good match for him. However, different issues often arise with counselors of different sexes.

With male counselors, the typical masculine interactional patterns often emerge. Men have been socialized to be especially competitive, unemotional, and invulnerable with other men. The male client may feel this pressure and act accordingly, making it difficult for the therapeutic work to proceed.

There is a high degree of intimacy in the counseling relationship. Sometimes it is higher than any other relationship the man has. It is not unusual for clients to feel warm and dependent toward the therapist, and these feelings may stimulate the client's homophobia (Heppner & Gonzales, 1987; Mintz & O'Neil, 1990).

With female counselors, these intimate feelings may also become sexualized, leading to confusion, distraction, or shame. Other feelings may arise in reaction to the power of the female therapist. Having been raised to feel superior to women, the man might try to dominate the counselor and/or exhibit the kind of childlike dependence that men sometimes have with their female partners. In a collaborative relationship, client and counselor can seek to understand and deal with these reactions in order to address the client's other concerns.

Research into the exact nature of the effects of therapist sex on the counseling process is far from extensive (Mintz & O'Neil, 1990), and more needs to be done in this area. The gender of the therapist is also important. There is an increasing awareness that it is vital for mental health professionals to be aware of their own issues. Counselors are not immune to the influences of the sex-typed culture, and they have gender biases like anyone else. For instance, in one study, counselors in training tended to react negatively to a male client who chose a nontraditional occupation (Fitzgerald & Cherpas, 1985). Robertson and Fitzgerald (1992) found that the diagnoses of experienced therapists were affected by the sex of the client. They suggested that therapists may also subtly exert pressure on male clients to conform their behavior to masculine standards.

Counselors must work hard to understand and deal with their emotional reactions to their male clients. Male counselors may find their homophobia stimulated with male clients. Female counselors may feel angry toward male clients as part of their general anger toward the oppressive culture of patriarchy. Both male and female therapists may find it harder to empathize with the pain of a male client, a reaction to the social notion that men are to be blamed for their problems and not seen as victims in any sense. Counselors of both sexes may feel uncomfortable when male clients show weakness or cry.

The counseling profession usually involves deeply personal activities. Counselors who fail to consider the gender issues involved with these activities do a disservice to their clients and perpetuate the negative aspects of gender-role socialization.

Psychological Services for Men

The specific techniques that a counselor would use with a male client depend on the individual's problem and the therapist's theoretical orientation, among other factors. It is hard to make sweeping generalizations about what techniques work with male clients. At the same time, some writers have identified certain approaches that are helpful in the treatment of many men, and a brief discussion of these approaches is appropriate.

Because the counseling environment is threatening for many men, several theorists have suggested that structured and psychoeducational approaches be considered as alternatives to traditional one-to-one psychotherapy. Robertson and Fitzgerald (1992) found that college men were more likely to say they would utilize workshops or seminars than personal counseling. Psychoeducational programs that offer self-help and problem-solving approaches allow men to do some psychological work in a masculine context.

As noted in Chapter Thirteen, men often need more structure than women in relationship situations. Several authors have designed workshops on specific, characteristically masculine problems. For example, Moore (1990) developed a structured, 10-week program for increasing emotional expressiveness. Levant (1990b) is involved with teaching fathering skills. Leafgren (1988) described a developmental program for college men around a wide range of men's issues. In all of these approaches, an environment is provided that allows men to do what they rarely do otherwise: share feelings, talk about the inner life, explore personal values, and express the parts of the self that are squelched by traditional masculinity.

In one-to-one counseling, as well as in the approaches just described, it is important to help men understand the effects of their gender training. In therapy, the client's presenting problem can often be viewed in terms of masculine socialization. For example, a man who is feeling very lonely following a breakup could understand his loneliness in the context of the social demands to be independent, nondisclosing, and task oriented. During this process, the mental health practitioner can help the man identify what he believes about masculinity and the sources of these beliefs. Then, the man can start to understand the ways in which he has been restricted by the narrow male gender role and begin the difficult task of freeing himself from masculine demands (Allen & Gordon, 1990). In this way, the counselor, lets the man know that his problems are understandable, that he need not feel shamed because he has problems, and that he can work toward feeling better.

In addition to helping male clients learn about the danger of avoiding certain behaviors, therapists can help men understand the value of behaviors that they have not learned. When men become clients, counselors often perform the educative role of helping them understand that self-disclosure and other nonsexual intimate behaviors are important for their mental health. The therapist communicates to the client that these behaviors are expected of him, but also acknowledges that they are difficult and anxiety provoking.

A major therapeutic task is to reintroduce men to the worlds of emotion and connectedness. This can be done in several ways. At the most elementary level, men often need to incorporate "feeling words" into their working vocabulary. Men who need structure in doing so can keep diaries in which they identify emotional reactions and record the situations in which the feelings occurred. Some men need a checklist of possible emotions because the identification of feeling is such a new task (Jacobson & Margolin, 1979). Moore (1990) published such a list. Lynch (1992) suggested that men at the most basic level start with basic emotions (mad, sad, glad, afraid) and build their affective vocabulary from there.

Therapists can also facilitate men's emotional education by confronting intellectualized interpretations of events and by communicating the expectation of emotional reaction. This can be done in a very matter-of-fact fashion, by saying in a nonjudgemental way, "I would think you'd have some feelings about . . . (whatever is being discussed)." Again, because most men need a little structure, the therapist is more successful if he or she talks about feelings in the context of some event rather than in the abstract (Ettkin, 1981).

Another strategy for helping men access their feelings is by attending to the physiological sensations that accompany emotions. The therapist can ask, "What's going on inside your stomach?" or "How does your face feel right now?" A jumpy stomach usually accompanies anxiety; a smile reflects pleasure. When the client is able to understand these connections and become more accepting of his natural emotional life, he may be able to resist the masculine propensity to dissociate the self from feeling. Eventually, he may learn to spontaneously identify his affective responses (Silverberg, 1986).

Therapists can also be helpful to their male clients by tapping into masculine modes of experience. Men who are working on emotional expression can view the development of these skills as a challenging task to accomplish. As most men are familiar with thinking in this kind of mode, this may reduce the threat. A man who has difficulty with learning emotional expression may feel incompetent (unmasculine). If the counselor frames the activity as a skill and connects it to other skills, the man's anxiety could be reduced. For example, the counselor might say to a client who plays golf, "Remember the first time you played golf? You weren't very good at that, either. But you practiced and you got better."

Interestingly, these masculine modes can be useful tools for breaking the client out of his constricted behavior if the therapist is skillful. Wong, Davey, and Conroe (1976) suggested an approach in which the base of positive masculinity is expanded to include other healthful behaviors. For instance, men value independence, and the therapist can help the man view nonconformism to stereotypic masculinity as a kind of independence. Men who value risk taking can learn to take risks with emotional self-disclosure. Men who value assertiveness can see objecting to sexist jokes or telling a male friend that he is valued as assertive communications. Men who are good at goal setting can set goals that are related to family, relationships, or play (Pasick, Gordon, & Meth, 1990).

A gender-aware approach to therapy with men involves giving them permission to be who they are and providing a safe atmosphere in which they can express the socially prohibited parts of the self. The therapy room can become a haven from the harsh demands of masculinity. In their exploration, male clients can discover which of these demands have been internalized and self-imposed and work toward a less restricted experience of the self. Then they become more prepared to take the changes they have made in counseling and expand them into the real world.

Summary

1. Mental health problems are related to gender from several perspectives. Definitions of mental health are culture bound, and gender stereotypes are a central feature of culture.

2. A positive relationship between mental health and psychological masculinity has been demonstrated by many research studies. However, relationships between male gender-role conflict and various psychological symptoms have also been demonstrated.

3. The proportions of males and females diagnosed in various categories of mental disorder vary significantly. Gender seems to be an important factor in determining how psychological distress finds expression. For adult men, the diagnoses of substance abuse, sexual disorders, behavior-control problems, and certain personality disorders are more common than for women.

4. Typically, male personality disorders tend to share the masculine

characteristics of hyperindependence, emotional restrictedness, self-absorption, and interpersonal exploitiveness. Men who exhibit these disorders display the most dysfunctional and destructive aspects of traditional masculinity.

5. The suicide rate for males is far greater than it is for females at every phase in the life cycle. Some theorists believe that this difference is related to the masculine values of aggression, task completion, denial of emotion, and the eschewal of help-seeking. The highest male suicide rates are found in adolescence, when males take masculine demands most seriously, and in old age, when the traditional masculine hallmarks of physical strength, self-reliance, and economic productivity are difficult to maintain.

6. Contrary to stereotypical beliefs, marriage seems to have the effect of protecting the mental health of men. The marital relationship may offer men's only avenue for meeting their intimacy needs. When marriages and other intimate relationships dissolve, men tend to have more psychological difficulties than women.

7. Male children are especially at risk for suffering negative effects from parental conflict and family separation. Sons witness more of their parent's marital conflict than daughters. This is thought to be a critical factor in the development of psychological distress. Child custody traditions place most sons with their mothers following divorce, although this practice is contraindicated by the research. Although connections between childhood father absence and mental health problems have not been convincingly demonstrated, it is clear that sons usually have powerful psychological issues around their relationships with their fathers.

8. Approaches to treating men in counseling and psychotherapy have recently placed an emphasis on the view of men as a special subgroup of clients. Well-trained therapists recognize that men bring characteristic issues to counseling, examine personal and societal biases about men and masculinity, and are aware of the impact of gender on the therapeutic relationship.

9. One-to-one psychotherapy does not provide a traditionally masculine environment. Vulnerability, emotional self-disclosure, and asking for help are connected with the sense that one is unmanly. Men are more likely than women to avoid psychological services and to drop out or otherwise shorten therapeutic relationships, even though men's need for therapeutic intervention is equal to or greater than that of women. Different counseling issues tend to emerge based on differences in therapists' sex and gender bias.

10. Because the counseling environment is uncomfortable for many men, other approaches to doing male psychological work have been developed. Workshops, seminars, and discussion groups provide for a

structured examination of men's issues. Mental health practitioners can help men to understand the effects of gender on their lives through these activities, as well as in the traditional therapy setting.

11. Many men have difficulty in dealing with the feminine areas of emotions and relationships. In counseling, a man can begin to reconnect with his feelings and intimacy needs. As a result, he can achieve a fuller experience and expression of the self.

Elizabeth Crews Photography

CHAPTER FIFTEEN

Struggles and Changes:
New Perspectives on Masculinity

> Won't you lift your head up to the mountain top,
> All your trials have not been in vain,
> There's a light that keeps shining up ahead of you,
> Every step of the way that you take.
> It's part of the plan
> For a new kind of man to come through.
>
> *Van Morrison "A New Kind of Man"*

It seems that gender roles are becoming archaic because they have aspects that limit human potential. The destructive characteristics of gender-based expectations negatively affect men as well as those around them. The need for changing gendered traditions is a quality-of-life issue for all human beings.

If we agree that the male gender-role needs to change (clearly, many people do not agree), then what aspects should be changed, and how do we go about it? These are controversial questions. As we shall see, there is a good deal of disagreement around these issues. Contrary to popular belief, there is no singular, unitary "men's movement."

Anyone who has ever tried to drop a bad habit will tell you that it is a difficult thing to do. Any psychotherapist who has ever tried to help a client change knows the challenge this task entails. And, effecting social change is always a slow, painstaking process. With regard to changing men, there are philosophical controversies and practical problems every step of the way.

Many people think that social problems are a result, not a cause, of changing gender roles—that we would all be better off if we would return to the time when, as fictional character Archie Bunker put it, "girls were girls and men were men." Among those who advocate change, some believe that men should reclaim "deep masculinity," some advocate androgyny, some think that gender roles should disappear altogether, and some just want men to "buck up" and take more responsibility.

When we begin to create methods for change, we find that gender roles are deeply ingrained in individuals, families, social customs, laws, and institutions—indeed in virtually ever facet of living. An agenda for change must therefore address multiple levels of intervention. To do so requires time, people, creativity, money, research, and other resources.

This may sound pessimistic, but it is not intended to be. However, we should appreciate the enormity of the tasks of individual and social change. At the same time, changes do happen. It is sometimes said that "the way to eat an elephant is one bite at a time." Because sexism and patriarchy are ingrained in the culture, and because they have existed for so long, they are rather formidable "elephants."

We have seen the processes of effecting social change in the crusades to end racism. People do what they can individually, and they organize to do what they can collectively. Antiracism efforts sometimes make progress, and they sometimes suffer setbacks. The people who believe in the value of racial equality continue to fight for it. Racism has not gone away, and so the efforts continue.

It is the same with sexism and patriarchy. The wheels turn slowly, sometimes they seem to be turning backward, and always there are disagreements about the directions in which the wheels should turn. In this final chapter, we look at the history of gender-role change efforts, the philosophies of individuals and organizations interested in these efforts, and the kinds of activities that address male gender-role issues in individual, social, and political contexts.

Versions of Men's Reality

Think about how strongly you agree or disagree with the following statements:

1. Modern men are a group of people who are alienated from their "true nature."

2. The innate differences between males and females go well be-yond reproductive roles.
3. Men are oppressed, mistreated victims of sexism.
4. Gender roles are a reflection of a natural order in which men are dominant.
5. Men should focus most on discovering and changing them-selves.
6. Men should focus most on eliminating sexism and patriarchy in the larger society.
7. Men should focus on eliminating sexism against men.
8. Men should gain a fuller appreciation of their privileged status, work to understand the worlds of people who have not been given such status, and strive to help women achieve equality.
9. Fundamental changes in men are not possible.
10. Feminism is men's enemy.

Theorists have taken differing positions on these issues, and thus there are varying perspectives on the nature of men and their agendas for change. Clatterbaugh (1990) described six such perspectives:

1. *Conservatives* believe that male dominance and traditional mas-culinity are natural and desirable. They often see feminism as dangerous. Therefore, they either oppose gender-role reforms or see these reforms as impossible.
2. *Profeminists* believe that traditional masculinity is destructive to women and men, in that order. Men ought to work to end pa-triarchy and men's violence and to foster equal rights for women. Men should also deal with the limitations of gender roles for themselves.
3. *Men's rights advocates* see men as victims of social and legal sex-ism. Their agenda is toward changing divorce, child custody, rape, and domestic violence laws that favor women. They also complain about "male bashing."
4. *Spiritual types* feel that males in modern society have been dis-connected from their "deep masculinity." They seek to reclaim this male essence through an agenda of self-development.
5. *Socialist theorists* see masculinity against the backdrop of capital-ist oppression. From this perspective, men control women be-cause men control most economic resources. Change in gender roles only comes from change in economic systems.
6. *Group-specific perspectives* emphasize that there is a basic flaw in the assumption that masculinity is universal across races, classes,

ethnicities, and sexual preferences. Masculinity interacts with racism, poverty, and heterosexism.

Various organizations and "movements" have come out of these different ways of viewing men's reality. In the United States, there appear to be four major foci of men's gender awareness and agendas for change: the mythopoetic movement, profeminism, men's rights, and men's studies.

One note is important before beginning a discussion of these various men's factions. There may be considerable disagreement among individual members of each of these perspectives. The situation is parallel to that of any ideological group. For instance, political conservatives may disagree with each other on certain issues, but the basic approach to and view of the world is similar across all group members. We are dealing, therefore, in somewhat stereotypic characterizations of each group.

The Mythopoetic Movement

When people speak of *the* men's movement, they are usually referring to the mythopoetic movement. It is by far the most popular and well publicized of men's gender-role-related activities. This movement leaped into the national spotlight in the early 1990s with two best-selling books: Robert Bly's (1990) *Iron John* and Sam Keen's (1991) *Fire in the Belly*. Bly is by far the most central figure in this movement. Tens of thousands of men from across the country have attended his seminars and read his books.

The mythopoetic movement comes out of the spiritual perspective just described. It has its theoretical roots in Jungian psychology (described in Chapter Four). The philosophical position is that modern men have lost the masculine roots that have been established and passed on from generation to generation since the dawn of humankind. This "deep masculinity" involves a fierce, mysterious, distinctly male energy. Being disconnected with this energy means being alienated from one's nature, and this is thought to have negative psychological consequences.

The mythopoetic contention is that deep masculinity has been eroded by several forces: the Industrial Revolution (which alienated men from their homes and disconnected them from the land), the loss of male initiation rites, the growing social disrespect of men and masculinity, and the frequent psychological distance between men and their fathers (Bly, 1990, 1991; Kimbrell, 1991). Some mythopoetic types seem to think that feminism has made things worse by devaluing the natural "wild man" quality of males. Men who buy into the feminist view of the world become "soft," female dominated, self-alienated "mama's boys."

For mythopoetic men, the agenda for change is mainly a personal one. They must separate from their mothers and be initiated into the world of men. Separating from the mother involves meeting in all-male groups. Small, somewhat intimate "ritual men's groups" meet regularly (see Liebman, 1991, for a description). "Men's councils" are larger groups of men who meet on a weekly or monthly basis for mythopoetic activity. A 1991 *Newsweek* article reported that there are at least 160 small groups and men's councils in the Northwest alone (Adler, Springen, Glick, & Gordon, 1991).

In the larger context, a variety of men's meetings and "wildman weekends" are regularly offered by Bly and others. Bly has sold out medium-sized auditoriums to men who pay $75 or more to spend the day with him and several hundred other men. Weekends are extended retreats in the service of exploring deep masculinity. Schwalbe (1992) estimated that over 100,000 men have attended a mythopoetic gathering in the past 10 years.

These meetings involve a variety of activities, including story telling, poetry reading, drumming, face painting, "sweat lodges," and other rituals. The philosophical position of the mythopoetics is that shared male ritual is the major avenue for accessing and reclaiming the rich inner experience of being a man. The lack of these rituals in modern society has left individual men disconnected from the larger community of men, and this prevents psychological growth.

A number of criticisms have been leveled against the mythopoetic movement, mostly from feminist perspectives. One of the major controversies concerns the mythopoetic doctrine of **essentialism**. The definition of deep masculinity as a guide to experience takes the position that there is a singular, important (essential) masculine quality.

The profeminist perspective rejects this notion. Its view is that gender is more of a social artifact than a "hard-wired" reality. The mythopoetic movement, with its emphasis on masculinity as transhistorical, transcultural, and transsituational denies the impact of patriarchy, misogyny, and power on the psychologies of men and women. Mythopoetic gatherings take place in a "ritual space" and allow men the luxury of a decontexualized journey into self.

Another criticism is that, because this journey usually costs money, mythopoetic types are most often men who have benefited from the economic advantages of patriarchy, racism, and classism. Brod (1992) characterized these people as men of privilege who "purchase community on the weekend." According to its critics, the mythopoetic movement has excluded large groups of oppressed people: women, people of color, and the poor. Gay, bisexual, and older men can be included if they have the money.

The response of mythopoetic leaders is that they have no intention of excluding men who are not affluent. In fact, small groups and men's councils do not require payment for participation. Even in the larger gatherings held by Bly and others, economic support is provided for some who are interested but lack the ability to pay. Critics respond by pointing out that, in fact, very few of these men are interested in participating in a gathering of white, middle-aged, upper-middle-class men who seem to have little in common with them.

The enormous appeal of the mythopoetic movement may well be due to feelings, in so many men, that they are disconnected from themselves and other men. Their desire to reconnect is in conflict with homophobia and socialized antifemininity. They sense that it is dangerous to introspect and be intimate with other men, yet they also sense that it is important to do so. Ritual seems to provide a comfortable structure that lowers the anxiety connected with the foreign world of feeling. Men have lots of rituals in sports, work, and all-male social gatherings. Mythopoetic assemblies provide new, ostensibly healthier rituals. The critics say that the exclusive and essentialist nature of mythopoetic work serves to reinforce patriarchy and misogyny. Supporters say that these activities tap a naturally masculine mode for doing important psychological work.

Profeminism

The profeminist men's movement embraces the philosophical tenets of feminism in its analysis of men's experience. Two major assumptions of this philosophy are, first, that all human beings share a similar need for self-expression and, second, that all human beings are entitled to choose their own behaviors in the service of self-expression. Gender roles are seen as destructive social forces that limit people's choices. The theoretical underpinnings of this point of view are closest to the phenomenological position described in Chapter Six.

Modern feminism has been a reaction against the male-dominated definition of human experience as well as to the social forces that limit the options of women. In the early 1970s, a few men began to write and talk about how gender demands limit men's options and harm women. This is an application of the feminist view of the world to the world of men.

The largest profeminist men's group is the National Organization of Men Against Sexism (NOMAS), formerly the National Organization of Changing Men (NOCM, 1984–1990) and the National Organization for Men (NOM, 1981–1984). NOMAS has formally sponsored an annual conference on men and masculinity since 1983, however, many of its members have been involved in this conference since it was first held in 1975. Without a doubt, this is the longest organized tradition of gender-aware dialogue about men.

In its statement of principles, NOMAS describes itself as "an activist organization supporting positive changes for men" and reflecting the value that "working to make this nation's ideal of equality real and substantive is the finest expression of what it means to be a man" (NOMAS, 1992, p. 7). This involves understanding the effects of masculine privilege; working to end injustices experienced by women, people of color, nonheterosexuals, and other oppressed groups; and challenging the self-destructive aspects of traditional masculinity. In short, this organization is self-described as "pro-feminist, gay-affirmative, enhancing men's lives" (p. 7). NOMAS supports these efforts, not only for individuals, but also in larger social contexts. For example, in 1991, NOMAS began to monitor and support legislation proposed to combat sexism (Funk, 1992).

The profeminist men's movement has taken a good deal of criticism from the mythopoetic movement, the men's rights movement, and sometimes from women. Because profeminist men reject essentialism and support and androgyny, mythopoetic types tend to view them as "soft" males who deny their natural masculine energy; they are "nice guys" but not "real men."

Mythopoetic men and men's rights advocates are often of the opinion that profeminists are overly focused on women and not focused enough on themselves. Some suggest that their annual conference has an atmosphere of guilt—a sense that men should change mostly for women and only secondarily for themselves. Mythopoetic men see this as a reflection of a lack of masculine pride. Profeminist Harry Brod (1992) responds, "I learned about male pride in NOMAS."

We see in the mythopoetic-profeminist debate an agreement that men need to change along with disagreements about directions and methods. Both factions seem invested in improving the quality of male-female relationships. The mythopoetic position seems to be that men need to be initiated into manhood by other men. As a result, they will become more free to express themselves and more psychologically healthy. At that point, they will be better prepared to enter into healthy relationships with others. The profeminist position seems to be that men need to take responsibiity for the destructiveness of their gender and spend time listening to women in a spirit of cooperation.

There is a good deal of common ground between these two approaches. Both reject violent masculinity and embrace introspective psychological development for men. Both affirm the need for men to find new ways to relate to other men that go beyond working and playing along side of each other. Both want to understand how to heal the destructive effects of harsh masculine socialization. While the mythopoetics emphasize a spiritual path for this process, profeminists emphasize dialogue and political action.

The men's rights position is that profeminists do not seem to understand the power of women over men (Williamson, 1985). As we shall see, their view is that men should be seeking to enhance their power, not to enhance the power of women.

Finally there are women who view the profeminist movement as paternalistic and as drawing attention away from women. They see profeminists as men who are learning how to act sensitive, but who are not really sincere about it (see Sattel, 1976). Williamson (1985) stated that profeminist men:

> have not convinced all feminist women of their sincerity. They have been accused of stealing the women's movement rhetoric in order to gain the limelight, or to trick women into going to bed with them. They have also been accused of adopting a new paternalism toward women by posing as the male protectors of women's liberation. (p. 312)

Women are understandably suspicious of men's groups. After all, the history of many such groups is steeped in the tradition of excluding and oppressing women. Women sometimes seem to be saying, "You have all the traditional male power, and now you want our power, too." As many women have suffered from men's dominance and inattention to their needs, it is difficult for them to believe that men want to change, much less to believe that it is possible for them to do so. It should be noted here that, of the three "movements" described, the profeminist movement is the most open to participation by and dialogue with women.

The Men's Rights Movement

In 1974, Warren Farrell's *The Liberated Man* was published. This was one of the most widely read profeminist books of its time. Farrell gave an insightful analysis of the male gender role and described the psychological benefits that men would accrue for changing in a more andryogynous direction.

Why Men Are the Way They Are was published 12 years later. This book was written by the same author, but this is hard to believe if you read both books. Rather than extolling the benefits of changing for men, Farrell (1986) was now describing men as victims of "the new sexism," a general lack of respect for men and lack of understanding for men's struggles.

Farrell's change from profeminism to the men's right perspective was a result of what he perceived to be a vilification of men by feminism. While feminists ostensibly support equal rights for all people, the National Organization for Women (NOW) opposed joint custody legislation in the late 1970s. For Farrell, this was a signal that the most influential U.S. feminist group was not so much a voice for human rights as it was a special-interest group for women's rights (Williamson, 1985). He now felt that someone should also be looking out for the rights of males.

The historical roots of the men's movement are in divorce and child custody reform efforts. In the 1960s, many men were beginning to feel that courts unfairly sided with divorcing wives in awarding alimony and child custody. They founded organizations to combat these perceived injustices. These groups never coalesced into a single national group. Williamson estimated that, as of 1985, there were 200 different "men's divorce societies" in the United States.

In the 1970s, a few men began to feel that men were being unjustly treated, not only by divorce courts, but also by the society at large. The most influential of these men was Herb Goldberg (1977), the author of *The Hazards of Being Male*. In this book, Goldberg described similarities between women's and men's issues by drawing parallels between abortion rights and the draft (control over bodies and choices) and between the sexual objectification of women and the work-and-success objectification of men.

Among groups that embraced this kind of thinking, the view that emerged was of men as a victimized and oppressed segment of the population. The most active of these organizations today are Men's Rights, Inc., and the Coalition of Free Men. Their position is that men should not accept women's interpretations of their experience. Feminists complain that men have too much power, yet these individual men do not feel powerful. Feminists claim that men are not oppressed, yet these men experience themselves otherwise.

Men's rights advocates have long lists of complaints. Following is a sample (in addition to the major issues already mentioned):

1. Social judgments that are positive for women but negative for men, for example, she has "physical needs," he's an animal; she raises her voice in frustration, he's out of control; she is homeless because society has abused her, he's a lazy bum (Speer, 1990).
2. The social acceptance of "male bashing" (Macchietto, 1991).
3. The demand that men always take the initiative, and therefore risk rejection, in heterosexual relationships (Farrell, 1986).
4. Lack of attention to male victims of spouse abuse, prison rape, war, and false accusations of rape or sexual harassment (Men's Rights, Inc., undated).

The men's rights movement is highly controversial and has been the target of criticism and ridicule. Feminists and profeminists tend to see the members of these organizations as men who do not understand or appreciate the cultural privilege of men and the legitimate anger of women. They view men's rights types as working to reinforce a patriarchy that is perceived as eroding. If you read their literature, you may get the feeling that the sexes are adversarial. Indeed, they seem to see feminists as man-hating and castrating.

With regard to an agenda for change, this movement takes the position that the emphasis should be on changing the social world's consideration of men. The only part of the traditional gender role they desire to change is the part that "takes it like a man" (silently) when mistreated.

While many feminists and profeminists reject the argument that the oppression of men is worthy of focus, mythopoetic types seem to accept it. Their differences with men's rights advocates is that they see oppression as an internalized quality that is changed through self-exploration. On the other hand, the men's rights movement sees oppression as a socially pervasive sexism against men, who will continue to be victimized unless something is done about it.

Goldberg (1977), who appears to be somewhat more moderate than the leaders of men's rights organizations, points out that there is no real contradiction between seeing women and men as oppressed at the same time. He concedes that women are more oppressed than men, but maintains that anyone who is being mistreated deserves relief. The amount of relative privilege and abuse received should not be a consideration. Sexism is sexism, regardless of its target. Goldberg's point seems well taken, although one must consider that, when finite resources are being allocated, the amount of mistreatment does of necessity become a consideration.

It is clear that these groups have differing versions of the male reality. Some synthesis of these views is possible, although the varying movements seem reluctant to enter into dialogues with each other. It might well be quite possible to do individual exploration, work for social justice for women and the same for men, and decry sexism, all at the same time. There may be appropriate settings for all-male (as well as all-female) groups to meet. In other settings, it seems quite important for mixed-sex, gender-aware dialogue to take place.

Men's Studies

In the last 30 years, feminist scholars have convincingly demonstrated that gender affects virtually every arena of life, including politics, family organization, literature, art, individual psychology, international relations, and views of history. *Women's studies* has emerged as a legitimate field of multidisciplinary intellectual interest. College and university courses, research programs, and even entire academic departments have been developed to place gender and women's perspectives into the male-dominated body of knowledge.

As men began to understand that gender has colored their views of the world, it became important to understand the effects of masculinity on the individual and society. The new field of *men's studies* has emerged as an effort in this direction.

The need for men's studies has been questioned. The most frequent objection is that nearly all study already *is* men's study, because of the pervasive influence of men in academia. Kimmel (1987), Brod (1987b), and others have responded to this objection by drawing a distinction between the study of men in the context of specific functions—as scientists, historical figures, artists, and so on—and the study of men *as men*. In the former approach, masculinity is a (usually unarticulated) backdrop of intellectual discourse. The latter approach brings masculinity into the *center* of inquiry.

The field of men's studies cuts across traditional academic disciplines. Femiano's (1991) directory of men's studies courses reveals that these courses are being taught out of a wide variety of academic departments, including psychology, sociology, English, religion, classics, history, education, anthropology, and philosophy. It was conservatively estimated that more than 200 such courses were being taught as of 1989 (Wiegand, 1989). Two interdisciplinary journals, *The Men's Studies Review* and *The Journal of Men's Studies*, are wholly devoted to this scholarship.

A number of psychological research endeavors have been described throughout this text. Following are some examples of men's studies questions from other disciplines:

1. How have the concepts of masculinity changed throughout history?
2. What do images of men in literature, art, and film tell us about masculinity?
3. How do we make sense of the reality of male patriarchal power and its seeming contradiction with the sense of powerlessness in the lives of so many men? (Kimmel, 1992)
4. What are the connections between masculinity and power, racism, sexism, heterosexism, and social class?
5. How does masculinity affect a nation's willingness to enter or avoid war?
6. What are the effects of male initiation rites in various cultures, and how are these rites similar or dissimilar? (Herdt, 1992; Gilmore, 1990)
7. How can the various "men's movements" be understood in historical, psychological, and political perspective? (Fiebert, 1987)
8. How has masculinity affected religious institutions and practices?
9. What kinds of techniques are useful in facilitating men's understanding of the impact of gender on their lives?
10. How does masculinity change and evolve in midlife and old age? (O'Neil & Egan, in press)

Most men's studies scholars come from profeminist or mythopoetic frames of reference. The general approach is to take seriously the influence of gender on men and articulate its effects. Profeminist-oriented writers are mainly interested in studying the changing character of masculinity and its consequences for individual men and social systems. Mythpoetic writers are mostly involved in writing (or writing about) stories, poems, and rituals that can be used to get closer to men's symbolic experience of their masculinity. The writing of men's rights advocates seems limited to demonstrating and criticizing perceived sexism against men.

Men's studies is controversial for many of the same reasons that the various men's movements are controversial. Some feminist scholars point out that the name "men's studies" implies a parallel with "women's studies." Once these two fields are seen as complementary, there may be a pressure to allocate resources more evenly between the two areas. Thus, the existence of men's studies may result in fewer jobs for women's studies scholars and a reinforcement of the institutional and economic power of men (Canaan & Griffin, 1990).

There is an implicit goal in much of women's studies to remove women's disadvantages and improve the quality of their lives. Many men's studies scholars have a similar goal for men. However, it is clear that men have enjoyed far-ranging advantages throughout history by virtue of their status as men. Some of men's studies is focused on the disadvantages of masculinity. Brod's (1987b) argument is that men who understand these disadvantages are more likely to discard destructive masculinity and the power that goes with it. This argument is unconvincing to some, who see this focus on disadvantage as drawing attention away from the obvious and more profound disadvantages of women in society and obscuring the overwhelmingly advantageous and unjust nature of masculine privilege.

In seeking to understand women's reactions to men's movements and men's studies, the image that may come to mind is of a schoolyard bully who beats up a child every day from Monday through Thursday, and then says he wants to be friends on Friday. Having been victimized by men for so long, women are understandably suspicious of these new efforts by men, just as the child would question the motives of the seemingly transformed bully.

Most women seem to want men to change. However, they may doubt whether men really want to (or have the ability to) change. A recent collection of women's reactions to men's efforts toward change begins with, "Make no mistake about it. Women want a men's movement. We are literally dying for it" (Steinem, 1992, p. v). The rest of the book contains expressions of various writers' doubts about whether this change is a reality, and, if so, whether it is one that will benefit women.

At the same time, there is a hopefulness that men will begin to move in a positive direction.

The notion that men should spend time understanding themselves seems to make a lot of women angry. The feeling is that men need to spend more time listening to and seeking to understand women. One of the assumptions behind gender-aware activity for men is that men's understanding of women is limited by their lack of self-understanding. The processes of individual exploration, challenging traditional stereotypes, productive dialogue between men and women, and working toward social change can and should take place all at the same time.

What is the future of masculinity? Hopefully, it is a new generation of men who feel less pressure to look, feel, and act like "real men" and more of an urgency to look, feel, and act like the people they truly are. It is a group of men who can hear the voices of women, children, other men, Nature, and the self, and who can connect more deeply with all of them. It is a group of men who can retain a vigorous masculine energy and direct it it into breaking the cycles of violence and self-destructiveness that have stood in place for centuries. It is a new generation of men who can love, work, and play in different ways. It is the reconnection of the masculine self with the human self.

Summary

1. There is a good deal of controversy around whether the male gender role should change or not. Among those who think that it should change, there are disagreements about the nature and direction these changes should take.

2. As gender is deeply ingrained in all social systems, the alteration of gender roles is a painstaking process. Differing opinions on men's reality result in differing opinions on the necessity and nature of change.

3. The position of the mythopoetic men's movement is that modern men have gotten out of touch with the spiritual essence of masculinity. This has resulted in self-alienation and destructive behaviors. The agenda for change, from this perspective, is to restore "deep masculinity" through male initiation rituals.

4. Major criticisms of the mythopoetic movement center around its assumption of essential masculinity and its removal of masculinity from its social contexts.

5. The profeminist men's movement emphasizes changing the aspects

of masculinity that limit freedom of choice for men and women. Profeminists are involved in a variety of individual and social activities concerned with the problems of sexism, racism, heterosexism, and other forms of injustice.

6. Critics of profeminism argue that these men are overly focused on masculine guilt. Some feminists have complained that profeminist men have drawn attention away from women's issues.

7. Men's rights advocates see men as oppressed victims of sexism. Perceived injustices include unfair divorce and child custody laws, the historical abuse of men in military service, the treatment of men as work and success objects, and "male bashing."

8. Critics of the men's rights movement see these men as ignorant of the privilege of patriarchy and unempathic with those who are truly oppressed.

9. There is a growing amount of research and scholarship on men and masculinity from a variety of perspectives. The academic interest in men's studies cuts across traditional disciplines.

10. Men's studies are controversial for many of the same reasons that the various men's movements are. Additionally, some women's studies scholars fear that men's studies will cut into the already scarce resources that are allocated to them.

11. The future of masculinity is in the reconnection of the masculine self with the human self.

References

Abbey, A. (1982). Sex differences in attributions for friendly behavior: Do males misperceive females' friendliness? *Journal of Personality and Social Psychology, 42,* 830–838.

Adams, C. H., & Sherer, M. (1985). Sex-role orientation and psychological adjustment: Implications for the masculinity model. *Sex Roles, 12,* 1211–1218.

Adler, J., Springen, K., Glick, D., & Gordon, J. (1991, June 24). Drums, sweat and tears. *Newsweek,* pp. 46–51.

Adler, T. (1992, February). Study links genes to sexual orientation. *APA Monitor,* pp. 12–13.

Adorno, T., Frenkel-Brunswik, E., Levinson, D., & Sanford, R. N. (1950). *The authoritarian personality.* New York: Harper.

Aiken, L. R. (1989). *Assessment of personality.* Boston: Allyn and Bacon.

Allen, B. (1974). A visit from uncle macho. In J. H. Pleck & J. Sawyer (Eds.), *Men and masculinity* (pp. 5–6). Englewood Cliffs, NJ: Prentice Hall.

Allen, J. A., & Gordon, S.(1990). Creating a framework for change. In R. L. Meth & R. S. Pasick (Eds.), *Men in therapy: The challenge of change* (pp. 131–151). New York: Guilford.

American Psychiatric Association (1968). *Diagnostic and statistical manual of mental disorders* (2nd ed.) (DSM-II). Washington, DC: Author.

American Psychiatric Association (1980). *Diagnostic and statistical manual of mental disorders* (3rd ed.) (DSM-III). Washington, DC: Author.

American Psychiatric Association (1987). *Diagnostic and statistical manual of mental disorders* (3rd ed.-revised) (DSM-III-R). Washington, DC: Author.

Ames, L. B. (1975). Are Rorschach responses influenced by society's change? *Journal of Personality Assessment, 39,* 439–452.

Anctil, J. (1992). Myths about gay men and lesbians. *Mentor, 22,* 31.

Angier, N. (1991, September 1). The biology of what it means to be gay. *The New York Times,* pp. 1–4.

Anderson, K. E., Lytton, H., & Romney, D. M. (1986). Mothers' interactions with normal and conduct-disordered boys: Who affects whom? *Developmental Psychology, 22,* 604–609.

Antill, J. K. (1983). Sex role complementarity vs. similarity in married couples. *Journal of Personality and Social Psychology, 45,* 145–155.

Antill, J. K. (1987). Parents' beliefs and values about sex roles, sex differences, and sexuality: Their sources and implications. In P. Shaver & C. Hendrick (Eds.), *Sex and gender* (pp. 294–328). Newbury Park, CA: Sage.

Archer, C. J. (1984). Children's attitudes toward sex-role division in adult occupational roles. *Sex Roles, 10,* 1–10.

Archer, J. (1984). Gender roles as developmental pathways. *British Journal of Social Psychology, 23,* 245–256.

Archer, J., & Rhodes, C. (1989). The relationship between gender-related traits and attitudes. *British Journal of Social Psychology, 28,* 149–157.

Arentewicz, G., & Schmidt, G. (1983). *The treatment of sexual disorders: Concepts and techniques of couples therapy.* New York: Basic Books.

Aries, E. J., & Johnson, E. L. (1983). Close friendship in adulthood: Conversational content between same-sex friends. *Sex Roles, 9,* 1183–1196.

Aries, E. J., & Oliver, R. R. (1985). Sex differences in the development of a separate sense of self during infancy: Directions for future research. *Psychology of Women Quarterly, 9,* 515–531.

Astin, A. W. (1985, January 16). Freshman characteristics and attitudes. *Chronicle of Higher Education,* pp. 15–16.

Astrachan, A. (1992). Men and the new economy. In M. S. Kimmel & M. A. Messner (Eds.), *Men's lives* (2nd ed.). New York: Macmillan.

Atkinson, J., & Huston, T. L. (1984). Sex role orientation and division of labor early in marriage. *Journal of Personality and Social Psychology 46,* 330–345.

Attorney General's Commission on Pornography (1986). *Final report of the Attorney General's Commission on Pornography.* Washington, DC: U.S. Government Printing Office.

Baca Zinn, M. (1980). Gender and ethnic identity among Chicanos. *Frontiers, 5*(2), 18–24.

Baca Zinn, M. (1992). Chicano men and masculinity. In M. S. Kimmel & M. A. Messner (Eds.), *Men's lives* (pp. 67–76). New York: Macmillan.

Bagby, R. M., Taylor, G. J., & Ryan, D. (1986). Toronto Alexithymia Scale: Relationship with personality and psychosomatic measures. *Psychotherapy and Psychosomatics, 45,* 207–215.

Bakan, D. (1966). *The duality of human existence.* Chicago: Rand-McNally.

Balkwell, C., Balswick, J., & Balkwell, J. (1978). On black and white family patterns in America: Their impact on the expressive aspects of sex-role socialization. *Journal of Marriage and the Family, 40,* 743–747.

Balswick, J. (1982). Male inexpressiveness: Psychological and social aspects. In

K. Solomon & N. B. Levy (Eds.), *Men in transition: Theory and therapy* (pp. 131–150). New York: Plenum.

Balswick, J. (1988). *The inexpressive male.* Lexington, MA: D. C. Heath.

Balswick, J., & Avertt, C. (1977). Differences in expressiveness: Gender, interpersonal orientation, and perceived parental expressiveness as contributing factors. *Journal of Marriage and the Family, 39,* 121–127.

Bandura, A. (1973). *Aggression: A social learning analysis.* Englewood Cliffs, NJ: Prentice Hall.

Bandura, A., Ross, D., & Ross, S. (1961). Transmission of aggression through imitation of aggressive models. *Journal of Abnormal and Social Psychology, 63,* 575–582.

Bandura, A., & Walters, R. H. (1963). *Social learning and personality development.* New York: Holt, Rinehart, and Winston.

Barash, D. P. (1979). *The whispering within.* New York: Elsevier.

Barash, D. P. (1982). *Sociobiology and behavior.* New York: Elsevier.

Barbach, L., & Levine, L. (1981). *Shared intimacies.* New York: Bantam.

Bardwick, J. M. (1979). *In transition.* New York: Holt, Rinehart, and Winston.

Barnett, R. C., & Baruch, G. K. (1987). Social roles, gender, and psychological distress. In R. C. Barnett, L. Biener, and G. K. Baruch (Eds.), *Gender and stress* (pp. 122–143). New York: Macmillan.

Barnett, R. C., Marshall, N. L., & Pleck, J. H. (1992). Adult son-parent relationships and their associations with sons' psychological distress. *Journal of Family Issues, 13,* 505–525.

Baruch, G., & Barnett, R. (1981). Fathers' participation in the care of their preschool children. *Sex Roles, 7,* 1043–1055.

Basow, S. (1986). *Gender stereotypes: Traditions and alternatives* (2nd ed.). Monterey, CA: Brooks/Cole.

Basow, S. (1992). *Gender: Stereotypes and roles* (3rd ed.). Monterey, CA: Brooks/Cole.

Beach, F. A. (1987). Alternative interpretations of the development of G-I/R. In J. M. Reinish, L. A. Rosenblum, & S. A. Sanders (Eds.), *Masculinity/feminity: Basic perspectives* (pp. 29–36). New York: Oxford University Press.

Beebe, J. (1989). Editor's introduction. In C. G. Jung, R. F. C. Hull (Trans.), & J. Beebe (Eds.), *Aspects of the masculine* (pp. vii–xvii). Princeton, NJ: Princeton University Press.

Beere, C. A. (1990). *Gender roles: A handbook of tests and measures.* New York: Greenwood.

Bell, A. P., & Weinberg, M. S. (1978). *Homosexualities: A study of diversity among men and women.* New York: Simon & Schuster.

Bell, A. P., Weinberg, M. S., & Hammersmith, S. (1981). *Sexual preference: Its development in men and women.* Bloomington: Indiana University Press.

Bem, S. L. (1974). The measurement of psychological androgyny. *Journal of Consulting and Clinical Psychology, 42,* 155–162.

Bem, S. L. (1981a). *Bem Sex-Role Inventory: Professional manual.* Palo Alto, CA: Consulting Psychologists Press.

Bem, S. L. (1981b). Gender schema theory: A cognitive account of sex-typing. *Psychological Review, 88,* 354–364.

Bem, S. L. (1985). Androgyny and gender schema theory: A conceptual and empirical integration. In T. B. Sonderegger (Ed.), *Nebraska symposium on motivation, 1984: Psychology of gender* (vol. 32, pp. 179–236). Lincoln: University of Nebraska Press.

Bem, S. L. (1987). Masculinity and femininity exist only in the mind of the perceiver. In J. M. Reinisch, L. A. Rosenblum, & S. A. Sanders (Eds.), *Masculinity/femininity: Basic perspectives* (pp. 304–314). New York: Oxford University Press.

Benbow, C. P., & Stanley, J. C. (1983). Sex differences in mathematical reasoning: More firsts. *Science, 222,* 1029–1031.

Berger, M., & Wright, L. (1980). Divided allegiance: Men, work, and family life. In T. M. Skovholt, P. Schauble, & R. David (Eds.), *Counseling men* (pp. 157–163). Monterey, CA: Brooks/Cole.

Berglass, S. (1986). *Success syndrome.* New York: Plenum Press.

Berk, R. A., Berk, S. F., Loseke, D. R., & Rauma, D. (1983). Mutual combat and other family violence myths. In D. Finkelhor, R. J. Gelles, G. T. Hotaling, & M. A. Straus (Eds.), *The dark side of families: Current family violence research* (pp. 197–212). Beverly Hills, CA: Sage.

Bernard, J. (1981). The good-provider role: Its rise and fall. *American Psychologist, 36,* 1–12.

Berndt, T. J. (1992). Friendship and friends' influence in adolescence. *Current Directions in Psychological Science, 1,* 156–159.

Berzins, J. I., Welling, M. A., & Wetter, R. E. (1978). A new measure of psychological androgyny based on the Personality Research Form. *Journal of Consulting and Clinical Psychology, 46,* 126–138.

Biernbaum, M., & Weinberg, J. (1991). Men unlearning rape. *Changing Men, 22,* 22–24.

Blazer, D. G., & Wiliams, C. (1980). The epidemiology of dysphoria and depression in an elderly population. *American Journal of Psychiatry, 137,* 439–444.

Bleier, R. (1984). *Science and gender: A critique of biology and its theories on women.* New York: Pergamon.

Block, J. D. (1980). *Friendship.* New York: Macmillan.

Block, J. H. (1984). *Sex role identity and ego development.* San Francisco: Jossey-Bass.

Block, J. H., Block, J., & Gjerde, P. F. (1986). The personality of children prior to divorce: A prospective study. *Child Development, 57,* 827–840.

Bloom, B. L., & Caldwell, R. A. (1981). Sex differences in adjustment during the process of marital separation. *Journal of Marriage and the Family, 43,* 693–701.

Blum, J. (1992, July 17). One-parent black households up. *The News Journal,* p. A12.

Blumenfeld, W. J. (1992). *Homophobia: How we all pay the price.* Boston: Beacon Press.

Blumstein, P., & Schwartz, P. (1983). *American couples.* New York: William Morrow.

Bly, R. (1988). A day for men. Workshop presentation.

Bly, R. (1990). *Iron John.* Reading, MA: Addison Wesley.

Bly, R. (1991). Father hunger in men. In K. Thompson (Ed.), *To be a man: In search of the deep masculine* (pp. 189–192). Los Angeles: Tarcher.

Bock, H. (1991, October 30). Officials find football safety tough to tackle. *The Free-Lance Star,* p. D1.

Bodenhausen, G. V. (1988). Stereotypic biases in social decision making and memory: Testing process models of stereotype use. *Journal of Personality and Social Psychology, 55,* 726–737.

Boss, M. (1963). *Psychoanalysis and daseinanalysis.* New York: Basic Books.

Boston Women's Health Book Collective (1992). *The new our bodies, ourselves* (3rd ed.). New York: Simon & Schuster.

Bowen, G. L., & Orthner, D. K. (1991). Effects of organizational culture on fatherhood. In F. W. Bozett & S. M. H. Hanson (Eds.), *Fatherhood and families in cultural context* (pp. 187–217). New York: Springer.

Boyd-Franklin, N. (1989). *Black families in therapy.* New York: Guilford.

Brannon, R. (1976). The male sex role: Our culture's blueprint of manhood, and what it's done for us lately. In D. David & R. Brannon (Eds.), *The forty-nine percent majority* (pp. 1–45). Reading, MA: Addison-Wesley.

Brannon, R. (1985). Dimensions of the male sex role in America. In A. G. Sargent, (Ed.), *Beyond sex roles* (2nd ed., pp. 296–316). New York: West.

Brehm, S. S., & Kassin, S. M. (1993). *Social psychology* (2nd ed.). Boston, Houghton Mifflin.

Bridges, J. S. (1989). Sex differences in occupational values. *Sex Roles, 20,* 205–211.

Briere, J., & Malamuth, N. M. (1983). Self-reported likelihood of sexually aggressive behavior: Attitudinal versus sexual explanations. *Journal of Research in Personality, 17,* 315–323.

Brod, H. (Ed.). (1987a). *The making of masculinities: The new men's studies.* Boston: Allen and Unwin.

Brod, H. (1987b). A case for men's studies. In M. S. Kimmel (Ed.), *Changing men: New directions in research on men and masculinity* (pp. 263–277). Newbury Park, CA: Sage.

Brod, H. (1992). *NOMAS panel: Mythopoetic men-profeminist men: A dialogue.* Panel discussion (with W. Liebman, J. Sternbach, & G. Murray) at the 17th National Conference on Men and Masculinity, Chicago, IL.

Broverman, I., Vogel, S. R., Broverman, D. M., Clarkson, F. E., & Rosenkrantz, P. S. (1972). Sex role stereotypes: A current appraisal. *Journal of Social Issues, 28,* 59–78.

Brownmiller, S. (1975). *Against our will: Men, women, and rape.* New York: Simon & Schuster.

Bruch, M. A. (1980). Holland's typology applied to client/counselor interaction: Implications for counseling with men. In T. M. Skovholt, P. Schauble, & R. David (Eds.), *Counseling men* (pp. 101–119). Monterey, CA: Brooks/Cole.

Brush, S. (1984). *Men: An owner's manual: A comprehensive guide to having a man underfoot.* New York: Simon & Schuster.

Buie, J. (1988, January). Divorce hurts boys more, studies show. *APA Monitor*, p. 5.

Burns, A., & Homel, R. (1989). Gender division of tasks by parents and their children. *Psychology of Women Quarterly, 13,* 113–125.

Burt, M. R. (1980). Cultural myths and supports for rape. *Journal of Personality and Social Psychology, 38,* 217–230.

Burt, M. R. (1991). Rape myths and acquaintance rape. In A. Parrot & L. Bechofer (Eds.), *Acquaintance rape: The hidden crime* (pp. 26–40). New York: Wiley.

Buss, D. M., (1990). Unmitigated agency and unmitigated communion: An analysis of the negative components of masculinity and femininity. *Sex Roles, 22,* 555–568.

Buss, D. M., & Barnes, M. (1986). Preferences in human mate selection. *Journal of Personality and Social Psychology, 50,* 559–570.

Busse, E. W. (1986). Treating hypochondriasis in the elderly. *Generations, 10* (3), 30–33.

Bussey, K., & Bandura, A. (1984). Influence of gender constancy and social power on sex-linked modeling. *Journal of Personality and Social Psychology, 47,* 1292–1302.

Bussey, K., & Perry, D. G. (1982). Same-sex imitation: The avoidance of cross-sex models or the acceptance of same-sex models? *Sex Roles, 8,* 773–784.

Butcher, J. N. (1987, September 21). *The Minnesota report for the Minnesota Multiphasic Personality Inventory.* Unpublished manuscript (individual testing report).

Byrne, D. (1977). Social psychology and the study of sexual behavior. *Personality and Social Psychology Bulletin, 3,* 3–30.

Caldwell, M. A., & Peplau, L. A. (1982). Sex differences in same-sex friendship. *Sex Roles, 8,* 721–732.

Canaan, J. E., & Griffin, C. (1990).   .1ew men's studies: Part of the problem or part of the solution? In J. Heain & D. Morgan (Eds.), *Men, masculinities, and social theory* (pp. 206–214). Cambridge, MA: Unwin Hyman.

Cancian, F. M. (1986). The feminization of love. *Signs, 11,* 692–709.

Cancian, F. M. (1987). *Love in America: Gender and self-development.* Cambridge, England: Cambridge University Press.

Candell, P. (1974). When I was about fourteen. . . . In J. H. Pleck & J. Sawyer (Eds.), *Men and masculinity* (pp. 14–17). Englewood Cliffs, NJ: Prentice Hall.

Carroll, J. L., Volk, K. D., & Hyde, J. S. (1985). Differences between males and females in motives for engaging in sexual intercourse. *Archives of Sexual Behavior, 14,* 131–139

Carson, R. C., & Butcher, J. N. (1992). *Abnormal psychology and modern life* (9th ed.). New York: Harper Collins.

Chafetz, J. S. (1978). *Masculine/feminine or human?* (2nd ed.). Itasca, IL: Peacock.

Chamberlain, D. B. (1989). Babies remember pain. *Pre- & Peri-Natal Psychology Journal, 3,* 297–310.

Chaze, W. (1981, June 29). Youth gangs are back—on old turf and new. *U.S. News and World Report,* pp. 46–47.

Chelune, G. T., Waring, E. M., Vosk, B. N., Sultan, F. E., & Ogden, T. K. (1984). Self-disclosure and its relationship to marital intimacy. *Journal of Clinical Psychology, 40,* 216–219.

Cherry, L. (1975). Teacher-child verbal interaction: An approach to the study of sex differences. In B. Thorne & N. Henley (Eds.), *Language and sex: Differences in dominance* (pp. 172–183). Rowley, MA: Newbury House.

Chodorow, N. (1978). *The reproduction of mothering: Psychoanalysis and the sociology of gender.* Berkeley: University of California Press.

Christenson, S. (1989, January/February). The invisible man. *American Health,* p. 63.

Chusmir, L. H. (1990). Men who make nontraditional career choices. *Journal of Counseling and Development, 69,* 11–16.

Clarke, D. (1992). *Suicide in the elderly.* Paper presented at the Annual Meeting of the American Association of Suicidology, Chicago, IL.

Clatterbaugh, K. (1990). *Contemporary perspectives on masculinity: Men, women, and politics in modern society.* Boulder, CO: Westview.

Cleary, P. D. (1987). Gender differences in stress-related disorders. In R. C. Barnett, & G. K. Baruch (Eds.), *Gender and stress* (pp. 39–72). New York: Macmillan.

Cleary, P. D., & Mechanic, D. (1983). Sex differences in psychological distress among married people. *Journal of Health and Social Beahvior, 24,* 111–121.

Cohn, L. D. (1991). Sex differences in the course of personality development. *Psychological Bulletin, 109,* 252–266.

Cohn, N. B., & Strassberg, D. S. (1983). Self-disclosure reciprocity among adolescents. *Personality and Social Psychology Bulletin, 9,* 97–102.

Colburn, D. (1991, January 29). The way of the warrior: Are men born to fight? *Washington Post Health,* pp. 10–13.

Coleman, E. (1990). Toward a synthetic understanding of sexual orientation. In D. P. McWhirter, S. A. Sanders, & J. M. Reinisch (Eds.), *Homosexuality/ heterosexuality: Concepts of sexual orientation.* New York: Oxford University Press.

Collier, H. V. (1982). *Counseling women: A guide for therapists.* New York: Macmillan.

Collins, G. (1979, June 1). A new look at life with father. *The New York Times Magazine,* pp. 30–31.

Comas-Diaz, L. (1990). Hispanic/Latino communities: Psychological implications. *Journal of Training and Practice in Professional Psychology, 4,* 14–35.

Commission on Obscenity and Pornography (1970). *The report of the commission on obscenity and pornography.* New York: Bantam.

Constantinople, A. (1973). Masculinity-feminity: An exception to the famous dictum? *Psychological Bulletin, 80,* 389–407.

Cook, E. P. (1985). *Psychological androgyny.* New York: Pergamon.

Cook, E. P. (1987). Psychological androgyny: A review of the research. *The Counseling Psychologist, 15,* 471–513.

Cook, E. P. (1990). Gender and psychological distress. *Journal of Counseling and Development, 68,* 371–375.

Cooper, D. E., & Holmstrom, R. W. (1984). Relationship between alexithymia and somatic complaints in a normal sample. *Psychotherapy and Psychosomatics, 41,* 20–24.

Copeland, A. R. (1987). Suicide among the elderly: The metro-Dade County experience, 1981–83. *Medicine, Science, and the Law, 27,* 32–36.

Corcoran, C. B. (1992). From victim control to social change: A feminist perspective on campus rape prevention programs. In J. Chrisler & D. Howard (Eds.), *New directions in feminist psychology* (pp. 130–140). New York: Springer.

Costa, P., & McCrae, R. (1978). Objective personality assessment. In M. Storandt, I. Siegler, & M. Elias (Eds.). *The clinical psychology of aging.* New York: Plenum.

Cozby, P. C. (1973). Self-disclosure: A literature review. *Psychological Bulletin, 79,* 73–91.

Crites, J. O., & Fitzgerald, L. F. (1978). The competent male. *The Counseling Psychologist, 7,* 10–14.

Culp, R. E., Cook, A. S., & Housley, P. C. (1983). A comparison of observed and reported adult-infant interactions: Effects of perceived sex. *Sex Roles, 9,* 475–479.

Cunningham, J. D., Braiker, H., & Kelley, H. H. (1982). Marital-status and sex differences in problems reported by married and cohabiting couples. *Psychology of Women Quarterly, 6,* 415–427.

Daly, M., & Wilson, M. (1983). *Sex, evolution, and behavior* (2nd ed.). Boston: Willard Grant.

Daly, M., & Wilson, M. (1985). Competitiveness, risk taking, and violence: The young male syndrome. *Ethology and Sociobiology, 6,* 59–73.

Daly, M., Wilson, M., & Weghorst, S. J. (1982). Male sexual jealousy. *Ethology and Sociobiology, 3,* 11–27.

Darwin, C. (1871). *The descent of man, and selection in relation to sex.* New York: Appleton & Co.

Davidson, B. J., Balswick, J., & Halverson, C. (1983). Affective self-disclosure and marital adjustment: A test of equity theory. *Journal of Marriage and the Family, 45,* 93–102.

Davis, F., & Walsh, W. B. (1988). *Antecedents and consequences of gender role conflict: An empirical test of sex role strain analysis.* Paper presented at the 96th Annual Convention of the American Psychological Association, Atlanta, GA.

DeAngelis, T. (1991, December). Sexual harassment common, complex. *APA Monitor,* p. 29.

Deaux, K. (1985). Sex and gender. *Annual Review of Psychology, 36,* 49–81.

Deaux, K., & Hanna, R. (1984). Courtship in the personals column: The influence of gender and sexual orientation. *Sex Roles, 11,* 363–375.

Deaux, K., & Kite, M. E. (1987). Thinking about gender. In B. B. Hess & M. M. Ferree (Eds.), *Analyzing gender: A handbook of social science research* (pp. 92–117). Newbury Park, CA: Sage.

Deaux, K., & Lewis, L. (1984). Structure of gender stereotypes: Interrelationships among components and gender label. *Journal of Personality and Social Psychology, 46,* 991–1004.

De Cecco, J. (1984). *Homophobia: An overview.* New York: Haworth.

Del Boca, F. K., & Ashmore, R. D. (1980). Sex stereotypes through the life cycle. In L. Wheeler (Ed.), *Review of personality and social psychology* (vol. 1, pp. 163–192). Beverly Hills, CA: Sage.

Derlega, V. J., & Chaikin, A. L. (1976). Norms affecting self-disclosure in men and women. *Journal of Consulting and Clinical Psychology, 44,* 376–380.

Derlega, V. J., Winstead, B. A., & Jones, W. H. (1991). *Personality: Contemporary theory and research.* Chicago: Nelson-Hall.

Devlin, P. K., & Cowan, G. A. (1985). Homophobia, perceived fathering, and male intimate relationships. *Journal of Personality Assessment, 49,* 467–473.

Dickemann, M. (1981). Paternal confidence and dowry competition: A biocultural analysis of purdah. In R. D. Alexander & D. W. Tinkle (Eds.), *Natural selection and social behavior.* New York: Chiron Press.

Division 17, American Psychological Association. (1979). Principles concerning the counseling and therapy of women. *The Counseling Psychologist, 8,* 21.

Dolnick, E. (1991, August 13). Why do women outlive men? *Washington Post Health,* pp. 10–13.

Donnerstein, E. (1983). Erotica and human aggression. In R. Green & E. Donnerstein (Eds.), *Aggression: Theoretical and empirical reviews.* New York: Academic Press.

Donnerstein, E. (1984). Pornography: Its effects on violence against women. In N. M. Malamuth & E. Donnerstein (Eds.), *Pornography and sexual aggression* (pp. 53–81). Orlando, FL: Academic Press.

Donnerstein, E., & Linz, D. (1986). Mass media sexual violence and male viewers: Current theory and research. *American Behavioral Scientist, 29,* 601–618.

Dosser, D. A., Jr. (1982). Male inexpressiveness: Behavioral intervention. In K. Solomon & N. B. Levy (Eds.), *Men in transition: Theory and therapy* (pp. 343–437). New York: Plenum.

Duneier, M. (1992). *Slim's table.* Chicago, IL: University of Chicago Press.

Eichorn, D., Clausen, J., Haan, N., Honzik, M., & Mussen, P. (1981). *Present and past in middle life.* New York: Academic Press.

Eisenstock, B. (1984). Sex-role differences in children's identification with counterstereotypical televised portrayals. *Sex Roles, 10,* 417–430.

Eisler, R. M., Blalock, J. A. (1991). Masculine gender role stress: Implications for the assessment of men. *Clinical Psychology Review, 11,* 45–60.

Ellis, L. (1989). *Theories of rape: Inquiries into the causes of sexual aggression.* New York: Hemisphere.

Emihovich, C. A., Gaier, E. L., & Cronin, N. C. (1984). Sex-role expectations changes by fathers for their sons. *Sex Roles, 11,* 861–868.

Equal Employment Opportunity Commission (1980). Discrimination because of sex under Title VII of the Civil Rights Act 1964, as amended; adoption of interim interpretive guidelines. *Federal Register, 45,* 25024–25025.

Erickson, R. J., & Gecas, V. (1991). Social class and fatherhood. In F. W. Bozett & S. M. H. Hanson (Eds.), *Fatherhood and families in cultural context* (pp. 114–137). New York: Springer.

Ettkin, L. (1981). Treating the special madness of men. In R. A. Lewis (Ed.), *Men in difficult times: Masculinity today and tomorrow* (pp. 36–46). Englewood Cliffs, NJ: Prentice Hall.

Fagot, B. I. (1984). Teacher and peer reactions to boys' and girls' play styles. *Sex Roles, 11*, 691–702.

Falbo, T., & Peplau, L. A. (1980). Power strategies in intimate relationships. *Journal of Personality and Social Psychology, 38*, 618–628.

Falicov, C. J. (1982). Mexican families. In M. McGoldrick, J. K. Pearce, & J. Giordano (Eds.), *Ethnicity and family therapy* (pp. 134–163). New York: Guilford.

Farr, K. (1988). Dominance bonding through the good old boys sociability group. *Sex Roles, 18*, 259–277.

Farrell, W. (1974). *The liberated man.* New York: Bantam.

Farrell, W. (1982, April). Risking sexual rejection: Women's last frontier? *Ms.,* 100.

Farrell, W. (1986). *Why men are the way they are: The male-female dynamic.* New York: McGraw-Hill.

Farrell, W. (1990). We should embrace traditional masculinity. In K. Thompson (Ed.), *To be a man: In search of the deep masculine* (pp. 10–16). Los Angeles: Tarcher.

Farrell, W. (1991, May/June). Men as success objects. *Utne Reader,* pp. 81–84.

Fasteau, M. F. (1974). *The male machine.* New York: McGraw-Hill.

Fausto-Sterling, A. (1985). *Myths of gender: Biological theories about women and men.* New York: Basic Books.

Federal Bureau of Investigation (1992). *Uniform crime reports of the United States.* Washington, DC: U.S. Government Printing Office.

Feirstein, B. (1982). *Real men don't eat quiche.* New York: Simon & Schuster.

Feldman, S. S., Biringen, Z. C., & Nash, S. C. (1981). Fluctuations of sex-related self-attributions as a function of stage in the family life cycle. *Developmental Psychology, 17*, 24–35.

Femiano, S. (1991). *Directory of men's studies courses taught in the United States and Canada.* Northampton, MA: (self-published).

Fiebert, M. S. (1987). Some perspectives on the men's movement. *Men's Studies Review, 4* (4), 8–10.

Fine, R. (1987). *The forgotten man: Understanding the male psyche.* New York: Hayworth.

Fiske, S. T., & Taylor, S. E. (1991). *Social cognition* (2nd ed.). New York: McGraw-Hill.

Fitzgerald, J. M. (1978). Actual and perceived sex and generational differences in interpersonal style: Structure and quantitative issues. *Journal of Gerontology, 33*, 394–401.

Fitzgerald, L. F., & Cherpas, C. C. (1985). On the reciprocal relationship between between gender and occupation: Rethinking the assumptions concerning masculine career development. *Journal of Vocational Behavior, 27*, 109–122.

Fogel, R., & Paludi, M. A. (1984). Fear of success and failure, or norms for achievement? *Sex Roles, 10,* 431–443.

Fox, M., Gibbs, M., & Auerbach, D. (1985). Age and gender dimensions of friendship. *Psychology of Women Quarterly, 9,* 489–502.

Frable, D. E. S. (1989). Sex typing and gender ideology: Two facets of the individual's gender psychology that go together. *Journal of Personality and Social Psychology, 56,* 95–108.

Frable, D. E. S., & Bem, S. L. (1985). If you're gender-schematic, all members of the opposite sex look alike. *Journal of Personality and Social Psychology, 49,* 459–468.

Frank, S. J., McLaughlin, A. M., & Crusco, A. (1984). Sex role attributes, symptom distress, and defensive style among college men and women. *Journal of Personality and Social Psychology, 47,* 182–192.

Frank, S. J., Towell, P. A., & Huyck, M. (1985). The effects of sex-role traits on three aspects of psychological well-being in a sample of middle-aged women. *Sex Roles, 12,* 1073–1087.

Frankel, M. T., & Rollins, H. A., Jr. (1983). Does mother know best? Mothers and fathers interacting with preschool sons and daughters. *Developmental Psychology, 19,* 694–702.

Frankl, V. (1960). *The doctor and the soul.* New York: Knopf.

Franzoi, S. L., & Davis, M. H. (1985). Adolescent self-disclosure and loneliness: Private self-consciousness and parental influence. *Journal of Personality and Social Psychology, 48,* 768–780.

Freiberg, P. (1991, March). Black men may act cool to advertise masculinity. *APA Monitor,* p. 30.

Freud, S. ([1910] 1989). Leonardo da Vinci and a memory of his childhood. In P. Gay (Ed.), *The Freud reader* (pp. 443–481). New York: Norton.

Freud, S. ([1915] 1989). Three essays on the theory of sexuality. In P. Gay (Ed.), *The Freud reader* (pp. 239–293). New York: Norton.

Freud, S. ([1924] 1989). The dissolution of the Oedipus complex. In P. Gay (Ed.), *The Freud reader* (pp. 661–669). New York: Norton.

Freud, S. (1925). *Collected papers.* London: Hogarth.

Freund, K., Nagler, E., Langevin, R., Zajac, A., & Steiner, B. (1974). Measuring feminine gender identity in homosexual males. *Archives of Sexual Behavior, 3,* 249–260.

Friedmann, E. A., & Orbach, H. L. (1974). Adjustment to retirement. In S. Arieti (Ed.), *American handbook of psychiatry. Vol. 1: Foundations of psychiatry* (2nd ed., pp. 609–645). New York: Basic Books.

Friend, T. (1991, October 21). Men and health: A deadly silence. *The News Journal,* p. B3.

Funk, R. E. (1992). *1992 legislative report to the National Organization for Men Against Sexism.* Unpublished manuscript.

Futuyma, D. J., & Risch, S. J. (1984). Sexual orientation, sociobiology, and evolution. *Journal of Homosexuality, 9,* 157–168.

Galambos, N. L., Almeida, D. M., & Peterson, A. C. (1990). Masculinity, femininity, and sex role attitudes in early adolescence: Exploring gender intensification. *Child Development, 61,* 1905–1914.

Garfinkel, P. (1985). *In a man's world: Father, son, brother, friend, and other roles men play.* New York: New American Library.

Garnets, L., & Pleck, J. H. (1979). Sex role identity, adrogyny, and sex role transcendence: A sex role strain analysis. *Psychology of Women Quarterly, 3,* 270–283.

Gatz, M., Smyer, M. A., & Lawton, M. P. (1980). The mental health system and the older adult. In L. W. Poon (Ed.), *Aging in the 1980's: Psychological issues* (pp. 5–18). Washington, DC: American Psychological Association.

Gelfand, D. E., & Kutzik, A. J. (Eds.) (1979). *Ethnicity and aging.* New York: Springer.

Gelman, D., Springen, K., Elam, R., Joseph, N., Robins, K., & Hagar, M. (1990, July 23). The mind of the rapist. *Newsweek,* pp. 46–53.

Gentry, W. D. (1984). Behavioral medicine: A new research paradigm. In W. D. Gentry (Ed.), *Handbook of behavioral medicine* (pp. 1–12), New York: Guilford.

Gilder, G. (1986). *Men and marriage.* London: Pelican.

Gilligan, C. (1982). *In a different voice: Psychological theory and women's development.* Cambridge, MA: Harvard University Press.

Gilmore, D. D. (1990). *Manhood in the making: Cultural concepts of masculinity.* New Haven, CT: Yale University Press.

Goldberg, H. (1977). *The hazards of being male.* New York: New American Library.

Goldberg, H. (1979). *The new male: From self-destruction to self-care.* New York: Morrow.

Goldfoot, D. A. & Neff, D. A. (1987). Assessment of behavioral sex differences in social contexts: Perspectives from primatology. In J. M. Reinisch, L. A. Rosenbaum, & S. A. Sanders (Eds.), *Masculinity/femininity: Basic perspectives* (pp. 179–195). New York: Oxford University Press.

Goldman, R. F. (1992). Questioning circumcision: A growing movement. *Wingspan, 6* (2), 12–13.

Gondolf, E. W. (1988). Who are those guys? Toward a behavioral typology of batterers. *Violence and Victims, 3,* 187–203.

Gondolf, E. W., & Hanneken, J. (1987). The gender warrior: Reformed batterers on abuse, treatment, and change. *Journal of Family Violence, 2,* 177–191.

Gonzales, A. (1982). The sex roles of the traditional Mexican family: A comparison of Chicano and Anglo students' attitudes. *Journal of Cross-Cultural Psychology, 13,* 330–339.

Good, G. E., Dell, D. M., & Mintz, L. B. (1989). Male role and gender role conflict: Relations to help seeking in men. *Journal of Counseling Psychology, 36,* 295–300.

Good, G. E., Gilbert, L. A., & Scher, M. (1990). Gender aware therapy: A synthesis of feminist therapy and knowledge about gender. *Journal of Counseling Psychology, 68,* 376–380.

Good, G. E., & Mintz, L. B. (1990). Gender role conflict and depression in college men: Evidence for compounded risk. *Journal of Counseling and Development, 69,* 17–21.

Gordon, B., & Allen, J. A. (1990). Helping men in couple relationships. In R. L. Meth & R. S. Pasick (Eds.), *Men in therapy: The challenge of change* (pp. 224–233). New York: Guilford.

Gough, H. G. (1957). *Manual for the California Psychological Inventory.* Palo Alto, CA: Consulting Psychologists Press.

Gould, R. E. (1974). Measuring masculinity by the size of a paycheck. In J. H. Pleck & J. Sawyer (Eds.), *Men and masculinity* (pp. 96–100). Englewood Cliffs, NJ: Prentice Hall.

Gould, R. L. (1978). *Transformations: Growth and change in adult life.* New York: Simon & Schuster.

Gove, W., & Tudor, J. F. (1973). Adult sex roles and mental illness. In J. Huber (Ed.), *Changing women in a changing society.* Chicago: University of Chicago Press.

Greely, A. M. (1981). *The Irish Americans.* New York: Harper & Row.

Green, R. (1987). Exposure to explicit sexual materials and sexual assault: A review of behavioral and social science research. In M. R. Walsh (Ed.), *The psychology of women: Ongoing debates* (pp. 430–440). New Haven, CT: Yale University Press.

Greenberg, J. S. (1990). *Comprehensive stress management* (3rd ed.). Dubuque, IA: Wm. C. Brown.

Greenberg, M., & Morris, N. (1974). Engrossment: The newborn's impact upon the father. *American Journal of Orthopsychiatry, 44,* 520–531.

Gregersen, E. (1982). *Sexual practices: The story of human sexuality.* New York: Franklin Watts.

Greif, E. B. (1976). Sex-role playing in preschool children. In J. S. Bruner, A. Jolly, & K. Sylva (Eds.), *Play.* Harmondsworth, England: Penguin.

Grimm, L., & Yarnold, P. R. (1985). Sex typing and the coronary-prone behavior pattern. *Sex Roles, 12,* 171–178.

Gross, A. E. (1992). The male role and heterosexual behavior. In M. A. Kimmel & M. S. Messner (Eds.), *Men's lives* (2nd ed., pp. 424–432). New York: Macmillan.

Groth, A. N. (1979). *Men who rape: The psychology of the offender.* New York: Plenum.

Groth-Marnat, G. (1990). *Handbook of psychological assessment* (2nd ed.). New York: Wiley.

Gustafson, R. (1986). Threat as a determinant of alcohol-related aggression. *Psychological Reports, 58,* 287–297.

Gutek, B. A., & Nakamura, C. Y. (1983). Gender roles and sexuality in the world of work. In E. R. Allgeier & N. B. McCormick (Eds.), *Changing boundaries: Gender roles and sexual behavior.* Palo Alto, CA: Mayfield.

Gutierrez, F. J. (1990). Exploring the macho mystique: Counseling Latino men. In D. Moore & F. Leafgren (Eds.), *Men in conflict* (pp. 139–151). Alexandria, VA: American Association for Counseling and Development.

Gutmann, D. (1977a). The cross-cultural perspective: Notes toward a comparative psychology of aging. In J. E. Birren & K. W. Schaie (Eds.), *Handbook of the psychology of aging* (pp. 302–326). New York: Van Nostrand Reinhold.

Gutmann, D. L. (1977b). Psychoanalysis and aging: A developmental view. In S. I. Greenspan & G. H. Pollack (Eds.), *The course of life: Psychoanalytic contributions toward understanding personality development. Vol. III: Adulthood and the aging process* (pp. 489–517). Washington, DC: National Institute of Mental Health.

Gutmann, D. (1987). *Reclaimed powers.* New York: Basic Books.

Habegger, C. E., & Blieszner, R. (1990). Personal and social aspects of reminiscence: An exploratory study of neglected dimensions. *Activities. Adaptation, and Aging, 14,* 21–38.

Hackett, T. P., Rosenbaum, J. F., & Cassen, N. H. (1985). Cardiovascular disorders. In H. I. Kaplan & B. J. Saddock (Eds.), *Comprehensive textbook of psychiatry/IV* (pp. 1148–1159). Baltimore: Williams and Wilkins.

Hall, C. S. (1954). *A primer of Freudian psychology.* New York: World Publishing.

Hall, C. S. & Lindzey, G. (1985). *Theories of personality* (4th ed.). New York: Wiley.

Hall, G. C. N. (1990). Prediction of sexual aggression. *Clinical Psychology Review, 10,* 229–246.

Hamilton, D. L. (1979). A cognitive-attributional analysis of stereotyping. *Advances in Experimental Psychology, 12,* 53–81.

Hamilton, J. B., Hamilton, R. S., & Mestler, G. E. (1969). Duration of life and causes of death in domestic cats: Influence of sex, gonadectomy, and inbreeding. *Journal of Gerontology, 24,* 427–437.

Hamilton, J. B., & Mestler, G. E. (1969). Mortality and survival: Comparison of eunuchs with intact men and women in a mentally retarded population. *Journal of Gerontology, 24,* 395–411.

Hansen, J. E., & Schuldt, W. J. (1984). Marital self-disclosure and marital satisfaction. *Journal of Marriage and the Family, 46,* 923–926.

Harney, P. A., & Muehlenhard, C. L. (1991). Rape. In E. Grauerholz & M. A. Koralewski (Eds.), *Sexual coercion: A sourcebook on its nature, causes, and prevention* (pp. 3–15). Lexington, MA: D. C. Heath.

Harris, I. (1992). Media myths and the reality of men's work. In M. S. Kimmel & M. A. Messner (Eds.), *Men's lives* (pp. 225–231). New York: Macmillan.

Harrison, J. B. (1978). Warning: The male sex role may be dangerous to your health. *Journal of Social Issues, 34,* 65–86.

Harrison, J., Chin, J., & Ficarotto, T. (1992). Warning: Masculinity may be dangerous to your health. In M. S. Kimmel & M. A. Messner (Eds.), *Men's lives* (2nd ed., pp. 271–285). New York: Macmillan.

Hartley, R. E. (1959). Sex role pressures and the socialization of the male child. *Psychological Reports, 5,* 457–468.

Hathaway, C. R. & McKinley, J. C. (1951). *Minnesota Multiphasic Personality Inventory.* New York: Psychological Corporation.

Haviland, M. G., Shaw, D. G., Cummings, M. A., & MacMurray, J. P. (1988). The relationship between alexithymia and depressive symptoms in a sample of newly abstinent alcoholic inpatients. *Psychotherapy and Psychosomatics, 50,* 81–87.

Hawke, C. C. (1950). Castration and sex crimes. *Journal of Mental Deficiency, 55,* 220–226.

Hawks, B. (1986). Personal communication.

Heiberg, A. N. (1980). Alexithymic characteristics and somatic illness. *Psychotherapy and Psychosomatics, 34,* 261–266.

Helgeson, V. S. (1990). The role of masculinity in a prognostic predictor of heart attack severity. *Sex Roles, 22,* 755–774.

Hendryx, M. S., Haviland, M. G., & Shaw, D. G. (1991). Dimensions of alexithymia and their relationships to anxiety and depression. *Journal of Personality Assessment, 56,* 227–237.

Heppner, P. P., & Gonzales, D. S. (1987). Men counseling men. In M. Scher, M. Stevens, G. E. Good, & G. A. Eichenfield (Eds.), *Handbook of counseling and psychotherapy with men* (pp. 30–38). Newbury Park, CA: Sage.

Herbert, A. (1976). Reciprocity of self-disclosure between adolescents and their parents. Unpublished doctoral dissertation, Columbia University.

Herdt, G. (1992). *Male initiation rituals across cultures.* Paper presented at the 17th National Conference on Men and Masculinity, Chicago, IL.

Herek, G. M. (1986). On heterosexual masculinity: Some psychical consequences of the social construction of gender and sexuality. *American Behavioral Scientist, 29,* 563–577.

Herzog, A. R., Bachman, J. G., & Johnson, L. D. (1983). Paid work, child care, and housework: A national survey of high school seniors' preferences for sharing responsibilities between husband and wife. *Sex Roles, 9,* 109–135.

Hetherington, E. M., Cox M., & Cox, R. (1976). Divorced fathers. *The Family Coordinator, 25,* 417–428.

Hetherington, E. M., Cox, M., & Cox, R. (1985). Long term effects of divorce and remarriage on the adjustment of children. *Journal of the American Academy of Child Psychiatry, 24,* 518–530.

Hetherington, E. M., Stanley-Hagen, M., & Anderson, E. R. (1989). Marital transitions: A child's perspective. *American Psychologist, 44,* 303–312.

Hill, J. P. (1986). Personal communication.

Hill, J. P. (1987). Research on adolescents and their families: Past and prospect. *New Directions for Child Development, 37,* 13–31.

Hodgkinson, H. L. (1985). *All one system: Demographics of education, kindergarten through graduate school.* Washington, DC: Institute for Educational Leadership.

Hoffman, J. (1992, February 16). When men hit women. *The New York Times Magazine,* pp. 23–27, 64–66, 72.

Holmes, T. H. & Rahe, R. H. (1967). The social readjustment rating scale. *Journal of Psychosomatic Research, 11,* 213–218.

Homans, G. C. (1974). *Social behavior: The elementary forms.* New York: Harcourt Brace Jovanovich.

Hood, J., & Golden, S. (1979). Beating time/making time: The impact of work scheduling on men's family roles. *The Family Coordinator, 28,* 575–582.

Horney, K. (1932). The dread of women: Observations on a specific difference in the dread felt by men and women respectively for the opposite sex. *International Journal of Psychoanalysis, 13,* 348–360.

Hosken, F. P. (1979). *The Hosken report. Genital and sexual mutilation of females* (2nd ed.). Lexington, MA: Women's International Network News.

Houseworth, S., Peplow, K., & Thirer, J. (1989). Influence of sport participation upon sex role orientation of Caucasian males and their attitudes toward women. *Sex Roles, 20,* 317–325.

Hrdy, S. B. (1981). *The woman that never evolved.* Cambridge, MA: Harvard University Press.

Huesman, L. R., Eron, L. D., Lefkowitz, M. M., & Walder, L. O. (1984). *The stability of aggression over time and generations.* Victoria, BC, Canada: International Society for Research on Aggression.

Hull, C. L. (1943). *Principles of behavior.* New York: Appleton-Century-Crofts.

Humphreys, A. P., & Smith, P. K. (1987). Rough and tumble friendship and dominance in school children: Evidence for continuity and change in middle childhood. *Child Development, 58,* 201–212.

Hunt, M. (1974). *Sexual behavior in the 1970's.* Chicago: Playboy Press.

Hussey, A. (1989). Neonatal circumcision: A uniquely American ritual. *Transitions, 9* (4), 18–22.

Huston, T. L., & Ashmore, R. D. (1986). Women and men in personal relationship. In R. D. Ashmore & R. K. Del Boca (Eds.), *The social psychology of female-male relations* (pp. 167–210). New York: Academic Press.

Huyck, M. (1992). *Evaluating the parental imperative in Parkville.* Paper presented at the Annual Meeting of the American Gerontological Society, Washington, DC.

Hyde, J. S. (1981). How large are cognitive gender differences? A meta-analysis using *v* and *d. American Psuychologist, 36,* 892–901.

Hyde, J. S., & Phyllis, D. E. (1981). Androgyny across the life span. *Developmental Psychology, 15,* 334–336.

Ickes, W., & Barnes, R. D. (1978). Boys and girls together—and alienated: On enacting stereotyped sex roles in mixed-sex dyads. *Journal of Personality and Social Psychology, 36,* 669–683.

Jacobson, N. S., & Margolin, G. (1979). *Marital therapy: Strategies based on social learning and behavior exchange principles.* New York: Brunner/Mazel.

James, S. (1984). *A dictionary of sexist quotations.* Totowa, NJ: Barnes and Noble.

Jolkovski, M. (1989). Personal communication.

Jones, G. P. (1990). The boy is father to the man: A men's studies exploration of intergenerational interaction. *Men's Studies Review, 7* (1), 9–13.

Jourard, S. M. (1971). *The transparent self.* New York: Van Nostrand.

Jung, C. G. (1933). *Modern man in search of a soul.* New York: Harcourt, Brace and World.

Jung, C. G. ([1959] 1989). Concerning the archetypes with special reference to the anima concept. In C. G. Jung, R. F. C. Hull (Trans.), & J. Beebe (Ed.), *Aspects of the masculine* (pp. 115–122). Princeton, NJ: Princeton University Press.

Jung, C. G. ([1963] 1989). The personification of the opposites. In C. G. Jung, R. F. C. Hull (Trans.), & J. Beebe (Ed.), *Aspects of the masculine* (pp. 85–187). Princeton, NJ: Princeton University Press.

Jung, C. G. ([1977] 1989). American men as sons of their wives. In K. Thompson (Ed.), *To be a man: In search of the deep masculine* (pp. 141–144). Los Angeles: Tarcher.

Kagan, J. (1964). Acquisition and significance of sex typing and sex role identity. In M. L. Hoffman & L. W. Hoffman (Eds.), *Review of child research* (vol. 1, pp. 137–169). New York: Russell Sage.

Kamarovsky, M. ([1940] 1971). *The unemployed man and his family: The effect of unemployment upon the status of the man in fifty-nine families.* New York: Dryden Press/Arno Press.

Kamarovsky, M. (1976). *Dilemmas of masculinity: A study of college youth.* New York: Norton.

Kanin, E. (1970). An examination of sexual aggression as a response to sexual frustration. *Journal of Marriage and the Family, 34,* 428–433.

Kanter, R. M. (1977). *Men and women in the corporation.* New York: Basic Books.

Kaplan, M. (1983). A woman's view of DSM-III. *American Psychologist, 38,* 786–792.

Kaprio, J., Koskenvuo, M., & Rita, H. (1987). Mortality after bereavement: A prospective study of 95,647 widowed persons. *American Journal of Public Health, 77,* 283–287.

Kardinger, A., & Linton, R. (1945). *The psychological frontiers of society.* New York: Columbia University Press.

Kart, C. S. (1981). *The realities of aging.* Boston: Allyn and Bacon.

Kaufman, S. R. (1986). *The ageless self: Sources of meaning in late life.* Madison: University of Wisconsin Press.

Kay, S. A. & Meikle, D. B. (1984). Political ideology, sociobiology, and the U.S. women's rights movement. In M. W. Watts (Ed.), *Biopolitics and gender* (pp. 67–96). New York: Hayworth.

Keen, E. (1970). *Three faces of being: Toward an existential clinical psychology.* New York: Appleton-Century-Crofts.

Keen, S. (1991). *Fire in the belly: On being a man.* New York: Bantam.

Kelly, J. B. (1988). Longer-term adjustment in children of divorce: Converging findings and implications for practice. *Journal of Family Psychology, 2,* 119–140.

Kemper, T. D. (1990). *Social structure and testosterone.* New Brunswick, NJ: Rutgers University Press.

Kenrick, D. T. (1987). Gender, genes and the social environment: A biosocial interactionist perspective. In P. Shaver & C. Hendrick (Eds.), *Sex and gender* (pp. 14–43). Newbury Park, CA: Sage.

Kenrick, D. T., Gutierres, S. E., & Goldberg, L. L. (1989). Influence of popular erotica on judgments of strangers and mates. *Journal of Experimental Social Psychology, 25,* 159–167.

Kilmartin, C. T. (1986). *Gender differences in child and adolescent self-disclosure.* Unpublished manuscript, Virginia Commonwealth University.

Kilmartin, C. T. (1987). *The male sex role: Suggestions for psychological consultation.* Unpublished manuscript, Virginia Commonwealth University.

Kilmartin, C. T. (1988). *Interpersonal influence strategies: Gender differences in response to nurturant behavior.* Unpublished doctoral dissertation, Virginia Commonwealth University.

Kilmartin, C. T., & Ring, T. E. (1991). *Understanding and preventing acquaintance rape on college campuses: Services for men.* Paper presented at the annual meeting of the Maryland College Personnel Association, College Park, MD.

Kimbrell, A. (1991, May/June). A time for men to pull together. *Utne Reader,* pp. 66–74.

Kimmel, M. S. (1987). Rethinking masculinity: New directions in research. In M. S. Kimmel (Ed.), *Changing men: New directions in research on men and masculinity* (pp. 9–24). Newbury Park, CA: Sage.

Kimmel, M. S. (1992). *Accountability in men's studies scholarship: The academic is political.* Remarks at the 17th National Conference on Men and Masculinity, Chicago, IL.

Kimmel, M. S., & Levine, M. P. (1992). Men and AIDS. In Michael S. Kimmel & M. A. Messner (Eds.), *Men's lives* (2nd ed., pp. 318–329). New York: Macmillan.

Kinder, B. N., & Curtiss, G. (1990). Alexithymia among empirically derived subgroups of chronic back pain patients. *Journal of Personality Assessment, 54,* 351–362.

Kinsey, A. C. Pomeroy, W. B., & Martin, C. E. (1948). *Sexual behavior in the human male.* Philadelphia: W. B. Saunders.

Kinsey, A. C., Pomeroy, W. B., Martin, C. E., & Gebhard, P. H. (1953). *Sexual behavior in the human female.* Philadelphia: W. B. Saunders.

Kipling, R. (1952). *Rudyard Kipling's verse: Definitive edition.* Garden City, NY: Doubleday.

Kleiger, J. H., & Jones, N. F. (1980). Characteristics of alexithymic patients in a chronic respiratory illness population. *Journal of Nervous and Mental Disease, 168,* 465–470.

Klerman, G. L. (1983). Problems in the definition and diagnosis of depression in the elderly. In L. D. Breslau & M. R. Haug (Eds.), *Depression and aging: Causes, care, and consequences* (pp. 3–19). New York: Springer.

Kohlberg, L. A. (1966). A cognitive-developmental analysis of children's sex-role concepts and attitudes. In E. E. Maccoby (Ed.), *The development of sex differences* (pp. 82–173). Stanford, CA: Stanford University Press.

Kohut, H. (1971). *The analysis of the self.* New York: International Universities Press.

Kohut, H. (1977). *The restoration of the self.* New York: International Universities Press.

Koss, M. P. (1983). The scope of rape: Implications for the clinical treatment of victims. *The Clinical Psychologist, 36,* 88–91.

Koss, M. P. (1990, August 29). Testimony before the United States Senate Judiciary Panel.

Koss, M. P., & Dinero, T. E. (1988). Predictors of sexual aggression among a national sample of male college students. In R. A. Prentky & V. L. Quinsey (Eds.), *Human sexual aggression: Current perspectives* (pp. 133–147). New York: New York Academy of Sciences.

Koss, M. P., Gidycz, C. A., & Wisniewski, N. (1987). The scope of rape: Incidence and prevalence of sexual aggression and victimization in a national sample of higher education students. *Journal of Consulting and Clinical Psychology, 55,* 162–170.

Koss, M. P., Leonard, K. E., Beezley, D. A., Oros, C. J. (1985). Nonstranger sexual aggression: A discriminant analysis of the psychological characteristics of undetected offenders. *Sex Roles, 12,* 981–992.

Kreuz, L. E., & Rose, R. M. (1972). Assessment of aggressive behavior and plasma testosterone in a young criminal population. *Psychosomatic Medicine, 34,* 321–332.

Kuniczak, W. S. (1978). *My name is million.* New York: Doubleday.

Kupferberg, T. (1986, July). Dumb records. *National Lampoon,* p. 18.

Kurdek, L. A. (1987). Sex role self schema and psychological adjustment in coupled homosexual men and women. *Sex Roles, 17,* 549–562.

Kurdek, L. A. (1988). Correlates of negative attitudes toward homosexuals in heterosexual college students. *Sex Roles, 18,* 727–738.

Kurdek, L. A., & Schmitt, J. P. (1986). Interaction of sex role self-concept with relationship quality and relationship beliefs in married, heterosexual cohabiting, gay, and lesbian couples. *Journal of Personality and Social Psychology, 51,* 365–370.

L'Abate, L. (1980). Inexpressive males or overexpressive females? A reply to Balswick. *Family Relations, 29,* 229–230.

Lambert, W., & Simon, S. (1991, July 30). Military discharges gay veterans of gulf. *The Wall Street Journal,* p. B8.

Lancaster, J. B. (1985). Evolutionary perspectives on sex differences in the higher primates. In A. Rossi (Ed.), *Gender and the life course* (pp. 3–27). New York: Aldine.

Landrine, H. (1988). Revising the framework of abnormal psychology. In P. Bronstein & K. Quina (Eds.), *Teaching a psychology of people: Resources for gender and sociocultural awareness* (pp. 37–44). Washington, DC: American Psychological Association.

Lange, A. J., & Jackubowski, P. (1976). *Responsible assertive behavior: Cognitive/behavioral procedures for trainers.* New York: Research Press.

LaRossa, R. (1989). Fatherhood and social change. *Men's Studies Review, 6* (2), 1–9.

Lavine, L. O., & Lombardo, J. P. (1984). Self-disclosure: Intimate and nonintimate disclosures to parents and best friends as a function of Bem sex-role category. *Sex Roles, 11,* 760–768.

Leafgren, F. (1988). Developmental programs. In R. J. May & M. Scher (Eds.), *Changing roles for men on campus* (pp. 53–65). San Francisco: Jossey-Bass.

Leafgren, F. (1990). Men on a journey. In D. Moore & F. Leafgren (Eds.), *Men in conflict* (pp. 3–10). Alexandria, VA: American Association for Counseling and Development.

Lederer, W., & Botwin, A. (1982). Where have all the heroes gone? Another view of changing masculine roles. In K. Solomon (Ed.), *Men in transition: Theory and therapy* (pp. 241–246). New York: Plenum.

Lee, C. C. (1990). Black male development: Counseling the "native son." In D. Moore & F. Leafgren (Eds.), *Men in conflict* (pp. 125–137). Alexandria, VA: American Association for Counseling and Development.

Lee, J. (1991). *At my father's wedding: Reclaiming our true masculinity.* New York: Bantam.

Lee, L. (1987). Rape prevention: Experiential training for men. *Journal of Counseling and Development, 66,* 100–101.

Lehne, G. (1976). Homophobia among men. In D. David & R. Brannon (Eds.), *The forty-nine percent majority* (pp. 66–88). Reading, MA: Addison-Wesley.

Lemann, N. (1991). *The promised land.* New York: Knopf.

Lemle, R., & Mishkind, M. E. (1989). Alcohol and masculinity. *Journal of Substance Abuse Treatment, 6,* 213–222.

Leong, F. (1986). Counseling and psychotherapy with Asian-Americans: Review of the literature. *Journal of Counseling Psychology, 33,* 196–206.

Lerner, M. J. (1980). *The belief in a just world: A fundamental delusion.* New York: Plenum.

Lester, J. (1974). Being a boy. In J. H. Pleck, & J. Sawyer (Eds.), *Men and masculinity* (pp. 32–35). Englewood Cliffs, NJ: Prentice Hall.

Letich, L. (1991, May/June). Do you know who your friends are? *Utne Reader,* pp. 85–87.

Levant, R. F. (1988). Education for fatherhood. In P. Bronstein & C. P. Cowan (Eds.), *Fatherhood today: Men's changing role in the family* (pp. 253–275). New York: Wiley.

Levant, R. F. (1990a). Coping with the new father role. In D. Moore & F. Leafgren (Eds.), *Men in conflict* (pp. 81–94). Alexandria, VA: American Association for Counseling and Development.

Levant, R. F. (1990b). Psychological services designed for men: A psychoeducational approach. *Psychotherapy, 27,* 309–315.

Levine, L., & Barbach, L. (1984). *The intimate male.* New York: Doubleday.

Levinson, D. J., Darrow, C. N., Klein, E. B., Levinson, M. H., & McKee, B. (1978). *The seasons of a man's life.* New York: Knopf.

Levy, C. J. (1992). ARVN as faggots: Inverted warfare in Vietnam. In M. S. Kimmel & M. A. Messner (Eds.), *Men's lives* (2nd ed., pp. 183–197). New York: Macmillan.

Lewis, E. T., & McCarthy, P. R. (1988). Perceptions of self-disclosure as a function of gender-linked variables. *Sex Roles, 19,* 47–56.

Lewis, M. (1987). Early sex role behavior and school age adjustment. In J. M. Reinisch, L. A. Rosenblum, & S. A. Sanders (Eds.), *Masculinity/femininity: Basic perspectives* (pp. 202–226). New York: Oxford University Press.

Lewis, M., & Weinraub, M. (1979). Origins of early sex-role development. *Sex Roles, 5,* 135–153.

Lewis, R. A. (1986). Men's changing roles in marriage and the family. In R. A. Lewis (Ed.), *Men's changing roles in the family* (pp. 1–10). New York: Haworth.

Liebman, W. (1991). *Tending the fire: The ritual men's group.* St. Paul, MN: Ally Press.

Liebow, F. (1980). Men and jobs. In E. H. Pleck & J. H. Pleck (Eds.), *The American man* (pp. 365–376). Englewood Cliffs, NJ: Prentice Hall.

Linz, D., & Donnerstein, E. (1992). Research can help us explain violence and pornography. *Chronicle of Higher Education, 39* (6), pp. B3–B4.

Lips, H. (1988). *Sex and gender.* Mountain View, CA: Mayfield.

Lisak, D. (1991). Sexual aggression, masculinity, and fathers. *Signs, 16,* 238–262.

Lisak, D., & Roth, S. (1988). Motivational factors in nonincarcerated sexually aggressive men. *Journal of Personality and Social Psychology, 55,* 795–802.

Lobel, T. E., & Winch, G. L.(1986). Different defense mechanisms among men with different sex role orientations. *Sex Roles, 15,* 215–220.

Lockwood, D. (1980). *Prison sexual violence.* New York: Elsevier.

Lombardo, J. P., & Fantasia, S. C. (1976). The relationship of self-disclosure to personality, adjustment, and self-actualization. *Journal of Clinical Psychology, 32,* 765–769.

Lombardo, J. P., & Lavine, L. O. (1981). Sex-role stereotyping and patterns of self-disclosure. *Sex Roles, 7,* 403–411.

Long, V. O. (1989). Relation of masculinity to self-esteem and self-acceptance in male professionals, college students, and clients. *Journal of Counseling Psychology, 36,* 84–87.

Loy, P., & Stewart, L. P. (1984). The extent and effect of the sexual harassment of working women. *Sociological Focus, 17,* 31–43.

Luria, Z., Friedman, S., & Rose, M. D. (1987). *Human sexuality.* New York: Wiley.

Lynch, J. R. (1992). Personal communication.

Lynn, D. B. (1959). A note on sex differences in the development of masculine and feminine identification. *Psychological Review, 66,* 126–135.

Lynn, D. B. (1966). The process of learning parental and sex-role identification. *Journal of Marriage and the Family, 28,* 466–477.

Lynn, D. B. (1969). *Parental and sex role identification: A theoretical formation.* Berkeley, CA: McCutchan.

Lynn, D. B. (1979). *Daughters and parents: Past, present, and future.* Monterey, CA: Brooks/Cole.

Lytton, H., & Romney, D. M. (1991). Parents' differential socialization of boys and girls: A meta-analysis. *Psychological Bulletin, 109,* 267–296.

Macchietto, J. (1991). Editor's comment: Hallmark learns about male-bashing: A slow but productive task. *Transitions, 11* (5), 2.

Maccoby, E. E. (1987). The varied meanings of "masculine" and "feminine." In J. M. Reinisch, L. A. Rosenblum, & S. A. Sanders (Eds.), *Masculinity/femininity: Basic perspectives* (pp. 227–239). New York: Oxford University Press.

Maccoby, E. E. (1988a). Gender as a social category. *Developmental Psychology, 24,* 755–765.

Maccoby, E. E. (1988b), *Gender as a social construct.* Paper presented at the Annual Meeting of the Eastern Psychological Association, Buffalo, NY.

Maccoby, E. E. (1990). Gender and relationships: A developmental account. *American Psychologist, 45,* 513–520.

Maccoby, E. E. & Jacklin, C. N. (1974). *The psychology of sex differences.* Stanford: Stanford University Press.

MacDonald, K., & Parke, R. D. (1986). Parent-child physical play: The effects of sex and age of children and parents. *Sex Roles, 15,* 367–378.

MacKinnon, C. A. (1985). Pornography, civil rights, and speech. *Harvard Civil Rights-Civil Liberties Law Review, 20,* 1–70.

MacLeod, L. (1980). *Wife battering in Canada: The vicious circle.* Hull, Quebec: Canadian Government Publishing Centre.

Macoby, M. (1976, December). The corporate climber. *Fortune,* pp. 98–101, 104–108.

Maddi, S. R. (1989). *Personality theories: A comparative analysis* (5th ed.). Chicago: Dorsey.

Maffeo, P. A. (1982). Gender as a model for mental health. In I. Al-Issa (Ed.), *Gender and psychopathology* (pp. 31–50). New York: Academic Press.

Majors, R., & Billson, J. M. (1992). *Cool pose.* New York: Lexington.

Makepeace, J. M. (1981). Courtship violence among college students. *Family Relations, 30,* 97–102.

Malamuth, N. M. (1981). Rape proclivity among males. *Journal of Social Issues, 37,* 138–157.

Malamuth, N. M. (1984). Aggression against women: Cultural and individual causes. In N. M. Malamuth & E. Donnerstein (Eds.), *Pornography and sexual aggression* (pp. 19–52). Orlando, FL: Academic Press.

Malamuth, N. M., & Check, J. V. (1981). The effects of mass media exposure on acceptance of violence against women: A field experiment. *Journal of Research in Personality, 15,* 436–446.

Maltz, D. N., & Borker, R. A. (1983). A cultural approach to male-female miscommunication. In J. A. Gumperz (Ed.), *Language and social identity* (pp. 195–216). New York: Cambridge University Press.

Markus, H., Crane, M., Bernstein, S., & Siladi, M. (1982). Self-schemas and gender. *Journal of Personality and Social Psychology, 42,* 38–50.

Marsh, H. W., Antill, J. K., & Cunningham, J. D. (1989). Masculinity and femininity: A bipolar construct and independent constructs. *Journal of Personality, 57,* 625–663.

Martin, C. L. (1987). A ratio measure of sex stereotyping. *Journal of Personality and Social Psychology, 52,* 489–499.

Mason, A., & Blankenship, V. (1987). Power and affiliation motivation, stress, and abuse in intimate relationships. *Journal of Personality and Social Psychology, 52*, 203–210.

Masters, W. H., & Johnson, V. E. (1970). *Human sexual inadequacy.* Boston: Little, Brown.

May, R. (1958). Contributions of existential psychotherapy. In R. May, E. Angel, & H. F. Ellenberger (Eds.), *Existence: A new dimension in psychiatry and psychology.* New York: Basic Books.

May, R. J. (1986). Concerning a psychoanalytic view of maleness. *The Psychoanalytic Review, 73*, 579–597.

May, R. J. (1988). The developmental journey of the male college student. In R. J. May & M. Scher (Eds.), *Changing roles of men on campus* (pp. 5–18). San Francisco: Jossey-Bass.

May, R. J. (1990). Finding ourselves: Self-esteem, self-disclosure, and self-acceptance. In D. Moore & F. Leafgren (Eds.), *Men in conflict* (pp. 11–21). Alexandria, VA: American Association for Counseling and Development.

Mazur, A. (1983). Hormones, aggression, and dominance in humans. In B. B. Svare (Ed.), *Hormones and aggressive behavior* (pp. 563–576). New York: Plenum.

Mazur, E. (1989). Predicting gender differences in same-sex friendships from affiliation motive and value. *Psychology of Women Quarterly, 13*, 277–292.

McAdams, D. P., Lester, R. M., Brand, P. A., McNamara, W. J., & Lensky, D. B. (1988). Sex and the TAT: Are women more intimate than men? Do men fear intimacy? *Journal of Personality Assessment, 52*, 397–409.

McAdoo, H. P. (1981). *Black families.* Beverly Hills, CA: Sage.

McCrae, R. R., & Costa, P. T., Jr. (1984). *Emerging lives, enduring dispositions: Personality in adulthood.* Boston, MA: Little, Brown.

McGadney, B. F., Goldberg-Glen, R., & Pinkston, E. M. (1987). Clinical issues for assessment and intervention with the black family. In L. L. Carstensen & B. A. Edelstein (Eds.), *Handbook of clinical gerontology* (pp. 354–375). New York: Pergamon.

McGhee, P. E. & Frueh, T. (1980). Television viewing and the learning of sex-role stereotypes. *Sex Roles, 6*, 179–188.

McGoldrick, M. (1982). Ethnicity and family therapy: An overview. In M. McGoldrick, J. K. Pearce & J. Giordano (Eds.), *Ethnicity and family therapy* (pp. 3–30). New York: Guilford.

McHale, S. M., & Huston, T. L. (1984). Men and women as parents: Sex role orientations, employment, and parental roles with infants. *Child Development, 55*, 1349–1361.

McKenry, P. C., & Price, S. J. (1990). Divorce: Are men at risk? In D. Moore & F. Leafgren (Eds.), *Men in conflict* (pp. 95–112). Alexandria, VA: American Association for Counseling and Development.

McKinney, K., & Maroules, N. (1991). Sexual harassment. In E. Grauerholz & M. A. Koralewski (Eds.), *Sexual coercion: A sourcebook on its nature, causes, and prevention* (pp. 29–44). Lexington, MA: D. C. Heath.

McLarin, K. J. (1992, July 19). Reaching out to black youth. *Philadelphia Inquirer,* pp. A1, A8.

Men's Rights, Inc. (undated). MR I.Q. Test (advertising brochure).

Meredith, D. (1985, June). Dad and the kids. *Psychology Today,* pp. 63–67.

Merriam, S. (1980). The concept and function of reminiscence: A review of the research. *The Gerontologist, 20,* 604–609.

Messner, M. A. (1992). Boyhood, organized sports, and the construction of masculinity. In M. A. Kimmel & M. S. Messner (Eds.), *Men's lives* (pp. 161–176). New York: Macmillan.

Meth, R. L. (1990). The road to masculinity. In R. L. Meth & R. S. Pasick (Eds.), *Men in therapy: The challenge of change* (pp. 3–34). New York: Guilford.

Miedzian, M. (1991). *Boys will be boys: Breaking the link between masculinity and violence.* New York: Doubleday.

Miller, A. (1949). *Death of a salesman.* New York: Viking.

Millon, T. (1981). *Disorders of personality: DSM-III, Axis II.* New York: Wiley.

Millon, T. (1986). The avoidant personality. In R. Michels & J. O. Cavenar, Jr., *Psychiatry* (vol. 1). New York: Basic Books.

Milos, M. F. (1992). Circumcision: Don't be conned by the pros. *Journeymen,* pp. 14–16.

Mintz, L. B., & O'Neil, J. M. (1990). Gender roles, sex, and the process of psychotherapy: many questions and a few answers. *Journal of Counseling and Development, 68,* 381–387.

Moitoza, E. (1982). Portuguese families. In M. McGoldrick, J. K. Pearce & J. Giordano (Eds.), *Ethnicity and family therapy* (pp. 412–437). New York: Guilford.

Mondykowski, S. M. (1982). Polish families. In M. McGoldrick, J. K. Pearce & J. Giordano (Eds.), *Ethnicity and family therapy* (pp. 393–411) New York: Guilford.

Money, J. (1987a). Propaedeutics of diecious G-I/R: Theoretical foundations for understanding dimorphic gender-identity/role. In J. M. Reinisch, L. A. Rosenblum, & S. A. Sanders (Eds.), *Masculinity/femininity: Basic perspectives* (pp. 13–28). New York: Oxford University Press.

Money, J. (1987b). Sin, sickness, or status? Homosexual gender identity and psychological neuroendocrinology. *American Psychologist, 42,* 384–399.

Money, J., & Ehrhardt, A. A. (1972). *Man and woman, boy and girl.* Baltimore: Johns Hopkins University Press.

Money, J., & Tucker, P. (1975). *Sexual signatures: On being a man or a woman.* Boston: Little, Brown.

Montague, D. K. (1988). *Disorders of male sexual function.* Chicago: Year Book Medical Publishers.

Moore, D. (1990). Helping men become more emotionally expressive: A ten-week program. In D. Moore & F. Leafgren (Eds.), *Men in conflict* (pp. 183–200). Alexandria, VA: American Association for Counseling and Development.

Moore, D., & Haverkamp, B. E. (1989). Measured increases in male emotional expressiveness following a structured group intervention. *Journal of Counseling and Development, 67,* 513–517.

Moore, D., & Leafgren, F. (Eds.). (1990). *Men in conflict.* Alexandria, VA: American Association for Counseling and Development.

Moore Hines, P., & Boyd-Franklin, N. (1982). Black families. In M. McGoldrick, J. K. Pearce & J. Giordano (Eds.), *Ethnicity and family therapy* (pp. 84–107). New York: Guilford.

Morawski, J. G. (1985). The measurement of masculinity and feminity: Engendering categorical realities. *Journal of Personality, 53,* 196–223.

Moreland, J., & Schwebel, A. I. (1979). A gender role transcendent perspective on fathering. *The Counseling Psychologist, 9,* 45–52.

Morgan, J., Skovholt, T., & Orr, J. (1978). Career counseling with men: The shifting focus. In S. Weinrach (Ed.), *Vocational counseling: Theory and techniques.* New York: McGraw-Hill.

Morin, S., & Garfinkle, E. M. (1978). Male homophobia. *Journal of Social Issues, 34,* 29–47.

Moses, A. E., & Hawkins, R. O. (1982). *Counseling lesbian women and gay men: A life-issues aproach.* St. Louis: C. V. Mosby.

Moses, S. (1991, March). Rape prevention "must involve men." *APA Monitor,* pp. 35–36.

Mosher, D. L., & Anderson, R. D. (1986). Macho personality, sexual aggression, and reactions to guided imagery of realistic rape. *Journal of Research in Personality, 20,* 77–94.

Mosher, D. L., & Tomkins, S. S. (1988). Scripting the macho man: Hypermasculine socialization and enculturation. *Journal of Sex Research, 25,* 60–84.

Mulcahy, G. A. (1973). Sex differences in patterns of self-disclosure among adolescents: A developmental perspective. *Journal of Youth and Adolescence, 2,* 343–356.

Naifeh, S., & Smith, G. (1984). *Why can't men open up? Overcoming men's fear of intimacy.* New York: Clarkson N. Potter.

Nathan, S. (1981). Cross-cultural perspectives on penis envy. *Psychiatry, 44,* 39–44.

National Center for Health Statistics. (1987). Advance report of final mortality statistics 1983. *NCHS Monthly Vital Statistics Report, 34,* (6, Suppl 2), 1985. Hyattsville, MD: U.S. Department of Health and Human Services.

National Gay and Lesbian Task Force. (1993). Correspondence to members.

National Organization for Men Against Sexism (NOMAS). (1992). *Statement of principles.* Published in conference schedule for "Coming Home to New Families": The 17th National Conference on Men and Masculinity, Chicago, IL.

National Organization of Circumcision Information Resource Centers. (1991). *Circumcision: Why?* (brochure).

Neilson, J. M. (1990). *Sex and gender in society: Perspectives on stratification* (2nd ed.). Prospect Heights, IL: Waveland.

Nelson, J. B. (1985). Male sexuality and masculine spirituality. *Siecus Reports, 13,* 1–4.

Nelson, J. B. (1988). *The intimate connection: Male sexuality, masculine spirituality.* Philadelphia: Westminster.

Nemiah, J. C., Fryberger, H., & Sifneos, P. E. (1976). Alexithymia: A view of the psychosomatic process. In O. W. Hill (Ed.), *Modern trends in psychosomatic medicine* (vol. 3, pp. 430–439). London: Butterworths.

Neugarten, B. L. (1968). *Middle age and aging.* Chicago: University of Chicago Press.

Neugarten, B. L. (1973). Personality change in late life: A developmental perspective. In C. Eisdorfer & M. P. Lawton (Eds.), *The psychology of adult development and aging.* Washington, DC: American Psychological Association.

Neugarten, B. L., & Gutmann, D. L. (1968). Age-sex roles and personality in middle age: A thematic apperception study. In B. L. Neugarten (Ed.), *Middle age and aging.* Chicago: University of Chicago Press.

Norrell, J. E. (1984). Self-disclosure: Implications for the study of parent-adolescent interaction. *Journal of Youth and Adolescence, 13,* 163–179.

Notarius, C., & Johnson, J. (1982). Emotional expression in husbands and wives. *Journal of Marriage and the Family, 44,* 483–489.

Nyquist, L. V., Slivken, K., Spence, J. T., & Helmreich, R. L. (1985). Household responsibilities in middle-class couples: The contribution of demographic and personality variables. *Sex Roles, 12,* 15–34.

Ochberg, R. (1988). Ambition and impersonality in men's careers. *Men's Studies Review, 1,* 10–13.

Oken, D. (1985). Gastrointestinal disorders. In H. I. Kaplan & B. J. Saddock (Eds.), *Comprehensive textbook of psychiatry/IV* (pp. 1123–1132). Baltimore: Williams and Wilkins.

Olds, D. E., & Shaver, P. (1980). Masculinity, academic performance, and health: Further evidence concerning the androgyny controversy. *Journal of Personality, 48,* 323–341.

O'Leary, K. D., Barling, J., Arias, I., Rosenbaum, A., Malone, J., & Tyree, A. (1989). Prevalence and stability of physical aggression between spouses: A longitudinal analysis. *Journal of Consulting and Clinical Psychology, 57,* 263–268.

O'Leary, K. D., & Curley, A. D. (1986). Assertion and family violence: Correlates of spouse abuse. *Journal of Marital and Family Therapy, 12,* 281–290.

Olweus, D. (1979). Stability of aggressive reaction patterns in males: A review. *Psychological Bulletin, 86,* 852–875.

O'Neil, J. M. (1981a). Patterns of gender role conflict and strain: Sexism and fear of femininity in men's lives. *Personnel and Guidance Journal, 60,* 203–210.

O'Neil, J. M. (1981b). Male sex role conflicts, sexism, and masculinity: Psychological implications for men, women, and the counseling psychologist. *Journal of Counseling Psychology, 9,* 61–80.

O'Neil, J. M. (1982). Gender role conflict and strain in men's lives. In K. Solomon & N. Levy (Eds.), *Men in transition: Theory and therapy* (pp. 5–43). New York: Plenum.

O'Neil, J. M. (1990). Assessing men's gender role conflict. In D. Moore & F. Leafgren (Eds.), *Men in conflict* (pp. 23–38). Alexandria, VA: American Association for Counseling and Development.

O'Neil, J. M., & Egan, J. (in press). Men's and women's gender role journies: Metaphors for healing, transition, and transformation. In B. Wainrib (Ed.), *Gender issues across the life cycle.* New York: Springer.

O'Neil, J. M., Fishman, D. M., & Kinsella-Shaw, M. (1987). Dual-career couples transitions and normative dilemmas: A preliminary assessment model. *The Counseling Psychologist, 15,* 50–96.

O'Neil, J. M., Helms, B. J., Gable, R. K., David, L., & Wrightsman, L. S. (1986). Gender-Role Conflict Scale: College men's fear of femininity. *Sex Roles, 14,* 335–350.

O'Rand, A. M. (1987). Gender. In G. L. Maddox (Ed.), *The encyclopedia of aging* (p. 271). New York: Springer.

Orlofsky, J. L., Ramsden, M. W., & Cohen, R. S. (1982). Development of the revised Sex-Role Behavior Scale. *Journal of Personality Assessment, 46,* 632–638

Osgood, N. J., & Thielman, S. (1990). Geriatric suicide behavior: Assessment and treatment. In S. J. Blumenthal & D. J. Kupfer (Eds.), *Suicide over the life cycle: Risk factors, assessment, and treatment of suicidal patients* (pp. 341–380). Washington, DC: American Psychiatric Press.

O'Sullivan, C. S. (1991). Acquaintance gang rape on campus. In A. Parrot & L. Bechofer (Eds.), *Acquaintance rape: The hidden crime* (pp. 140–156). New York: Wiley.

Pagelow, M. D. (1984). *Family violence.* New York: Praeger.

Palkovitz, R. (1984). Parental attitudes and fathers' interactions with their 5-month old infants. *Developmental Psychology, 20,* 1054–1060.

Pankratz, L., & Kofoed, L. (1988). The assessment and treatment of geezers. *Journal of the American Medical Society, 259,* 1228–1229.

Pantony, K. L., & Caplan, P. J. (1991). Delusional dominating personality disorder: A modest proposal for identifying some consequences of rigid masculine socialization. *Canadian Psychology, 32,* 120–135.

Parke, R.D., & Sawin, D. B. (1976). The father's role in infancy: A reevaluation. *The Family Coordinator, 25,* 365–371.

Parke, R. D., & Tinsley, B.R. (1981). The father's role in infancy: Determinants of involvement in caregiving and play. In M. Lamb (Ed.), *The role of the father in child development* (2nd ed., pp. 429–457), New York: Wiley.

Parnes, H. S., & Nestel, G. (1981). The retirement experience. In H. S. Parnes (Ed.), *Work and retirement* (pp. 155–197). Cambridge, MA: MIT Press.

Parrot, A. (1991). Recommendations for college policies and procedures to deal with acquaintance rape. In A. Parrot & L. Bechofer (Eds.), *Acquaintance rape: The hidden crime* (pp. 368–380). New York: Wiley.

Parrot, A., & Bechofer, L. (1991). *Acquaintance rape: The hidden crime.* New York: Wiley.

Pascoe, A. W. (1981). Self-disclosure and marital satisfaction. *Dissertation Abstracts International, 42* (3A), 1013.

Pasick, R. S. (1990). Raised to work. In R. L. Meth & R. S. Pasick (Eds.), *Men in therapy: The challenge of change* (pp. 35–53). New York: Guilford.

Pasick, R. S., Gordon, S., & Meth, R. L. (1990). Helping men understand themselves. In R. L. Meth & R. S. Pasick (Eds.), *Men in therapy: The challenge of change* (pp. 152–180). New York: Guilford.

Paul, W., Weinrich, J., Gonsiorek, J., & Hotvedt, M. (Eds.). (1982). *Homosexuality: Social psychological, and biological issues.* Beverly Hills, CA: Sage.

Payne, B. D. (1981). Sex and age differences in the sex-role stereotyping of third- and fifth-grade children. *Sex Roles, 7,* 135–144.

Pedersen, F. A. (Ed.). (1980). *The father-infant relationship: Observational studies in the family setting.* New York: Praeger.

Pellegrini, A. (1992). S(h)ifting the terms of hetero/sexism: Gender, power, homophobias. In W. Blumenfield (Ed.), *Homophobia: How we all pay the price* (pp. 39–56). Boston: Beacon Press.

Penwell, L. W. (1992). Personal communication.

Peplau, L. A. (1979). Power in dating relationships. In J. Freeman (Ed.), *Women: A feminist perspective* (2nd ed.). Palo Alto, CA: Mayfield.

Perry, D. G., & Bussey, K. (1979). The social learning theory of sex differences: Imitation is alive and well. *Journal of Personality and Social Psychology, 37,* 1699–1712.

Peskin, H. (1992). *Shifts in uses of the past in the Intergenerational Longitudinal Studies.* Paper presented at the Annual Meeting of the Gerontological Society of America, Washington, DC.

Petrie, R. (1986). Personal communication.

Pharr, S. (1988). *Homophobia: A weapon of sexism.* Little Rock, AR: Chardon.

Piaget, J. (1954). *The construction of reality in the child.* New York: Basic Books.

Pietropinto, A., & Simenauer, J. (1977). *Beyond the male myth: What women want to know about men's sexuality.* New York: Times Books.

Pinderhughes, E. (1982). Afro-American families and the victim system. In M. McGoldrick, J. K. Pearce & J. Giordanao (Eds.), *Ethnicity and family therapy* (pp. 108–123). New York: Guilford.

Pleck, J. H. (1975). Masculinity-feminity: Current and alternative paradigms. *Sex Roles, 1,* 161–178.

Pleck, J. H. (1976). The male sex role: Definitions, problems and sources of change. *Journal of Social Issues, 32,* 155–164.

Pleck, J. H. (1978). The work family role system. *Social Problems, 24,* 417–427.

Pleck, J. H. (1981a). *The myth of masculinity.* Cambridge, MA: MIT Press.

Pleck, J. H. (1981b, September). Prisoners of manliness. *Psychology Today,* pp. 24–27.

Pleck, J. H. (1985). *Working wives / Working husbands.* Beverly Hills, CA: Sage.

Pleck, J. H. (1987). American fathering in historical perspective. In M. S. Kimmel (Ed.), *Changing men: New directions in research on men and masculinity* (pp. 83–97). Beverly Hills, CA: Sage.

Pleck, J. H. (1988, October). Letter to the editor. *APA Monitor,* p. 2.

Pleck, J. H., & Rustad, M. (1980). *Husbands' and wives' time in family work and paid work in the 1975–76 study of time use.* Wellesley, MA: Wellesley College Center for Research on Women.

Pomerleau, A., Bolduc, D., Malcuit, G., & Cossette, L. (1990). Pink or blue: Environmental stereotypes in the first two years of life. *Sex Roles, 22,* 359–367.

Powell, G. N. (1986). Effects of sex role identity and sex on definitions of sexual harassment. *Sex Roles, 14,* 9–19.

Preston, K., & Stanley, K. (1987). "What's the worst thing . . . ?" Gender-directed insults. *Sex Roles, 17,* 209–219.

Priest, D. (1993, January 12). U.S. is urged to view AIDS as a racial issue. *Washington Post,* p. A3.

Prosser-Gelwick, B., & Garni, K. F. (1988). Counseling and psychotherapy with college men. In R. J. May & M. Scher (Eds.), *Changing roles for men on campus* (pp. 67–77). San Francisco: Jossey-Bass.

Pryor, J. B. (1987). Sexual harassment proclivities in men. *Sex Roles, 17,* 269–290.

Rabins, S., Lucas, M. J., Teitelbaum, M., Mark, S. R., & Folstein, M. F. (1983). Utilization of psychiatric consultation for elderly patients. *Journal of the American Geriatrics Society, 31,* 581–585.

Rapp, S. R., & Davis, K. M. (1989). Geriatric depression: Physician's knowledge, perceptions, and diagnostic practices. *The Gerontologist, 29,* 252–257.

Rapp, S. R., Parisi, S. P., & Walsh, D. A. (1988). Psychological dysfunction and physical health among elderly medical inpatients. *Journal of Consulting and Clinical Psychology, 56,* 851–855.

Rappaport, B. M. (1981). Helping men ask for help. *Public Welfare,* 22–27.

Raskin, P. A., & Israel, A. C. (1981). Sex-role imitation in children: Effects of sex of child, sex of model, and sex-role appropriateness of modeled behavior. *Sex Roles, 7,* 1067–1077.

Raymond, D. (1992). "In the best interests of the child": Thoughts on homophobia and parenting. In W. J. Blumenfeld (Ed.), *Homophobia: How we all pay the price* (pp. 114–130). Boston: Beacon Press.

Reedy, M. N. (1977). *Age and sex differences in personal needs and the nature of love: A study of happily married young, middle-aged, and older adult couples.* Unpublished doctoral dissertation, University of Southern California.

Renaissance Education Association (1987, October). *Reasons for male-to-female crossdressing.* Background paper no. 2.

Rensberger, B. (1992, March 1). Science and sensitivity: Primates, politics, and the sudden debate over the origins of human violence. *The Washington Post,* p. C3.

Resnick, J. L., Resnick, M. B., Packer, A. B., & Wilson, J (1980). Fathering classes: A psycho/educational model. In T. M. Skovholt, P. Schauble, & R. David (Eds.), *Counseling men* (pp. 173–182). Monterey, CA: Brooks/Cole.

Reynolds, G. (1992). The rising significance of race. *Chicago Magazine, 41* (12), 81–85, 126–130.

Richardson, L. R. (1981). *The dynamics of sex and gender: A sociological perspective* (2nd ed.). Boston: Houghton-Mifflin.

Ring, T. E., & Kilmartin, C. T. (1991). Man to man about rape: A rape prevention program for men. *Journal of College Student Development, 33,* 82–84.

Ritter, M. (1991, October 25). Elderly suicides on rise. *The Free-Lance Star,* p. 21.

Roark, M. L. (1987). Preventing violence on college campuses. *Journal of Counseling and Development, 65,* 367–371.

Roberts, T. (1991). Gender and the influence of evaluations on self-assessments in achievement settings. *Psychological Bulletin, 109,* 297–308.

Robertson, J. M., & Fitzgerald, L. F. (1992). Overcoming the masculine mystique: Preferences for alternative forms of assistance among men who avoid counseling. *Journal of Counseling Psychology, 39,* 240–246.

Robins, E. (1985). Suicide. In H. I. Kaplan & B. J. Sadock (Eds.), *Comprehensive textbook of psychiatry/IV* (4th ed., pp. 1311–1315). Baltimore, MD: Wiliams and Wilkins.

Rochlin, C. (1982). The heterosexual questionnaire. *Changing Men, 13,* 1.

Rodin, J., & Ickovics, J. R. (1990). Women's health: Review and research agenda as we approach the 21st century. *American Psychologist, 45,* 1018–1034.

Rogers, C. R. (1957). The necessary and sufficient conditions of therapeutic personality change. *Journal of Consulting Psychology, 21,* 95–103.

Rogers, C. R. (1959). A theory of therapy, personality, and interpersonal relationships, as developed in the client-centered framework. In S. Koch (Ed.), *Psychology: A study of a science. Volume 3: Formulations of the person and the social context* (pp. 184–256). New York: McGraw-Hill.

Rogers, C. R. (1961). *On becoming a person.* Boston: Houghton-Mifflin.

Rogers, C. R. (1980). *A way of being.* Boston: Houghton-Mifflin.

Rose, R. M., Gordon, T. P., & Bernstein, I. S. (1972). Sexual and social influences on testosterone secretion in the rhesus. *Psychosomatic Medicine, 34,* 473.

Rosen, B., & Jerdee, T. H. (1973). The influence of sex-role stereotypes on evaluations of male and female supervisory behavior. *Journal of Applied Psychology, 57,* 44–48.

Rosen, B., & Jerdee, T. H. (1974). Influence of sex role stereotypes on personnel decisions. *Journal of Applied Psychology, 59,* 9–14.

Rosenblum, L. A. (1987). The study of masculinity/femininity from a comparative developmental perspective. In J. M. Reinisch, L. A. Rosenblum, & S. A. Sanders (Eds.), *Masculinity/femininity: Basic perspectives.* New York: Oxford University Press.

Rosenstein, M., & Milazzo-Sayre, L. J. (1981). *Characteristics of admissions to selected mental health facilities, 1975: An annotated book of charts and tables.* Washington, DC: U.S. Government Printing Office.

Rosenzweig, M. R., & Leinan, A. L. (1989). *Physiological psychology* (2nd ed.). New York: Random House.

Rotter, J. B. (1954). *Social learning and clinical psychology.* Englewood Cliffs, NJ: Prentice Hall.

Royner, S. (1992, February 4). What men won't tell. *Washington Post Health,* p. 10.

Rozee, P. D., Bateman, P., & Gilmore, T. (1991). The personal perspective of acquaintance rape prevention: A three-tier approach. In A. Parrot & L. Bechofer (Eds.), *Acquaintance rape: The hidden crime* (pp. 337–354). New York: Wiley.

Rubin, Z., Peplau, L. A., & Hill, C. T. (1981). Loving and leaving: Sex differences in romantic attachments. *Sex Roles, 2,* 821–835.

Ruble, T. L. (1983). Sex stereotypes: Issues of change in the 1970's. *Sex Roles, 9,* 397–402.

Ruiz, R. (1981). Cultural and historical perspective in counseling Hispanics. In D. W. Sue (Ed.), *Counseling the culturally different: Theory and practice* (pp. 186–214), New York: Wiley.

Russell, D., & Howell, N. (1983). The prevalence of rape in the United States revisited. *Signs, 8,* 688–695.

Rybarczyk, B. D. (1992). *The reminiscence interview: Using volunteers to help older patients cope with stressful medical procedures.* Paper presented at the Annual Meeting of the Gerontological Society of America, Washington, DC.

Rybarczyk, B. D., & Auerbach, S. M. (1990). Reminiscence interviews as stress management interventions for older patients undergoing surgery. *The Gerontologist, 30,* 522–528.

Rybarczyk, B., Gallagher-Thompson, D., Rodman, J., Zeiss, A., Gantz, F. E., & Yesavage, J. (1992). Applying cognitive-behavioral psychotherapy to the chronically ill elderly: Treatment issues and case illustration. *International Psychogeriatrics, 4,* 127–140.

Saal, F. E., Johnson, C. B., & Weber, N. (1989). Friendly or sexy?: It may depend on whom you ask. *Psychology of Women Quarterly, 13,* 263–276.

Sadalla, E. K., & Kenrick, D. T. (1987). Dominance and heterosexual attraction. *Journal of Personality and Social Psychology, 52,* 730–738.

Sadker, M., & Sadker, D. (1985). Sexism in the classroom of the '80s. *Psychology Today, 3,* 54–57.

Sanday, P. R. (1981). The socio-cultural context of rape: A cross-cultural study. *Journal of Social Issues, 37,* 5–27.

Sanday, P. R. (1990). *Fraternity gang rape: Sex, brotherhood, and privilege on campus.* New York: New York University Press.

Satinover, J. (1986). The myth of the death of the hero: A Jungian view of masculine psychology. *The Psychoanalytic Review, 73,* 553–565.

Sattel, J. (1976). The inexpressive male: Tragedy or sexual politics? *Social Problems, 23,* 469–477.

Saurer, M. K., & Eisler, R. M. (1990). The role of masculine gender role stress in expressivity and social support network factors. *Sex Roles, 23,* 261–271.

Sawrie, S. M., Watson, P. J., & Biderman, M. D. (1991). Aggression, sex role measures, and Kohut's psychology of the self. *Sex Roles, 25,* 141–161.

Scher, M., Stevens, M., Good, G., & Eichenfield, G. A. (Eds.). (1987). *Handbook of counseling and psychotherapy with men.* Newbury Park, CA: Sage.

Schneider, W., & Lewis, I. A. (1984, February 16). The straight story on homosexuality and gay rights. *Public Opinion,* pp. 20, 59–60.

Schumm, W. R., Barnes, H. L., Bollman, S. R., Jurich, A. P., & Bregaighis, M. A. (1986). Self-disclosure and marital satisfaction revisited. *Family Relations, 34,* 241–247.

Schwalbe, M. (1992). *The mythopoetic men's movement and male-female relations.* Paper presented at the 17th National Conference on Men and Masculinity, Chicago, IL.

Sekeran, U. (1986). Self-esteem and sense of competence and moderators of the job satisfaction of professionals in dual career families. *Journal of Occupational Behavior, 7,* 341.

The Sentencing Project (1990). *Young black men and the criminal justice system.* Washington, DC: Author.

Shabsigh, R., Fishman, I, & Scott, F. (1988). Evaluation of erectile impotence. *Urology, 32,* 83–90.

Sharabany, R., Gershoni, R., & Hofman, J. E. (1981). Girl friend, boy friend: Age and sex differences in development of intimate friendships. *Developmental Psychology, 17,* 800–808.

Sharpe, M. J., & Heppner, P. P. (1991). Gender role, gender-role conflict, and psychological well-being in men. *Journal of Counseling Psychology, 38,* 323–330.

Sheehy, G. (1976). *Passages.* New York: E. P. Dutton.

Sheppard, H. L. (1976). Work and retirement. In R. M. Binstock & E. Shanas (Eds.), *Handbook of aging and the social sciences* (pp. 286–309). New York: Van Nostrand Reinhold.

Sherif, C. W. (1982). Needed concepts in the study of gender identity. *Psychology of Women Quarterly, 6,* 375–398.

Sherman, E. (1991). *Reminiscence and the self in old age.* New York: Springer.

Sherman, J. (1978). *Sex-related cognitive differences.* Springfield, IL: Charles C. Thomas.

Shinar, E. H. (1978). Person perception as a function of occupation and sex. *Sex Roles, 4,* 679–693.

Siegel, J. M., & Kuykendall, D. H. (1990). Loss, widowhood, and psychological distress among the elderly. *Journal of Consulting and Clinical Psychology, 58,* 519–524.

Siegler, I. C., George, L. K., & Okun, M. (1979). Cross-sequential analysis of adult personality. *Developmental Psychology, 15,* 350–351.

Sifneos, P. E. (1972). *Short-term psychotherapy and emotional crisis.* Cambridge, MA: Harvard University Press.

Silverberg, R. A. (1986). *Psychotherapy for men: Transcending the masculine mystique.* Springfield, IL: Charles C. Thomas.

Skinner, B. F. (1974). *About behaviorism.* New York: Knopf.

Skovholt, T. M. (1990). Career themes in counseling and psychotherapy with men. In D. Moore & F. Leafgren (Eds.), *Men in conflict* (pp. 39–53). Alexandria, VA: American Association for Counseling and Development.

Skovholt, T. M., & Hansen, A. (1980). Men's development: A perspective and some themes. In T. M. Skovholt, P. Schauble, & R. David (Eds.), *Counseling men* (pp. 1–39). Monterey, CA: Brooks/Cole.

Sluser, R., & Kaufman, M. (1992). *The White Ribbon Campaign: Mobilizing men to take action.* Paper presented at the 17th National Conference on Men and Masculinity, Chicago, IL.

Smeaton, G., & Byrne, D. (1987). The effects of R-rated violence and erotica, individual differences, and victim characteristics on acquaintance rape proclivity. *Journal of Research in Personality, 21,* 171–184.

Smetana, J. G., & Letourneau, K. J. (1984). Development of gender constancy and children's sex-typed free play behavior. *Developmental Psychology, 20,* 691–696.

Smith, K. (1971). Homophobia: A tentative personality profile. *Psychological Reports, 29,* 1091–1094.

Snell, W. E., Jr. (1989). Development and validation of the Masculine Behavior Scale: A measure of behaviors stereotypically attributed to males vs. females. *Sex Roles, 21,* 749–767.

Snell, W. E., Jr., Belk, S. S., & Hawkins, R. C. II (1986). The masculine role as a moderator of stress-distress relationships. *Sex Roles, 15,* 359–366.

Snow, M. E., Jacklin, C. N., & Maccoby, E. E. (1981). Birth-order differences in peer sociability at thirty-three months. *Child Development, 52,* 589–595.

Solomon, K. (1981). The depressed patient: Social antecedents of psychopathologic changes in the elderly. *Journal of the American Geriatrics Society, 29,* 14–18.

Solomon, K. (1982a). The masculine gender role: Description. In K. Solomon & N. B. Levy (Eds.), *Men in transition: Theory and therapy* (pp. 45–76). New York: Plenum.

Solomon, K. (1982b). The older man. In K. Solomon & N. B. Levy (Eds.), *Men in transition: Theory and therapy* (pp. 205–240). New York: Plenum.

Sorenson, S. B., Stein, J. A., Siegel, J. M., Golding, J. M., & Burnam, M. A. (1987). The prevalence of adult sexual assault: The Los Angeles epidemiologic catchment area project. *American Journal of Epidemiology, 126,* 1154–1164.

Speer, J. (1990). Office politics and men's liberation. *Transitions, 10* (1), 18–19.

Spence, J. T., Helmreich, R. L., & Holahan, C. K. (1979). Negative and positive components of psychological masculinity and femininity and their relationship to self-reports of neurotic and acting out behaviors. *Journal of Personality and Social Psychology, 37,* 1673–1682.

Spence, J. T., Helmreich, R. L., & Stapp, J. (1974). The Personal Attributes Questionnaire: A measure of sex role stereotypes and masculinity-femininity. *JSAS Catalog of Selected Documents in Psychology, 4* (43) (MS no. 617).

Stapley, J. C., & Haviland, J. M. (1989). Beyond depression: Gender differences in normal adolescents' emotional experiences. *Sex Roles, 20,* 295–308.

Stearns, P. N. (1990). *Be a man! Males in modern society.* New York: Holmes and Meier.

Stearns, P. N. (1991). Fatherhood in historical perspective: The role of social change. In F. W. Bozett & S. M. H. Hanson (Eds.), *Fatherhood and families in cultural context* (pp. 28–52). New York: Springer.

Steinem, G. (1992). Foreword. In K. L. Hagan (Ed.), *Women respond to the men's movement* (pp. v–ix). San Francisco: HarperCollins.

Stepp, L. S. (1992, July 17). Anti-gay bias OK by Vatican. *The News Journal,* p. A2.

Stericker, A. B., & Kurdek, L. A. (1982). Dimensions and correlations of third through eighth graders' sex-role self-concepts. *Sex Roles, 8,* 915–929.

Stevens, M., & Gebhardt, R. (1984). *Rape education for men: Curriculum guide.* Columbus: Ohio State University.

Stevenson, M. R. (1991). Myth, reality, and father absence. *Men's Studies Review, 8* (1), 3–8.

Stewart, A. J., & Salt, P. (1981). Life stress, life-styles, depression, and illness in adult women. *Journal of Personality and Social Psychology, 40,* 1063–1069.

Stillion, J. M. (1985). *Death and the sexes: An examination of differential longevity, attitudes, behaviors, and coping skills.* Washington, DC: Hemisphere.

Stillion, J. M., McDowell, E. E., & May, J. H. (1989). *Suicide across the life span: Premature exits.* New York: Hemisphere.

Stillson, R. W., O'Neil, J. M., & Owen, S. V. (1991). Predictors of adult men's gender-role conflict: Race, class, unemployment, age, instrumentality-expressiveness, and personal strain, *Journal of Counseling Psychology, 38,* 458–464.

Stoddart, T., & Turiel, E. (1985). Children's concepts of cross-gender activities. *Child Development, 56,* 1241–1252.

Stokes, J., & Levin, I. (1986). Gender differences in predicting loneliness from social network characteristics. *Journal of Personality and Social Psychology, 51,* 1069–1074.

Straus, M. A., & Gelles, R. J. (1986). Societal change and change in family violence from 1975 to 1985 as revealed by two national surveys. *Journal of Marriage and the Family, 48,* 465–479.

Stroebe, M. S., & Stroebe, W. (1983). Who suffers more? Sex differences in health risks of the widowed. *Psychological Bulletin, 93,* 279–301.

Strong, S. R. (1986). Interpersonal influence theory and therapeutic interactions. In F. J. Dorn (Ed.), *Social influence processes in counseling and psychotherapy.* Springfield, IL: Charles C. Thomas.

Struckman-Johnson, C. (1991). Male victims of acquaintance rape. In A. Parrot & L. Bechofer (Eds.), *Acquaintance rape: The hidden crime* (pp. 192–213). New York: Wiley.

Struckman-Johnson, C., & Struckman-Johnson, D. (1992). Acceptance of male rape myths among college men and women. *Sex Roles, 27,* 85–100.

Sue, D., Sue, D., & Sue, S. (1990). *Understanding abnormal behavior* (3rd ed.). Boston: Houghton-Mifflin.

Sue, D. W., Bernier, J. E., Durran, A., Feinberg, L., Pedersen, P., Smith, E., & Vasquez-Nattall, E. (1982). Position paper: Cross-cultual counseling competencies (Education and Training Committee, Division 17, American Psychological Association). *The Counseling Psychologist, 10,* 45–52.

Sugarman, D. B., & Hotaling, G. T. (1989). Violent men in intimate relationships: An analysis of risk markers. *Journal of Applied Social Psychology, 19,* 1034–1048.

Sun, L. H. (1991), November 17). A growth industry in China: Inch by inch, this surgeon is making a name for himself. *The Washington Post,* pp. F1, F8.

Swim, J., Borgida, E., Maruyama, G, & Myers, D. G. (1989). Joan McKay versus John McKay: Do gender stereotypes bias evaluations? *Psychological Bulletin, 105* 409–429.

Symons, D. (1987). An evolutionary approach. In J. H. Geer & W. T. O'Donahue (Eds.), *Theories of human sexuality* (pp. 91–125). New York: Plenum.

Tangri, S., Burt, M. R., & Johnson, L. B. (1982). Sexual harassment at work: Three explanatory models. *Journal of Social Issues, 38*, 33–54.

Tannen, D. (1990). *You just don't understand: Women and men in conversation.* New York: Morrow.

Tavris, C. (1992). *The mismeasure of woman.* New York: Simon & Schuster.

Tavris, C., & Offrir, C. (1977). *The longest war: Sex differences in perspective.* New York: Harcourt Brace Jovanovich.

Taylor, G. J. (1984). Alexithymia: Concept, measurement, and implications for treatment. *American Journal of Psychiatry, 141*, 725–732.

Taylor Gibbs, J. (1991). Young black males in America: Endangered, embittered, and embattled. In M. S. Kimmel & M. A. Messner (Eds.), *Men's lives* (pp. 50–66). New York: Macmillan.

Taylor, S. E. (1981). A categorization approach to stereotyping. In D. L. Hamilton (Ed.), *Cognitive processes in stereotyping and intergroup behavior.* Hillsdale, NJ: Lawrence J. Erlbaum.

Terkel, S. (1992). *Race: How blacks and whites think and feel about the American obsession.* New York: The New Press.

Terman, L. M., & Miles, C. C. (1936). *Sex and personality: Studies in masculinity and femininity.* New York: McGraw-Hill.

Thompson, E. H. (1990). Courtship violence and the male role. *Men's Studies Review, 7* (3), 1; 4–13.

Thorne, B. (1992). Girls and boys together . . . but mostly apart: Gender arrangements in elementary schools. In M. S. Kimmel & M. A. Messner (Eds.), *Men's lives* (2nd ed., pp.108–123). New York: Macmillan.

Thorne, B., & Luria, Z. (1986). Sexuality and gender in children's daily worlds. *Social Problems, 33*, 176–190.

Tiger, L. (1969). *Men in groups.* New York: Random House.

Tillich, P. (1952). *The courage to be.* New Haven, CT: Yale University Press.

Tobin, J. (1991, December 15). In modern politics, big boys really do cry. *The New Journal*, p. A2.

Toby, J. (1966). Violence and the masculine mystique: Some qualitative data. *Annals of the American Academy of Political and Social Science, 36* (4), 19–27.

Toch, H. (1992). *Violent men: An inquiry into the psychology of violence.* Washington, DC: American Psychological Association.

Trezona, R. R., Jr. (1991). Assessment and treatment of depression in the older rehabilitation patient. In R. J. Hartke (Ed.), *Psychological aspects of geriatric rehabilitation* (pp. 187–210). Gaithersburg, MD: Aspen Publications.

Tschann, J. (1988). Self-disclosure in adult friendship: Gender and marital status differences. *Journal of Social and Personal Relationships, 5*, 65–81.

Turner, R. (1970). *Family interaction.* New York: Wiley.

Tyler, D. C. (1988). Pain in the neonate. *Pre- & Peri-Natal Psychology Journal, 3*, 53–59.

Tyson, P. (1986). Male gender identity: Early developmental roots. *The Psychoanalytic Review, 73*, 405–426.

United States Bureau of the Census (1991). *Statistical abstract of the United States* (111th ed.). Washington, DC: U.S. Government Printing Office.

Unites States Department of Labor (1991). *Employment and earnings, February 1991.* Washington, DC: U.S. Government Printing Office.

United States Merit Systems Protection Board (1981). *Sexual harassment in the Federal workplace. Is it a problem?* Washington, DC: U.S. Government Printing Office.

Urberg, K. A. (1982). The development of the concepts of masculinity and femininity in young children. *Sex Roles, 8*, 659–668.

Utne, M. K., Hatfield, E., Traupmann, J., & Greenberger, D. (1984). Equity, marital satisfaction, and stability. *Journal of Social and Personal Relationships, 1*, 323–332.

Vaillant, G. E. (1977). *Adaptation to life.* Boston: Little, Brown.

Valdes, L. F., Baron, A., Jr., & Ponce, F. Q. (1987). Counseling Hispanic men. In M. Scher, M. Stevens, G. Good, & G. A. Eichenfield (Eds.), *Handbook of counseling and psychotherapy with men* (pp. 203–217). Newbury Park, CA: Sage.

van den Berghe, P. L. (1979). *Human family systems: An evolutionary view.* New York: Elsevier.

Vasta, R., Haith, M. M., & Miller, S. A. (1992). *Child psychology: The modern science.* New York: Wiley.

Wade, C., & Cirese, S. (1991). *Human sexuality.* San Diego: Harcourt Brace Jovanovich.

Waldron, I. (1976). Why do women live longer than men? *Journal of Human Stress, 2*, 1–13.

Walker, E., Bettes, B. A., Kain, E. L., & Harvey, P. (1985). Relationship of gender and marital status with symptomatology in psychotic patients. *Journal of Abnormal Psychology, 94*, 42–50.

Walker, L. S., & Wright, P. H. (1976). Self-disclosure in friendship. *Perceptual and Motor Skills, 42*, 735–742.

Wallerstein, J. S., & Blakeslee, S. (1989). *Second chances: Men, women, and children a decade after divorce.* New York: Ticknor and Fields.

Wallerstein, J. S., & Kelly, J. B. (1980). *Surviving the breakup: How children and parents cope with divorce.* New York: Basic Books..

Walsh, F. (1980). The family in later life. In E. A. Carter & M. M. McGoldrick (Eds.), *The family life cycle: A framework for family therapy* (pp. 217–238). New York: Gardner.

Walsh, M. R. (1987). Is pornography harmful to women? In M. R. Walsh (Ed.), *The psychology of women: Ongoing debates* (pp. 427–429). New Haven, CT: Yale University Press.

Watson, P. J., Biderman, M. D., & Boyd, C. (1989). Androgyny as synthetic narcissism: Sex role measures and Kohut's psychology of the self. *Sex Roles, 21*, 175–207.

Watson, P. J., Taylor, D., & Morris, R. J. (1987). Narcissism, sex roles, and self-functioning. *Sex roles, 21,* 175–207.

Watts, D. L., & Courtois, C. A. (1981). Trends in the treatment of men who commit violence against women. *Personnel and Guidance Journal, 81,* 245–249.

Waxman, H. M., & Carner, E. A. (1984). Physician's recognition, diagnosis, and treatment of mental disorders in elderly medical patients. *The Gerontologist, 24,* 593–597.

Weiss, R. S. (1990). *Staying the course: The emotional and social lives of men who do well at work.* New York: Macmillan.

Weiten, W. (1992). *Psychology: Themes and variations.* Monterey, CA: Brooks/Cole.

Wellesley College Center for Research on Women (1984). Men at home: Fathers' participation in family life. *Research Report, 4* (1), 1–4.

Welts, E. P. (1982). Greek families. In M. McGoldrick, J. K. Pearce & J. Giordano (Eds.), *Ethnicity and family therapy* (pp. 269–288). New York: Guilford Press.

Whiting, B. (1965). Sex identity conflict and physical violence: A comparative study. In L. Nader (Ed.), *The ethnography of law* (pp. 123–140). Menasha, WI: American Anthropological Association.

Whiting, B., & Edwards, C.P. (1973). A cross-cultural analysis of sex differences in the behavior of children aged three through eleven. *Journal of Social Psychology, 91,* 171–188.

Whiting, B. B., & Edwards, C. P. (1988). *Children of different worlds: The formation of social behavior.* Cambridge, MA: Harvard University Press.

Whitley, B. E., Jr. (1984). Sex-role orientation and psychological well-being: Two meta-analyses. *Sex Roles, 12,* 207–225.

Whitley, B. E., Jr. (1987). The relationship of sex role orientation to heterosexuals' attitudes toward homosexuals. *Sex Roles, 17,* 103–113.

Wiegand, G. (1989, November 27). His-tory lessons: Men's studies gaining favor on campus. *Washington Post,* p. B5.

Wilkie, J. R. (1991). The decline in men's labor force participation and income and the changing structure of family economic support. *Journal of Marriage and the Family, 53,* 111–122.

Williams, D. G. (1985). Gender, masculinity-femininity, and emotional intimacy in same-sex friendship. *Sex Roles, 12* 587–600.

Williams, J. E., & Best, D. L. (1990). *Measuring sex stereotypes: A multination study.* Newbury Park, CA: Sage.

Williamson, T. (1985). A history of the men's movement. In F. Baumli (Ed.), *Men freeing men: Exploding the myth of the traditional male* (pp. 308–324). Jersey City, NJ: New Atlantis Press.

Wilson, E. O. (1975). *Sociobiology: The new synthesis.* Cambridge, MA: Harvard University Press.

Wilson, W. J. (1978). *The declining significance of race.* Chicago, IL: University of Chicago Press.

Wilson, W. J. (1987). *The truly disadvantaged.* Chicago, IL: University of Chicago Press.

Wilson-Schaef, A., & Fassel, D. (1988). *The addictive organization.* New York: Harper Religious Books.

Winstead, B. A., Derlega, V. J., & Wong, P. T. P. (1984). Effects of sex-role orientation on behavioral self-disclosure. *Journal of Research in Personality, 38,* 541–553.

Wiswell, T. E., & Geschke, D. W. (1989). Risks from circumcision during the first month of life compared with those for uncircumcised boys. *Pediatrics, 83,* 1001–1005.

Wong, M. R. (1982). Psychoanalytic-developmental theory and the development of male gender identity: A review. In K. Solomon & N. B. Levy (Eds.), *Men in transition: Theory and therapy.* New York: Plenum.

Wong, M. R., Davey, J., & Conroe, R. M. (1976). Expanding masculinity: Counseling the male in transition. *The Counseling Psychologist, 6,* 58–64.

Ziff, B. (1990, December 15). (Letter to Ann Landers). *Washington Post,* p. D10.

Zilbergeld, B. (1992). *The new male sexuality.* New York: Bantam.

Zillmann, D., & Bryant, J. (1982). Pornography, sexual callousness, and the trivialization of rape. *Journal of Communicaiton, 32,* 10–21.

Zuckerman, D. M., Singer, D. S., & Singer, J. L. (1980). Children's television viewing, racial, and sex-role attitudes. *Journal of Applied Social Psychology, 10,* 281–294.

NAME INDEX

SUBJECT INDEX

Academic problems, 86
Accidents, 153
Achievement, 7, 9, 11–13, 35, 41–42, 66, 79,
    86, 104, 109, 115, 119–22, 126, 137, 163,
    171, 174–76, 178–80, 190, 215, 246–47,
    255, 260
Actualizing tendency, 98
Adam/Eve principle, 49
Advertising, 159, 161, 175–76
African American men, 11, 126–30, 154,
    163, 178
  health problems, 127–28, 153, 163
  homicide victims, 154
Agentic orientation, 74–75, 85, 139, 216
  unmitigated, 74, 216
Aggression. See Violence
Aging men, 114–21, 259, 266, 281
  mental health problems, 117–20, 259
  reminiscence, 120–21
  suicide, 118–20, 158, 259
Agricultural societies, 169–70
AIDS, 153, 162, 195, 198
Alcohol abuse, 125, 127, 155, 157, 160, 163,
    217, 230–31, 256
Alcoholism, 120, 175
Alexithymia, 143–44
ANDRO scale, 40
Androgen, 48–49, 51
Androgen insensitivity syndrome, 49
Androgyny, 31–33, 37, 40–41, 74, 77, 116,
    121, 137, 240, 243, 255–56, 278, 283–84
  and cross-sex friendship, 240
  and marital satisfaction, 243
  and mental health, 33, 75, 255–56
  measurement of, 40–41
  and self-disclosure, 138
Anger rape, 228
Anima archetype, 78–80
Animus archetype, 78
Antifemininity, 9, 72–73, 87, 89–90, 104,
    138, 141, 182, 189, 214–15, 237–38, 240,
    242, 264, 282
Antisocial personality disorder, 257–59
Anxiety disorders, 257
Archetype, 78–79
Assertiveness, 147
Athletics. See Sports

Behavioral threshold, biological, 54–55, 214
Bem Sex Role Inventory (BSRI), 40–41, 254
Bisexuality, 197, 266, 281
Borderline Personality Disorder, 257
Boxing, 157, 160
Breadwinner role. See Provider role
British men, 123

California Psychological Inventory (CPI),
    38–39
Cancer, 153, 159–60
Castration, 156–57
Castration anxiety, 68–70
Cathexis, 63–64
Child care, 57–58, 245–47
Child custody, 263–64, 285
Childhood Mental Disorders, 257
Cholesterol, 156
Chromosomes, 48–51, 155–56
Circumcision, 195–96
Clitoris, 49–50
Coalition of Free Men, 285
Cognition, 88–94
Cognitive developmental theory, 91–92
Cohort effects, 115
Communal orientation, 74–75, 85, 139
  unmitigated, 74
Compensatory masculinity, 71, 218
Competition, 7, 11, 13, 22, 33, 41–42, 54,
    56, 67, 86, 93, 103, 105, 141, 146–47,
    163, 167, 170, 172, 175–77, 190, 193,
    212–13, 216, 219, 236–37, 245, 255–56,
    260, 269
Complementarity, 142
Conditions of worth, 99
Congenital microphallus, 192
Conscience, 65–66
Consciousness raising, 95, 146
Conservative position on men, 279
"Cool pose" 128–29, 163
Corporate environment, 140, 176–77
Counseling, 265–72
  approaches with male clients, 270–72
  effects of sex and gender, 265–66,
    268–70
Counseling psychology, 265
Crime, 66, 126–27, 129, 178, 182, 211–12,
    222
Cross-gender behavior. See Out-role be-
    havior

Death of a Salesman 179–80
"Deep masculinity" 62, 278–81
Defensive style, 142–43, 216
Depression, 118–19, 252, 257
  in older men, 118–19
Diagnostic and Statistical Manual of Mental
    Disorders, 252–53, 258
Differential treatment, 84–87
Division, 17
  American Psychological Association,
    265
Division of labor, 58, 168–72

335